AA

Explorer
India

Fiona Dunlop

AA Publishing

Front cover
Top: *The Taj Mahal*
(Douglas Corrance)
Middle (left to right): *A
street vendor* (Douglas
Corrance); *Cycling from
Jhule Point* (Steve
Watkins); *A traditional
instrument played at
Chettiar Hindu Temple*
(Ken Paterson); *Taxi
driver in Delhi* (Douglas
Corrance)
Spine
Taj Mahal (Douglas
Corrance)
Back cover
Left: *Lamjung Himal*
(Steve Watkins). Right:
*Tourists on the walls at
Jaisalmer* (Douglas
Corrance)
Page 2: *P ortrait of a
sadhu (ascetic) at the
holy city of Varanasi*
Page 3: *Gateway into
Jaipur's City Palace,
Rajasthan*
Page 4: *A boy with a
model of the Taj Mahal*
Page 5: *(a)* Dhobi
wallahs *(washermen)
washing clothes in the
Yamuna River, Uttar
Pradesh; (b) women buy-
ing votive offerings at
Varanasi*
Page 6: *(a) Members of a
nomadic tribe; (b) a holy
man, Tamil Nadu*
Page 7: *Local boys next to
a decorated rickshaw in
the town of Bundi*
Page 8: *Women cooking
at Varanasi, Uttar
Pradesh*
Page 9: *(a) Udaipur,
Rajasthan; (b) portrait of
a Rajput from Jodhpur,
Rajasthan*

Written by Fiona Dunlop
Updated by Robin Barton

Published by AA Publishing (a trading name of Automobile
Association Developments Limited, whose registered office
is Fanum House, Basing View, Basingstoke, Hampshire,
RG21 4EA. Registered number 1878835).

ISBN-10: 0-7495-4831-2
ISBN-13: 978-0-7495-14831-5

The contents of this publication are believed correct at the time of
printing. Nevertheless, AA Publishing accept no responsibility for
errors, omissions or changes in the details given, or for the
consequences of readers' reliance on this information. This does not
affect your statutory rights. Assessments of the attractions, hotels and
restaurants are based upon the author's own experience and contain
subjective opinions that may not reflect the publishers' opinion or a
reader's experience. We have tried to ensure accuracy, but things do
change, so please let us know if you have any comments or correc-
tions.

A CIP catalogue record for this book is available from the British
Library.

Colour separation by M.R.M. Graphics Ltd. Bucks, UK
Printed and bound in Italy by Printer Trento srl

Find out more about AA Publishing and the wide range of
travel publications and services the AA provides by visiting
our website at www.theAA.com/travel

First published 1998.
Reprinted 2004 (twice). Information verified and updated.
Reprinted May 2005
Reprinted 2006. Information verified and updated

Titles in the Explorer series:
Australia • Boston & New England • Britain • Brittany
California • Canada • Caribbean • China • Costa Rica
Crete • Cuba • Cyprus • Egypt • Florence & Tuscany • Florida
France • Germany • Greek Islands • Hawaii • India • Ireland
Italy • Japan • London • Mallorca • Mexico • New York
New Zealand • Paris • Portugal • Provence • Rome
San Francisco • Scotland • South Africa • Spain • Thailand
Tunisia • Turkish Coast • Venice • Vietnam

A02698

How to use this book

ORGANIZATION

India Is, India Was
Discusses aspects of life in modern India and places the country in its historical context, exploring past events whose influences are still felt.

A–Z
Breaks down the country into regional chapters, and covers places to visit. Within this section fall the Focus On articles, which consider a variety of topics in greater detail.

Travel Facts
Contains the strictly practical information that is vital for a successful trip.

Hotels and Restaurants
Lists recommended establishments in India, giving a brief summary of their attractions.

ADMISSION CHARGES
Inexpensive: up to 50 rupees
Moderate: 50–200 rupees
Expensive: over 200 rupees

ABOUT THE RATINGS
Most places described in this book have been given a separate rating. These are as follows:

▶▶▶   **Do not miss**

▶▶   **Highly recommended**

▶   **Worth seeing**

MAP REFERENCES
To make the location of a particular place easier to find, every main entry in this book is given a map reference, such as 53C2. The first number (53) indicates the page on which the map can be found; the letter (C) and the second number (2) pinpoint the square in which the main entry is located. The maps on the inside front and inside back covers are referred to as IFC and IBC respectively.

Contents

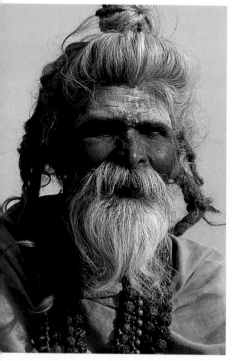

A–Z

Fiona Dunlop has written books on Spain, Paris, Mexico, Costa Rica, Singapore, Malaysia and Vietnam. In researching this guide, she combed the subcontinent from north to south to assess its countless offerings, and select the best.

My India

'Are you roaming?' one man enquires politely as I whirl through the great Indian subcontinent researching this book. Time there is circular, or perhaps elliptical, and the very air, the meandering sacred cows and the roadside *chai*-stands (tea-stands) hardly stimulate decisive action. It is a country that invites contemplative visiting, and one whose soul takes time to absorb. So woe to this guide-researcher, propelled ever onwards by the demands of encompassing the entire sweep.

Luckily, humanity here is great, not just in size but in quality. Communication is constant, drawing any traveller into the complex embrace of a nation riddled with history, with foreign legacies, with gaping inequalities, with on-going eruptions of unexpected and deadly violence, but above all with philosophy. For in no other country in the world have I had such deeply abstract conversations. It was the Indians, after all, who invented the concept of zero over 2,000 years ago. Aeons of Hindu rumination have permeated Muslims, Buddhists and Christians alike, creating an analytical predisposition that easily flips over into ironic humour. Yet dynamism is there too, in the will to survive of a ragged boy sweeping the railway-carriage, in the ploys of hardened stall-holders in the bazaars and in the equanimity of a woman transporting her worldly possessions on the crowded night-train to war-torn Kashmir. And then there are the IT supremos, the Bollywood cariactures and, of course, the bureaucrats. India is infinite.

Sugar-sweet movie *ghazals* (songs) crackle from transistor radios, heady perfumes drift from floral garlands, unidentifiable *thali* flavours subtly assault the palate, Mughal palace-forts loom on the horizon, Rajasthani women-workers in bright saris flash dazzling smiles, incense billows in staggeringly crafted temples, and exhaust fumes envelop the passengers of auto-rickshaws roaring through the cities. India is a drug in itself. I shall be back again, next time to truly roam.

Fiona Dunlop

India Is

Generous of spirit, land, culture and people, India is in a state of flux. Freedom, democracy and tolerance are its treasures, but are under pressure: India's population will soon overtake China's. From mountains to plains, coasts to deserts, the subcontinent presents a staggering density of humanity, and an extraordinary variety of forms, colour and history.

10

❏ Caste distinctions are deeply embedded in Indian society. In the past, relative social back-wardness led the *dalits* (lower castes) to suffer discrimination in silence. Today, with a marked absence of central ideological leadership, India is experiencing the rise of the *dalits* both in government and in militant ethnic groups. ❏

Fifty million years ago the giant island that became India was rammed into the Asian mainland, heaving the Himalayas up to their icy heights and unfurling fertile, river-threaded plains at their base. This was the birth of the subcontinent. With the world's highest mountains to the north and the Indian Ocean

Hindu pilgrims bathe in the holy River Ganga (Ganges) at Varanasi

washing its coasts, it undergoes the extreme weather cycles of the monsoon winds. For three months of the year they bring essential rains that sometimes swell into devastating floods. If they fail, there is drought, although the tragic famines of only a few decades ago are being avoided because the infrastructure is better.

Within this immense territory of over 3 million sq km (1,158,000 sq miles)—a third of the size of the USA, 13 times larger than the UK, live around a billion souls, fatalistic and fervent, Hindu and Muslim, peasant and industrialist, rich and poor. No other nation is such a dazzling kaleidoscope of humanity.

CULTURAL TAPESTRY Dust, poetry, sweat, human misery, splendour, belief: these are just some of the threads that have combined to make India over the last 5,000 years or so. Deeply woven into the tapestry are the shadows of past invaders: Greeks, Turks, Persians, Afghanis, Portuguese and British—all left their mark on the social fabric and psyche. In the background rise minarets, domes, impregnable forts, churches, palaces and extrava-gant railway stations, each pointing to a cultural priority that may or may not have endured. What has remained, despite the horrors of partition that saw the world's greatest migrations, is a mesmerizing multi-culturalism. Veiled Muslim women flit past Hindus weaving perfumed garlands of flowers outside a Siva shrine; pork is eschewed by the one

and beef by the other; turbanned, bearded, sword-bearing Sikhs chant from their sacred scriptures, the Granth, while pacifistic Buddhists and Jains meditate and pray. Religious belief is omnipresent, and occasionally omni-divisive.

LIE OF THE LAND In the north are the mighty Himalayas, with their colonial hill-stations, Buddhist monasteries and lakes (notably in turbulent Kashmir). Skirting the mountains is the Gangetic plain, India's most highly populated and industrialized region. Stretching between the contrasting cities of Delhi and Kolkata (Calcutta), it includes Hinduism's holiest cities, the Mughals' greatest monument—the Taj Mahal—and Bodh Gaya, the fount of Buddhism. To the west unfolds the Thar Desert, home of the Rajputs, and Gujarat, a Jain stronghold. South of the plains, the forested Aravalli and

Sunset over the sandstone city of Jaipur lends a romantic look to the city

Vindhya hills shelter wildlife sanctuaries and majestic forts.

Halfway down the subcontinent starts the vast, boulder-strewn Deccan plateau, which embraces the cultural highlights of Ajanta, Hyderabad, Hampi and Mysore, as well as the burgeoning city of Bangalore. Along the coastline to the east is culturally rich Orissa; to the west lie Mumbai (Bombay) and Goa. Finally comes the magical deep south, home to India's ancient Dravidian people. Here Hindus built astounding temples, early Christians erected churches, the British created Madras (Chennai) and the Keralans revel in their lush garden of Eden. The subcontinent ends at Kanniyakumari, where each April the moon can be seen rising as the sun sets.

India is the world's largest democracy and its fifth largest economy. In the decades following Independence, its development was successively steered by Jawaharlal Nehru and his daughter, Indira Gandhi. Today the Congress party they dominated has been weakened, and the country is governed by unstable coalitions.

When Nehru became independent India's first Prime Minister in 1947, he headed a Constituent Assembly representing 275 million Hindus, 50 million Muslims, 7 million Christians, 6 million Sikhs, 100,000 Parsis and 24,000 Jews. The only common tongue among the 15 official languages and 845 dialects was English, soon replaced by Hindi, although even today much of the south understands little of this northerners' tongue. In 1950 the constitution (the world's longest) became law, embodying the principles of democracy, secularism and equality. India's parliament has a lower house (Lok Sabha) and an upper house (Rajya Sabha), complemented by state governments.

NEHRU'S INDIA Intent on creating an egalitarian socialist nation, Nehru embarked on abolishing prejudice against low caste Hindus or 'untouchables' (one of Gandhi's pet aims), improving women's status and, above all, building up industry and agriculture. By his death in 1964, India's food production was booming. For 17 years, Nehru had been a popular figurehead, whose honesty and dedication to his country were undisputed, but he was dogged by external problems that continued under the premiership of his daughter, Indira Gandhi. Nehru's greatest achievement in foreign policy was the promotion of non-alignment with world powers. The still unresolved Kashmir issue has led to three wars with Pakistan; in 1948 (resulting in Kashmir's 'temporary' division), 1965 and 1971 (which led to the creation of Bangladesh). Despite repeated negotiations, the situation remains potentially explosive and again, in May 2002, produced a moment of global panic with nuclear threats from both sides. Relations with China, complicated by the occupation of Tibet, resulted in a Chinese invasion in 1962.

INDIRA'S EMERGENCY The euphoria that met Indira Gandhi's election victory in 1967 gradually evaporated. With a divided Congress party losing votes to the right wing, a Marxist coalition ruling Bengal, and Naxalite terrorist activities, India was nearing crisis. Social unrest was fuelled by nationalizations, drought, the cost of the 1971 war against Pakistan, the oil

crisis and Indira Gandhi's high-handedness. In 1975 she imposed a dictatorial state of emergency. The press was censored and over 10,000 people were arrested, including opposition leaders. Indira's youngest son, Sanjay Gandhi, assumed increasing powers, implementing a controversial sterilization programme. Although the 1977 elections gave the Janata party a majority and even saw a humiliated Indira arrested for corruption, the phoenix rose again to carry off the 1980 elections. However her political astuteness had faded, and the massacre of 700 Sikhs at Amritsar's Golden Temple, and ensuing bloody riots, resulted in her assassination in 1984.

DESTINY Sanjay having died in a plane-crash, Indira's successor was her eldest son, Rajiv, whose charisma and sincerity did not succeed in solving Hindu–Muslim confrontations, trouble in the northeastern states and the Punjab, or the Tamil issue in Sri Lanka. In turn, he was assassinated by a Tamil fanatic in 1991 and the baton of the Nehru dynasty passed to Rajiv's widow, Italian-born Sonia Gandhi, President of the Congress Party, which won the 2004 elections. Sonia's daughter, Priyanka, has now entered politics and her career wil be followed with interest.

BOOM Since 1991, India has been governed by coalitions that include the Bharatiya Janata Party (BJP), Congress and the Communists, a tradition repeated in the 1998 election result—which led to the leadership of Ata Behari Vajpayee. An economic volte-face came in the early 1990s during the premiership of Narashima Rao, whose reforms attracted a flood of foreign capital. The newly buoyant economy fuelled new enterprises and resulted in the expansion of a prosperous educated middle class. However this economic dynamism exists alongside widespread child labour, poverty, illiteracy, corruption and religious conflicts (such as the bloody 1992–3 Ayodhya riots, when deep-rooted tensions between Hindus and Muslims resurfaced and reemerged in Gujarat in 2001 and 2002). Nehru's dream state has yet to be realized, although democracy endures.

Indira Gandhi (above) in September 1970 Modern India is still to realize Nehru's dream (below)

From birth to death, the lives of devout Hindus are punctuated by ceremony. Food, hygiene, marriage and worship all fall into a prescribed pattern that has existed for some 3,000 years, although this is being increasingly eroded by Western lifestyles in the cities. Muslim ritual keeps a far lower profile.

At Hindu marriages the bridegroom traditionally rides a white horse

The prescribed rituals of ancient Vedic texts steer the daily lives of hundreds of millions of Hindus today. Faith runs deep, and evidence of it can be seen everywhere. *Sadhus* (Hindu ascetics) travel the roads, and wayside shrines are filled with offerings of flowers. Cows are sacred, as are certain plants. Meditation and cremation are important ritual practices, and numerous rites are performed to promote fertility. Muslim ritual is far less visible. Prayer is the most obvious practice, with the faithful called five times a day by the distinctive wail of the *muezzin* (crier) from the minaret. The principal event in the Muslim religious calendar is the month-long festival of Ramadan, when eating or drinking between sunrise and sunset is forbidden.

MARRIAGE Central to traditional Hindu society is the family, welded together by arranged marriages in which adolescent girls bring negotiated dowries to the selected husband. Such marriages join not simply two individuals but also two families, clans or even communities. Money, land, tradition and social convenience all play a part. Times are changing though. With education and birth control more widely available, women now have far greater control over their own lives, and love marriages are increasingly accepted by the middle classes.

BIRTH Rituals surrounding fertility range from making offerings at *naga* shrines (dedicated to the snake-god, symbol of fertility) to donating black stones to an ancient cactus at Calcutta's Kali temple. When a desert woman in Rajasthan dons a *pido*, a yellow veil with a large red spot, it announces her pregnancy and acceptance by the community. Simply being fertile, however, is not enough. Vedic verses honour sons followed by more sons, but never daughters. When a boy is born, conch shells are blown in Bengal and Assam, and drums are beaten in Maharashtra. When a girl is born, the women of Rajasthan retreat behind their veils and wail. In traditional Hindu households throughout India, an ancient rite to produce a male child is still performed over pregnant women.

❏ In 2006 a study estimated that 10 million female feotuses had been aborted in India in the last 20 years, an average of 500,000 a year. ❏

❏ The cows that meander through every Indian street are identified with Mother Earth: both are sources of food, fuel and fertilizer. The cow is said to be an embodiment of the benevolence of the gods, and its five products (*pancagavya*)—milk, curd, *ghee*, urine and dung—are believed to have purifying properties. Hindus will touch the forehead of a passing cow and utter a prayer in a gesture of devotion and respect. ❏

Some groups in Indian society perform ritual body piercing

DEATH In the philosophical Vedic text the *Bhagavad Gita*, Krishna explains that at death, the soul passes into another body. Hindus traditionally cremate their dead on funeral pyres, preferably on the banks of sacred rivers such as the Ganga (Ganges), where the ashes are later scattered so that the cycle of reincarnation can be broken. Seemingly indifferent to the emotions of the bereaved families, priests bargain over the price of each verse of the *Vedas* (sacred texts) to be recited while the body burns. The first son performs the last rite at his parents' cremations, thereby guaranteeing their release from this world. *Sati*, the rite of a widow throwing herself on her husband's pyre, was banned by the British in 1829; this left widows who

were shunned by society, unable to remarry whatever their age. Though illegal, *sati* is performed on rare occasions and in rural communities widows are still stigmatized.

Muslims, unlike Hindus, believe in resurrection after death, and in the existence of heaven and hell. It is customary for Muslims to bury, rather than cremate, their dead.

15

A woman prepares a ritual offering or puja

Brahma, Siva and Vishnu head the Hindu pantheon of millions of gods, reflecting the basic cycle of life, death and rebirth. Their multiple incarnations and consorts play out the eternal and divine ordering of the cosmos as revealed in the Vedas, *or sacred texts, and have inspired a stream of completely fantastic and often paradoxical myths.*

The notion of a divine triad is rooted in early Indian belief, perhaps in a cult of the sun, which creates with its warmth, preserves with light and destroys with scorching rays. Over the centuries the members of the triad evolved, and during the Brahmanic period (see page 33) they finally assumed their present identities of Brahma (standing for creation), Vishnu (standing for preservation) and Siva (standing for destruction and reproduction); in other words, a trinity symbolizing life, death and rebirth.

16

Hindu holy man or sadhu *in a yogic meditative trance (below)*
A statue of Brahma, the creator (right)

BRAHMA As creator and progenitor of the human race, Brahma is often perceived as the first of the gods, framer of the universe and guardian of the world. When recognized as an equal to Vishnu and Siva, he was represented as the god of wisdom,

❏ While Brahma and Vishnu were quarrelling, a fiery pillar appeared. They set off to find its origins, an investigation that took 1,000 years. Vishnu followed the column downwards in the guise of a mighty boar, while Brahma travelled upwards as a swan. When neither reached the end, they wearily returned to their starting point. Then Siva stepped in to reveal that the column was his *lingam* (phallus), proving himself the greatest of the trinity. ❏

with the four *Vedas* springing from his head. His powers were later interpreted as those of merely creator and therefore inferior to those of other members of the trinity. This inferiority is illustrated in a myth in which Brahma is the victim of a demon, a situation in which Vishnu or Siva must intervene. Born with one head, Brahma acquired four more in order not to lose sight of the female partner he had created, but Siva reduced this by one. Brahma is usually depicted with four arms astride a goose.

VISHNU As the preserver of the universe and cosmic order (*dharma*), Vishnu embodies mercy and goodness. He is the cosmic ocean, Nara, which existed before the creation of the universe. As Narayana ('moving in the waters') he is represented in human form asleep on the coiled serpent, Ananta, floating on the ocean, a posture he resumes after every destruction of the universe. Vishnuite worshippers claim that his mild self-assurance proves that he is the greatest of gods. Vishnu, a handsome young man with blue skin, dressed in regal attire, is often depicted with his much revered wife, Lakshmi, goddess of fortune, reclining on the serpent, seated on a lotus or riding his bird-man steed, Garuda. As preserver, Vishnu periodically descends to earth in human form to re-establish the balance of good and evil. His *avatars* (incarnations) so far total nine. The eighth, Krishna, inspired a huge body of mythology related in the lengthy

Mahabharata and is a popular god in his own right. The ninth *avatar* was Buddha, an astute attempt to subordinate Buddhism to Hinduism. The tenth and last has yet to come.

SIVA The trinity's most popular god is Siva the destroyer, a development of the terrifying Vedic god of fire, Rudra, and the pre-Aryan Lord of Beasts, the bull. Siva's activity as destroyer is essential to his role as reproducer: Siva is Supreme Lord, and the *lingam* is the phallic symbol of his creative power. He repeatedly demonstrated the mastery of austerities, gained through yoga, as the source of power, and is described wandering for thousands of years as an ascetic. Demon-slayer, giver of long life, distributor of India's seven holy rivers, creator of *amrita* (ambrosia) to strengthen the gods against the demons, god of storms, dancer of death: Siva is the most complex deity. With his vehicle Nandi, the bull, and his wife Parvati (depicted in numerous forms), he embodies omnipotent force.

Granite statue of Siva's bull, Nandi, on Chamundi Hill in Mysore

17

Much of the majestic architecture of India is closely linked with its numerous religions, and it can be viewed as three-dimensional odes to gods and beliefs. Centuries of outside influences, from Turks, Mughals, the British and others, have also contributed to a unique and idiosyncratic architectural legacy.

From delicate chalk-paintings on tribal mud-huts to sprawling palaces bristling with turrets, Indian domestic architecture is incredibly varied. There are the elaborately carved and painted merchants' *havelis* (courtyard houses) of northwest India, beautiful Keralan Nayar houses in tropical hardwoods, Portuguese-inspired Goanese dwellings and British colonial bungalows. Whether Rajput forts, Mughal palaces or thatched tribal huts, buildings display a love of decoration. In the domain of temple architecture, wonders of the world may be seen, each period inspiring the next.

BEGGING-BOWL STYLE For the Buddhists, the *stupa* (dome) was the ultimate symbol, its generous shape a reflection of the holy Mount Meru or, alternatively, an overturned begging-bowl. The earliest of the Buddhists' soaring rock-cut *chaityas* (worship halls) date from the 2nd century BC, and some 1,200 examples were to be carved by Jains and Brahmans in the following centuries, as were *viharas* (literally shelters, but used to mean very simple, austere monasteries). The best examples are the *stupas* at

The 5th-century Dhamekh stupa *at Sarnath (above)*
Decorative wall painting, Great Rann of Kachchh (below left)

Sanchi and Sarnath, and the *chaityas* and *viharas* of Ajanta and Ellora. Hundreds of years later, Buddhism also produced the staggering monasteries of the Himalayas.

WRITHING FAÇADES Hindu temple architecture developed from the forms evolved by the Chalukya people (6th–8th centuries) around Badami. These inspired the great southern dynasty, the Pallavas, whose influence spread well beyond India. Mamallapuram and Kanchipuram are the places to see their work. Their techniques and vision were further refined by the neighbouring Cholas in

18

The exquisitely carved interior of a Jain temple, Ranakpur (above)
Erotic sculpture, a hallmark of Hindu temple architecture (left)

Chittaurgarh. It is often said that Jain temples reflect a more serene metaphysical approach, but in fact the interiors show bold combinations of features, in a kind of Indian baroque. The prosperous Jain community ensures that the temples are well maintained. Another major circuit of Jain temples exists in Karnataka, where Jain was once the state religion, its finest work the 10th-century colossus of Shravanabelgola.

Thanjavur and the Hoysalas around Mysore. For filigree carving, the temples here are unsurpassed, and the writhing sculptures that face their lofty *gopurams* (gatehouses) became a hallmark of all southern temples. Other major Hindu architectural schools were developing to the north, in Khajuraho and Orissa, both perfecting the design of gently curved, ribbed and carved towers. Erotic imagination and sculptural skills culminated in the breathtaking Surya temple at Konark, in the 13th century.

NOT SO PLAIN JAIN Contemporary with these were the Jain temples. Rajasthan and Gujarat's astounding examples include the exquisitely carved marble interiors of Ranakpur and Mount Abu, as well as important structures at Jaisalmer, Osiyan and

ALLAH IS GREAT Turkish invaders in the 13th century brought Islamic architectural traditions to India. Mosques, *minars* (towers) and mausoleums rose from the rubble of Hindu and Jain shrines. Under the Mughals India's greatest imperial monuments were created. The Red Fort and tombs of Delhi, the Taj Mahal, Fatehpur Sikri and Golconda Fort are just the cream of a decorative style that blanketed northern and central India, producing delightful pockets such as Mandu, and infusing Rajput palaces with Persian decorative detail. It also produced vast monuments such as Hyderabad's Jama Masjid. British architects of the Raj took inspiration from Islamic structures for their Indo-Saracenic style, which can be seen in a range of colonial structures.

Inventive, skilful, ingenious and immensely varied, whether produced in mud-huts or urban factories, handicrafts are among India's greatest attractions. Persuasively marketed across the country, they make compelling viewing on the great subcontinental trail.

The basis of India's crafts industry is an enormous and cheap labour force, employed in cottage industries or mass-production to churn out the symbols of the nation's cultural diversity. When a Western visitor carries away a hard-bargained-for carpet, he or she should bear in mind that it may have been produced by under-paid children. Ethics aside, the wealth of handicrafts is such that it becomes confusing. A choice is difficult; should it be a Kashmir shawl or a rosewood carving from Kerala, a bronze statue of dancing Siva or an inlaid sandalwood box from Mysore?

❑ India's cheap, stylish clothing is perfectly adapted to the climate. Few female visitors don a sari, however beautiful its fabric, but many adopt the *salwar kameez*, a long-sleeved dress and matching trousers originally worn only by Punjabi Muslims. This makes an acceptably modest outfit for less-visited areas and is also practical. Cotton *kurtas* (the long tunics worn by Indian men) are another practical item for male and female visitors, as are Nehru-style waistcoats. Indian tailors are everywhere and adept at copying clothes to order. ❑

BIG-CITY BUYS The finest-quality goods usually find their way to the bazaars and emporia of Delhi, Mumbai (Bombay), Kolkata (Calcutta) and Chennai (Madras). Thousands of 'craft-shops' are run for foreigners in tourist towns, with many items actually designed as tourist souvenirs. Foreign visitors can also shop for craft items alongside locals, in pricey antique shops, state emporia or stalls in local bazaars. The main centres of large-scale production are Rajasthan (producing fabrics, jewellery, glass, pottery, miniature paintings, rugs, brass and wood inlay, camel-hide products and embroidered slippers), and Kashmir, which despite its turbulent political situation still manages to produce fine carpets, shawls, embroidery and decorative papier-mâché objects. Kashmiri merchants have spread throughout

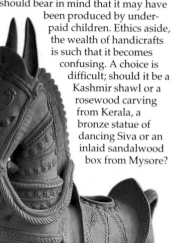

A selection of typical Indian handicrafts

India and are often the wiliest and toughest businessmen, but they generally have quality stock.

MINORITY ARTS Some of India's most intriguing crafts are produced by its many tribal communities. They include the fine wire animal *tarakashi* of Orissa, and Nagaland's larger bronze sculptures. Specialities abound: one-off tribal weavings in Assam, Mizoram's bamboo hats and the Khachchhs's mirror embroideries and copper-bells. In the Himalayas, a vast amount of Tibetan and Ladakhi silver, turquoise and coral jewellery is available, some of it, sadly, once the property of Tibetan refugees. This mountainous area is also the source of an endless supply of woollen shawls of wildly varying quality.

GLITTER Indian jewellery shops specialize in the very bright 22-carat gold that is popular throughout Asia. Tribespeople often trade in their traditional silver jewellery for this seemingly more attractive investment, and jewellers may have sacks full of chunky silver bracelets and anklets under the counter. They are usually sold by weight. Less pricey brass and copperware is superbly worked as trays, cups or plates. The

Traditional silver jewellery worn by a tribeswoman in Rajasthan

Camels are frequently the subject of folk art in Rajasthan

best was made in Varanasi a few decades ago and is still available. Bidriwork, a Deccan speciality of Aurangabad and Hyderabad, is a matte gun-metal alloy finely inlaid with silver and gold, that is used to make boxes, vases and *huqqas* (water-pipes). Stainless steel kitchenware, a great bargain that has the added advantage of being extremely light, is sold throughout India.

Music, the mirror of India's soul, encompasses classical Hindustani ragas, melodramatic cinema sound-tracks and the sound of a solo flautist on the ramparts of a Rajput fort. Dancers, enacting a form of worship, obey rigid rules, whether carrying a pot of fire or using minute gestures to subtly convey emotions.

The colourful Bharat Natyam Dance of Orissa (above)
Traditionally, playing musical instruments was a male preserve (right)

❏ Rajasthan is one of the most richly rewarding regions for folk dances, devotional songs and music. Professional tribal performers in brilliantly coloured costumes entertain villages throughout the state, with mesmerising fire-dances, dramas on mock horses and cymbal and drum-dances, to the accompaniment of haunting ballads and hand-crafted instruments. ❏

In spellbinding solos or group displays of swirling colour, glittering ornaments and fluid movements, Indian dance forms can be enjoyed purely for their visual appeal. At the other extreme are the intent, almost motionless groups of cross-legged musicians who pluck the spirit and emotions as they create a melodic build-up of rhythms that, although improvised, conforms to predetermined movements. Behind both forms lies India's diverse regional cultures and historic fusion of Vedic, Turkish and Persian musical traditions.

DEVOTIONAL DANCE Originating from the chanted hymns of the sacred *Vedas*, music evolved to express the seasonal cycle and the rhythm of agricultural work, becoming interlinked with dance forms to celebrate the harvest, greet a particular season or worship a specific god. Classical dance rules were set down in the 2nd century BC, categorizing three aspects: *nritta* (pure dance); *nrittya* (emotional expression) and *natya* (drama). Young dancers became a part of worship, performing in Hindu and Jain temples and inspiring countless sculptural renderings (*apsaras*) of their ritualized positions. Orthodox Hinduism later came to frown on what bordered on seduction, even prostitution, and temple dancing was eventually banned. The few events that show Hindu dance in its original home, the temple precinct, include the Khajuraho Dance Festival held in March, the Konark Dance Festival and that of Mamallapuram, both in December.

STAR TURNS Of the many dance forms of worship, each with its own vocabulary of emotions, poses and steps, the best known is the dramatic and colourful Kathakali of Kerala. This is a male-only dance form, with larger-than-life characters symbolically made-up. Equally captivating is Odissi, Orissa's ancient dance form.

Odissi performances of Hindu myths in extravagant costumes and jewellery, accompanied by musicians and singers, are sometimes staged in Puri's Jagannath temple and may be seen every November during the Konark Dance Festival.

MUSLIM MOODS The courts of the Turks and Mughals gave rise to the tradition of the *ragas*, melodic structures of between five and twelve notes within which musicians improvise. *Ragas* are defined and played according to the time of day and season and their suitability for a masculine or feminine audience, and players try to match the ambient mood. Within each *raga* are several movements, each of which would once have lasted for hours but is now reduced to suit shorter concentration spans. The final movement, subdivided into three sections, introduces percussion, in complex patterns of sound and rhythm. Although instruments were traditionally a hereditary male domain, women contributed as vocalists and are now becoming musicians in their own right. Southern India's Carnatic music developed in the 18th century in Thanjavur, and, although following the *raga* structure, is livelier and uses modified versions of the traditional instruments. Major music festivals are held in New Delhi, Mumbai (Bombay) and Chennai (Madras), with Gwalior's Tansen Festival a highlight every December.

❑ String instruments include the sitar, invented in the 13th century, its smaller version the sarod, the sarangi (said to be one of the most difficult instruments in the world as its 40-odd strings are held by the finger-nails), and the santoor, a zither of Persian origin. The shahnai is the main wind instrument, similar to an oboe, and bamboo flutes are widely played. Percussion is dominated by the versatile tabla, whose invention is attributed to the creator of the sitar. ❑

23

Countless festivals pepper the Indian calendar. They may be devoted to gods, seasonal agricultural celebrations, political events, culture, camels or the anniversary of a philosopher, but all are excuses for re-enacting customs that may date back hundreds, if not thousands, of years, and offer mesmerizing images drawn from India's deep-rooted beliefs.

India's festival calendar is enviable. Whether the occasion is a desert camel festival in Rajasthan, the Onam festival snake-boat races in Kerala, kite-flying in Ahmedabad, dragging Lord Jagannath's chariot in Puri or a monastery ceremony in Ladakh, the size and enthusiasm of the crowd will probably be enormous. Traditional festivals are now rivalled by sports fixtures, and hundreds of thousands will turn out to cheer on their cricket heroes. For visitors, some festivals make pleasant chance interludes, but others should be firmly fixed on the itinerary.

The paint-splattered face of a Hindu during the riotous festival of Holi

HINDU FANFARES Each religious group in India has its own calendar of major festivals. For Hindus, the beginning of winter (late October to November) is marked by Diwali (Deepavali), the festival of lights, inspiring the lighting of millions of oil-lamps in the home and firecrackers outside. These celebrate the homecoming of the hero Rama and his wife Sita (the subjects of the epic poem, the *Ramayana*), while prayers are made to Lakshmi, goddess of wealth, and boxes of sweets are exchanged between friends, families and business associates. This five-day festival is the Hindu equivalent of Christmas, also widely celebrated. Spring brings Holi, a riotous festival in which coloured water and paint are liberally scattered, leaving most people who venture into the street doused in pink, blue and silver (a pigment which happens to be toxic). Northern India in particular revels in the social levelling that occurs during Holi. Specific gods have their festivals: Siva has Shivatri, Ganesh has Ganesh Chaturthi, celebrated in

Maharashtra, and Durga, Durga Puja, celebrated in Bengal for nine days.

PROPHETS AND SAINTS The Muslim community holds major celebrations for Id-E-Milad, the birthday of Mohammed, as well as for Muharram, the Islamic New Year and Idul Fitr, the feast that ends the 28-day Ramadan fast. Saints' shrines, for example at Ajmer, give rise to particularly fervent anniversary celebrations. Sikhs pay annual homage to each of their ten gurus, with processions to *gurudwaras* (places of worship), readings of the holy Granth and feasting. The biggest Jain festival celebrates the birth of the religion's founder, Mahavir in April, and Buddha's birthday at full moon in May is marked by major processions in Sarnath and Bodh Gaya. The Parsis celebrate Jamsedi Navoroj, their new year, in March–April.

CAMELS AND ELEPHANTS Pushkar's camel fair is one of the most popular regional festivals; others take place at Tarnetar in Gujarat and at Bikaner. These are social focal points for local tribal people and present unparalleled images of India at its most exotic.

The Great Elephant March at Thrissur, Kerala (above)
Sikhs celebrating outside a gurudwara, *in the Punjab (above left)*

The south has its own fabulous celebrations: Onam is the August and September harvest festival, marked by snake-boat races through Keralan backwaters. Spring (March/April) brings numerous *pooram* festivals complete with elephant pageants and musicians. Tamils go wild in January for Pongal, also celebrated in Karnataka and Andhra Pradesh, with processions of cows whose horns and bodies have been brilliantly painted. *Ragolis* (chalk floordrawings) are renewed, and a sweet porridge is consumed.

❏ The festival of Kumbh Mela is held every three years in one of four holy towns: Nasik, Ujjain, Allahabad or Haridwar. According to Hindu mythology, drops of pure ocean water fell on them en route to the Himalayas. The number of pilgrims is estimated at about 12 million each time. ❏

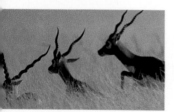

Habitats ranging from the snowy Himalayas in the north to the rainforests of the south give India a unique selection of wildlife. This rich world is threatened by poaching and the growing population. If conservation measures are not strictly enforced, much of it will soon be relegated to history.

❑ Squawking vultures and crows monopolize urban birdlife—head for the hills to watch bulbuls, flycatchers, wagtails and pheasants. In the mountains, eagles and other birds of prey circle through the skies. Elsewhere, India's national bird, the peacock, is ubiquitous, while grasslands nurture storks, minas, drongos, hoopoes and weavers, and the marshes have cormorants, cranes and storks. Flocks of brilliant green parakeets are a sure sign that you have reached subtropical climes. ❑

India plays host to an astonishing 350 mammal species, 2,100 bird species, and thousands of different amphibians, reptiles and fish. Concern over animals and their habitat is ages old,

Visitors watch animals at a pool in the National Park of Ranthombre

as much of Indian mythology and ritual is inextricably linked to the deification of creatures and plants. Emperor Ashoka (3rd century BC) called upon his subjects to conserve forests, which were reserved for meditating ascetics and saints, and to refrain from slaughtering wildlife. Today, India boasts 572 reserves, including 89 national parks, 16 bird reserves and 22 UNESCO biosphere reserves. Yet the magnificent tiger is only just surviving (see page 100).

GOING, GOING... As forests diminish by an estimated 1,500sq km (580sq miles) each year to make way for farms, mines, hydro-electric projects, human occupation or just for fuel, wildlife is directly jeopardized. Only an estimated 13 per cent of the subcontinent remains under dense forest cover and even this is subject to fires which propel tigers and elephants into nearby villages to create havoc, if not to kill. In 2002 Asam witnessed an extraordinary

case of rampaging wild elephants, fired by consuming vast amounts of local liquor, which led to human fatalities. Respect for wildlife is greatest amongst the traditional inhabitants of the forest, usually tribal people who have an intuitive understanding of animal habits. During the days of the Raj, they were favoured as trackers and *mahouts* (elephant handlers). At the other extreme are gangs of poachers working with smugglers. Elephants are massacred for their ivory tusks, tigers for their skins and other parts prized in China and elsewhere as aphrodisiacs. Despite stiffer penalties introduced in 2002, poorly equipped forest rangers are unable to stop the slaughter.

SURVIVING GLORIES What remains is a fabulous array. The Himalayas are home to the legendary snow leopard, yak, musk deer, ibex and a variety of pheasants. There are chinkara stag, black buck, barking deer and bear on the higher slopes, and musk deer, red pandas and blue sheep lower down. The varied vegetation of the vast Gangetic plain harbours herbivores such as elephants, sambar deer, wild boar and chital (spotted) deer, as well as leopards and tigers, and fresh-water dolphins in the rivers. The rare one-horned rhinoceros is found only in Assam, while Gujarat, to the west, harbours the last 300 Asiatic lions. The barren wastes of the Thar Desert are home to the Indian bustard, wild asses, black buck and nilgai (blue bull) as well as domesticated camels, commonly seen chewing leaves off roadside shrubs. In the wetter, subtropical south, rainforests are home to monkeys, civet cats, elephants, sloth bears, tigers and leopards.

Monkeys such as Hanuman langur live in both towns and forest

NATIONAL PARKS You are never very far from one of India's national parks. They offer the best chance of seeing wildlife; start in the cool of dawn if you can. The isolation of many parks makes access tricky, phones do not always function and booking schedules constantly change: the best bet for independent travellers is often simply to turn up and hope for a cancellation. Bird sanctuaries are richest from November to February when they fill with migratory species. Most parks close down during the monsoon months.

Who said curry? In India, this dish does not exist. Instead, there are countless aromatic regional dishes reflecting historical influences. With rich meat dishes in the north and subtle vegetarian mixtures in the south, gastronomic experiences are high on the list of Indian pleasures and few visitors are disappointed.

Pulses, nutritious and inexpensive, feature in many Indian dishes

Other countries may have Indian restaurants, but these usually have only a pale and partial imitation of the real thing. In India itself you can sample succulent roadside *pakora* (vegetable pasties), have a feast of *thali* (small servings of several dishes) served by attentive waiters, slurp a Tibetan noodle-soup or crack open a lobster straight from the Indian Ocean. As varied as everything else in the subcontinent, Indian cuisine can be subtly spiced or chilli-hot, succulent meat or purely vegetarian, savoury or sweet, simply baked or simmered in rich sauces of yoghurt and coconut. The much misused word 'curry' may come from the Tamil *kari*, one of the plants that contributes to the spicy masala sauce favoured in the south. Another misused word is chutney: the

real Indian thing is a divinely fresh, herbal concoction that has little to do with the sweet bottled variety.

SPICES At the heart of Indian cooking are spices: black pepper, cardamom, cinnamon, cloves, cumin, ginger, turmeric, nutmeg, and others, all of which grow on the fertile slopes of the Western Ghats. In the 16th and 17th centuries, western countries fought wars over the spice trade, fortunes were made and lost, empires were created and spices far exceeded gold in value. Many were first used for medicinal purposes, as they act as both appetite stimulators and digestives. They also help the body cope with long periods of heat, a property shared by numerous varieties of chilli.

SOUTHERN APPETITE South India, more strongly Hindu than the north, has a predominantly vegetarian cuisine, accompanied by rice flavoured with coconut or lime. *Thalis* were once served on banana-leaves, but now come on a tray packed with steel bowls and are generally eaten with fingers and *chapatis* (unleavened bread) to mop up more liquid sections. *Masala dosa*, a puffy rice pancake filled with potato and spiced vegetables, is the south's favourite snack and is eaten for breakfast. Other fillers that start the southern day are *iddli*

Rich and creamy buffalo milk, purified by boiling (above)
Spicy snacks, eaten for breakfast (left)

sambar (steamed rice cake with a spicy lentil and vegetable sauce), *oopma*, a spicy semolina, and its sweeter cousin *kesari* (syrupy semolina with raisins). India's equivalent of pizza is *uttapam*, a filling rice-flour pancake topped with onions. Fish is widely consumed, including pomfret, shark, kingfish, prawns, crab and lobster.

MUGHAL FLAVOURS Hyderabad, with its long Muslim traditions, is a gastronomic highlight. Mumbai (Bombay), too, has a wide range, including the pungent Bombay Duck, which is actually dried bummalo fish. The north has a tradition of very rich cooking, much influenced by Mughal cuisine and characterized by the use of yoghurt (*dahi*), cream, fried onion, nuts and saffron in meat dishes. Mildest of all is *biryani* (rice cooked with saffron or turmeric, lamb or chicken and dried fruits). *Tandoors*

(clay ovens) are used for baking chicken, lamb or fish marinated in yoghurt, herbs and spices. Other outstanding dishes include *gushtaba*, spicy meatballs, *paneer*, cubes of cottage cheese, fried and served in a butter-based sauce or with vegetables, and the omnipresent *dal* (lentils), consumed with rice and *roti* (unleavened bread). *Dal* is the staple diet of India's poorer inhabitants.

❏ Typical sweets are *kulfi*, ice cream flavoured with cardamom, pistachio nuts and saffron, *rasgulla*, cream-cheese balls in syrup, *gulab jamun*, ground almond balls with honey, and *firnee*, a richly flavoured rice pudding. Ancient Ayurvedic culinary principles stressed the importance of all six *rasas* (flavours): sweet, salty, bitter, astringent, sour and pungent. ❏

India's version of Silicon Valley has propelled it to the forefront of world computer technology. This is the most obvious reason not to consider India as a backward agricultural country. Abstract thought, when it is applied to something other than the complexities of Hindu metaphysics, is a potentially profitable national talent.

Information technology attracts multinational investment

Bangalore is the undisputed capital of information technology in India, flourishing in the middle of Karnataka's cotton and millet fields. The city is the proof of India's technological progress, and is the world's third-largest assembly of scientific and technological manpower. Television-assembly plants, satellites, millions of new telephone lines, nuclear submarines, combat aircraft and rockets are among the many items produced and/or designed as a result of the consistent technological research and development spearheaded by India's first nuclear test in 1974. Hyderabad, too, follows closely behind.

BANGALORE BRAINS Large foreign companies have flooded to Bangalore to make use of low-cost data-processing. Clients include numerous inter-national banks and accountancy firms. Savings can be substantial as salaries paid to Indian accounting staff are about one-fifth of those paid in the West, while improved communications systems and computer networks mean that advantage can be taken of time differences across the world.

India's fast-growing computer industry increased software exports by over 70 per cent in the 1990s and seems set to continue. As an additional claim to fame, the Pentium chip and Hotmail were the creations of home-grown talent.

❑ One of the offshoots of the Indian proclivity for computers is a widespread trade in illegal unbranded products. Homemade computers are assembled by engineer whizzkids from circuits boards, hard disks, CD readers and other peripherals purchased at markets in Mumbai (Bombay) and elsewhere. The machines are about 25 per cent cheaper than brand-name computers and, according to purchasers, their performance is equally satisfactory. However, this activity is being targeted by the authorities and there are signs that it is now being curbed. ❑

India was

Around 4,500 years ago, a sophisticated urban civilization emerged in the Indus Valley. It eventually succumbed to Aryan invaders and their rulers, priests, rituals and Sanskrit language. Aryan literature, especially the **Vedas,** *formed the religious and social foundations of the Hindu system that still endures today.*

India's earliest traces of human activity date back to 400,000–100,000BC but it was only around 7000–5500BC that crudely made brick houses, agriculture, pottery and jewellery appeared. Excavations in Baluchistan, the western province of Pakistan, have revealed more sophisticated craftwork and workshops dating from 4000–3000BC. These represent the genesis of a cultural unity that encompassed Baluchistan, Afghanistan, southern Turkmenistan and the fertile Indus Valley.

HARAPPAN CIVILIZATION The mighty Indus river, flowing down from the mountains of Kashmir to the Arabian Sea, nurtured this sophisticated civilisation that reached its zenith in 2500–2000BC. Urban settlements emerged, at Mohenjodaro and Harappa (both now in Pakistan),

A copper vase, over 4,000 years old, dating from the Harappan period

Rajasthan's Kalibangan and Gujarat's trading-ports of Lothal and Maliya Miyana near Rajkot. Evidence survives of brick-built citadels, *tanks* (artificial lakes), drainage, irrigation and two-storeyed houses. Finds have included steatite seals engraved with enigmatic animal designs, terracotta figures and bullock-carts, toys, bronze statues, and jewellery, made or inlaid with semi-precious stones, shell, ivory, gold and copper. By no means isolated, the so-called Harappan civilization traded as far away as the Arabian Gulf, but its pictogram script composed of over 400 signs still remains undeciphered.

ARYAN ADVANCE The end came around 1700BC, brought about by both environmental changes and Aryan invaders from the northwest. The latter brought a hierarchical system that was to form the basis of India's castes. They also brought Sanskrit and India's oldest literary source, the *Rig Veda*, probably composed over a long period starting in 1300BC. It consists of 1,028 hymns guiding priestly activities, and is the origin of the influential Vedic culture that persists today. From their regional base between the Yamuna and Sutlaj rivers (roughly corresponding to the Punjab and Rajasthan), the Aryans gradually subjugated local Dravidian peoples, enslaving them, intermarrying or driving them south. Their

❏ Vedic rituals stemmed from the notion of *agnihotra*, the basic reciprocal relationship between man, the gods and the universe. They included drinking fresh milk before sunrise and after sunset, animal and even human sacrifice, and the consumption of the sacred liquid *soma*. This was probably a hallucinogenic obtained from mushrooms, which led to a state of heightened consciousness. ❏

political system was based on a *raja* (ruler) who shared sovereignty with two tribal consultants (of undefined roles), a military general and a priest, who performed sacrifices to ensure each tribe's prosperity and victories.

CASTE DIVISIONS It was during the Vedic era that the four divisions of society appeared: the *Brahmins* (priests); the *Kshatriyas* (warriors); the *Vaishyas* (merchants) and the *Sudras* (serfs). Each *varna* (colour) was sub-divided into a multitude of sub-groups (*jâtis*) that correspond to castes. At the basis of Aryan society was the family unit, patriarchal and monogamous, dependent on a mixed economy of cattle and agriculture,

with horses used for battle, and goats and sheep for wool. Their ritualistic religion was dominated by three divinities, Mitra, Varuna and Indra. Boys were initiated at seven years' old to receive religious instruction and learn the rites and oral formulas of the *veda* (knowledge) until, at the age of 17, they were ready to marry. Girls were not instructed.

POSTVEDIC As the centuries rolled by, another body of Vedic literature took shape, the *Brahmanas*, whose legends included the story of Janaka, king of Videha, father-in-law of Rama and protector of sages, propagated in the new mystic doctrines of the *Upanishads*. These Sanskrit sacred texts probably date from 600–400BC and reflect an evolved post-Vedic society which had also produced the great epic poems, the *Mahabharata* (including the Bhagavad Gita, much consulted by Gandhi) and the *Ramayana*. Originally transmitted orally they were written down centuries later. Aryan society was thus poised for its first great dynasty, the Mauryas.

*Limestone die (right)
Harappan bangles and ear studs (below)*

33

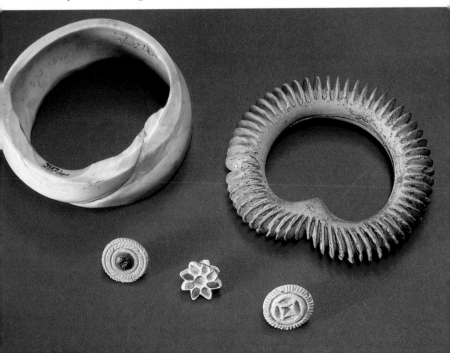

Within a key period of two centuries, India witnessed the birth of two religions, Buddhism and Jainism, saw influences brought by Alexander the Great from Persia and Greece, and produced its most influential dynastic emperor the Mauryan Ashoka.

Alexander the Great invaded India and settled troops there

Valley in 326BC from his vast Persian and Mediterranean empire. The last of Alexander's garrisons was forced to leave India in 317BC but their impact was such that, even 70 years later, Greek was still widely spoken in north-west India. The relatively short-lived Mauryan dynasty filled the political vacuum left by relentless battles and alliances between Persians, Greeks and Indians. Greeks were employed in Persia's administration and army and, according to one ancient text, became accepted as *Kshatriyas* (warriors), despite them being non-Brahmans and therefore impure.

The Mauryan dynasty ruled over most of the subcontinent from about 320 to 185BC, and was much influenced by the statecraft of Alexander the Great, who invaded the Indus

❏ The first Persian incursions into India took place during a major crisis in Brahmanism in the 6th century BC. This was also when Buddhism and Jainism first appeared. Buddha and Mahavir (founder of Jainism) underwent their *nirvanas* (enlightenments) in around 527BC and 498BC respectively. Both taught in northeastern India, in what is now Bihar, which consequently became more important. ❏

RISE TO POWER Alexander the Great had been advised by Chandragupta Maurya to advance to the Ganga (Ganges) and attack the powerful but unpopular Nanda dynasty, whose rule stretched to Bengal. In the event it was Chandragupta himself who deposed the Nandas. From his capital at Pataliputra (in today's Bihar), the sovereign expanded his kingdom, built up a centralized bureaucracy supported by efficient judicial and espionage systems, and used Sanskrit as the official language. Buddhism and Jainism were meanwhile gaining ground and Chandragupta retired to a Jain monastery, leaving the state in the hands of his son. The empire spread into the Deccan, and in about 272BC, Emperor Ashoka came to the throne. He was to leave a lasting legacy throughout India.

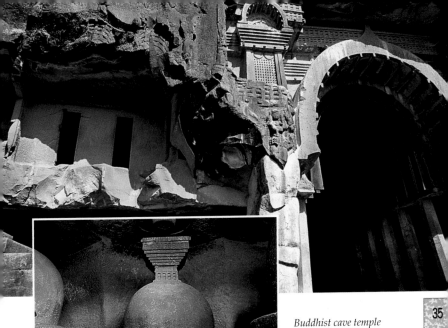

*Buddhist cave temple
c200BC at Bhala*

**GENESIS OF INDIAN
ART** At the same time,
the foundations of
Indian art were being
laid. Magnificent stone capitals
surmounted the enormous pillars
inscribed with Ashoka's edicts. Proof
of their lasting impact is that, in 1947,
the lion capital at Sarnath was chosen
to be the emblem of independent
India. Not only pillars but thousands
of *stupas*—reputedly 84,000—were
erected. Each contained a relic com-
memorating events such as a miracle,
Buddha's *nirvana*, his death, or even
marking one of his footprints. These
masterpieces in stone, visible in all
their glory at Sanchi, are the first
substantial relics of Indian art. Indian
architecture, too, developed during
Ashoka's reign. Cave-temples reminiscent of Persian tombs were carved
into the Barabar Hills in Bihar, north
of Bodh Gaya, as retreats for Buddhist
monks. These temples initiated a
tradition that was to produce the
marvels of Ajanta and Ellora and last
over 1,000 years.

THE FIRST EMPEROR Ashoka's
momentous reign is well recorded by
his inscriptions. These are a boon for
historians as they clearly define his
principles. Soon after his accession,
Ashoka's declarations became
infused with the Buddhist doctrine
of *dharma*, and discouraged his
citizens from killing (although insist-
ing on the need to 'reform' the people
of the forest). Government methods
became more flexible, assuming a
paternalistic tone, animal sacrifices
were forbidden and pilgrimages to
Buddhist sites replaced hunting expeditions. Though Ashoka was tolerant
of all religious beliefs, it was during
his reign that Buddhist canons
written in Pali were taken by missions
throughout Asia.

Ashoka's death, in 232BC, sparked
off a war of succession among his
sons, and the administrative strength
of Mauryan rule was eroded. The
empire fragmented and, in 185BC, the
last Mauryan emperor was killed.

❑ The Pali script, derived from
Sanskrit, appeared in the 3rd
century BC and became the
language of ancient Buddhist
texts. It is still used in Sri
Lanka, Myanmar (Burma), Laos,
Thailand and Cambodia. ❑

The fall of the Mauryan empire marked the end of Indian unity, as rival powers fought over the different regions. Initially the strongest was the Kushan dynasty; later the Gupta empire was predominant. The arts flourished as never before but could not stop India's next invaders, the Huns.

By the beginning of the Christian era, orthodox Hinduism using Vedic sacrifices was developing as a counter to Buddhism. Some time after the first century AD, a doctrine based on the *Upanishads* was codified into the *Vedanta* ('end of the Vedas'). This contained the Brahma Sutras, still revered in modern intellectual Hinduism today.

Another important element to emerge was yoga, a physical and mental discipline leading to self-knowledge. It represented the concept of self-denial and penance performed by Siva, at that time still perceived as the Vedic god Rudra.

KUSHANS North India was again beset by foreign invaders. Bactrian Greeks, Scythians and Yueh-Chi (southern Mongols) fought over tiny kingdoms but were overcome by the Kushans from Afghanistan, whose greatest leader, the Buddhist Kanishka (1st century AD) controlled a

The Ajanta caves, near Aurangabad, were chiselled from layered granite rock

> ❑ Gandhara's Buddhists originated the changes that ultimately produced Mahayana Buddhism, a more humanistic faith that split from the monastic Therevada Buddhism. ❑

vast empire from Central Asia to Varanasi. His immense power was celebrated in his three titles: the Indian Maharaga (great king), the Iranian King of Kings, and the Chinese Son of Heaven. From their capital in Peshawar (Pakistan), the Kushans promoted the art of statuary, notably in the Greek-influenced schools of Gandhara and Mathura. This was also the most important era of the Silk Road, the great trading route from China to Rome. Alternative routes taken by camel caravans connected the high plateaux of Central Asia with the ports of Gujarat.

SOUTHERN TURMOIL Meanwhile, the south saw endless bloody battles between the Cholas, the Ceras and the

Pandiyas, despite the pacifist presence of numerous Buddhists and Jains. Under the Sungas and Andhras, who controlled much of the Deccan, Buddhist *stupas*, *viharas* and *chaityas* multiplied, becoming increasingly sophisticated in structure, proportion and sculpture. Sanchi's magnificent *toranas* (gateways) date from the Andhra period as does the Great Stupa at Amaravati, where the first image of the figure of Buddha was made, cAD200. With the decline of Andhra power in the Deccan, Brahmanism again came to dominate the centre and south.

GUPTA ART In about AD320 Chandra Gupta founded a dynasty in northern India which for the next 150 years witnessed a new sophistication in Hindu art, literature and science. During this crucial period the foundations of India's Classical Age were laid; concepts developed over the previous centuries ripened and took fresh life from the new spiritual outlook of Brahmanism. Buddhism was by no means eclipsed: the serene Buddha figures of Mathura were carved at this time, and at Sarnatha a wealth of sculptures embodying an increasingly refined and perfected style was produced. Around AD400, this artistry overflowed into Gupta Hindu art, and some of the first examples of Indian painting were made at Ajanta.

RISE AND FALL Chandra Gupta II (376–415) propelled the Guptas to their zenith, expanding his kingdom over most of northern India and the Deccan, and estab-

lishing his capital at Ujjain. During his reign, the works of the great poet and writer, Kalidasa, outlined the Hindu ideal, and a new calendar system was elaborated to commence with the Vikrama era. Prosperous and efficiently run, the empire encouraged poets, philosophers and artists, even organizing literary competitions. Although the Guptas were orthodox Vishnuites who upheld Vedic sacrifices and the caste system (only the lower castes and untouchables ate meat, for instance), they also tolerated Buddhism, which continued to flourish, notably at Ajanta. This harmonious era was not to last. Under Kamaragupta, successor to Chandra Gupta II, the Huns started attacking the north. Both victories and defeats followed, but Gupta power had definitively declined by AD550.

37

Below: A statue of a Hindu goddess with a man killing a lion

As the Gupta empire disintegrated, India became a patchwork of independent kingdoms that went on to produce some of central and southern India's greatest temples and finest sculpture. While their influential styles spread overseas, rival empires flourished and declined as they fought for internal power.

By the 7th century AD, Hinduism was firmly established in the south and in the Deccan, giving rise to the fabulous temples of the Chalukyas, Pallavas, Cholas, Hoysalas and Pandiyas. Jainism flourished under the Chalukyas and Hoysalas, leaving a string of important shrines. The south was unaffected by the advance of Islam in the north, and was able to nurture an unrivalled and unhindered flowering of Hindu and Tamil culture.

Gatehouse at Kamakshi Aman temple,

CHALUKYAN From successive capitals around Badami between the 6th and 8th centuries, the Chalukyan dynasty carried out India's first great experiments in temple building. Evolving from the earlier *chaitya* and *vihara* forms (see pages 18–19), the increasingly imaginative designs had a far-reaching influence. *Mandapas* (pillared halls) and *shikharas* (towers marking the location of the deity), both became dominant features in Hindu temples. Although confirmed Vishnuites, the Chalukyas encouraged Sivaite and Jain worship. At their most powerful they controlled a vast empire extending to Kanchipuram and Orissa. It included Ajanta and propelled their fame as far as Persia, but this affluence and power attracted enemies who eventually destroyed them. Their successors in the Deccan from around 750, the Rashtrakutas, were responsible for the wonders of Ellora's rock-cut Kailasa temple.

PALLAVAS One of Badami's attackers was the great Pallava dynasty. Since the 4th century, the dynasty—whose people were renowned as great traders and seamen—had held sway over southeast India from Kanchipuram. They were to spread their influence to much of Southeast Asia, and there is evidence of early links with Greece and Rome. Originally Buddhist, they converted to Brahmanism in the 5th century. Over the next three

Chola bronzes from the 10th century

centuries they developed a style of cave-temples, carved granite monoliths and astounding bas-reliefs that is still visible today at Mamallapuram (its name means 'place of the wrestler', referring to the great Narasimha Varman I). The Pallavas disappeared in the 9th century when they were conquered by the neighbouring Cholas.

CHOLAS This dynasty had already experienced periods of power from its base at Thanjavur, but enjoyed a renaissance around 850 that began 300 years of momentous expansion. Sweeping through Pandiya and Cera territory, the Chola kingdom eventually encompassed today's Tamil Nadu, Kerala, Sri Lanka, the Lakshadweep and Maldive islands, southern Andhra Pradesh and Karnataka, Orissa and part of Bengal. Their zenith was during the reigns of Rajaraja (985–1014) and Rajendra (1014–44), when naval expeditions accomplished the partial occupation of Myanmar (Burma), Malaysia and Sumatra, as well as control of the profitable trade routes of the Indian Ocean. This political stability, accompanied by economic prosperity, encouraged a blossoming of the arts and Tamil culture.

❏ Cholan artistry survives in their extraordinary Sivaite temples at Thanjavur, incorporating refined versions of Pallavan stone sculpture, and above all in their bronze sculpture. Cast with the lost-wax technique using clay moulds, Cholan bronzes reached unsurpassed heights of grace, symbolism and detail. ❏

LAST GASPS By the mid-13th century the Cholas had been superseded by their old enemies, the Pandiyas of Madurai in the south and, to the west, the Hoysalas. The Pandiyas, too, had been a great trading power from the first centuries AD, establishing links with Greece, Rome and China. They also fostered a flowering of Tamil literature. Their new supremacy lasted only until 1364, when they were absorbed by the spreading Vijayanagar empire of Hampi. The Hoysalas, originally a group of hill chieftains who had been feudal subjects of the Chalukyas, are known for their temples at Halebid, Belur and Somnathpur, whose ornate filigree carvings are totally different from the geometric style of early Pallavan structures.

Rajputs, Palas, Turks and Arabs were the chief protagonists of northern India's turbulent 'medieval' period. While Islamic invaders were encroaching on the north, Hindu and Buddhist temple architecture experienced a last period of flowering quite unaffected by Islamic styles.

Carved chariot wheel at the Surya (Sun) Temple at Konark—crowning glory of Orissan medieval art

Of the numerous rulers and short-lived dynasties that immediately followed the Guptas in northern India, there is little significant trace, except in the case of the philosophically inclined Harsa (606–47). Both the poet Bana and the Chinese pilgrim Hsuan Tsang made detailed accounts of his kingdom, which stretched from Gujarat to Bengal. Hsuan Tsang relates that Buddhism was noticeably declining and that new practices such as *sati* and Tantric cults had appeared in Hinduism. From the 8th to the 10th centuries, two dynasties shared the spoils of northern India: the Palas of Bihar and the Rajputs of Rajasthan. Obsessive power struggles eroded their power, and their domains eventually fragmented into numerous vulnerable kingdoms.

PALA POWER The height of Pala power in Bihar was reached under King Dharmapala (770–810) who revived Buddhism and even exported it to Tibet. Surrounded by a sea of Brahmanism, only the Buddhist sites of Bodh Gaya, Nalanda and Sarnath still functioned, supported by streams of Buddhist pilgrims from Southeast Asia in search of *darshan* (mystic ecstasy). The monastery of Nalanda reached heights of splendour, vividly described by Hsuan Tsang who stayed there in the 7th century. Pala sculptors expanded the Bodhisattva pantheon and created numerous symbolic icons, yet their style became increasingly lifeless and stylized. By the 12th century, Buddhism and Brahmanism started to overlap, and Buddha was even accepted by Hindus as the ninth incarnation of Vishnu.

TEMPLE TRYST Parallel to this decline in Buddhism, Hinduism was creating

□ From the 7th century onwards, Tantric ideas permeated both Buddhist and Brahmanic philosophies. Tantra asserted that *shakti* (the female principle) was the dominant force in the universe through its power to energize the dormant male force, a belief that gave rise to the agitated consorts of the Hindu trinity. The notion of ecstatic bliss achieved through sexual union led to the formation of secret Tantric groups but was eventually suppressed by Hindu orthodoxy. Muslim invaders were particularly efficient at effacing its images. □

spectacular temples in Orissa, including the Kesari dynasty's countless structures at Bhubaneshwar and the Ganga dynasty's masterpieces at Puri and Konark (c1240). The distinctive Orissan style was the climax of centuries of development and was the last great expression of Hinduism before the influences of Islam were felt. Erotic sculptures at Konark and at Khajuraho, a product of the Rajput dynasty of the Chandelas (10th–13th centuries) point to the rise of Tantric thought at this time.

RAJPUTS Thought to be descended from the Huns and their accompanying Central Asian tribes, the bellicose Rajputs (meaning 'sons of kings') held sway over Rajasthan and part of Gujarat from the 7th century onwards, but were never able to maintain a united front. Despite being constantly embroiled in war, these warriors built stupendous forts that peppered the hills and desert of Rajputana. Individual princely states rose and fell but the Rajput clan (the warrior caste) went on, instilling fear even in the Mughals and the British.

ISLAM ARRIVES After gathering strength throughout Central Asia and conquering Sind in 712, the Arabs consolidated their power and that of Islam, but it was not until 988 that India was deeply affected. In that year Mahmud of Ghazhi, the son of a

Lavishly carved marble columns at Mount Abu, Rajasthan (above)
Hindu temple complex, Bhubaneshwar, Orissa (top)

Turkish slave and self-promoted champion of Sunnite Islam, was employed by the Caliph to rid the Indus Valley of all Hindus. Increasingly motivated by the immense wealth he found, he made several raids, including attacks on Mathura in 1017, Delhi in 1018 and Somnath in 1026. Later Turkish invaders defeated the Rajputs in 1192, and then attacked Gwalior, Varanasi (Benares) and Lahore. In 1206 Delhi fell to the Turks, and by 1236 Turkish domination of north India was complete.

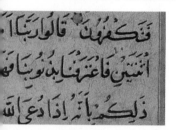

For some 300 years India endured the oscillating power of the Sultans of Delhi. Whether barbarous or enlightened, illiterate slaves or erudite nobles, these Turkish rulers maintained a firm hold on their conquests, suffering at the hands of the Mongols but only finally destroyed by internal rivalries. Meanwhile, Hinduism saw its last great dynasty at Vijayanagar.

The Qutb Minar marks the triumph of
Islam in Delhi (left)
Genghis Khan (below)

❑ Urdu, the Muslim language of India and Pakistan, evolved in the military camps of India's first Turkish invaders (the English word 'horde' comes from 'urdu'). It was later written down in the Arab-Persian alphabet and, although an Indo-Aryan language, incorporates numerous Arab and Persian terms. ❑

A slave-soldier named Iltumish seized power in 1211 and consolidated Turkish rule. The Mongols, led by Genghis Khan, swept through central Asia, causing a stream of Turkish and Persian refugees to join the Turkish administration in Delhi. In 1221 the Mongols reached the Indus Valley, where they turned back. In 1296, another Mongol advance to the Indus led to the rise of a new Turkish dynasty, the Khaljis, whose Sultan Ala-ud-din extended the Sultanate across the Deccan and Gujarat. Although non-literate, Ala-ud-din nurtured architecture and the arts, and made Urdu the official tongue.

UPS AND DOWNS Rebellions, assassinations and death in battle were common events of the Sultanate, which went into marked decline

under the Tughluqs (1320–1414). Under the threat of Mongol and Chinese invaders from the north, they set up a second capital at Daulatabad. Gradually the Sultanate fragmented as the Vijayanagar kingdom grew stronger and numerous independent sultanates appeared, such as those in Bengal, Kashmir and Madurai. From 1351 an interlude of peace and prosperity under Firuz saw the introduction of free hospitals and aid to the poor, and even the translation of 1,500 Sanskrit manuscripts into Persian. Indian Muslims governed and Hindus were employed in their administrations.

TURKISH FINAL Central power was definitively on the decline, however, and was helped on its way by the Mongol Timur, an adept at devastation, pillage and butchery, who reached Delhi in 1398. An estimated 5 million people died in the ensuing genocide, and the resultant famines and plagues accelerated the end of the Sultanate. The Sayyids in 1414 were followed by the Lodis in 1451. Under the Lodis, Afghan nobles became an influential force of dissent, causing Ibrahim Lodi to turn to the Punjab governor for support. The latter's decision, in his turn, to call on Babur, the ruler of Kabul for help, opened the doors to India's next great conquerors, the Mughals.

VIJAYANAGAR Meanwhile southern India was witnessing the rule of one of its greatest Hindu dynasties, the Vijayanagar, who had emerged after a revolt against the Tughluq governor

The Jama Masjid in Old Delhi

in 1336. Their adopted name came from a Vedic master, Vidyarana, who was the spiritual guru of two young local Hindu princes. Successive Vijayanagar rulers oversaw a new Hindu renaissance and expanded their territory, governing from a glorious and prosperous capital, the ruins of which can be seen at Hampi. It was financed by tribute from vassal states that by the early 15th century spread south to Madurai. Devaraya I (1406–22) employed Muslim soldiers for whom he built a mosque.

DAZZLING Inexorably, internal ambitions frittered away Vijayanagar power. Nevertheless, Krishna Deva Raya (1509–29) was described by early Portuguese accounts as a magnanimous king, wrathful yet inclined towards poetry, ruling from (Hampi, see pages 220–1) and head of a powerful army of elephants and javelin-throwers. Vijayanagar provinces were ruled by Nayaks who oversaw the rajahs of small territories; all were obliged to attend the grand festivities held in the capital and some were permanent courtiers. Public order was maintained with the help of mutilation, impalement and hanging. Rice was exported to the Persian Gulf and sugar to Southeast Asia, while cotton, diamonds, pearls and tropical hardwoods were also produced. Krishna Deva's successors saw Vijayanagar power crushed by the combined forces of the Deccani sultanates, and led by Akbar in 1565 they ransacked the majestic capital.

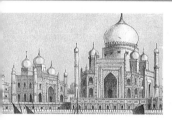

The Mughal empire made monumental changes in Indian culture, religion and government. Islam dominated, but enlightened rulers ensured religious tolerance, while artists, writers and craftsmen received imperial patronage—until the religious fanatic Aurangzeb provoked the empire's downfall.

44

Babur, founder of the Mughal dynasty, was descended from the ferocious Mongol Timur and also from Genghis Khan. 'Mughal' derives from the Arab-Persian word for Mongol, but Babur's immediate origins lay in the hills of Turkestan from where he conquered Kabul. In 1526 he defeated Ibrahim Lodi, the last of the Delhi Sultans. Although unimpressed by his Indian conquest, he laid the foundations of political and military power and established courtly traditions of the arts that were adopted by all subsequent Mughal emperors.

AKBAR'S EXPANSION At Babur's death in 1530, he was succeeded by his son Humayun, who was equally well educated but less militarily astute, and was ousted by an Afghan chief, Sher Shah, within a decade. In 1556 Humayun recaptured Delhi but, plagued by bad luck, died accidentally a month later, leaving

Anup Talao pavilion, part of Akbar's ambitious capital at Fatehpur Sikri

a 13 year-old son as heir. This was Akbar, who in the years to come was to prove himself as a great statesman, conqueror and mystic. From 1561 onwards he launched assaults that reduced the power of the Rajput (who later became allies), annexed the maritime states of Gujarat and Bengal, and swallowed up Bihar and Orissa. In 16 years he had constructed the Mughal empire.

ECLECTIC TALENTS Under Akbar's rule (1556–1605), the empire was strengthened. Power was centralized, a reformed administration introduced fairer taxation and rents, the *durbar* (public audience hall) became a feature of court rituals, and religious tolerance prevailed. Endless philosophical debates led Akbar to found a new religion combining several beliefs and much influenced by *Sufism.* Among his other passions were elephant fighting, music, poetry, painting (nurtured during his childhood in Persia) and architecture (reflected in the ceremonial capital of Fatehpur Sikri and the fort-palace of Agra).

ART AND OPIUM In 1605 Akbar was succeeded by his son, Jehangir, whose upbringing in his father's scintillating court inclined him towards the arts rather than warfare. Jehangir later wrote his memoirs and commissioned countless works of art and literature. His adored Persian wife, Nur Jahan, a highly intelligent, artistically inclined princess, assumed a significant hold on state affairs from 1622 onwards, as Jehangir succumbed increasingly to the pleasures of alcohol and opium.

URBAN PLANNER Jehangir's death brought his son, Shah Jahan (1628–58), to the throne. Far from being a pronounced aesthete like his father, Shah Jahan set about renewing Mughal military conquests, west into Central Asia

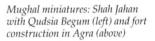

Mughal miniatures: Shah Jahan with Qudsia Begum (left) and fort construction in Agra (above)

and south into the Deccan. Yet he also had his more refined traits: he built the legendary Taj Mahal, and the new walled city of Shahjahanabad, better known as Old Delhi, as well as enriching the forts of Agra and Lahore.

THE ZEALOT Despite these marvels, the Mughal empire was disintegrating, and its last ruler, Aurangzeb, lacked the scheming qualities which had helped his predecessors to hold it together. This son of Shah Jahan, usurped his brother, the designated heir, in front of their dying father. He then used all his military and political skills to try and strengthen the unwieldy empire. However, his religious zeal led to the introduction of orthodox Islamic laws, destroying Hindu temples and withdrawing imperial patronage of the arts. On his death, in 1707, the Mughal empire shrank to the environs of Delhi and from then on its power was a mere charade.

❏ The Mughal school of painting originated in a state workshop founded by Akbar. It employed about 100 artists, mainly Hindu, working under two Persian masters brought to India by Humayun. By the time of Akbar's death his library held about 24,000 illuminated manuscripts. The Akbari style blended Persian art with Indian elements, using extended space, lively action and even European realism, inspired by illustrated bibles brought by Portuguese Jesuits from Goa. ❏

45

While the Mughals were developing Islamic civilization inland, India's coastline was increasingly encroached upon by European powers. After the Portuguese came the English, establishing strong bases that, through astute manipulation, eventually led to the hegemony of the East India Company.

British king, William III's Grant of Arms to the New East India Company dated 1698

In 1498, Vasco da Gama laid anchor at Calicut, on India's Malabar Coast, inadvertently opening the gates of India to European powers. The arrival of Alfonso de Albuquerque as Portuguese viceroy in 1508 gave the impetus for the establishment of strategic west coast trading-posts, and above all for the development of the capital at Goa, all of which remained under Portuguese control until 1961. Close on their heels, in 1605, came the Dutch East India Company (VOC), but its Javanese interests left little time for expansion in southern India.

TURNING-POINT The commercial appetite of the British had been awakened by tempting tales of spices, silks and sandalwood. A landmark victory over the Portuguese off Surat, in 1612, led to their being accorded trading rights at Surat by Emperor Jehangir. Within 40 or so years, the British had established effective control over southeast India (founding Madras, modern Chennai, in 1639) and Bengal. Control over the latter was confirmed by Robert Clive (once known in British schoolbooks simply as Clive of India) in 1757 at the battle of Plassey. This was a crucial point in British involvement, which was centred on the burgeoning city of Calcutta (now Kolkata).

Vasco de Gama

CONFLICT AND EXPANSION Relations with the Mughals in north India were much aided by the East India Company's habit of paying for cloth in silver bullion. In the south, ongoing wars between minor kingdoms gave the British the perfect opportunity to practise 'divide and rule' tactics, allying with one ruler against another in exchange for trading rights and taxes. In 1799, the British carved up the state of Mysore, ending more than a century of Franco-British rivalry in India, which had started when the French established a trading-post at Pondicherry in 1674. War broke out in 1744, giving France temporary supremacy in Madras and expanding its influence in the Deccan and Orissa. In 1758 a

VASCO DE GAMA.

46

❏ A treaty signed with the Mughal emperor in 1765 gave Clive (representing the East India Company) control over taxation in Bengal, Orissa and Bihar. Under Governor Warren Hastings, nominated in 1772, the Company gained monopolies over salt, opium and saltpetre. In Britain, the 1784 India Act gave the government authority over Company governor-generals. ❏

Lord Clive, who turned the East India Company into a military power

new governor was given the task of seizing all British possessions. The taking of Madras by the the British in 1760 put an end to Gallic ambitions in the subcontinent outside existing French *comptoirs* (trading-posts). It also ended the ambitions of Hyder Ali and his son, Mysore's hero, Tipu Sultan, who was previously allied with the French. He died in battle against Arthur Wellesley, later Duke of Wellington, in 1799.

MUGHAL VICTIMS Meanwhile, the Mughal emperors had been under threat from the Marathas to the south ever since the latter's Hindu leader, the ruthless Sivaji, had killed the Nawab of Bijapur and set up a powerful base at Pune. Sivaji's death, in 1680, put an end to Marathi aspirations for a while, but they resurfaced under the Maratha confederacy, which united under the banner of Maharashtra nationalism (still simmering today). Land to the south was unassailably dominated by the Nizam of Hyderabad, but to the north, the weak Mughal empire offered better pickings (this weakness had already been exploited by a Persian invader in 1739, who massacred thousands and looted treasures from Delhi's palaces). By the 1750s, Delhi's gates were simultaneously threatened by the Marathas from the south and Afghans from the north. A battle between these two forces left the Afghans victorious, but they were forced by internal problems to retreat, while the Maratha confederacy fell apart. Seizing their opportunity, the British stepped in. By the early 19th century, British control over India was virtually complete.

British power was strengthened through the East India Company, until the Uprising of 1857 precipitated momentous change. Queen Victoria was appointed Empress of India, and the subcontinent became the legendary 'jewel in the crown' of the world's largest empire. Inevitably, though, colonialism nurtured a desire for independence.

After definitively quashing the Marathas (see page 47) in 1818, gaining Assam through war with Myanmar (Burma), and taking control of Sind, Punjab and Lower Burma (Myanmar) in 1852, the British had complete supremacy over India. A network of princely states were supposedly independent allies, but a law introduced by Lord Dalhousie (Governor-General 1848–56) stipulated that the state of any ruler who died without a male heir would automatically be annexed. Thus Oudh, the last major independent state of north India, passed into East India Company control in 1856.

REFORMS The East India Company had lost its commercial monopoly in 1813 but expanded its political and

Storming of Delhi in 1857, *by George McCulloch*

military role. It controlled the taxation system, appointed British officers to lead the *sepoys* (Indian soldiers) of the army, and appointed governor-generals. After centuries of war, India's infrastructure was in ruins. The countryside was terrorized by *dacoits* (bandits) and *thuggee* (who ritually sacrificed their victims in the name of Kali, goddess of destruction). From the 1820s, governor-generals began to instigate reforms, some stimulated by humanist thinking at home. *Sati* was abolished and attempts were made to eradicate *thuggee*. Western-style schools and colleges were founded, English ousted Persian as the official language, and canals, roads, railways and telegraph systems were developed.

THE UPRISING India's first war of independence was sparked off in 1857. Hindu and Muslim sepoys

❏ Some 3,000 people (mainly British families and their loyal Indian servants and soldiers) were besieged for three months at Lucknow in 1857. When finally freed by a battalion of Scots and Sikhs, only 1,000 were alive. ❏

were offended by having to bite gun cartridges which they believed to be greased with cow and pig fat (respectively counter to their religious tenets). From Meerut, the mutineers marched on Delhi and gained the backing of the last Mughal emperor, Bahadur Shah, then in exile in Kanpur, and the royal family of the recently annexed Oudh, in Lucknow. The rebellion spread fast, igniting the latent fears of Indians who had been undergoing radical changes to their traditional lifestyle. There were atrocities on both sides. Within a year the British regained control and executed thousands of Indians. Bahadur Shah was exiled to Rangoon.

BRITISH RAJ The momentous result of the Uprising was the abolition of the East India Company and establishment of British government control through a viceroy. In the new organization, local maharajas and nawabs were cosseted as never before: their territorial sovereignty was assured, and their egos were polished by medals and cannon-salutes. The 1858 India Act also established the Indian Civil Service. The Indian Army played a major role not only in regional conflicts against Afghanistan and Myanmar (Burma), but also worldwide, anywhere British interests were at stake. Queen

Regal statue of Queen Victoria as Empress of India in Calcutta

Victoria's coronation as Empress of India in 1877 marked the zenith of the British Raj.

RUMBLING DISCONTENT A new, western-educated, Indian élite arose, including businessmen, civil servants and landlords, who saw the short-comings of a political system that negated Indian identity, and of an economic system exploiting India's raw materials and its huge market for British manufactured goods. A British initiative produced India's first political party, the Indian National Congress, in 1885. Wary of Hindu dominance in the country, the Muslim community formed its own associations, leading, in 1906, to the creation of the Muslim League. Then, in 1915, a certain Mohandas Gandhi returned to his country from South Africa.

Gandhi's return to India gave impetus to a struggle marked by civil unrest, riots and repression, as well as the radicalism of Nehru's Congress party. The Quit India campaign and the violence resulted, in 1947, in Lord Mountbatten's preparations for independence.

God is Truth. MKGandhi

show of silent resistance. The protesters were not all silent, and in Amritsar, General Dyer's troops fired into the crowds, killing 379 and wounding another 1,200. This notorious event set the fuse of resistance alight. The writer and philosopher Rabindranath Tagore returned his knighthood to the Viceroy, riots erupted all over India, and martial law was imposed. Gandhi initiated non-cooperation, including the boycotting of schools and law courts, and the burning of British textiles. He soon found himself in prison, not for the last time. In 1921 he took to wearing the homespun *dhoti* (loincloth).

Mohandas Gandhi had spent 21 years in South Africa, masterminding the use of *satyagraha* ('strength of the truth'), or passive resistance to government, to oppose apartheid. Back in India, he found a country ripe for revolt. Britain, fully aware of the mounting threat, instigated more administrative autonomy but, soon after, tightened repression through imprisonment without trial.

AMRITSAR MASSACRE In 1919, Gandhi's first overt act of opposition was to organize a *hartal* (day of mourning), in fact a general strike and

PROGRESS The 1930s began with the Congress party's declaration of Independence Day, inspired by a combative Nehru who had now assumed leadership, and by Gandhi's well-publicized salt-march (see page 84). Demonstrations, strikes and political imprisonments increased until finally Viceroy Irwin and Gandhi struck a truce, and the latter, clad in his *dhoti*, travelled to London for talks. The Government of India Act of 1935 gave increased power to Indian ministers within the context of a federation, yet kept finance and defence in the hands of the Viceroy. This advance helped Congress in the 1937 elections.

Left: Gandhi—known as Mahatma, meaning sage
Right: Nehru with Lord and Lady Mountbatten

CRACKS India's Muslim community was far from happy, however. The first riots between Hindus and Muslims took place in 1930, and the leader of the Muslim League postulated the formation of a Muslim state, Pakistan, to encompass Punjab, Afghania, Kashmir and Sind. When Congress did not share power, after its 1937 electoral successes, in provinces with substantial Muslim minorities, the Muslim League leader, Mohammed Ali Jinnah, became the unyielding advocate of the creation of Pakistan.

ESCALATION In World War II, the Indian Army played a major role for the Allies, but British prime minister Winston Churchill remained hostile towards Indian independence. In 1942, Gandhi and Nehru encouraged Congress's adoption of the Quit India Resolution, which resulted in the imprisonment of most party leaders. Tension was exacerbated when countless people died in the 1943 famine in Bengal, and a further 10,000 were killed there in riots. There was also widespread violence in the Punjab.

FREEDOM AT A PRICE In 1947, when the new viceroy, Lord Mountbatten, was instructed to negotiate independence, India was on fire. Gandhi, Nehru and Patel (Congress's other leader) agreed on the need for speed, but Jinnah's demand for Pakistan proved an obstacle. Consensus was finally reached: India was to be partitioned, with Bengal and the Punjab becoming East and West Pakistan. In the following months, over 10 million people were uprooted, as Hindus moved into India and Muslims into Pakistan. Between 500,000 and one million were brutally killed in circumstances described by Mountbatten as 'sheer madness'. However, on 14 August, Nehru's words as India's first Prime Minister rang out to a delirious, free nation.

❑ 'Long years ago we made a tryst with destiny...At the stroke of the midnight hour, while the world sleeps, India will awake to life and freedom. A moment comes, which comes but rarely in history, when we step out from the old to the new, when an age ends, and when the soul of a nation, long suppressed, finds utterance...'
Jawaharlal Nehru, New Delhi, 14 August 1947. ❑

51

Delhi

53

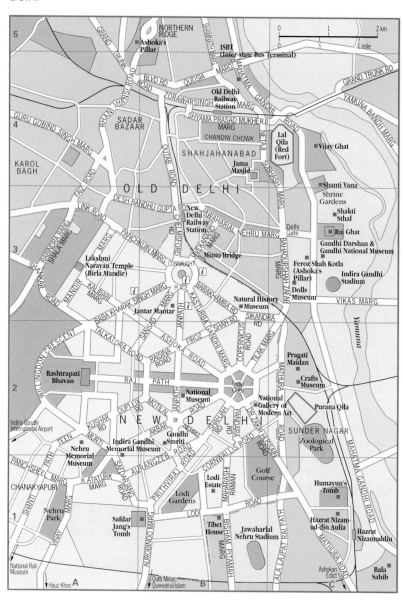

Previous pages: A panoramic view of the city from the Jama Masjid, India's largest mosque

DELHI Of all India's cities, the capital, Delhi, is the most accessible and rewarding for first-time visitors. Parks and gardens are plentiful, street life is colourful, the people outgoing and amenities wide-ranging. Above all, the immense sweep of the city's turbulent history has left magnificent monuments dating to the 12th century and up to the 20th century (the elegant results of Lutyens's urban planning and colonial buildings that marked the transfer of the capital from Calcutta in 1931). Today, Delhi has 14 million inhabitants, and sprawls haphazardly over 485sq km (187sq miles) of verdant avenues, traffic-choked back streets and pungent markets packed with stalls.

Although beggars still occasionally accost cars at traffic-lights and plead with pedestrians, this is a prosperous city experiencing the benefits of India's recent growth. As such it provides a fascinating cultural introduction to this multi-faceted country.

Chandni Chowk, Old Delhi (above)
In the Red Fort (below)

LAYOUT Traditionally said to be formed out of seven successive cities, Delhi is an agglomeration of numerous districts, each with its own history and character. At the centre is a triangle formed by Connaught Place (the commercial hub), India Gate (the war-memorial and symbol of freedom), and Rashtrapati Bhavan, the Presidential residence and symbol of authority. To the north lies Old Delhi, site of the massive Red Fort, the Jama Masjid and the narrow lanes of the bazaars. Here too is Old Delhi Railway Station and, closer to Connaught Place, New Delhi Railway Station. Southeast of India Gate is another cluster of sights, including Purana Qila, the zoo and several museums, ending at Humayun's Tomb in the district of Nizamuddin. West of here stretch leafy residential areas starting at the Lodi Gardens and continuing to the Diplomatic Enclave and luxury hotels of Chanakyapuri. Further south is trendy Hauz Khas and, further still, Delhi's oldest monument, the Qutb Minar. Almost due west of here is the airport.

Delhi

INDEPENDENT DELHI
'Temples, mosques and
Sikh gurudwaras were out-
lined in garlands of light
bulbs. So, too, was the
Red Fort of the Moghul
emperors. New Delhi's
newest temple, Birla
Mandir, with its curlicue
spires and domes hung
with lights, looked to one
passerby like a hallucina-
tion of Ludwig of Bavaria.
In the Bangi Sweepers
Colony, among whose
Untouchables Gandhi had
often dwelt, independence
had brought a gift that
many of those wretched
people had never known—
light.'
Larry Collins and
Dominique Lapierre,
Freedom at Midnight,
1975

HISTORY Although legend and archaeological excavations point to the Purana Qila as the site of an early settlement dating from around 1000BC, the first Delhi was founded by the Rajput Tomar kings in the 8th century AD (see page 41). Four centuries later came the first Muslim sultan and Delhi's longest surviving monument, the Qutb Minar. Under Humayun, the second Mughal Emperor, the walls of the Purana Qila were built; later his widow built his domed tomb, an architectural landmark. Major transfor-mations came when Shah Jahan (see page 45) constructed Old Delhi, an ambitiously planned walled city that still claims India's largest mosque, and includes a palace that evokes the grandeur of his reign and the zenith of Mughal arts. From the late 17th century until the early 20th century, Delhi slumbered while foreign powers were developing India's port cities. Then in 1911, George V announced that the capital of the British Raj would move from Calcutta to Delhi. Sir Edwin Lutyens was appointed to plan the new city (see page 64), and so the leafy imperial avenues and whitewashed residences that still characterize New Delhi. The official inauguration

Gateway to the 16th-century citadel of Purana Qila (above)
Busy, narrow streets typical of Old Delhi (right)

took place in 1931. Just 16 years later Independence provided the first massive celebrations in the new capital.

TODAY'S FACE Lutyens designed the city for some 70,000 inhabitants, and it now has a population of over 200 times that figure, which creates havoc with the overstretched infrastructure. Attempts are being made to cater for the poor, whether with public housing (usually cheaply built concrete apartment blocks) or night dormitories for the homeless. Few tourists see the living conditions of an estimated 30 per cent of the population, squeezed into shacks around the perimeter, although sleeping bodies on the streets of the centre are a common sight. Just as typical are shining new sports stadiums, the ubiquitous mobile phone, golf clubs, a brand new subway sytem (Delhi Metro, see panel opposite) and buses and taxis running on CNG (compressed natural gas). This is India's duality: prosperity and modern technology alongside low quality of living. It is a city worth giving time to, as it effortlessly encapsulates so many stark contradictions together with millennia of history.

DELHI METRO
All three of Delhi's new Metro systems are open. Line One runs from Shahdara to Rithala, Line Two from Vishwa Vidyalaya to Cental Secretariat, and Line Three, inaugurated on 30 December 2005 by Prime Minister Manmohan Singh, connects Barakhamba Road with Dworka via the first stretch of underground railway in the country. When complete the project will have cost Rs10,500 (105 billion rupees). Some 1.5 million passenger journeys are made from 6am to 10pm daily with 250 drivers sharing shifts.

57

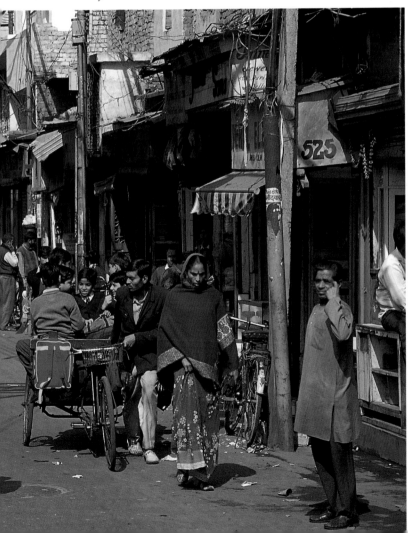

Delhi

VILLAGE IN THE CITY

The Crafts Museum has steered clear of freezing objects in the past. Instead, it interweaves past and present, so following the timeless traditions of Indian crafts. Fragments are displayed in glass cases without captions, so that India's dense craft history is left open to interpretation. Charles Correa's architecture adds to the sense of spontaneity, while the presence of 50 artists and craftspeople (fewer during the monsoon when they must work indoors), who are invited on a monthly basis, gives a living dimension. The adjoining village complex, a remnant of an exhibition set up in 1972, has been decorated by visiting tribal and rural painters.

Statue of Gandhi, Gandhi Darshan and Gandhi National Museum

▶▶▶ Crafts Museum   54C2

Pragati Maidan, Bhairon Marg
Open: Museum Tue–Sun 10–5. Village and craft demonstrations daily 10–5.30. Admission: free

This exemplary complex, a relative new-comer on the Delhi cultural scene, gives a fabulous view of India's multifarious crafts. Innovatively designed by contemporary Indian architect Charles Correa, the museum is meant to resemble an Indian street, with tiled roofs, courtyards, shrines, passages and carved doors. A large courtyard is set aside for invited craftspeople to demonstrate and sell their creations. Whatever your preference—the giant 18th-century *bhuta* figures from Karnataka, the fine tribal bronzes of Orissa, sacred Jain cloth paintings or the entire carved courtyard house from Gujarat—it is an exceptional display. Leave plenty of time to explore the village dwellings, and don't miss the excellent, well-priced selection of handicrafts in the shop.

▶▶ Gandhi Darshan and Gandhi   54C3
National Museum

Raj Ghat
Open: Tue–Sun 9.30–5.30. Admission: inexpensive

This park on the banks of the Yamuna river is where Mahatma Gandhi, Indira Gandhi (who was Nehru's daughter) and her son Rajiv were all cremated: memorials commemorate them. Immediately opposite stand pavilions with photographs, letters and paintings illustrating the life of the Mahatma and his inestimable contribution to India's independence struggle, that tragically ended with his assassination by a Hindu militant in 1948.

▶▶▶ Indira Gandhi Memorial Museum   54A2

Safdarjang Road
Open: Tue–Sun 9.30–5. Admission: free

The elegant whitewashed house where Indira Gandhi lived out her political career now houses a fascinating photographic display covering her life. Visitors flock here at weekends, ending the carefully defined tour at the spot in the garden where she was assassinated in 1984. Photos, excerpts from her speeches, letters, personal accounts (including the premonitory one made shortly before her death) and press coverage are presented beside selected memorabilia (including her spectacles and blood-stained sari). There are views into the family rooms from the exterior. Her close relationship with her father, Jawarharlal Nehru, and her sons, Sanjay and Rajiv, is apparent. The last room is devoted to the tragedy of Rajiv's own life and assassination in 1991. Altogether the museum paints a captivating picture of the woman who did so much to shape contemporary India.

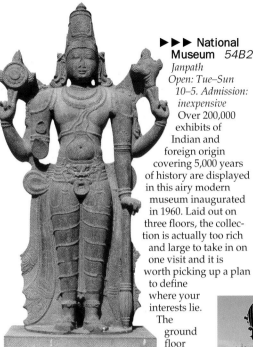

►►► National Museum 54B2
Janpath
Open: Tue–Sun
10–5. Admission:
inexpensive
Over 200,000
exhibits of
Indian and
foreign origin
covering 5,000 years
of history are displayed
in this airy modern
museum inaugurated
in 1960. Laid out on
three floors, the collec-
tion is actually too rich
and large to take in on
one visit and it is
worth picking up a plan
to define
where your
interests lie.
The
ground
floor
covers
India's early civilizations, from the Indus Valley
to Gandhara and Gupta pieces, Cholan bronzes
and Tantric art. An extensive Buddhist gallery
includes the relics of Buddha unearthed in
Piprahwa and over 80 superb *thangkas* (Buddhist
scrolls), sculptures and terracottas.

The decorative arts section contains some
outstanding exhibits, such as an intricately
carved ivory screen, an elaborate silver *huqqa*
(water-pipe) and a room full of jewellery that no
maharana would reject. Upstairs are miniatures (17th
century–1850), and manuscripts, while the more limited
top floor covers pre-Columbian art. The displays are often
reshuffled to accommodate temporary exhibitions.

►► Nehru Memorial Museum 54A2
Teen Murti Bhavan, Teen Murti Marg
Open: Tue–Sun 10–5. Admission: free
This imposing 1930s palace surrounded by lawns and
rose-gardens is devoted to the life of Jawarharlal Nehru,
India's first Prime Minister from 1947 to 1964. Less
dynamic in spirit than the museum devoted to his daughter Indira Gandhi (see opposite), it nevertheless offers
insights, through the photographic display, into Nehru's
education at Harrow and Cambridge, his prodigious
interests and the early years of the independence
movement.

Formal reception rooms, his study and the bedroom
where he died, packed with hundreds of books and
memorabilia, add to the portrait of this far-sighted statesman. His interest in astronomy is recalled in the neighbouring planetarium, where English language shows are
staged on Tuesday and Sunday at 11.30am and 3pm.

This Hindu statue (left)
stands in the gardens of
the National Museum

RAILWAY BAZAAR
At the southern end of
Chanakyapuri and a short
rickshaw ride from the
Indira Gandhi Memorial
Museum is a railway
enthusiast's paradise,
the National Rail Museum
(*Open* Oct–Mar Tue–Sun
9.30–5; Apr–Sep
9.30–7). Whether or not
you have experienced
the wonders of India's
rail transport, this is an
excellent way to learn
about its background.
Outside stands a
collection of vintage
locomotives and
carriages that include
gilded Maharaja specials
and India's first train, an
1855 steam engine.
Model trains are
displayed in the indoor
section.

Above: Humayun's Tomb, a Mughal masterpiece
Right: the beautifully colonnaded Quwwat-al-Islam mosque, dating back to the 12th century

HUMAYUN'S CONTRIBUTION
The history of Delhi from the late 12th century is one of a succession of conquerors, each leaving an important mark on the face of the city. With the advent of the first Mughal ruler, Babur (1526–30), Indo-Islamic culture began to blossom, but it was thanks to his son, Humayun, that the art of miniature painting was adopted and developed in India. This was a result of Humayun's enforced exile by the Afghan rebel Sher Shah, which led him to spend 15 years at the Persian court. Here he became enamoured of the art of miniatures. On recapturing Delhi in 1556 he was accompanied by two Persian masters who were to found the new Mughal school of Indian miniatures.

▶▶▶ **Humayun's Tomb**   54C1
Mathura Road, Nizamuddin
Open: daily dawn–dusk. Admission: expensive
This was the first example of a Mughal garden-tomb in India and remains Delhi's best-preserved Mughal structure. The gardens are now undergoing full restoration. It was completed in 1573, by Humayun's widow, who camped on site during construction and was later buried beside her husband. The 38m-high (125ft) double dome, arches and symmetrical layout of the water-channels and walled garden (*char-bagh* or quartered garden) were all later copied, notably at the Taj Mahal, but their origin lies in Central Asia. The tomb was also the final refuge of Delhi's last emperor, Bahadur Shah II, before he capitulated to the British in 1857. Humayun's white marble tomb itself lies inside the towering octagonal structure of red sandstone inlaid with white and black marble. Lattice screens of stone and marble and endless arches enhance the rhythmic geometry of the building. Several other tombs at the site on the shady lawns create a pleasant retreat from Delhi traffic, and are far less visited than Old Delhi's equivalent, the Red Fort.

▶ **Lodi Gardens and Tombs**   54B1
Lodi Road
Open: daily dawn–dusk. Admission: free
Another escape route from pollution lies in these delightful and historic gardens and tombs built by the Sayyid and Lodi dynasties (see page 43). Flowers, lawns and squirrels surround a cluster of 15th- and 16th-century tombs, with joggers and young cricketers weaving their way in between. The largest, most central structure is the low-domed Bara Gumbad (1494) and its adjacent mosque. About 50m (55yd) north of this lies the Sheesh Gumbad. The tomb of Mohammed Shah (1450), the third Sayyid ruler, prefigures the Mughal style of Humayun's tomb.

▶▶ **Purana Qila**   54C2
Mathura Road
Open: daily dawn–dusk. Admission: moderate
This 16th-century walled citadel was built on the

legendary site of Indraprastha, the 1000BC Aryan capital, by the rival emperors Humayun and Sher Shah. The picturesque stone ramparts, gateways and *chhatris* (domed, open-sided pavilions) dominate Mathura Road, where the main entrance leads through the imposing Bara Darwaza. Inside stands Sher Shah's most outstanding monument, the well preserved Qila-i-Kuhna mosque (1541), built in typical Mughal style of sandstone inlaid with marble. Immediately south stands a two-storey octagonal tower, probably used as a library and observatory. This is where Humayun accidentally met his death in 1556, reputedly rushing to the call of the *muezzin*. Overgrown paths and the occasional *sadhu* add to the fort's atmosphere of crumbling glory.

▶▶▶ Qutb Minar

Aurobindo Marg, Mahrauli
Open: daily dawn–dusk.
Admission: expensive
Delhi's oldest monument, dating from the 1190s, takes some getting to as it is now engulfed by an inglorious suburb served by potholed roads on the far southern outskirts. Yet it is a striking memorial to the triumphant arrival of Islam. The tapered

minar (main tower), 73m (239ft) high with a base diameter of over 14m (46ft), still dominates the area, 800 years on. It was built as a victory monument by Qutb-ud-din-Aibak, the successor of the Afghan conqueror Muhammed Ghuri.

From the main entrance a path leads through the verdant complex to the tower. It is faced with Koranic inscriptions, above which it rises in sections to the summit. These are a result of its lengthy construction period and successive patrons. The 379 steps inside are now closed to the public following various fatal accidents.

Adjoining the tower are the beautiful colonnaded courtyards of the Quwwat-al-Islam mosque, built in the same period using stone from demolished Hindu and Jain temples and twice extended later. At the centre stands a 4th-century relic of the Gupta period, a black iron pillar that was originally part of a Vishnu temple. Immediately to the north stands the rough beginnings of another tower, the Ala'i Minar, initially intended to rise above the Qutb Minar but stopped at just over 25m (82ft). Other structures of interest include the Ala'i Darwaza (south gate—1311AD), several tombs and a *madhrasa* (Islamic college). Guides, drinks and snacks are easily available.

THE IRON ENIGMA
The secret of the iron pillar in the Qutb Minar complex has yet to be unlocked. Sanskrit inscriptions on the pillar reveal that it honoured Vishnu in memory of a 4th-century Gupta king, and it was once crowned by a *Garuda*, the mythical bird-man that Vishnu rides. However no one has fathomed how it came to this spot nor how the cast iron has remained so impeccably rust-free over a period of some 1,600 years. Legend has it that whoever manages to stretch his arms backward and embrace the pillar—as many have done —will have good fortune, but it is now fenced off.

Muslim girl at the Jama Masjid

MUGHAL INSIGHTS
The exhibits of the archaeological museum offer some interesting insights into the Mughal dynasty. A large collection of superb celadon porcelain imported from China is a reminder of justifiable imperial paranoia: it was believed that celadon would break if poison was mixed into the food served on it. Another curiosity is a 17th-century celadon beard-washer. The school of miniature painting, introduced by Humayun and at its zenith under Shah Jahan, shows a notable decline under Aurangzeb, a religious bigot whose disregard for the arts culminated in most of the artists leaving for the more hospitable provincial courts of Rajasthan.

OLD DELHI Despite its name, Old Delhi is far from being the oldest part of the capital, as it dates from the mid-17th century when Shah Jahan moved to Delhi from Agra. A decade of frenetic building produced a walled city, Shahjahanabad, punctuated by 14 gates and crossed by the main shopping street, Chandni Chowk. India's largest mosque, the Jama Masjid, was built near by and the Lal Qila (Red Fort) erected on the banks of the Yamuna River. Only five of the gates still stand and the fortress-palace is suffering from neglect and tourists, but Chandni Chowk and the Jama Masjid continue to function as if the centuries had never been.

▶▶▶ Jama Masjid   54B4
Open: daily dawn–dusk. Admission: free
The so-called 'Friday Mosque', dating from 1656 and an integral part of Shah Jahan's plan, stands south of Chandni Chowk by Delhi Gate. A vast open courtyard is enclosed by a low arcade with three massive gates on the north, east and south sides, each approached by exterior stairs where visitors should remove their shoes. To the west, the direction of Mecca, rise three generous domes and two towering minarets overshadowing the covered prayer-hall and *mihrab* (prayer-niche). It is possible to climb the southern tower (small admission charge) for a fabulous view over Delhi. At the centre of the 900sq m (1,076sq yd) courtyard is a large pool where Muslims perform their ablutions before prayer. Beside it stands a platform designed so that a second prayer-leader could copy the main *imam* inside, although today's loudspeakers have made this redundant.

▶▶▶ Lal Qila (Red Fort)
54C4
Netaji Subhash Marg
Open: daily dawn–dusk.
Admission: expensive
The main entrance to this huge palace of 1648 lies on the west side by a car-park and through Lahore Gate. Beyond this is a covered bazaar, Chatta Chowk, now lined with the predictable souvenir shops. From here an open space stretches to the pretty red sandstone Hathi Pol (Elephant Gate, also called Drum Gate), where visitors once dismounted from their traditional transport before entering the royal palace, serenaded from the musicians' gallery above.

With long overdue renovation under way, access to certain structures may be limited. A path leads between lawns to the Diwan-i-Am, a raised, colonnaded hall dominated by a spectacular marble throne where the ruler gave public audiences. Today's bare aspect belies its original opulence when it was draped in fine cloths and silk carpets, and the

polished plaster surfaces were painted with intricate floral designs. From here a path leads left (north) through the gardens, which were originally landscaped as a *char-bagh*, with fountains and canals dividing the symmetrical layout. At the far northern end of the gardens stand pavilions, including the octagonal Shahi Burj in the northeast corner.

Walking south from here along the walls that once overlooked the Yamuna River (it has since shifted), you come to the tiny Moti Masjid, an ornate white mosque built by Emperor Aurangzeb *c*1660. Next are the *hammam* (bath) rooms, with water-channels laid into the floor and fountains that once spouted rose-water. Beyond stands the finest structure of the fort, the white marble Diwan-i-Khas, where the emperor held private audiences. Although the inlaid precious stones and gold and silver ceiling have disappeared, the delicate structure has echoes of its early grandeur. The adjoining Khas Mahal served as the emperor's private palace and has some remarkable carved marble screens separating the different areas.

Next, to the south and fronting a garden is the Rang Mahal (Palace of Colour) where the extensive harem was housed. Again, most of its extravagant decoration (mirror mosaic, gold and silver inlay, fine paintwork) has long since gone, although the cooling 'stream of paradise' remains, but is now waterless.

Completing the circuit is the Mumtaz Mahal (Palace of Jewels), once an annexe of the women's palace and now converted into a small museum with a wide variety of archeological and other exhibits (*Open* 10–5). From here, a path leads past a drinks stand back to Hathi Pol.

THE SUN AND THE MOON

The southernmost room of the Khas Mahal, known as the Tosh Khana (Robe Room), displays a superb filigree marble screen. Looking from the north (that is, facing the throne-room of the Diwan-i-Khas) you can see a bas-relief of the scales of justice surrounded by small suns. The sun was a symbol of royalty, much used by the Rajputs of Rajasthan and also by Shah Jahan's French near-contemporary, Louis XIV. When viewed from the south, the scales of justice are surrounded by moons.

63

Lal Qila, or Red Fort, is so named because of its red sandstone walls

For nearly 20 years Sir Edwin Lutyens struggled to produce a style of architecture in keeping with India's Imperial status and reflective of its context. Hampered by the demands of officialdom and obsessed with classicism, he nevertheless created a green capital long before the concept became fashionable elsewhere.

VICEROY'S HOUSE

Now renamed Rashtrapati Bhavan and occupied by the President of India, this vast palace suffers from one of Lutyens' mistakes, as he himself confessed. Miscalculating the gradient of Raisini Hill, he realized too late that the palace would not be entirely visible from the base of the processional route on Rajpath. Nor did his concerns include the number of servants needed to keep the 340 rooms shipshape and the 130ha (321 acres) of gardens manicured. Under Mountbatten, over 400 gardeners were employed, including 50 bird-chasers. More successful than Lutyens' perspective calculations, the central dome recalls that of the Buddhist *stupa* at Sanchi.

Rashtrapati Bhavan, formerly the Viceroy's House, in New Delhi was designed by Lutyens

Sir Edwin Lutyens (1869–1944) was an architect steeped in the imperial grandeur of the Edwardian years. This made him the ideal candidate for drawing up an urban plan for the new Delhi—an architect's dream project as it was to include monumental symbols of the Empire. Working beside Lutyens was his friend Herbert Baker, who in 1912 became responsible for the design of the Secretariat and the Legislative Assembly, leaving the Viceroy's House to Lutyens.

Clash of wills Their task was far from simple, as opinions ranged from that of George V, demanding something resembling the style of the Mughal landmarks, to the Viceroy Hardinge, who wanted a western design with 'oriental motifs'. Add to these the liberal voice of Bernard Shaw advocating a totally Indian approach, and you have stylistic and conceptual conflict. Lutyens himself took an obstinate stand: 'Personally, I do not believe there is any real Indian architecture or any great tradition. There are just spurts by various mushroom dynasties with as much intellect as there is in any other art nouveau.'

Fancy dress Lutyens insisted that there were two ways of transferring Western ideas into an alien environment, either to produce 'fancy dress' (meaning a hybrid design) or to create 'an Englishman dressed for the climate'. The latter he achieved in the elegant residential bungalows of the Lodi Estate where the English style is clad in Indian, Persian, Palladian or Grecian clothing. For his government buildings, Lutyens bowed to pressure by adding the odd *chhatri* and other local features to what were essentially grandiose English buildings.

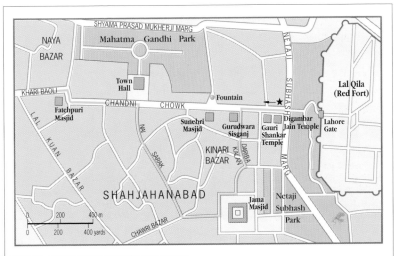

Walk

Old Delhi

Start at the southeastern corner of Chandni Chowk at the Digambar Jain temple. This red sandstone temple (1656) houses a bird hospital from which, in true Jain life-preserving style, the cured patients are released to liberty. There is also some impressive decoration surrounding the main shrine dedicated to Parshvanath, the 23rd manifestation of Mahavir. Immediately west, and announced by mounds of fragrant garlands, is the marble Gauri Shankar temple, Delhi's most sacred Siva temple, sheltering an ancient 12th-century *lingam*.

Following Chandni Chowk west through the mayhem of shoppers, vendors and traffic, the next spiritual landmark is the Gurudwara Sisganj, a Sikh temple. This stands just beyond the corner of Dariba Kalan, a turn to the left that runs through the heart of the Kinari Bazar. Here the lanes are crammed with tiny shops—including glittering jewellers' and specialists in festival finery—food-stalls

and shoppers. The dilapidated Hotel Meru stands on the corner. Follow Dariba Kalan south until it ends at the massive Jama Masjid. After visiting the mosque, go to its western corner and turn into Chawri Bazar, once famed for dancing girls but now specializing in papermaking and selling metalwork. Turn right into Nai Sarak. This is another main artery, with shops dealing in books, stationery, blankets, fabrics and sarees. These offer endless bargains.

Continue back to Chandni Chowk, turn left and head west to Naya Bazar on Khari Baoli. This pungent spice market is the main wholesale centre for Delhi, so traffic in this area is dense. After glimpsing Fatehpuri Masjid, hail a rickshaw and head back to New Delhi.

Shoppers taking advantage of one of the many rickshaws in Old Delhi

Oberoi Maidens, Old Delhi, providing atmospheric, colonial-style luxury

SWINGING NIGHTS?

For a capital city, Delhi has a severely limited nightlife. Clubs and late-night drinks are the preserve of the luxury hotels and are expensive. Annabelles at the Inter-Continental, My Kind of Place at the Taj Palace, EAU Bar and Lounge at Le Méridien and Djinns at the Hyatt nightspots are the city's top dance floors. Other good evening spots are the Maurya Sheraton's Jazz Bar (with live jazz), Le Méridien's Le Belvédère restaurant (live band nightly, until 1am) and the Rodeo restaurant (karaoke and live music Wed, Fri and Sat after 7.30pm on Connaught Place). Live entertainment is also in the Village Bistro Complex.

Accommodation

Delhi, like Mumbai (Bombay), is far from being a budget-traveller's paradise. Accommodation follows the pattern of real-estate and comes at a price, about twice to three times that of the rest of India. There are four main areas to choose from: Old Delhi, Connaught Place, Sunder Nagar and the expensive hotel district of the Lodi Estate and Chanakyapuri. Delhi's sights are scattered, but transport remains inexpensive (after bargaining) and each quarter has its attractions, so ultimately your decision will depend on budget and room availability. Mid-range and luxury hotels can be booked on arrival at the airport and railway station tourist offices, but for budget accommodation just hire a rickshaw and search.

CENTRAL Old Delhi has the atmospheric Oberoi Maidens at the top of the range, and peeling hovels with shared bathrooms at the bottom. There is not much choice in the middle except for the Broadway, well placed between Old Delhi and Connaught Place. In busy Paharganj, near New Delhi's railway station, there is a concentration of budget hotels, mostly insalubrious and with shared facilities. Exceptions are the Metropolis and Star Palace Hotel, both of which benefit from the lively atmosphere of the Main Bazaar. Further south around Connaught Place, Delhi's commercial hub, lies a wide range of accommodation, for example the popular Nirula's and the large Hotel Marina and, further south down Janpath, the plushly refurbished Imperial, complete with pool and gardens. This area is particularly convenient for restaurants and shopping.

SOUTHWARDS Southeast of here, a handful of small hotels surround the shops and gentrified residences of Sunder Nagar. This convenient location is much favoured by businessmen, and if there were more restaurants it would make an excellent tourist base. Here, too, is the illustrious Oberoi. Southwest of India Gate lies a nucleus of luxury hotels, including the traditional Claridges, the reliable Taj Mahal, Ashok and, further afield in Chanakyapuri, the Maurya Sheraton and the Taj Palace.

Restaurants

Delhi's eating places are as varied as its history, ranging from roadside stalls selling samosas to top-class restaurants in the luxury hotels. Although prices are high at the latter establishments, many serve excellent value lunchtime buffets. Most mid-range restaurants are gloomy, indoor affairs (though with air conditioning); if you want to eat outside, the best choices are hotels such as the Imperial with its pleasant garden bar and restaurant.

EATING HOURS
The more expensive restaurants are usually open 12.30–3 and 7.30–11.30. Some hotel coffee-shops have 24-hour service. Establishments around Connaught Place are open from breakfast until 11pm or midnight and serve anything from a coffee or a Kingfisher beer to a full-blown meal.

CENTRAL EATS Connaught Place has a concentration of restaurants, coffee shops and fast-food outlets that are as popular with office-workers as with tourists. Most have Western-style cuisine beside the North Indian classics and also serve beer. The United Coffee House is particularly lively and has excellent service. Non-smokers and vegetarians might enjoy the neighbouring Kovil, a stylishly decorated South Indian restaurant. The Rodeo offers a complete contrast: tequila slammers to wash down the tortillas and waiters in cowboy gear. The ever-popular Nirula's has several different restaurants while Delhi Coffee Home, squeezed between the state emporiums, is an excellent budget destination with an outdoor terrace.

North towards Lal Qila (Red Fort), is the excellent Chor Bizarre in the Hotel Broadway where delicious Kashmiri and Tandoori dishes are served in eccentric surroundings complete with a vintage car. South down Janpath, Le Méridien houses Delhi's best French restaurant, the classic Pierre, and also offers Continental and Indian dinners at Le Belvédère.

SUBURBAN SAMPLING South of India Gate in the smarter residential areas there is a vast choice of restaurants. The Ambassador Hotel has Dasaprakash, a highly recommended South Indian restaurant, and a Chinese Room that serves both Szechuan and Cantonese cuisine. Make the effort to reach the gentrified area of Hauz Khas and you will have a wide choice at the popular restaurant complex of the village Bistro, near the Deer Park. Dilli Haat , to the southwest, is recommended for its complex of regional cuisines, while Defence Colony has an equally tempting choice.

A cup of hot, sweet tea or chai is never far from hand in Delhi

OPENING HOURS

Government emporia open 10–6; private shops operate 9.30–7.30, and often close for a one-hour lunch. All shops around Connaught Place, Janpath, Sunder Nagar, Chandni Chowk and the Santushti Arcade are closed on Sundays. This is the day to head south for the market and shops at Lajpat Nagar (closed Monday) or Hauz Khas (closed Tuesday).

SON ET LUMIÈRE

Soak up Delhi history in sound and light shows at Lal Qila (covering 326 years) or Purana Qila (from the *Mahabharata* to Independence). English performances, lasting an hour, begin from 7.30pm to 9pm depending on the season. Book through Government of India Tourist Office or ITDC for Lal Qila and DTDC for Purana Qila (*Admission: moderate*).

Traders sell a wide range of merchandise, but be prepared to bargain

Shopping

Delhi is full of places that tempt you to empty your wallet. Bargaining is part of any transaction except in fixed-price state emporia and the more expensive shops, places which for some visitors will be a relief. Avoid being whisked away to a 'special address' by your rickshaw- or taxi-driver as drivers' commissions are built into the price you will pay, adding on 20–40 per cent.

Visitors interested in handicrafts should visit the Crafts Museum (see page 58) as its shop and the resident crafts-people have a range of quality goods at reasonable prices. Near here, at Sunder Nagar is a string of specialist shops where you can stock up on anything from carved chairs to bronze Buddhas—all at a price. A favourite for quality furnishings, clothes and contemporary Indian designs is the Santushti Shopping Arcade, NWC Race Course near Chanakyapuri, where individual shops are dotted around a pretty garden. Just south of Sarojini rail station is Dilli Haat, a market for crafts (and cuisine) from many regions. Even further south, and equally fashionable with the local clientele, are the excellent and varied shops of Hauz Khas Village.

Back in the centre, Connaught Place is always a useful area for a variety of goods, including a wide selection of books at Bookworm (B-29) and the New Book Depot (B-18). Street stalls on Connaught Place and along the pedestrian street off Janpath are packed with cheap and cheerful goods. Two blocks down Janpath opposite a string of so-called 'Tibetan' shops is the government-run Central Cottage Industries Emporium, with a wide selection of handicrafts, carpets, household goods and fabrics.

More spread out but with an even greater choice are the various state emporia and the excellent shops selling *khadi* (hand-made, hand-printed cloth) along Baba Kharak Singh Marg running south-west of Connaught Place. To get a feel for the hustle and bustle of shopping here check out the bazaar area of Old Delhi, where you will find the best everyday domestic goods, saris and spices.

Practical details

One of Delhi's ubiquitous black-and-yellow taxis

WARNING At New Delhi railway station deal *only* with the International Tourist Bureau on the first floor—staircase to the left of the main information board. Ignore anyone, however plausible, who tells you it is somewhere else.

MOBILITY For a quick overview of Delhi's scattered and numerous monuments, take a guided tour. The ITDC (tel: 2332 0031), and Delhi Tourism (tel: 2331 5322/4229), offer similar tours, lasting a half-day or full day. Otherwise Delhi's vast expanse is best covered by taxi or auto-rickshaw, as buses are overcrowded and favourite haunts of pickpockets. Although taxis are metered, it is rare to find a driver who uses the meter for foreigners. If your time is short, negotiate a half-day or full-day rate: this saves energy. Hotel staff will give advice on a reasonable current rate. In 2002, the Delhi metro was inaugurated, connecting Connaught Place with the railway stations of Old and New Delhi, Chandni Chowk and the inter-state bus station.

GUIDES There is no shortage of English-speaking guides at each monument but ask to see their official identification as unofficial guides are legion, usually loitering around the ticket offices outside.

MONEY Delhi banks are open Mon–Fri 10–4 and Sat 10–1. Outside these hours you can change money at Thomas Cook's at the Imperial Hotel, at the Ashok Hotel's Central Bank or at the airport. Otherwise there are authorized money-changers at large hotels and certain shops. ATMs are plentiful in Connaught Place. Avoid street touts—an apparent gain is generally a loss.

CULTURE To get the most out of Delhi and to get a flavour of Indian cultural life, sample the art exhibitions, concerts, dance and yoga courses. The best source of information is the weekly listings magazine, *Delhi Diary*, available at large hotels or from news stands on Connaught Place.

TOURIST OFFICES
India Tourism Delhi, 88 Janpath (*Open* Mon–Fri 9–6, Sat 9–4.30; tel: 011 2332 0005/0008/0342, fax: 011 2332 0109, email: goitodelhi@ tourism.nic.in,www.incre dibleindia.org). Counters at airports.
ITDC, L-Block, Connaught Place (*Open* daily 7am–9pm; tel/fax: 011 2332 0331).
DTTDC, N-36 Connaught Place (*Open* Mon–Sat 10–6; tel: 011 2331 5322, tel/fax: 011 2331 3637, email: info@delhitourism.nic.in, www.delhitourism.nic.in). State Emporia Complex, Baba Kharak Singh Road (*Open* daily 7am–9pm).

AIRPORT TAXI WARNING
Extra care should be taken with taxis from the airport. Ensure you have two copies of the pre-paid taxi receipt including the taxi registration number. Insist on going to your chosen hotel, not the driver's recommendation. In emergencies, call the police on 2337 8888 (24 hours).

The Northwest

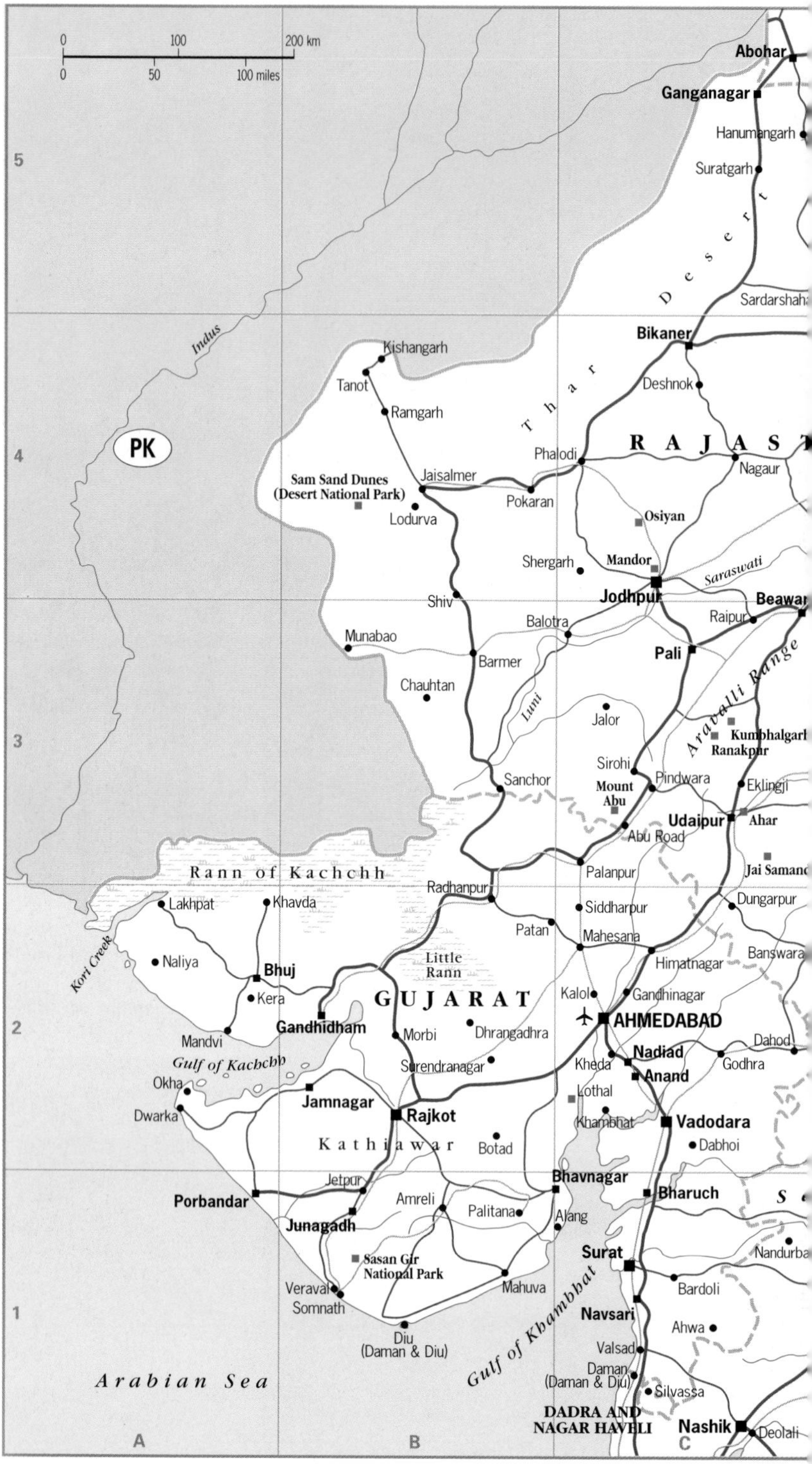

72

The Northwest

0 100 200 km
0 50 100 miles

Abohar

Ganganagar

Hanumangarh

Suratgarh

Sardarshah

Thar *Desert*

Indus

PK

Kishangarh

Tanot

Ramgarh

Bikaner

Deshnok

Jaisalmer

Phalodi

R A J A S

Sam Sand Dunes
(Desert National Park)

Lodurva

Pokaran

Nagaur

Osiyan

Shergarh

Mandor

Saraswati

Shiv

Jodhpur

Beawa

Munabao

Balotra

Raipur

Aravalli Range

Barmer

Pali

Luni

Chauhtan

Jalor

Kumbhalgarl
Ranakpur

Sanchor

Sirohi

Pindwara

Eklingji

Mount
Abu

Udaipur

Ahar

Abu Road

Rann of Kachchh

Radhanpur

Palanpur

Jai Samand

Kori Creek

Lakhpat

Khavda

Patan

Siddharpur

Dungarpur

Naliya

Little
Rann

Mahesana

Banswara

Bhuj

Kera

G U J A R A T

Kalol

Himatnagar

Gandhidham

Morbi

Dhrangadhra

Gandhinagar

AHMEDABAD

Dahod

Mandvi

Surendranagar

Kheda

Nadiad

Godhra

Gulf of Kachchh

Okha

Jamnagar

Rajkot

Lothal

Anand

Dwarka

Khambhat

Vadodara

K a t h i a w a r

Botad

Dabhoi

Porbandar

Jetpur

Amreli

Palitana

Bhavnagar

Bharuch

S

Junagadh

Alang

Sasan Gir
National Park

Mahuva

Surat

Nandurba

Veraval
Somnath

Gulf of Khambhat

Bardoli

Diu
(Daman & Diu)

Navsari

Ahwa

Arabian Sea

Valsad
Daman
(Daman & Diu)

Silvassa

DADRA AND
NAGAR HAVELI

Nashik

Deolali

A

B

C

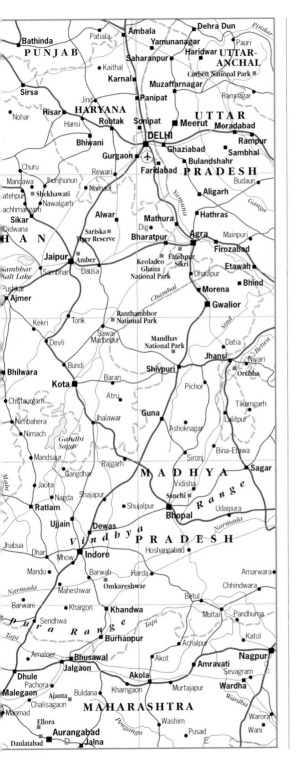

Previous pages: Celebrating Rajput style, Jaipur Rajasthani woman dressed in dazzling colours (below)

The Northwest

74

PALATIAL TRAINS

Rajasthan and Gujarat have two luxury train services, best described as first-class travelling hotels, that recall a glorious past.

The Palace-on-Wheels uses replicas of carriages originally built for maharajas and the British viceroys, and operates week-long tours. Starting at Delhi, it rattles to Jaipur, Amer, Jaisalmer, Sam dunes, Jodhpur, Ranthambhor, Chittaurgarh, Udaipur, Bharatpur, Fatehpur Sikri, Agra and back to Delhi. Travel is overnight with the day free for sightseeing and shopping. This is a marvellous way to cover the major sights of India's most popular tourist area. It runs every Wednesday, September to April.

The equally stylish Royal Orient, also takes a week Delhi to Delhi, visiting Chittaurgarh, Udaipur, Junagadh, Somnath, Sasan Gir, Diu, Palitana, Sarkhej, Ahmadabad, Jaipur and Amer.

These top-price tours can be booked through Palace-on-Wheels, RTDC, Bikaner House, Pandara Road, New Delhi (tel: 011 2338 1884, fax: 011 2338 2823; www. rajasthantourism.gov.in) or Royal Orient, Gujarat Tourism, A-6 State Emporium Complex, Baba Kharak Singh Marg, New Delhi (tel: 2374 4015; fax: 2336 7050, email: delhi@ gujarattourism.com).

UK agents for both: Sd Enterprises, 103 Wembley park Drive, Wembley, Middlesex HA9 8HG (tel: 020 8903 3411; fax: 020 8903 0392; email: info @indiarail.co.uk).

US agents:Palace on Wheels, 20 Nassau Street, Suite 412, Princeton, NJ08542 (tel: 609683-5018; fax: 609/683-9772; email: bookings@palaceon-wheels.net.

NORTHWEST Nudging India's border with Pakistan are two major states: Rajasthan and Gujarat. Desert, scrub and forested hills are their terrain, and palaces, forts and Jain temples are their landmarks. Rajasthan is the most visited Indian state and Gujarat one of the least visited, but both are now suffering from the effects of a long drought.

CONTRASTS Rajasthan's Thar Desert ends to the east at the Aravalli Range and to the south in Gujarat's Kathiawar peninsula. These geographical frontiers outline the desert provinces of Jaisalmer, Jodhpur, Bikaner and Kachchh, with sparse but breathtaking outposts. Beyond the Aravallis is a dense concentration of former Rajput principalities, their hunting reserves converted into wildlife sanctuaries, their monkey-ridden forts into museums and their maharajas' palaces into luxury hotels. Here too are fabulously painted *havelis*, such as in the crumbling villages of Shekhawati, and the jewel-like lake-city of Udaipur. The less scenic Kathiawar peninsula and Kachchh region of Gujarat saw tragedy close up in January 2001 when an earthquake devastated most of Bhuj, the villages of the Rann of Kachchh and severely damaged Ahmadabad's residential blocks. Tragedy resurfaced in March 2002 when hundreds were killed and thousands made homeless by clashing Hindu and Muslim mobs, and it remains a flashpoint.

CROSSROADS Both states have a strong history of trading that enabled wealthy rulers, nobles and merchants to pour profits into fabulous mansions and palaces. In Gujarat, the Portuguese traded at the ports of Diu and Daman in the 16th century, and, soon after, the first British outpost was established at Surat. For centuries earlier these ports were used by pilgrims to Mecca and traders from Arabia, Africa and Central Asia. The harsh desert climate has inspired some monumental structures, such as the golden sandstone ramparts of Jaisalmer, the exquisite fort-palaces of Jodhpur and Bikaner, and the mirror-encrusted, whitewashed mud huts of the Kachchh's Rabari tribe.

CITY LIFE The only large cities are Jaipur, capital of Rajasthan, and Ahmadabad, former (and still unofficial) capital of Gujarat. Both cities offer fascinating cultural introductions to their states. Ahmadabad in particular is a vibrant combination of old and new, though somewhat marred by industrialization and congestion. Jaipur is the crafts capital *par excellence*, where numerous specialist bazaars trade in embroidery, fabrics, miniature painting, pottery, leather ware or carpets.

PILGRIMAGES Jains have a high profile in this region, with major temple complexes at Palitana, Osiyan, Mount Abu, Ranakpur, Jaisalmer and Bikaner. Mount Abu and Ranakpur have 11th-century temples featuring spectacular carving. Palitana's 863 temples beckon from a summit reached after a climb up more than 3,000 steps; steps also lead to the temples on Mount Girnar at Junagadh. Osiyan, remote and requiring effort to visit, has the region's oldest Jain structures.

BACK TO NATURE There are relaxing beaches on the little island of Diu in Gujarat. The northwest also has numerous wildlife sanctuaries, with Asiatic lions at Sasan Gir, tigers at Ranthambhor and Sariska, and prolific birds at Keoladeo (Bharatpur). The scrub and sand dunes of the Thar Desert itself offer plentiful sightings of desert foxes and cats, black buck, eagles and the great Indian bustard.

BALANCE The dynamism of Rajasthan's tourist services, its rich and romantic heritage, the temptations of palace-hotels and the added draw of riotous festivals mean that little can stop the inexorable advance of tourism. While its main towns feel increasingly artificial, a trip into the more low-key Gujarat helps to redress the balance.

ANCIENT BEADS
The Indus Valley, home of the 5,000-year-old Harappan civilization and India's earliest known settlements, has its riverbed in Pakistan but includes part of Rajasthan and Gujarat. One of the most impressive sites is at Lothal, south of Ahmadabad near the Gulf of Khambhat. Mud-brick ruins clearly delineate this port and citadel, laid out in a grid pattern, where finds have included beads, gold and copper jewellery, ivory work and board-games. From its harbour, boats loaded with semi-precious stones sailed to Iraq, Arabia and Egypt. The more recently excavated Dholavira, in the Rann of Kachchh, is targeted to become Gujarat's main archaeo-logical attraction. Access is from Bhuj. Dholavira reveals all three stages of the Harappan culture.

75

The golden city of Jaisalmer (above), perched above the Thar Desert
A shop in Pushkar, Rajasthan (below)

STEP-WELLS

The step-wells (*vav*) of Gujarat demonstrate how local people have coped imaginatively with adverse climatic conditions. The simple early wells had stone walls which were gradually strengthened with surrounding platforms and corridors. Stairs led down one side, enabling people to reach low water levels, and incorporated intermediary landings on which pavilions were built. As step-wells were considered the abodes of gods and spirits, their ornamentation was increased, and as they became more refined they were used as underground retreats from the long hot summers. One of the best examples is the 15th–16th-century Adalaj Vav, 20km (12 miles) from Ahmedabad. The largest is an 11th-century wonder decorated with some 500 sculptures and reliefs at Patan in northern Gujarat. Despite major earthquake damage elsewhere in Patan, Raniki Vav survived completely unscathed.

Ahmedabad, with a foreground of marigold—much used in Hindu worship (below)
The 'shaking minarets' of Sidi Bashir (right)

Gujarat

▶▶ Ahmedabad 72C2

The hot, dusty and chaotic city of Ahmadabad ('Ahmbad') was replaced as Gujarat's capital in 1970 by the new city of Gandhinagar, about 32km (20 miles) to the north. However it is Ahmadabad that reveals the spirit, dynamism and history of Gujarat through a wealth of fine museums and an exceptional crafts tradition developed by the Mughals. At its heart, on the right bank of the wide Sabarmati river (often completely dry), is the old fortified city erected in the early 1400s by Ahmed Shah, ruler of Gujarat. Several original gates survive, as do traditional *havelis*, while veiled Muslim women, markets, mosques, camels and fax-offices coexist picturesquely. West of the river is the administrative new town, bristling with modern architecture. Many hotels lie just across Nehru bridge in Khanpur, a lively part of the old town. Ahmedabad's traffic is appalling and the scattered sights are not always known by auto-rickshaw drivers, so allow plenty of time for travelling. Earthquake damage was mainly limited to cheaply built residential complexes, affecting 4,000 families and resulting in a tragically high death toll, which, some say, could have been avoided.

Textile mania First priority for any visitor should be the fabulous **Calico Museum▶▶▶** (*Open* Thu–Tue. *Admission: free*, only on guided tours; in English at 10.30 and 2.45, lasting about two hours), at Shahibag in the northeast of the city. This exemplary private foundation is housed in a superb 17th-century *haveli* standing in lovely gardens. It displays a superlative collection of textiles, embroidery, carpets and costumes alongside a gallery of miniatures and bronzes, and a research centre. The highly informative tours explain the background to the priceless exhibits, many of which originated in the imperial workshops established by Akbar at Agra, Lahore and Ahmedabad.

Folk customs South of the city, across Sardar bridge, is the **Kite Museum▶** (*Open* Tue–Sun 11–8. *Admission: free*),

with hundreds of exhibits reflecting the city's obsession with kites, which culminates in a kite-flying festival every 14 January. Everyday items are the focus of a quirky private collection in the **Utensils Museum▶** in the Vishalla restaurant complex, Sarkatj Road (*Open* daily 11–3, 4.30–11). Among the exhibits in the **Institute of Indology Museum▶**, based at Gujarat University (*Open* Tue–Sun 11–5.30. *Admission: free*) is an outstanding collection of items connected with Jainism.

Folk traditions are explored in depth at the **Shreyas Folk Museum▶▶**, Shreyas Hill (*Open* Tue–Sun 10.30–1, 2–5.30. *Admission: inexpensive*), which has a fabulous collection of toys, costumes, jewellery, furniture, utensils and metalwork. Tribal traditions are also explored at the **Tribal Museum▶**, Gujarat Vidyapith, Ashram Road (*Open* Mon–Fri 11–2.30, 3–6, Sat 11.30–2.30). North along this road is Gandhi's **Sabarmati Ashram▶▶** (*Open* daily 9–5.30), where he lived between 1917–30, and now a monument to him. Gandhi's living room was badly damaged by the 2001 earthquake, has now been repaired.

Within the walls The lively old city radiates from Ahmed Shah's Bhadra fort (1411). Now mostly administrative offices, it is surrounded by Ahmed Shah's mosque, the later, more attractive **Sidi Sayid mosque▶** (1570s)

and the striking, but always crowded **Jami Masjid▶▶** (1423) that rises to the east. Beyond this is **Manek Chowk▶▶**, a maze of traditional cloth shops and jewellers and the site of the **Rani-ka-Hazira**, the tombs of Ahmed Shah and his wives. On the eastern periphery, near the railway station, stand the last surviving 'shaking minarets'—15th-century *minars* built by Sidi Bashir to withstand earthquakes. Their soft sandstone foundations allow them to sway, and this can be tested from an upper balcony of the nearby Bibi-ki-Masjid minaret (1454); sadly, part of this legendary complex did actually suffer earthquake damage in 2001. Other sights of the old city include the equally ingenious **Dada Harini Vav▶▶** (*c*1500), an elaborately conceived step-well (see panel), the large lavishly carved Hathi Singh (1848), one of Ahmedabad's many Jain temples, and the **Rani Rupmati mosque▶**, that combines Hindu and Islamic features of the early 1500s.

TOURIST OFFICES
Gujarat Tourism, (TCGL) HK House, Ashram Road (*Open* Mon–Fri 10.30–1.30, 2–6, also first and third Sat each month, tel: 079 2658 9172/9683, fax: 079 2658 2183; email: www.ahmedabad@ gujarattourism.com). Large hotels have better information. Counters at the airport and railway station may be useful and try the website www.ahmedabadcity.org.

Nomadic tribal people can still be seen in Gujarat, though many have settled in villages

SHOPPING
Kachchhi tribes produce some of India's most exuberant and intricately worked textiles (see pages 86–87), including bandhani tie-dye in earthy colours, heavily embroidered Ahir mirrorwork and simpler block-printing. One of the best showcases for local textile work is an annual fair normally held in early March in Bhuj. This draws a colourful crowd of traders, craftspeople and their wares. However, in view of the earthquake and its Kachchhi victims (70 per cent of the artisans in one village died), local production has been severely reduced. With rebuilding and aid to artisans, normality should return.

► **Bhavnagar** 72C1

Although of no historical interest, the port of Bhavnagar (founded 1743) is sometimes a necessary stopover on the long Gujarat trail. It has a handful of decent hotels, from a ritzy palace to an extraordinarily decrepit one crowned by a clock tower in the heart of the bazaar. This atmospheric old part of town, south of the railway station, continues its craft traditions and specialist trades, in sharp contrast to the region's greatest economic asset, **Alang►**, 50km (31 miles) south. This is the ship cemetery of the world, its high tides used by captains from all over the world to beach obsolete ships and so create an immense scrapyard. After thoroughly picking over the soon-skeletal vessels, local dealers break them up and sell the metal.

Some 65km (40 miles) north of Bhavnagar lies **Velavadar National Park►** which can be visited on a day trip by taxi or book lodgings through the Sanctuary Superintendent in Bhavnagar (tel: 0278 2426425). The sole predators in the national park are wolves, and the grasslands are home to blackbuck, deer, jackal and the rare 'sarus' crane (*Admission: expensive*).

► **Bhuj** 72A2

Bhuj, a remote medieval town in the desert-like Rann of Kachchh on the Pakistani border, was a magical town of 200,000 inhabitants where life drifted by in a maze of narrow, vibrant streets full of cows, bicycles and glittering textiles. It was ruled by the Khengarji family from 1548 until independence in 1947, and boasted three palaces, a hill-fort, an excellent museum and impressive city walls.

Earthquake On 26 January 2001 tragedy struck when Bhuj found itself at the epicentre of a devastating earthquake. Within minutes, 90 per cent of the buildings in this once beautiful town were in ruins, victims of a quake that measured 7.5 on the Richter scale. Human losses were even more tragic, rising to over 20,000 all told throughout Gujarat, while hundreds of thousands of people in more than 300 villages of the Kachchh region were made homeless and some 166,000 were injured. Aftershocks, followed by a somewhat lesser earthquake two weeks later, only increased the trauma.

Prosperous Gujarat, the second most industrialized state in India and once boasting a superior infrastructure of good roads and communications, suddenly foundered. Although relief poured in from the outside world, efforts were seriously hampered by the absence of telephone lines and the destruction of roads. Four local hospitals were among the estimated 339,000 buildings which collapsed, killing staff and patients inside. Despite this, doctors and volunteers operating without any real infrastructure or hygiene managed to treat some 8,000 victims in northern Gujarat within three days of the earthquake.

Reconstruction For the people of Bhuj, a mixture of Kachchhi tribespeople and Muslim, Jain and Hindu Gujaratis, life started again in temporary tents amid the debris of the past. Yet resilience and economic necessity prevailed and within a short time women could be seen doing traditional embroidery in their basic shelters while makeshift shops sprang up in the ruins. Reconstruction started slowly, hampered by a lack of coordination and communications but a new city eventually emerged, leaving the old one in ruins.

Few of the main monuments can be restored, such was the force of the destruction, but the Indian government aims to achieve at least partial restoration. Other than structural losses (which included the 1877 Kachchh Museum in its entirety), most of the palace treasures (rare Chinese ceramics, drawings by Hogarth, royal portraits, European glass, Dutch clocks) were obliterated.

Ramsingh's prowess Visitors to the region today will see very little of the extraordinary Aina Mahal, a mid-18th century palace devised by the enlightened Maharao Lakhpatji with his Dutch-trained craftsman, Ramsingh. It was Ramsingh who was responsible for founding glass and tile factories that not only furnished the palace but also had a lasting influence on Kachchhi architecture, enamelwork, jewellery and interior decoration.

His *pièce de resistance* was the Hall of Mirrors, which made masterful use both of reflected light and considerable engineering prowess. The white marble walls, faced with gilt-framed mirrors and lit by elaborate Venetian chandeliers, surrounded a tile-lined pool.

The former gateway into Aina Mahal, famed for its elaborate interior decoration; much is now in ruins

The Northwest

KACHCHHI HANDICRAFTS
Rogan, the art of cloth-painting, is now practised only by a father-son duo in the remote village of Nirona. Delicate *soof* embroidery is a cottage industry at Sumrasar, where 180 workers wield their needles. Leather embroidery, lacquerwork on wooden utensils, beadwork and copper bell-making are other regional crafts, as are the weaving, dyeing and embroidery of camel wool and cotton textiles.

Excursion

Rann of Kachchh►► Bounded by sea to the south and west, and by sand to the north and east, this arid, inhospitable terrain has long been plagued by sandstorms, tornadoes, drought and earthquakes, the latest in January 2001 which obliterated dozens of villages. Despite this, the Rann of Kachchh is home to formerly nomadic cattle-breeders and shepherds, as well as the makers of some of Gujarat's most elaborate textiles. Essential services such as roads, electricity, water and telecommunications have been restored, but as government bodies still struggle to provide accommodation other than makeshift shelters and tents, it will be some time before any tourism returns.

Bordering extensive salt-flats to the east is the Little Rann, site of the Wild Ass Sanctuary, best visited from Adeser. The southern Kachchh is oddly affluent in places. Many of the large modern houses here belong to

Thatched houses decorated with dried cow dung and mirrors are typical in the Kachchh, although many were destroyed in the earthquake

Gujaratis living in Britain, in particular the enormous Patel family, which has its opulent Swaminaryan temple in Kera.

Tribal peoples The word 'Banni' covers the groups living to the north of Bhuj, whose heavily encrusted embroidery and mirrorwork are among the region's finest. Among them are the Muslim Jats who migrated from Persia some 500 years ago, the dairy-farming Ahir who came from Pakistan, and the mysterious, semi-nomadic Rabaris. They are thought to have come from Afghanistan via Baluchistan and Rajasthan. The heavily bejewelled women make and wear brilliantly coloured embroidery, while the turbanned men don beautifully pleated white shirts, baggy pants and *puttees* (cloths wound round the legs). The immaculate thatched huts, as well as their clothes, are elaborately decorated with mirrors.

Temples You can see the crumbling 10th-century walls and Siva temple of the former Kachchh capital at **Kera▶**. Here you will also find **Kotai temple▶**, notable for its eroded sandstone statues and bell-shaped roof. The most evocative structure in the area is **Than monastery▶▶**, whose shrines, cells and halls sprawl up a hillside.

81

▶▶ **Diu**   *72B1*

Alcohol is forbidden in Gujarat, except in the former Portuguese colony of Diu, which has separate status, a tiny, elongated island (barely 35sq km/13.5sq miles) off the south coast of the Kathiawar peninsula. The branching palms along the access road from the fortified town of Goghla are unique, having been introduced from Africa centuries ago. Beyond a checkpoint and across the bridge lined with beer-bars, an unmistakably Portuguese fort and white churches rise over tiled rooftops. Dating back to the 16th century, the pretty, winding streets are lined with whitewashed houses, palm-trees, banyans and a few hotels. An old city wall ends between the southeastern beaches of **Jallandhar and Chakratirth▶**, an easy walk or bicycle-ride from the centre.

Short circuit To the west is the popular tourist beach of **Nagoa▶**, a tree-lined crescent offering camel-rides and watersports. The north is mainly mud- and salt-flats with good birdwatching. Diu is usually quiet, but has a high season from October to early January, with daily flights from Mumbai (Bombay).

Military might The impressive **fort▶▶** (*Open* daily 8–6. *Admission: free*) was built between 1535–41 and covers a vast 57,000sq m (67,830sq yd) washed by the sea on three sides. The solid walls and bastions, plus a few cannons, are still intact but much of the interior is overgrown, with vegetation creeping through the cracks of the old chapel, and 16th-century tombstones lying in fragments. **Panikot fort▶** stands on a tiny island in mid-channel: this can be visited by boat from the main jetty.

The island of Diu, a relaxing break from the Gujarati interior

CATHOLIC CRISIS
Although many Diu inhabitants are distinctly Portuguese, Catholicism is fighting a losing battle. Of the three picturesque though peeling churches, only St. Paul's (1691) still functions. The Jesuit St. Francis of Assisi is now a hospital and St. Thomas's has become a museum. The latter is well worth visiting (*Open* daily 8am–8pm. *Admission: free*) for its evocative collection of carved wooden statues, silver reliquaries, crucifixes and a recumbent Jesus whose pierced hand gratefully accepts donations from visitors.

TOURIST INFORMATION
Department of Tourism, Marine House (tel: 02875 252653; email: info@diuindia.com.

*Mosque domes and
minarets characterize the
skyline of Junagadh*

▶▶ **Junagadh**   72B4

The small, ancient town of
Junagadh lies at the base of the
Girnar Hills, a rare undulation in
the otherwise monotonous flatness
of the Kathiawar peninsula. It had
an illustrious early history as the
capital of Gujarat under the
Buddhist Mauryas (see page 34).
After Ashoka's death, in the 3rd
century BC, Junagadh was successively ruled by Hindu, Rajput and
Muslim dynasties. Today it functions as a market-centre for the
region. Its colourful history is
reflected in Buddhist caves, the
ruins of Uparkot citadel and above
all the sacred Mount Girnar, whose shrines and temples
draw streams of Hindu and Jain pilgrims.

Main sights The town centre is full of character, with
lively bazaars, city gates, mosques, mausoleums and
attractive old buildings. Regal relics are exhibited in the
Durbar Hall Museum▶ (*Open* Thu–Tue 9–12.15, 3–6.
Admission: inexpensive) inside the old nawabs' palace. To
the northwest stand the ornate, 19th-century **muqbara▶**
(mausoleums) of Junagadh's Muslim rulers. To the northeast, up a cobbled street curling around to the main triple
gateway, is the **Uparkot citadel▶▶** (*Open* daily
7am–6.30pm. *Admission: inexpensive*). Above are a huge
tank, water-wheel and gardens with paths leading to the
roofless but stunningly situated Jama Masjid
and, further north, the Adi Chai Vav, a 15th-
century step-well. Deeper still is the 11th-
century Navghan Kuva. To the west are the
remains of 3rd-century BC Buddhist caves,
and earlier rock-cut temples and a *stupa* lie in
the vicinity. As all these sites are scattered
and overgrown, making them difficult to
find, a local guide is particularly useful.

Mystical climb Junagadh's oldest monument
is an Ashokan rock-edict (*c*250BC), 4km (2.4
miles) east at the base of **Mount Girnar▶▶**.
This 1,000m-high (3,280ft) volcano is hewn
with several thousand well-trodden steps,
past stalls offering *chai* and water, up to Jain
and Hindu shrines and temples, and exceptional views. Allow three hours for the
ascent, and start early to avoid the heat.
Below the summit is a complex of 16 marble
Jain temples, some beautifully carved, which
were built in the 12th and 13th centuries. The
oldest is dedicated to Neminath, the 22nd
Tirthankara (Jain prophet), said to have died
here. Looming above and scattered over the
ridge are Hindu shrines, including the Amba
Mata temple and one dedicated to the
goddess Kalika (Durga) that attracts fervent
sadhus with an interest in the rites of death.
There is also a Muslim shrine.

▶▶▶ Palitana 72B1

Open: daily 6:30–5. Admission: free

Little can equal the architectural grandeur of the 863 Jain temples at Palitana, crowning a hilltop wreathed in Jain legends. The town below exists almost solely for pilgrims, and is monopolized by their guest houses. Even the Edwardian-style palace, the Hawa Mahal, was built with the taxes levied on Jain visitors. Like Mount Girnar, Palitana entails a long, hot haul to the top. The fact that you cannot see the temple complex as you climb up is discouraging, as is being overtaken by energetic Jain nuns, but there are shady trees, sweeping views and stalls serving spring water on the way. The ascent up to 600m (1,968ft) covers 4km (2.4 miles), taking under two hours. At the gates of the complex, creamy buffalo-curd in terracotta bowls restores energy. *Dhooli*-chairs are available.

Victory Shatrunjaya, the name of the hill, means 'place of victory' and it does have the air of a citadel; a walled complex encloses multiple towers, domes and courtyards, with bells and flags marking the breezes. To the left of the shady main courtyard are the more recent, ostentatiously decorated temples favoured by the pilgrims, while high up on the right is the more peaceful, older section. The oldest temple may date from the 11th century and is dedicated to Lord Adinath, the first Jain Tirthankara. The Chaumukha temple houses his four-faced image. Jain prosperity is evident in the conservation and ongoing restoration of these temples, and Jain regard for every form of life is reflected in the numerous resident birds and constant sweeping by the yellow-robed priests (see panel).

JAIN RULES

The strict tenets of Jainism make it an extremely puritanical religion, despite the gaudily decorated dancing-halls in some temples. The buffalo-curd available at the entrance to Palitana is not for Jains, as they must not touch dairy products nor wear leather. Every living creature is considered sacred, a belief that results in the wearing of mouth masks (so as not to swallow an insect) and the sweeping of floors (so as not to tread on one). Meat, smoking and alcohol are strictly prohibited, and fasting should be practised four times a month. The Jains' complex metaphysics involve the rejection of objective truth, which allows for an infinite number of viewpoints on everything.

83

Shatrunjaya at Palitana is a sacred place of pilgrimage for Jains

The Northwest

84

SALT-MARCH
Gandhi's salt-march was organized from Ahmedabad in March 1930 and was a turning-point in the independence movement. In protest against the British Raj's monopoly of the production and sale of salt, Gandhi and some 80 followers set off on foot towards Danti, a small coastal town 320km (198 miles) to the south near Surat. One month later, they arrived and set about boiling sea-water to produce salt in an overtly subversive act that was followed by a symbolic sale of their produce. Widespread protests and police aggression culminated in Gandhi's imprisonment without trial. His release, in January 1931, was followed by the Gandhi–Irwin pact and negotiations for India's independence.

Asiatic lion

▶ **Porbandar**
72A1

Due west of Junagadh and about two hours away by road lies Porbandar, known above all as the birthplace of Gandhi in 1869. This is just one of his many close associations with Gujarat, as he attended school in Rajkot, university in Bhavnagar, began his mass civil disobedience movement in Bardoli (Surat) and began his salt march at Ahmedabad (see panel). His 200-year-old ancestral house is in the western promontory of Porbandar, but the main attraction is the neighbouring **Kirti Mandir**▶▶, (*Open* dawn–dusk. *Admission: free, but tip guide*), where a museum illustrates Gandhi's life through photographs, memorabilia and a prayer-hall with a bookshop. This house was where his wife, Kasturba, was born. Southeast of here on the seafront is the Hazur palace, now a college. It was built by the ruler of Bhavnagar as part of his daughter's dowry when she married the Jethwa prince of Porbandar in 1902.

▶ **Rajkot**
72B2

Plum in the centre of the Kathiawar peninsula is Rajkot, founded by the Jadeja Rajputs in the 16th century and later the scene of numerous clashes between its ruling nawab and the British. Two relics of this period are the **Watson Museum**, Jubilee Gardens (*Open* Mon–Sat 9–1, 2–6. *Admission: inexpensive*) and the adjacent **Lang Library**, both grandiose Victorian edifices surrounded by lawns. The museum has a collection of rare regional exhibits, from Indus Valley artefacts to sculptures, bronzes, manuscripts and Rajput miniatures. Rajkot's numerous temples, mosque and bazaar were among Gujarat's earthquake casualties in 2001 and many surrounding villages were devastated.

▶▶ **Sasan Gir National Park**
72B1

Open: mid-Oct to mid-Jun, usually 6–11, 3–5.
Admission: expensive

The national park, halfway between Junagadh and Somnath, is the last habitat of the Asiatic lion, a species that was almost extinct at the beginning of the 1980s. The story goes that the Viceroy Lord Curzon was invited on a lion hunt by the local nawab but that, after public outcry, the trip was cancelled with Curzon, instead, advising the nawab to protect this rare animal. Spread over 1,400sq km (540sq miles) of undulating terrain, the park consists of savannah, dry deciduous thorn forest and some evergreens. Apart from lions, estimated at close to 300

The temple at Somnath was once one of the richest in India

and usually found in prides of eight to ten, there are black buck, hyenas, sambar, panthers, spotted deer, chinkara gazelles, langurs and marsh crocodiles. There is a crocodile-rearing centre by Sindh Sadan.

Lion-tracking At the heart of the sanctuary is a core 'interpretation zone' for which permits are required. These are issued at the park headquarters, where a wide range of accommodation is based next to the lively hamlet of Sindh Sadan. Jeeps and guides set off at dawn or late afternoon to explore rather well-covered terrain, stopping at observation towers during the three-hour circuit. Longer trips can be made outside this zone, though rough road surfaces discourage the majority of visitors. Wildlife and termite mounds are abundant but the lions remain elusive, despite sporadic attacks on villagers.

▶ Somnath 72B1

Just outside the port town of Veraval, the temple of Somnath has an illustrious place in Hindu history, but the structure you see today dates from 1950 and reflects little of its original magnificence. It is said to have been built by the moon god, Somraj, in gold, silver, wood and stone to redeem himself in the eyes of Siva, who had laid a curse on him. Its legendary wealth led to repeated plundering by Muslim invaders from the 11th century onwards, but it always rose again. Veraval was for a long period the region's main port for Muslim pilgrims sailing to Mecca, and traditional *dhows* (ships) are still built here. Today's Sivaite temple faithfully reflects the original architectural style with a soaring central tower that shelters one of India's 12 highly sacred *jyotirlingas* (miraculously formed *lingams* surrounding which there are many myths). A museum (*Open* Thu–Tue 10–6. *Admission: inexpensive*) displays fragments and sculptures from Somnath's former incarnations.

AFRICAN FACES
Porbandar's historical trading links with East Africa may account for the entire villages of 'Siddis'—people of African origin—that exist between Sasan Gir and Porbandar. It is thought that they were bought from Arab slave-traders by local rulers, the women to work as palace servants and the men as hunters. Another version is that the Siddis came as slaves of invading armies, while still another suggests that slaves were imported by the rulers of Bengal in the early 15th century but were eventually driven out and settled in the far west. Certainly Mahmud of Ghazni, the Turk who sacked Somnath in 1024, employed Siddis as drummers in his army.

For many people India quite simply means textiles. Fine muslin, calico, chintz, embroidery, ikat, block-prints, silk brocades and tie-and-dye cottons are all specialities of the subcontinent, resulting in a dazzling, diaphanous array at every bazaar. Above all, Rajasthan and Gujarat produce a bewitching range, painstakingly made by hand or more profitably by machine.

IKAT

The *ikat* technique has long existed from Persia to Indonesia and flourishes in Central America. The word itself comes from the Malay meaning to tie or bind, referring to the threads on a loom that are bound with dye-resistant fibres. Successive plunges into dye-vats create different tones, with new ties being added each time to create the overall pattern. The cloth is subsequently woven by hand or machine. Apart from the silk saris made in Patan (Gujarat), *ikat* is most widely produced in Andhra Pradesh.

India's textile history is a lengthy one, with evidence of exports by land and sea to China, Mesopotamia and Rome as far back as the 1st century AD. Fragments of Gujarat cotton have been excavated in Egypt, while Java's royal courts had a particular penchant for *patola*, silk lengths woven using the complex double-*ikat* technique, also a Gujarati speciality. Desert people such as the Jats and Rabari have been using needles artistically to decorate textiles for centuries, producing embroidered and mirror-encrusted quilts, hangings and tunics that enliven the monotonous sandy tones of their environment. Today, both Jaipur and Ahmedabad sell a fantastic variety of fabrics, still much sought after by the Western market.

Trading textiles Indian muslins have long been coveted, their different qualities leading to poetic names such as abrawan ('running water', which when immersed in a stream became invisible); baft hava ('woven air', as it floated like a cloud); and shabnam ('evening dew'). The Romans admired them, and handspun, handwoven Indian muslins continued to be prized in Europe even after the rise of machine-made imitations, as the former's yarn had

far greater strength. The astute East India Company also traded in fine embroideries from Bengal and Gujarat, the latter peaking in popularity during the 17th and 18th centuries. Marco Polo (1254–1324) referred to the exquisite Gujarati embroideries 'depicting birds and beasts in gold and silver thread sown very subtly on leather'. Leather covers were later replaced by heavy silk sewn with decorative chain-stitch, first acquired from Cambay and subsequently from Surat.

Calico and chintz Further south, from Calicut, came a cotton fabric that became known by European traders as calico. This fabric was

block-printed and hand-painted by Persian craftsmen, and eventually evolved into chintz (from the Hindi *chintz* meaning 'variegated'), which was often decorated with adapted European designs. This was an area exploited by British manufacturers and soon their imitations were indistinguishable from Indian originals. Chintzes were also produced by machine in the larger textile centres of Ahmedabad and Mumbai (Bombay). It was only Gandhi's *swadeshi* (home-produced goods) movement that revived the domestic market for hand-made production in the 1920–30s. Indian brocades (mainly from Ahmedabad and Varanasi) were also imitated, but were more prized than European lookalikes because of their enduring colour and the lustre of the fabric.

Bandanna The spotted bandanna worn (in pictures if not in real life) by pirates, gypsies, cowboys and bandits from Britain to the Wild West actually originated in India, from where it was exported from the 18th century onwards. Bandanna derives from *bandhani* which means 'tying' in Sanskrit, a succinct description of the laborious process originally involved in producing the spots. Some of India's most fabulous textiles, generally silk in Gujarat and cotton in Rajasthan, are made in this way.

Knotting The process used in tie-dyeing is basically the same today, except that chemical dyes are used. The most widely used motif in *bandhani* is the simple dot formed by pinching and knotting a small area of cloth; after dying, the thread is removed to reveal either a white circle or the previously dyed colour. Jamagar in Gujarat is considered to be where the most elaborate and accomplished silk *bandhani* is produced, but this widely used technique is also applied to coarse wool, as among Kachchhi tribes. The finished product, which might be a *odhani* (head-cloth), *layariya* (turban) or *duppatta* (scarf), is often sold still tied up in a coil, giving the customer the assurance that it is genuine and not a printed imitation.

MIRROR, MIRROR
Gujarat and Rajasthan tribes excel in creating brilliantly coloured embroidery incorporating tiny mirrors, used for skirts, quilts or wall-hangings. A tribal girl spends her early years learning basic patterns and colour combinations from older women, and the rest of her life embroidering the contents of her tiny home. The finest work is produced by the Banni community north of Bhuj, where minuscule mirrors are combined with dense embroidery.

87

The Rann of Kachchh has a long tradition of embroidery

The annual camel fair brings thousands of camels to Pushkar

Rajasthan

▶ Ajmer
73D4

Ajmer's turbulent history since the defeat of the Chauhan Rajputs by Sultan Mohammed Ghauri in 1193 has left it with a rich mixture of Hindu and Islamic monuments. At the heart of the city and its bazaar is the **Dargah▶▶**, the much revered tomb complex of the Sufi saint Khwaja Muin-ud-din (who died in 1236), extended over the centuries by the Mughal emperors. Its many mosques include an elegant structure erected by Shah Jahan, and the tomb itself stands in a domed marble pavilion. The Dargah is considered a second Mecca by South Asia's Muslims. It is a place of intense religious fervour especially during the annual Urs celebrations, when people commemorate the saint's death with six days of non-stop music. If you sign the 'visitor book' you are committing yourself to a hefty donation!

North of this stands the **Adhai-din-ka-Jhonpra▶** (*Open* Sat–Thu 10–5. *Admission: free*) Its name refers to the two-and-a-half days allegedly taken by Ghauri, in 1193, to build the present mosque. Pillars from at least 30 Hindu and Jain temples are incorporated into this early example of Indo-Islamic architecture. Ajmer's remarkable past is illustrated by sculpture and Mughal and Rajput miniatures at the museum (*Open* Sat–Thu 10–4.30. *Admission: inexpensive*), housed in Akbar's palace, the Daulet Khana, in the Daulat Bagh. These lovely gardens include an artificial lake full of thousands of flamingoes.

Excursion

Pushkar▶▶ A scenic drive through dry hills 11km (7 miles) northwest of Ajmer goes to the site of the camel fair (see panel). Pushkar is a delightful lakeside town though

Vinay Vilas Mahal, in Alwar, stands in splendour by a vast tank

no longer the peaceful haven of a few years ago; commerce and tourists have taken their toll. However, its legendary creation by Brahma, who dropped a lotus-flower into the desert to make a sin-purifying lake, gives it a poetic start. The Brahma Mandir is always thronged with pilgrims, but the priests make forceful demands for donations. In return they issue a 'Pushkar passport', a red braid that you can flourish to ward off other demands. Both Saivitri Mandir and Gayitri Mandir crown a hilltop and respectively have beautiful sunset and sunrise views.

▶ Alwar   73D4

Alwar's proximity to imperial Delhi inspired in its Mewar inhabitants a rebellious and bellicose character until Sultan Baban (1267–87) crushed their resistance. In 1770 a Kachhwaha Rajput won back Alwar and created his own principality. The picturesque town nestles in a valley of the Aravalli hills where lakes and woods nurture wildlife, and is watched over by a fort on a rocky ridge. Most of the fort's structures are dilapidated, and entry is restricted. Inside the walled city below stands the grandiose late 18th-century **Vinay Vilas Mahal▶▶**, an extravagantly decorated palace fronting a large *tank*. The museum upstairs (*Open* Sat–Thu 10–4.30. *Admission: inexpensive*) displays a fascinating regal hotchpotch including a silver dining-room table, rare Arabic, Persian and Sanskrit manuscripts and an exceptional collection of Rajput and Mughal miniatures. Behind the palace, temples edge the lake, including lovely **Moosi Maharani Ki Chhatri▶** and the **Purjan Vihar▶▶** (Company Garden) laid out in 1868.

Tiger country 37km (23 miles) southwest of Alwar lies **Sariska Tiger Reserve▶▶** (*Open* daily all year, Oct–Feb 7–4, otherwise 6.30–5, but minimal wildlife Jul–Aug. *Admission: expensive*), offering good opportunities for spotting nilgai (blue bull), sambar, chital, four-horned antelopes, wild boar and abundant monkeys. The sanctuary of mainly dry deciduous forest was established in 1955 and in 1979 joined Project Tiger (see page 100), however, a 2005 World Wildlife Fund survey found no evidence of tigers whatsoever. Jeep-safaris are organized by the Forest Reception Centre, opposite the Lake Palace Hotel, Jaipur Road.

TOURIST OFFICES
Tourist Reception Centre, Hotel Khadim, Savitri Girls College Road, Ajmer (*Open* Mon–Sat 8–noon, 3–6; tel: 0145 2627426). Counter at rail station. Tourist Office, opposite the railway station, Alwar (*Open* Mon–Fri 10–1.30, 2–5; tel: 0144 2347348).

*Hand prints at Junagarh
Fort, a lasting memorial
to the widows who
performed* sati

SHIPS OF THE DESERT
India's only camel-breed-
ing and research centre
(*Open* Mon–Sat 3–5.
Admission: free) lies
8km (5 miles) south of
Bikaner. Since it was set
up in 1975 it has become
the main source for the
country's camels. In
1993 Bikaner
inaugurated an annual
January camel fair to
encourage local camel
craftsmen. The two-day
event includes camel-
races and plenty of music
and dance. Camel-safaris
are also plentiful here.

▶▶ Bikaner   72C4

Bikaner, lost in the dry, flat scrub of the Thar Desert, is
India's camel capital (see panel). Despite bleak surroundings, Bikaner's location on the caravan route into India
from Central Asia made it a great trading centre and since
its founding by a prince from Jodhpur in 1486, the fortified
town has become Rajasthan's fourth largest city. Overtly
hardworking, with scattered sights and a business
community of astute Marwari traders (see page 106), it is
little touched by tourism and makes a .welcome change
from Rajasthan's more commercialized destinations.

Fort of palaces Towering dramatically over the town is
Junagarh Fort▶▶▶ (*Open* daily 10–4.30. *Admission:
moderate*, including guide). Inside the fort that was never
conquered are 37 palaces, private temples and pavilions
built between 1588 and 1943, an architectural range
that is also immaculately conserved.
Projecting balconies, *jali* (latticed) screens
and oriel windows add grace to the
façade rising above 9m (30ft) thick walls,
although Bikaner's pink sandstone is less delicately carved than that of Jaisalmer (see pages
96–97), because it is harder. The main entrance
through Suraj Pol (Sun Gate) takes you past
the hand prints of 59 wives who performed
sati on the death of their husbands, the last
dating from 1837. Of the numerous interlock-
ing palaces, the most lavish is the Anup Mahal
(1788–1828), where marble columns painted
by Persian artists, lacquerwork and inlaid
mirrors add to the opulence of the red and
gold coronation room.
    Maharaja Gaj Singh's Chandra Mahal (Moon
Palace) and Phul Mahal (Flower Palace) offer
interesting decorative contrasts. Phul Mahal has delicately
lacquered floral paintings and marble, while gloom
pervades the Chandra Mahal, which is used for prayer
and meditation. The palace of the enlightened Maharaja
Ganga Singh (1887–1943), with its vast Durbar Hall (accessible by Rolls-Royce), has been converted into a museum
housing some extraordinary and varied exhibits, including a World War I fighter plane.

More luxury Visitors who have enough energy after touring the fort's amazing sights can also visit **Lalgarh
Palace▶** (*Open* Thu–Tue 10–5. *Admission: moderate*), about
3km (2 miles) north. This early 1900s design in sandstone
by Sir Swinton Jacob became part hotel and part royal residence. A museum and the Anup Sanskrit Library are
housed here; the latter displays old photographs, wildlife
trophies and manuscripts. Bikaner also has Jain
merchants' *havelis*, concentrated in Rampuria Street in the
ramshackle old city. On one façade reliefs depict the
British King George V and Queen Mary. Surrounding
Kote Gate is the huge old **bazaar▶**, where camel-hide
products, rugs and lacquerwork abound.
    Southwest of here are the 16th-century **Bhandasar and
Sandeshwar Jain temples▶▶**, built by two brothers with
elaborate decoration using mirrorwork, frescoes, enamel
and gold leaf.

Rats Deshnok is 30km (18 miles) away and is home to the 17th-century **Karni Mata temple**►► (*Open* daily 6am–9.30pm. *Admission: free*), dedicated to an incarnation of the goddess Durga (see page 252). It has become a sanctuary for thousands of plump rats, believed to hold the souls of Karni Mata's devotees. There are also two gigantic cauldrons, used during its biannual festival to feed 7,000 people.

►►► Chittaurgarh 73D3

Between 1303 and 1567, Rajasthan's oldest fort (*Open* daily dawn–dusk. *Admission: inexpensive*) three times witnessed the Rajput ritual of *jauhar* (the mass suicide of women by fire), before their men plunged into a hopeless battle. The fort actually dates from the 7th century, and was the capital of Mewar in the 15th and 16th centuries. High above the modern town, 5km (3 miles) of walls encircle the ruined citadel, its palaces, towers and temples abandoned since Akbar's siege in 1567. Of outstanding interest are the richly carved, 37m (121ft) high Vijay Stambh (victory tower) built to commemorate a 1440 victory, and the 22m (72ft) Kirti Stambh (tower of fame). The latter was the work of a Jain merchant in the 12th century, dedicated to Adinath and plastered with his images. At the southern end stands Padmini's Palace in its pool. Padmini was a Rajput beauty whose image, glimpsed in a mirror, seduced the Sultan of Delhi in 1303. He attacked the fort to win her, but only inspired Padmini and her women to perform the fort's first incidence of *jauhar*.

Sacred rats at Karni Mata temple (above)
Chittaurgarh (below)

SHOPPING
Jaipur is India's shopping destination *par excellence*. Any purchase needs hard bargaining but no other city in India offers such a wide choice. Silks, cottons, jewellery, gemstones, enamelwork, puppets, blue pottery, quilts, marbleware, carpets, *dhurries* and 'antiques' are churned out in back-street workshops or in larger factories on the outskirts and at Sanganer. Chandpol Bazar is the marble and stone-carving centre, while Johari Bazar, Nehru Bazar, Bapu Bazar and Tripoliya Bazar sell leatherware, jewellery, fabrics and ornaments. Tourist shops along Mirza Ismail (MI) Road to the south stock plenty of pricey antiques, and the Rajasthali Government Emporia have an excellent range of fixed-price goods.

▶▶▶ Jaipur   73D4

The pink capital of Rajasthan, traffic-choked, dynamic, highly commercialized and not to be missed, was founded by the Rajput Maharaja Jai Singh II in 1727. The grid layout, sandstone palaces, *havelis*, avenues and bazaars of the old walled city offer an unrivalled harmony, although Jaipur now sprawls chaotically outwards to encompass two and a half million inhabitants. To the north are the ruins of the hilltop Nahargarh Fort and to the south the Ram Niwas gardens, with various later monuments, institutions and hotels. Much of Jaipur's attraction lies in its wealth of atmospheric hotels converted from old *havelis* standing in spacious gardens.

Royal centre Dominating the central grid is the **City Palace▶▶▶** (*Open* daily 9–4.30. *Admission: expensive*) composed of the Chandra Mahal (Moon Palace), still the residence of the former ruling family, and several other edifices converted into a museum. Picked out with delicate white patterns, the sandstone walls and arches, marble columns and guardian elephants offer a wonderful fusion of Hindu and Mughal styles. Exhibits throughout the pavilions are all of superlative quality, whether costumes, textiles, arms, manuscripts, miniatures, carpets, furniture or astronomical instruments. In the beautiful courtyard of the Diwan-i-Khas (1730) stand the much photographed giant silver urns commissioned by Madho Singh II to carry holy water from the Ganga (Ganges) on a trip to England.

Royal fantasies Opposite the main entrance to the palace is the **Jantar Mantar**▶▶▶ (*Open* daily 9–4.30. *Admission: inexpensive*), the biggest of Jai Singh's five remarkable observatories. Constructed of stone and marble between 1728–34, these large, highly complex structures were designed by Jai Singh himself to prove to the Mughal Emperor that Hindu astrology was based on precise scientific calculations. Their curiously modernistic appearance adds to the fascination. East of here, rising above the main north–south avenue and bazaar, is the fabulous façade of the **Hawa Mahal**▶▶▶ (*Open* Sat–Thu 9–4.30. *Admission: inexpensive*). This dates from around 1800, when it was built for the ladies of the harem by the poet-king, Pratap Singh. The name means 'palace of the winds', and the lavish five-storey structure was designed to catch the breeze through the multiple *jali* screens, balconies and arches. A popular **Govindji temple**▶, devoted to Lord Krishna, Jai Singh's family deity, stands in gardens north of the palace.

Open space The **Ram Niwas Gardens**▶ lie south of the frenetic walled city. This park with zoo, aviary, herbarium and sports grounds was built under Ram Singh II in 1868 as a famine relief project. Rising from the lawns is the impressive Indo-Saracenic 'Albert Hall', designed by Sir Swinton Jacob and opened as a museum in 1887. This **Central Museum and Art Gallery**▶▶ (*Open* Sat–Thu 10–4.30. *Admission: inexpensive*) displays sculptures, miniatures, metalware, decorative art, natural history and Rajasthani folk art. It also runs the Ravindra Rangmanch, containing a modern art gallery (*Open* Sat–Thu 10–4.30. *Admission: free*), auditorium and open-air theatre.

TOURIST OFFICES
Government of India, State Hotel, Khasa Kothi (*Open* Mon–Fri 9–6, Sat 9–1; tel/fax: 0141 2372200; email: goito-jpre @raj.nic.in). Helpful and arranges tours including Amer. It is well worth hiring a guide to explain the intricacies of Jaipur's colourful history. Some guides are specialists in the City Palace.
Tourist Reception Centre, Paryatan Bhavan Tourist Hotel, MI Road (*Open* Mon–Sat 10–5, closed second Sat each month;, www.rajasthantourism. gov.in). Supplies brochures. Tourist counters also at railway station and airport.

93

Hawa Mahal (top left), where, from behind jali *screens, women could observe without being observed*
One of the many emporiums that make Jaipur a shoppers' paradise (bottom left)

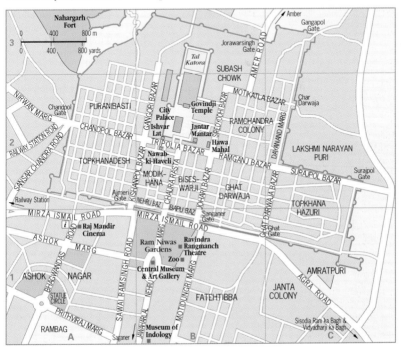

Excursions

Amber, the former capital of the Kachhwaha rulers, lies 11km (7 miles) north of Jaipur, reached by a scenic rural road that passes the Man Sagar lake, and its elegant water palace, the Jal Mahal (1735). Now being restored, this is likely to become a major tourist attraction once visits are possible. Not far away is **Kanak Vrindavan**, a complex of renovated temples and gardens. Opposite lies **Gaitore▶**, the royal cremation ground where the cenotaphs of Jaipur's rulers are dominated by that of Jai Singh II. Near the Ramgarh crossroads stands the queens' memorial ground, the **Maharana-ki-Chhatri▶**.

Amber▶▶▶ (*Open daily 9–4.30. Admission: moderate*). The palace complex of Amber is stunningly set, with its sandy colour blending into a backdrop of rocky hills overlooking the Maota lake at its feet. Monkeys are constant companions and the main sections are often filled with tour groups, but it remains exceptional. Building started in 1037; what remains today is the work of Raja Man Singh (which was begun in 1592) and subsequent rulers until Jai Singh II moved on to create Jaipur. Access to the hillside palaces, pavilions, gardens, temples and walls is by a long steep path. Elephants and jeeps are available, but hard bargaining is needed.

Public domain The huge front courtyard, entered through the Suraj Pol (Sun Gate) is edged by steps leading up through the Singh Pol (Lion Gate). To the right is the green marble temple devoted to Shila Mata, Kali's incarnation as goddess of war, whose image was brought from East Bengal, and ahead is the spectacular pillared hall of the Diwan-i-Am (1639). Rising at the southern end of this courtyard is the massive, three-storey painted gateway, the Ganesh Pol, that divides public from private areas. The rooftop and upper chambers has fabulous views over the site.

Private domain Beyond the corridors and galleries on either side of a small *char-bagh* garden are, to the right, Sukh Niwas, a pleasure pavilion with water-channels and inlaid doors, and, to the left, the Jai Mandir or Sheesh Mahal (mirror palace) conceived as the private audience hall. This and the upper floor, known as Jas Mandir (1630s), form the apex of Jai Singh I's palace, displaying dazzling fine glass mosaics, mirror-work, stucco, stained glass and exquisitely carved marble *jali* screens, all harmoniously blending Mughal decorative features with a Rajput setting. The older, simpler structures at the far end were built under Raja Man Singh in the late 16th century. A pretty arched pavilion at the centre of this labyrinthine palace was used as a meeting-place for the palace ladies.

Village and fort North of the palace are the ruins of its prosperous settlement of nobles and craftsmen. There is little to recall the former inhabitants apart from the beautifully decorated **Jagat Shiromani temple►►**, which has an image of Lord Krishna, the old temple of Narsingh and the impressive step-well, Panna Mian-ki-Baoli. In contrast, the **Jaigarh fort►►** (*Open* daily 9–4.30. *Admission: inexpensive*), whose battlements loom high on the western ridge, is a remarkably well-preserved structure, its watch towers having witnessed hardly any military action. The huge complex commands breathtaking views as well as housing several temples, a cannon foundry, a small museum and one of India's largest cannons, the Jai Ban. It is a long, hot haul to reach the fort from Amber village but there is direct road access from below. This same road eventually leads to **Nahargarh Fort►**. This is mainly in ruins, apart from some 19th-century additions offering wonderful views south over Jaipur. A path leads down directly into the old city.

Agra Road Several sights lie northeast of Jaipur on the busy Agra road. Most notable are the landscaped gardens constructed by kings and nobles in the 18th and 19th centuries. The largest, the **Sisodia Rani ka Bagh►** was built by Jai Singh II for his Sisodia queen and contains terraced gardens with fountains, water-channels and painted pavilions. Equally well preserved is the Vidyadharji Ka Bagh, a garden laid out by Jaipur's brilliant 18th century urban planner, Vidyadhar.

RAJASTHANI CRAFTS
Despite devoting so much energy to wars, Rajasthan developed a rich crafts tradition under the patronage of its numerous kings and nobles. The parched landscape may have stimulated the desire to decorate the walls of buildings, from simple mud-huts to *havelis*, forts and palaces. Hardworking Rajasthani women wear heavy jewellery, from nose-rings to anklets, even while carrying hods of earth or tilling the fields. Courtly jewellery became more refined and was much influenced by skilled enamel workers brought by Man Singh from Lahore. The delicate art of enamelling is known as *meenakari*. Jaipur's other glittering speciality is *lac* bangles, often inlaid with glass.

95

Tours of Amber Palace can be made on caparisoned elephants (below and left)

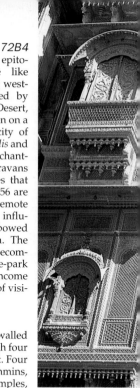

DESERT FESTIVAL

Full moon in late January or early February is the time of Jaisalmer's three-day desert festival, with a sound and light show, Gair dancers, fire-dancers, puppet shows, turban-tying competitions, camel races and the Mr Desert contest, with a grand finale of moonlight festivities at Sam sand dunes. Hotel rates rocket, and all accommodation must be booked in advance.

▶▶▶ Jaisalmer   72B4

No other town in Rajasthan epitomizes the desert culture like Jaisalmer. Isolated in the far western wastelands characterized by the sand-dunes of the Thar Desert, perched in spectacular fashion on a high outcrop, this golden city of winding lanes, exquisite *havelis* and burgeoning crafts is an enchantment. Yet the days of caravans loaded with silks and spices that inspired its foundation in 1156 are long gone, and Jaisalmer, remote and untouched by outside influences for centuries, has now bowed to the demands of tourism. The magic remains but it is fast becoming a museum, a Rajput theme-park that now derives all its income from the omnipresent army of visitors. Touts abound.

The crown Dominating the walled city is the fort, entered through four successive gates from the east. Four thousand people, mainly Brahmins, live within its walls among temples, palaces, hotels and shops. Parts of the towering **Maharaja's Palace**▶▶ (*Open* daily Oct–Feb 8–6, Mar–Sep 9–6. *Admission: moderate*) date from the early 1500s, and other sections were added by successive rulers until the late 19th century. There are some exceptional details—Italian and Chinese tiles, stone doors carved to resemble wood, mirrorwork, intricate *jali* screens and carved balconies—but renovation is limited and much has deteriorated. Far better maintained are the nearby **Jain temples**▶▶▶ (*Open* daily 11–2. *Admission: free*), their sandstone and marble imaginatively and profusely carved between the 12th and 15th centuries. The Parsvanath temple is outstanding, with lively images including Hindu gods. Palm-leaf manuscripts that are among India's oldest and other items of ancient Jain culture are preserved in a 1,000-year old library, called the Gyan Bhandar.

Havelis Outside the fort gate is the busy main marketplace, the Manak Chowk, from where a maze of atmospheric streets spreads northwards. These lead to Jaisalmer's fabulous **havelis**▶▶▶, their oriel windows and columns rising three to five storeys around central courtyards, and all minutely carved out of Jaisalmer's honey-coloured sandstone. Most were built between the mid-18th and late 19th centuries by wealthy merchants and money-lenders. The Nathmal *haveli*, the work of two Muslim brothers in the 1880s, displays seven ornate balconies, each carved from a single stone, with stone elephants and an asymmetrical façade due to fraternal rivalry. Five adjoining houses, the Patwa *havelis* (*Open* daily 10.30–5. *Admission: inexpensive*), built by one family in 1800–60, have a magnificent display of verandas, fountains, niches, pillars, gold-painted ceilings

SHOPPING

Jaisalmer is famed for its handicrafts, including embroidery, superbly embroidered soft leather slippers, camelhide stools and silver jewellery. Good places to start are the Rajasthani Government Emporium and the Khadi Emporium, where fixed prices prevail. On Asani Road, Vijay Leatherworks has slippers, belts and bags and Geeta Jewellers stock antique tribal ornaments and Kundan jewellery and Dhanraj Sweets, in Bhatia Market, is a speciality sweetmaker.

and frescoes. East of the fort gates is the extraordinary Salim Singh *haveli* (Moti Mahal) with six storeys sprouting 38 balconies. It was built in the late 18th century by a prime minister who tyrannized Jaisalmer and even its royal family. (*Open* daily 10.30–5. *Admission: inexpensive*).

Outskirts Gadisar lake►, 2km (1 mile) southeast of the citadel, was the town's only source of water before the completion of the 1987 canal. Edged by delicately carved pavilions and temples, some dating back to the 14th century, it makes a peaceful spot that attracts numerous waterbird species. Close by stands the **Jaisalmer Folk Museum►►** Gadi Sagar (*Open* daily Oct–Mar 9–6, Apr–Sep 9–noon, 3–6. *Admission: moderate*), the work of an inspired local teacher who has been collecting and documenting regional folk art since 1984. His Desert Cultural Centre (*Open* daily 9–8. *Admission: inexpensive*), next to the Tourist Reception Centre, stages music and dance performances in season.

Desert sights West of the town lie the **Sam sand dunes►**, 42km (26 miles) away, where the rolling dunes of the Desert National Park unfold. An ideal spot for 'sunset camel-rides' with drum and flute accompaniment, it also has accommodation for those enamoured of the desolate drifting sands. An afternoon circuit by car can take in **Bada Bagh►** (ruined 16th-century gardens and royal cenotaphs), **Amar Sagar's►** *tanks* and temples, and **Lodurva►►**, (*Admission: free*), the desert-bound remnants of the capital before Jaisalmer replaced it in the 11th century, site of a lovely Jain temple rebuilt in the 1600s.

Jaisalmer's merchants prospered from its position on a camel-caravan route and invested in their houses

TOURIST OFFICES
Tourist Reception Centre, Gadisar Road, 500m (550yd) from the rail station, on southern perimeter of citadel (*Open* Mon–Sat 10–5; tel: 02992 252406). Exchange, post office, rest rooms, travel and ticket arrangements. Guides and cars available. Half-day tours. Also counter at railway station (open to meet trains).
Bicycles are available for rent, and are a good way of touring the nearby sights.

▶▶ Jodhpur
72C4

Nearly 10km (6 miles) of city walls and countless bastions give Rajasthan's second largest city an aura of invincibility, and the traditional trades of cattle, camels, wood, salt and crops remain its mainstays. It is also distinctive for its 'blue city', a sprawl of indigo-coloured houses originally occupied by Brahmins but now also inhabited by other people. Painting a house indigo deflects heat from sandstone walls, keeping the interior relatively cool, and blue houses can now be found dotted throughout Jodhpur.

Fort In 1459, advised by a sage to establish an impregnable base, Rao Jodha, ruler of Marwar, moved his capital from Mandore to this towering outcrop and built one of Rajasthan's most impressive places, with walls rising up to 36m (118ft). **Fort Mehrangarh▶▶▶** (*Open* daily 9–5: conservation may close parts of the fort occasionally. *Admission: moderate*) dates mostly from the

TOURIST INFORMATION
Tourist Reception Centre, Hotel Ghoomar, High Court Road (*Open* Mon–Sat, theoretically 8–6, but 10–5 with a lunchbreak is more realistic; tel: 0291 2545083). The tourist bureau at the rail station has toilets and a shower. Marwari hospitality can be enjoyed through their Paying Guest scheme. Village 'safaris' make a circuit of local craftspeople, Bishnoi villages and desert wildlife.

17th century and consists of a rambling complex of palaces and courtyards, all impeccably conserved or restored. Fine filigree sandstone *jali* screens for the women's quarters, and silvered hand prints of women who performed *sati* (at the Loha Gate) indicate the strong Rajput traditions.

Regalia Outstanding exhibits include arms, miniatures, *howdahs* (seats for riding on elephants) and *palanquins* (covered litters), jewellery, costumes, musical instruments, furniture, elaborate cradles, silverware and model trains in ivory, all displayed in suitably regal settings. Among the numerous palaces, the mid 18th-century Phool Mahal (Flower Palace) has delicate gilded wall-paintings and coloured glass inlays; the Takhat Vilas has an outrageously decorated Maharaja's bedroom (mid-19th century) with suspended glass baubles; the Sheesh Mahal (early 18th century) has mirrorwork; and its contemporary, the vast Moti Mahal, boasts a Durbar Hall to beat them all, with mirrored and gold casement ceilings designed to reflect flickering oil-lamps and candles in wall-niches. Well-geared to visitors, the fort has a resident palmist, bookshop, restaurant turbanned guards who will give evocative flute recitals for a tip, and even an elevator to the top.

Art deco In contrast, the British-influenced **Umaid Bhawan palace►** was designed in the 1920s by London architects and stands among lawns and bougainvillea. It was commissioned by the Maharaja to provide employment for famine relief, and building lasted 14 years. Today it is partly inhabited by descendants of the royal family, partly a museum and partly a hotel. The museum (*Open daily 9–5. Admission: moderate*) has an idiosyncratic collection of arms, clocks, glass, tableware, polo trophies and model planes. The lofty domed atrium, throne room frescoes by Norblin, and modernist washrooms are particularly impressive.

Past and present Close to the fort at **Jaswant Thada►** (*Open daily 9–5. Admission: inexpensive*) is a cluster of elaborate white marble cenotaphs built in 1899. The **Government Museum►** (*Open Sat–Thu 10–4.30. Admission: inexpensive*) in Umaid Park, has exhibits ranging from stuffed animals to textiles. Jodhpur's lively central market areas, the **Girdikot and Sardar bazars►►** sprawl north and south of the landmark clocktower, a British relic of 1912. Narrow dusty streets, lined with old houses and courtyards in terracotta and blue hues, offer a dazzling array of goods.

The interior of Fort Mehrangarh (top)
The Hall of Heroes at Mandor (above)
Jodhpur's clock tower (left)

Excursion
Mandor►► This ancient capital lies north of Jodhpur and contains the grandiose cenotaphs of Marwar's rulers, beautifully sculpted in dark red sandstone. In a pillared compound is the Hall of Heroes, a shrine to Hinduism's 330 million gods. More enticing are the lush gardens surrounding the hall that are much enjoyed by picnicking families.

MARWAR FESTIVAL
Traditional Marwar music and dance are celebrated during Jodhpur's annual festival. It is held each October, but the dates vary considerably, so check before planning a trip around it.

India's tiger population is now estimated at around 3,500, an improvement on the dramatic figures of a decade ago. Project Tiger has, in some places, increased numbers, but poaching and the shrinkage of natural habitat remain overwhelming problems. Is the roar of this magnificent wild animal destined to disappear?

100

FEROCIOUS, FELINE, IMPERIAL

'The ultimate wild things are incidentally dangerous—white sharks, harpy eagles, polar bears—and unpredictable. Even the most gorgeous tiger is less athletic, more complicated than a leopard, say, which may sometimes seem like a single, lengthy muscle. But the tiger's spirit, when ferocious, feline and imperial, can parallel ours...Tigers are less heartbreaking than the beleaguered elephant, because they are not social creatures, are reactive, not innovative. But they are an apex, a kind of hook the web of nature hangs from. To know them marked my life.'
Edward Hoagland, *Wild Things*, 1996

The tiger (*Panthera tigris*) is incontestably the most splendid of India's beasts, and stalks through a wide range of the subcontinent's habitats: the Himalayas, the mangrove swamps of the Sunderbans, the Gangetic plain, the sandalwood forests of Karnataka and Rajasthan's national parks. Tigers were the favoured quarry of every self-respecting maharaja, nawab or Mughal emperor, and *shirkar* (tiger-hunting) was adopted by the British as a true *pukka sahib's* (gentleman's) sport. At the beginning of the 20th century, there were an estimated 40,000 tigers, but by 1947 this number had already been halved.

Awakening Despite the example set by individuals such as Jim Corbett (see page 124) and certain enlightened maharajas, the post-Independence years saw the tiger population plummeting even further. This was mainly due to the widespread destruction of forests and to poaching. By the early 1970s fewer than 2,000 tigers survived. Prime Minister Indira Gandhi stepped in to declare a total ban on tiger-shooting and set up Project Tiger.

Project Tiger Initially nine areas of forest were declared reserves. Their human inhabitants were resettled with compensation, and armed rangers employed to keep poachers at bay. Now 23 such sites exist, with a marginal improvement in numbers. Poaching remains a serious problem as rangers in remote areas are ill equipped to combat the forces of the lucrative trade in much coveted tiger products. The tiger in the wild may soon be a thing of the past.

▶▶ Keoladeo Ghana
National Park (Bharatpur)

Open: daily 6am–6pm. Admission: expensive, including guide and transport.

Declared a national park in 1983, this reserve was one of the world's best for waterbirds, with over 350 bird species but drought has affected this. Before converting it into a sanctuary in 1956, the local Maharaja used it as his hunting reserve. The shallow marsh water, lakes and partly submerged thorny babul trees are favoured by migratory birds in November to January. The most common native species are the open-billed stork, painted stork, egret, pelican, ibis, cormorant, darter or snake-bird, spoonbill and grey heron. Migrants arrive from Siberia, including the rare Siberian crane, Central Asia and Tibet.

Easy viewing As well as birds, Keoladeo has sambar, black buck, chital, nilgai, feral cats, hyenas, otters and mongoose. Pythons are easily visible at Python Point. Unusually for an Indian national park, Keoladeo can be visited independently by bicycle (easily rented in town) or even by rickshaw; knowledgeable rickshaw-drivers and guides are available at the entrance and, a little further on, a boat jetty offers lake tours. Dawn and dusk are the best viewing times. Binoculars can be rented.

In town The reserve is sometimes known as Bharatpur after the adjoining town—which is easily reached from Agra (56km/35 miles)—and is much visited by tourists on whistlestop tours. Few visitors make it to the 18th-century **Lohagarh Fort▶** whose ingenious defence mechanisms consistently repelled attacks by the British. Little remains of the walls but there are three adjoining palaces in a sunken garden, blending Mughal and Rajput architecture. The central wing houses the **Government Museum▶** (*Open Sat–Thu 10–4.30. Admission: inexpensive*), displaying fine Jain sculptures, arms and manuscripts. An excursion can be made 32km (20 miles) north to **Dig (Deeg)▶▶**, once the summer resort of Bharatpur's royal family, with superb palaces, gardens and a fort beside a lake.

Painted storks nesting at Keoladeo Ghana National Park

101

TOURIST OFFICE
Tourist Reception Centre, Hotel Saras, Agra Road, Bharatpur (*Open* Mon–Sat 10–5 closed second Sat of month. tel: 05644 222542), paying guest list.

The Northwest

DESERT DWELLERS

The Bishnoi community are the desert-dwellers of the Jodhpur/Jaisalmer/Bikaner triangle. They live according to 29 rules, of which the first is to protect flora and fauna. Their immaculate round mud-huts crowned by conical thatched roofs are usually grouped in compounds with sheep and goats. They use camels for transport. The notoriously arduous desert climate ranges in temperature from 0°C (32°F) during winter nights to highs of 40–50°C (104–122°F) in April and May when the *loo* (desert-wind) blows. Sandstorms and the scarcity of water-sources are other major challenges.

Chillies drying in the sun in the Osiyan region

►► Mount Abu 72C3

This holy mountain and Jain pilgrimage site lies at the southern extremity of the rugged Aravalli hills, overlooking the arid, rocky plains of the Gujarat border. The steep, 1,220m (4,000ft) climb up the mountain twists through a wildlife sanctuary where dense vegetation interspersed with sculptural boulders is alive with langurs and birds. The town of Mount Abu itself, sprawling among palm-trees, has something of the atmosphere of an oasis about it. For centuries it has been a retreat for sages and seers, who have left a trail of legends in their wake. Its main sights are its beautiful Jain temples. Streams of honeymooners and weekending Gujaratis are drawn here also by the cool, fresh air, boating lake and endless souvenir-stands.

Jain prowess Half hidden by mango groves, the five **Dilwara temples►►►** (*Open daily noon–dusk. Admission: free*) lie about 4km (3 miles) northeast of the town centre on the road to Achalgarh. Their façades were purposely kept simple in order to deceive Muslim attackers. The fabulously worked interiors are in total contrast. The earliest, Vimal Vasahi, was started in 1031, allegedly employing 1,500 masons and 1,200 labourers for 14 years. They created a feast of sculpted white marble that illustrates the 24 stages of Mahavir (the founder of Jainism), with cusped arches, ornate capitals, dome rosettes carved with exquisite dancers and elephants, and a colonnaded transept and ambulatory lined by 52 small shrines, each housing a statue. In front stands an elephant hall (1147) in homage to the hard labour involved.

The other masterpiece is the Vastupal and Tejpal temple (1231), named after its two founding brothers and dedicated to Neminath, the 22nd Tirthankara. Door-casings, friezes, architraves, pillars and porticoes are all intricately carved, and rivalry between the brothers' wives is indicated in two tilting female heads sculpted above the lateral altars. At the back, the priests' prayer-hall can be spied through a lattice wall. Less interesting are the unfinished Risah Deo temple, and the Chaumukhi temple at the entrance, where the stone quality is mixed and carvings distinctly inferior.

Views About 500m (550yd) beyond the temples is **Trevor's Tank►**, a small wildlife reserve with slothful-seeming crocodiles, pheasants, partridges and peacocks. The 11km (7 mile) road from here to the ruined 14th-century fort of **Achalgarh►** and its 15th- to 16th-century temples, traverses beautiful countryside, alternating between wild landscapes of rocks and cacti, and wheatfields and farms roamed by donkeys. A little further looms the highest point in Rajasthan, Guru Shikhar, with a small Sivaite shrine at the top of 300 steps. The views from here are superb, and at sunset the open-air café below fills up with shy honeymooning couples. Their other favourite destinations are west of town at Sunset Point, Honeymoon Point and above all Nakki Lake, specializing in kitsch souvenirs, photo-opportunities and boating.

▶▶ Osiyan   72C4

Magical and remote, this ancient Brahmanical and Jain centre lies 65km (40 miles) north of Jodhpur. Flat desert scrub dotted with camels, black buck, goats and Bishnoi hamlets suddenly ends with dramatic hills. These announce the temple town of Osiyan. Of the couple of dozen temples, three are outstanding: the Surya (Sun) temple (early 8th century); the still functioning Sachiya Mata temple (11th–12th centuries) and the main Mahavir temple. This last is a riotous mixture of styles, with vaulted ceiling, gold leaf, pillars that are between three and 500 years old and 7th-century Pali inscriptions. The interior of the Sachiya Mata temple, its *shikhara* rising out of a cluster of turrets, displays 19th-century mirrorwork, tiles, coloured glass and an altar to Durga (see page 252). A separate group of Harihara temples dating from the 8th and 9th centuries stands south of the town centre by the bus-stand. Decorative features include carved spiralling serpents, goddesses and extensive friezes.

TOURIST OFFICE
Tourist Reception Centre, opposite bus-stand, Mount Abu (*Open* in peak season Mon–Sat 8–11, 4–8; otherwise 10–1.30, 2–5; tel: 02974 235151). Also at Abu Road railway station. Helpful with guides, taxis, half-day tours. Paying guest list.

The Mahavir temple in Osiyan

103

No two pillars of the Chaumukha temple are the same. The temple is carved from creamy white marble

MEWAR SCHOOL OF PAINTING
The school of Mewar, based in Udaipur (see page 108) was at the forefront of art, architecture, music and devotional literature, especially under the Maharanas Kumbha and Sanga. Illustrated manuscripts were produced from the 13th century onwards and by the early 17th century sets of miniatures were being painted in a well-defined, bold and colourful style. These were followed by large court paintings showing the Maharana in processions, on hunting expeditions or attending religious festivities. Portraits, folk legends and divinities extended the subject matter. A good selection is displayed at Udaipur's City Palace Museum, and copies are produced in the back streets.

▶▶▶ Ranakpur   72C3

Peacefully set in a beautiful valley at the western end of the Aravalli hills, Ranakpur requires a special effort to visit. This is repaid in full by its remarkable temple complex, one of the five holiest Jain sites, dating from 1439. Entering the main **Chaumukha temple**▶▶▶ (*Open daily 12–5. Admission: free*) is like walking through three-dimensional lace: every conceivable surface of the white marble walls, pillars and ceilings is carved with unbelievable intricacy and imagination. The only element not in marble is the stone floor that supports this symphony of domes, arches, towers and 1,444 pillars, of which no two are alike. The central open-sided sanctuary, rising majestically on three storeys, contains a quadruple image of Adinath, the first Tirthankara (Jain prophet), surrounded by four subsidiary shrines. Altogether 29 halls and 66 shrines crowned by spires, and five monumental *shikharas*, their flags and bells moved by the breeze, make up this staggering celebration of Jain beliefs.

Images include floral designs, animals and superb human figures, including erotic figures on the façade of the 14th-century **Parsvanath temple**▶▶. Here, equally astounding carving surrounds a black marble image of Parsvanatha and, nearby, another beautiful temple honours **Surya**▶ the sun god. Ranakpur monkeys are aggressive, so watch out.

Mighty fort A day trip to Ranakpur from Udaipur (90km/56 miles) can also include the remote, impregnable and evocative fortress of **Kumbhalgarh**▶▶. Dominating 13 surrounding hills that now form a wildlife sanctuary, its 36km (22 miles) of ramparts enclose 365 ruined temples, shrines and a palace. There are Hindu temples dating from the 14th century, but the majority are Jain structures, some going back to the 3rd century BC when it is thought a grandson of Emperor Ashoka ruled here. The Nilkanth Mahadev temple dedicated to Siva houses a black marble *lingam* surrounded by finely fluted, tapering pillars, and there are some royal *chhatris* nearby.

Looming above the temples and reached by a steep path through seven sturdy gateways is the Badal Mahal (Cloud Palace), founded in 1415 by Maharana Kumbha of Udaipur and rebuilt and extended in 1813. The palace is semi-derelict but retains lovely colours, floral murals and features such as the royal toilet, revealing a precipitous drop below. A roaring wind and rattling shutters promote a suitably desolate atmosphere, reinforced by sweeping views of the once powerful state of Mewar.

▶▶ Ranthambhor National Park   *73D3*

Open: daily Oct–Jun. Three hour safaris begin Oct–Feb at 7am and 2.30pm; Mar–Jun at 6.30am and 3.30pm.
Admission: expensive

This popular wildlife reserve of 392sq km (151sq miles) lies 12km (7 miles) from the town of Sawai Madhopur on the main Delhi–Mumbai (Bombay) railway. Its focus is a 10th-century fort that had a turbulent history under Delhi sultans, Rajput and Mughal rulers before it was taken over by the Maharaja of Jaipur in the early 18th century. From then on, it was a royal hunting reserve used by such illustrious visitors as Queen Elizabeth II. The fort's unique style of construction means that it is barely visible from afar: the walls follow the ridge lines winding up the forested, sheer precipice. Apart from a temple devoted to Ganesha, who receives sacks of fan-mail and wedding invitations daily, the interior structures are mostly in ruins but offer wonderful views. There is a range of accommodation just outside the park, and all hotels organize jeep safaris, or cheaper minibuses, for visitors.

Fauna Since joining Project Tiger in 1979 (see page 100), Ranthambhor has supplied frequent sightings of tigers, now thought to number about 30. Poaching is by no means unknown. The undulating dry deciduous forest also shelters sambar, chital, nilgai, wild boar, chinkara, jackal and langur, most of which are favoured by tigers as prey. Over 120 bird species are attracted by the many lakes and *tanks*, including laggar falcon, several types of eagle, and migratory birds such as sandpipers, black storks, lapwings and geese.

TOURIST INFORMATION
Tourist Reception Centre,
Project Tiger office,
within RTDC's Vinayak
Tourist Complex,
Ranthambhor Road,
Ranthambhor
(*Open* Mon–Sat 10–1.30,
2–5; tel: 07462 220808,
fax: 07462 220702).
Park information, jeep
and minibus hire and
RTDC hotels.

The battlements of Kumbhalgarh fort, stretching out over the Aravalli hills

GARDEN OF SHEKHA
In the early 15th century the childless Mokal Singh, ruler of a tiny principality called Barwara, was advised to consult a *fakir* (religious mendicant) named Sheikh Burman in order to produce a son. The consultation accomplished, Mokal Singh did finally produce an heir who in honour of the *fakir* was named Shekha. Shekha ascended the throne in 1433 at the tender age of 12 to begin a reign that was to last 43 years. His kingdom came to be known as Shekhawati ('garden of Shekha').

▶▶ Shekhawati 73D4

The 20 or so towns and villages of Shekhawati have a wealth of superbly painted *havelis* and forts that make this semi-arid region well worth exploring. They were the unintended result of heavy taxation by the East India Company, which drove the entrepreneurial Marwaris away from here to create trading-houses and industries elsewhere in India (the Birlas being the most famous). They sent their profits back home, and the result is an astonishing abundance of traders' mansions handpainted with unique images that make a lavish visual record of social history between 1750 and 1930. Today, apart from pockets of nascent tourism, Shekhawati has returned to being a sleepy backwater with many *havelis* permanently shuttered-up or crumbling gracefully.

Practicalities Rough roads mean its slow-going, all the better for observing neatly walled mud-hut compounds of desert tribes, camel-carts, brilliantly appliquéd saris, and the surrounding countryside. Some villages are mere

sandy streets where a few shops and derelict *havelis* front piles of rubble picked over by peacocks, but others have more majestic sights, with whimsical decoration that demands hours to decipher. The best way to enter Shekhawati is either from NH11 between Jaipur and Bikaner or directly from Delhi, about 150km (93 miles) to the northeast. Most accomodation is in superb but scattered forts, and public transport is limited, so a car is essential if you want to make the most of the region.

Themes *Havelis* were built around courtyards that offered safety, privacy for women and protection from the harsh climate. Several generations lived together under one roof. Early frescoes were made with crushed lime, marble and natural pigments on wet plaster, as in Italy, but chemical dyes and PVA paints are widely used for restoration. The most prolific period for Shekhawati wall-painting was 1830–1900, when mythological frescoes were interspersed with illustrations of local legends, daily life, animals, portraits, and hunting and wrestling scenes. These were gradually replaced by a broader range of images influenced by European lithographs and photographs. *Chiteras* (artists) would depict trains, gramophones, planes or cars without ever having seen them, and the gods became strolling *sahibs* and *memsahibs* with dogs on leashes.

Starters In the capital of Shekhawati, **Jhunjhunun▶▶** is the beautiful Khetri Mahal (Wind Palace) alongside the accessible havelis of Marugh Das Tibriwal, Mehau Das Modi and Khaitan, all displaying ornate wall-paintings. There are more frescoes at the Bihariji temple, and the domed and turreted structures of the Birdi Chand well are also worth seeing. Southwest of here is **Dighal▶**, where a beautiful century-old *haveli* on the main square comes as a complete surprise. Typically, its owners now live in Mumbai (Bombay), returning only once a year to a modern house nearby. Central **Fatehpur▶**, although not the most attractive town of Shekhawati, was founded by Muslim nawabs in the mid-15th century and its prosperous merchants later funded some unrivalled frescoes. Indian and Western styles fuse in the Devra and Singhania *havelis*, with mirrorwork and Japanese tiles depicting Mount Fuji adding to the eclecticism.

Fort towns Far more dramatic are fort towns such as **Lachhmangarh▶**, **Mukundgarh▶**, a town built around a temple square and known for its *bandhani* fabrics and brassware, and **Nawalgarh▶▶▶**. This last has two forts, a palace hotel, decorative temples, countless crumbling *havelis* and, best for frescoes, the Senior Secondary School. This much restored masterpiece displays a wealth of striking, idiosyncratic images. Atmospheric **Mandawa▶▶** has a fort-hotel with a magnificent interior, some notable *havelis* and a Siva temple with rock crystal *lingam*.

Shekhawati is like a huge open-air art gallery, with superbly painted havelis as the works of art (above and left)

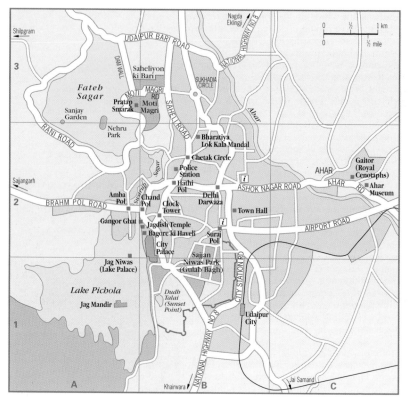

TOURIST OFFICES

Tourist Reception Centre, Fateh Memorial, near Suraj Pol (*Open* Mon–Sat 10–1.30, 2–5, tel: 0294 2411535).

Also counters at airport and at railway station. Well organized, with guide and car services. Half- and full-day tours include Chittaurgarh. Paying Guest scheme accommodation.

▶▶▶ Udaipur
72C3

Romance and magic fill the air of this city of lakes, palaces, gardens, *ghats*, temples, craftspeople and painted houses. It was named after its founder, Maharana Udai Singh who, on being forced out of his citadel of Chittaurgarh by Akbar in 1567, consulted a *sadhu* and was advised to move to Lake Pichola. Nestling in a beautiful valley rimmed by verdant hills, Udaipur developed around three lakes, to become the last and greatest capital of Mewar. Still dominated by gregarious, meat-eating Rajputs, Udaipur now generates 60 per cent of its income from tourism, but the influx of foreign visitors does little to change the aura of this enchanting town.

Palatial genesis Dominating the east bank of Lake Pichola is the majestic **City Palace**▶▶▶ (*Open* daily 9.30–4.30. *Admission: expensive*) that expanded from the late 16th century onwards to become Rajasthan's largest palace. It is well worth hiring a guide to explain the intricacies and stories behind each structure. The approach is through Tripolia (triple gate), with its eight carved arches. This is the spot where rulers were weighed in gold or silver whose value was distributed as food to the poor. Behind the balconies and turrets of the towering façade is a succession of restored palaces: the Sheesh Mahal is characterized by beautiful mirrorwork, Krishna Vilas by superlative frescoes, Moti Mahal by mirrors, coloured glass and inset paintings, Chini Chitrasala by blue-and-white

Chinese and Dutch tiles, Bhim Vilas by wall-paintings of the Radha-Krishna stories, Mor Chowk by vivid mosaics of peacocks, and the Mosaic Gallery by stained glass portraits and panoramic city views. A museum near the entrance displays royal armour, arms and toys. Through the courtyard of the Queen's Palace at the southern end is the residence of the royal descendants. A neglected government museum (*Open* Sat–Thu 9.30–4.30. *Admission: inexpensive*) in the northwestern corner displays miniatures and regional temple sculptures including a superb 8th-century head of Siva.

The **Fateh Prakash Palace** has a **Crystal Gallery►►** (*Open* daily 10–1, 3–8. *Admission: expensive*) displaying extraordinary 19th-century items made of crystal—including furniture. It overlooks the **Durbar Hall►**, now a dining-room with huge chandeliers, royal portraits and weapons.

Heart of Udaipur Just to the north is a 1651 **Jagdish temple►►** dedicated to Vishnu as Lord Jagannath and replete with carved marble columns and sculptures. Jagdish Temple Road, Udaipur's attractive main shopping street, runs northeast from here past the Clock Tower to end at Hathi Pol (Elephant Gate). Downhill and northwest from the crossroads is **Gangor Ghat►►**, a picturesque archway framing the lakeshore where women and children habitually bathe, swim and thwack laundry. Through a courtyard on the left is the

Mosaic glasswork in the City Palace (inset) and views of the City Palace and Shiv Niwas from Udaipur's Lake Pichola

109

Coloured glass characteristic of Moti Mahal, in Udaipur's City Palace

THE SUN KINGS
A golden sun with a moustached human face is a recurring image throughout Udaipur. This is the emblem of the Mewar rulers whose last capital was Udaipur. Former capitals were Ahar, Nagda and Chittaurgarh, established by the Sisodia Rajputs, head of the 36 royal clans. Claiming descent from Lord Rama, King of Ayodhya and hero of the Ramayana epic dating from around 500BC, the Sisodia Rajputs trace an unbroken line of kings of Mewar from AD144. Their dynasty became more firmly established in the 8th century when Bappa Rawal, a legend-inspiring king, defeated the prince of Chittaurgarh and founded an enlarged kingdom that was to blaze a trail of Rajput valour through Indian history.

Haveli Museum (*Open* daily 10–7. *Admission: inexpensive*) inside the **Western Zone Cultural Centre►**, newly converted to exhibit crafts and stage music and dance performances. The most atmospheric streets of old Udaipur meander south of here parallel to the lake. Whitewashed houses with colourful murals, tiny shutters and balconies rise to precipitous heights with shrines squeezed in between, while aromas of incense, food, fruit and flowers waft through the air. Many have been converted into budget hotels and restaurants.

Lake Pichola In the lake are two island palaces, the 18th-century Jag Niwas, now a luxury hotel, and the 17th-century **Jag Mandir►►**, where Shah Jahan once took refuge from his father. The domed sandstone pavilion contains some beautiful rooms fronted by stone elephants and gardens. Boat trips round the lake (some solar powered) stop here, with magical views of the shore at sunset.

Fateh Sagar lake Sights north of the centre on the eastern shore of the shrinking Fateh Sagar lake include the lush, peaceful **Saheliyon ki Bari►►** (*Open* daily 9–7. *Admission: inexpensive*), laid out in the early 18th century with pools, fountains (no longer working), delicate pavilions and marble elephants. These gardens were designed to amuse 48 young ladies-in-waiting sent as part of a royal dowry. Another promenading-spot close by is the hilltop **Pratap-Smarak►** (*Open* daily 9–6. *Admission: inexpensive*). Here a statue of the heroic Maharana Pratap on his beloved steed looks out across the thirsty lake-bed to distant hills. Fateh Sagar's island contains **Nehru Park**. In the new town east of here the main sight is **Bharatiya Lok Kala Mandal►►** (*Open* daily 9–5.30. *Admission: inexpensive*), a museum of folk art displaying masks, *thapas* (finger-paintings), a mobile temple, costumes, musical instruments and photographs of India's tribal peoples and their art. Amusing puppet shows, an Udaipur speciality, are held daily at 6pm with shorter versions during the day. (For information, tel: 0294 2529296.)

East and west Another of Udaipur's delights is its wealth of sights scattered outside the town. These include the rather artificial though revealing **Shilpgram►►** (*Open* daily 11–7. *Admission: inexpensive*), about 3km (2 miles) west, an arts-and-crafts village of 26 traditional huts from Gujarat, Goa, Maharashtra and Rajasthan where some mesmerising performances are held. A little further through idyllic rural landscapes looms the **Sajjangarh►** (Monsoon Palace). It is closed and derelict, and shares its strategic hilltop site with a telecommunications station, but the courtyard and ramparts have fabulous views. East of Udaipur lies **Ahar►**, the ancient capital of the Sisodias who created Mewar. This forest of crumbling white marble *chhatris* includes the royal cenotaphs of Mewar and a museum (*Open* Sat–Thu 10–4.30. *Admission: inexpensive*) that houses a rare collection of 4,000-year-old artefacts.

North Some 20km (12 miles) northeast of town, beyond a long stretch of marble workshops, lie the ruins of another former capital, **Nagda▶**, where three 11th-century temples survive in a peaceful lakeside spot. Intricate sandstone and marble carvings surround the main porch of the Saas-Bahu temple, the intricate carving continues inside the building while ribbed, carved towers curve gracefully behind. The façades are alive with countless gods, *apsaras* (dancers), floral designs and some erotic couples.

Two kilometres (1 mile) further lies **Eklingji▶▶**, a tiny village that is centred on a huge temple complex dating from 734 but rebuilt in the 15th century. No fewer than 108 shrines and temples are discreetly enclosed behind high walls, all devoted to Eklingji, an aspect of Siva and the deity of the Maharanas of Mewar whose descendants still come here to worship. Pilgrim souvenirs, flowers and garland-sellers line the entrance that leads to the white marble main temple, faced by a statue of Bappa Rawal, the 8th-century Mewar hero. Sculpted friezes depict musicians, a few erotic couples, elephants and *apsaras*. Inside, engraved silver screens shield the altar faced by a solid silver *nandi*. Eklingji has plenty of bicycle-rental shops offering the possibility of some very pleasant pedalling and sightseeing around its rural environs.

South One of Asia's largest artificial lakes, **Jai Samand ▶**, lies 48km (30 miles) to the southeast. It was created by Maharana Jai Singh in 1685. The scenic *ghats* are lined with graceful marble *chhatris* and on either side are the queens' summer palaces. The Bhils, a local tribe, still inhabit the islands in the lake, and a wildlife sanctuary shelters many species including panther, wild boar, deer, antelope, mongoose and flocks of migratory birds.

FESTIVAL TIME
Every March–April, Udaipur welcomes the spring with the riotously colourful Mewar festival of Rajasthani culture. Songs, dances, processions, devotional music and firework displays keep the city's 400,000 or so inhabitants and tourists entranced. In the evening the Gangor procession takes place— groups of women dressed in brilliant yellow, green, purple and scarlet saris carry images to Gangor Ghat, while boat processions bring the horizon alive.

111

A family at work on an Udaipur street stall

Rajputana, land of the bellicose Rajputs, possesses a legacy of palaces and forts which is among the greatest cultural riches of the subcontinent. With a history veering from courageous deeds to preposterous extravagance (a Maharaja who shot crane from his private plane), the Rajputs are people of intensity, vivid legends and larger-than-life characters.

Rajput opulence in interior decoration

According to legend, the Rajputs were born from the fire offering of the gods on Mount Abu. In reality they emerged in the 6th century from Scythian and Hun invaders to become the fearsome rulers of Rajputana. By appointing themselves *kshatriyas* within the ancient Vedic system, a move supported by the priestly caste of Brahmins, they gained a semi-divine status and claimed descent from the sun (in Udaipur) or the moon (in Jaisalmer). Reaping the rewards of their feudal system, the Rajput princes constructed daunting forts and developed a warriors' code of honour and fearlessness. Whether they were fighting neighbouring kingdoms, Turks, Delhi Sultans or Mughals, they were unrivalled for their military prowess and heroism. Proof of their ferocity is the fact that the Mughals, and the British after them, sought conciliation rather than do battle with them, with some notable and bloody exceptions.

Chivalry and valour Honour came first for the Rajputs, and countless men and women sacrificed themselves rather than lose it. If a battle was turning definitively against them, the mass suicide by fire of the women would accompany the men's final and equally suicidal onslaught. The notions of retreat and surrender were unknown, and defeat was intolerable to them. A classic Rajput legend describes Maharana Pratap being so traumatized by his family's loss of Chittaurgarh that he abandoned the comfortable Udaipur palaces to haunt the forests of the Aravalli hills, relentlessly but unsuccessfully attempting to win back the capital city from the Mughal conquerors.

Extravagances After Britain's haphazard, piecemeal conquest of India, most Rajput rulers retained their autonomy in exchange for ceding control of foreign affairs and

defence. They indulged in hunting, polo matches, bejewelled elephants, private railway carriages, Rolls Royces,
marble palaces, harems and glittering banquets, and
jewels were an obsession. The fabulous treasure of the
Maharaja of Jaipur was so precious that it was buried in a
hillside and guarded by a particularly fearsome Rajput unit.
Each maharaja would visit the hoard to select one item for
his reign; the choice ranged from a three-tiered necklace of
egg-sized rubies to three giant emeralds weighing 90
carats. A Maharaja of Jodhpur sported diamond eyebrows;
the Maharaja of Bharatpur preferred ivory masterpieces,
and his favourite car was a silver-plated Rolls Royce. More
extraordinary still was the Maharaja of Alwar's self-styled,
gold-plated Lancaster, with a steering wheel of carved
ivory and a body designed as a replica of the English coronation coach.

Social sustenance Visiting the palaces of Rajasthan gives
an idea of the anachronistic, often eccentric lifestyle that
continued unabated until Independence, among silver
cradles, inlaid ivory beds, Bohemian glass chandeliers,
golden *howdahs* and endless wildlife trophies. There was
another, paternalistic side to these rulers, though, that
sometimes gave their peoples
benefits and privileges unknown elsewhere in India.
Enlightened rulers invested in improving the state infrastructure and industrial technology, as with Ganga Singh of
Bikaner who brought rail-
ways, elevators, mining
and the world's longest
concrete-lined canal to his
parched state in 1925–27.
In addition, various famine
relief projects were instigated—one example of
these was the construction
of Jodhpur's Umaid Bhawan
palace.

113

*Hunting was considered
essential proof of valour
by the Rajputs*

The North

115

116

Previous pages: Hindu faithful bathing in the sacred waters at Varanasi A Hindu sadhu, *in a yogic position (below)*

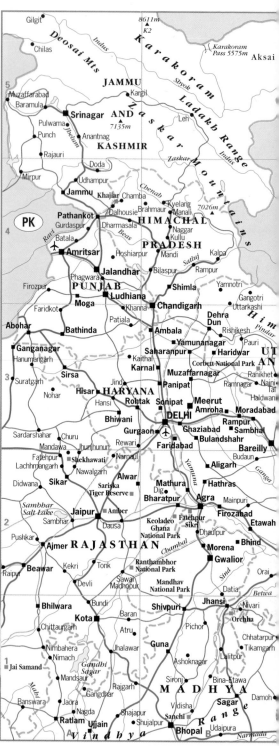

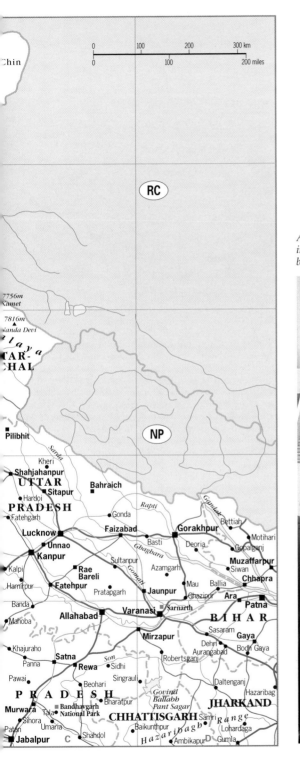

0 100 200 300 km

0 100 200 miles

Chin

RC

NP

7756m
Kamet

7816m
Nanda Devi

alaya

TAR-
HAL

Pilibhit

Kheri

Shahjahanpur

UTTAR

Hardoi · Sitapur

PRADESH

Fatehgarh

Bahraich

Gonda

Rapti

Gandak

Bettiah

Lucknow

Faizabad

Gorakhpur

Motihari

Unnao

Basti

Deoria

Gopalganj

Kanpur

Ghaghara

Sultanpur

Azamgarh

Muzaffarpur

Siwan

Kalpi

Rae
Bareli

Gomati

Mau

Ballia

Chhapra

Hamirpur

Fatehpur

Pratapgarh

Jaunpur

Ghazipur

Ara

Patna

Banda

Allahabad

Varanasi · Sarnath

BIHAR

Mahoba

Mirzapur

Sasaram

Gaya

Khajuraho

Dehri

Aurangabad

Bodh Gaya

Satna

Son

Sidhi

Robertsganj

Panna

Rewa

Pawai

Beohari

Singrauli

Daltenganj

Hazaribag

PRADESH

Bharatpur

Govind
Ballabh
Pant Sagar

JHARKAND

Murwara

Bandhavgarh
National Park

CHHATTISGARH

Samri

Range

Sihora

Tala

Baikunthpur

Lohardaga

Paten

Umaria

Hazaribagh

Jabalpur

C

Shahdol

Ambikapur

Gumla

A Sikh holy man, wear-
ing the ritual dagger,
bracelet and turban

Above: A man ties a prayer flag to a post at Mustang in the Himalayas
Below: Tibetan refugee in Dharmsala

NORTH Radiating northwards and eastwards from Delhi, the North reaches from the densely populated Gangetic plain to the towering Himalayas that feed it from their snows and glaciers. The fertile plain was the original heartland of India, where hunter-gatherers became farmers along the Indus, Yamuna and Ganga (Ganges) rivers some 5,000 years ago. The original Dravidian people were driven to the deep south by fair-skinned Aryans who introduced Sanskrit and the fundamental texts of Hindu philosophy and religion. Persians, Greeks and Mughals were successively seduced by this region, long before the British made Delhi their capital and chose the western Himalayas for their summer retreats.

HIGH CONTRAST It is a region of stark contrasts, that includes the desolate heights of Ladakh, the blossoming valleys of Himachal, the Mughal glories of Agra, the erotic temples of Khajuraho, the tigers of Corbett National Park and the tumultuous human hordes descending on the holy sites of the Ganges. Such variety puts demands on visitors, who need considerable mental and physical energy, respect for the climate, and, in Kashmir, awareness of political developments. Places in northern Madhya Pradesh that can be combined with destinations in Uttar Pradesh are included in this section. Amritsar, capital of the comparatively colourless Punjab, is home to the spectacular Golden Temple, the Sikhs' most sacred monument.

PILGRIMS AND PYRES Uttar Pradesh, India's most heavily populated state, dominates national culture through its language (Hindi). It is of immense importance to Hindus as site of India's holiest city—Varanasi (Benares). Here Mother Ganges is treated with infinite respect: it is believed that to be cremated by the river at Varanasi releases the body from the endless cycle of rebirths. Cremations account for a fraction of the daily activity on the *ghats*, however, and Varanasi also maintains an illustrious cultural and crafts tradition. Closer to its source in the Himalayas, the Ganges has also fostered Haridwar and Rishikesh, two smaller but equally intense pilgrimage destinations.

ARCHITECTURAL HERITAGE Varanasi, Haridwar and Rishikesh are spiritual centres. Agra is much more worldly: you could give it a miss were it not the site of the Taj Mahal, built in the 17th century at the zenith of the Mughal artistic and architectural prowess. This had its genesis in the earlier Agra Fort and the architecturally imaginative, but abandoned, town of Fatehpur Sikri. Also deserted are the atmospheric palaces and temples of Orchha, dating from the same period and now an increasingly popular destination. Between the two is the magnificent fort of Gwalior, started long before any of the above. To the east are the fabulous temples of Khajuraho, created as a Hindu celebration of erotic pleasures as a way to self-deliverance.

UNADULTERATED NATURE The end (or the beginning?) of the North lies in the Himalayas. In the foothills lies the very beautiful national park, Corbett, and from there the terrain rises abruptly into Himachal Pradesh and its new sister state, Uttranchal. Rolling pine-clad hills, rivers, orchards and small hill-towns like Shimla, Dalhousie, Chamba, Manali and Dharmsala, are bordered to the north by the violence-prone state of Jammu and Kashmir. The plateaux of the Western Himalayas here hover around 3,500m (9,840ft) and snowy peaks tower above to 6,000m (19,680ft). The highest town is Leh in the bleak, magnificent Ladakh. Buddhism rules here and in the Tibetan community of Dharmsala, but Islam is strong in Kashmir. This is perhaps India's most dangerous flashpoint, where troops fire at Pakistanis over the border, bringing sporadic threats of nuclear war. However Srinagar has quietened and a few visitors are returning. From spiritual esctasy to spiritual conflict, the North has the whole gamut.

Uttar Pradesh has a dense network of buses and trains serving its large population. The fast Shatabdi Express covers Delhi, Agra, Gwalior and Jhansi (for Orchha). The Delhi–Agra–Khajuraho–Varanasi air route is quick too, but is often booked up months in advance by tour groups. Even if you have a confirmed ticket, you may not have a seat. Leh's short season also creates overbooking havoc. Himachal Pradesh has airports at Shimla and Kullu; from there, buses and jeep-taxis are the only way to go—slowly. An alternative is the night-train from Delhi to Pathankot, giving easy access to Jammu, Dharmsala and Dalhousie. HPTDC in Delhi also operates direct buses.

119

Temples at Khajuraho

The North

TOURIST INFORMATION
India Tourism, 191 The Mall (*Open* Mon–Fri 9–5.30, Sat 9–1; tel: 0562 2226378, email:goitoagr@sanchrnet.in). Guides and cars. Also counter at airport. UPTDC, 64 Taj Road (*Open* Mon–Sat 10–5, but closed second Sat of month; tel: 0562 2226431). Tours. A counter at Cantonment rail station is open daily 8–8.

TOURIST TICKET
The Taj Mahal, Agra Fort, Fatehpur Sikri and Etmad-Ud-Daula and Sikandra are covered by a pricey tourist ticket valid for one day only. All monuments are open dawn–dusk. The Taj Mahal closes on Fridays but not Agra Fort or Fatepur Sikri.

▶▶▶ Agra 116B2

Agra's prominence on the tourist trail is due to one monument alone, the Taj Mahal. This is the glory of Mughal India, its white marble façade, domes and minarets glowing in a projection of grandeur that is far from the reality of India today. Built as an expression of love, it is now surrounded by a polluted, industrialized city whose heart beats to the commercial rhythms of tourism. The best advice is to see the monuments, and head to Fatehpur Sikri.

Capital Agra's history really started when Sultan Sikander Lodi moved his capital here from Delhi in 1504 to keep a closer eye on his extensive but war-prone kingdom to the south. His city rose on the eastern banks of the Yamuna river, but just 22 years later the Sultanate was crushingly defeated by Babur, the first of the Mughal emperors, and his son, Humayun (see pages 44–45). With the construction of the fort by Humayun's son, Akbar, Agra reassumed its role as capital, this time of the Mughal empire. So it remained for a further century, except for the short, ill-fated interlude of Fatehpur Sikri. In the 17th century Shah Jahan built his labour of love, the Taj Mahal (see pages 122–123), at Agra, but his ambitions led him to redevelop Delhi and move to its expanded Red Fort. It was in Agra Fort that he ended his days, however, imprisoned by his merciless son, Aurangzeb. This last Mughal emperor definitively adopted Delhi as his capital and Agra was later successively taken by the Jats, the Marathas and, in 1803, by the British.

Practicalities This city of nearly two million inhabitants is relatively easy to get around. Its main monuments, the Taj and the fort, rise above the banks of the Yamuna. Hotels are mainly in the central cantonment area, south of the fort, with budget lodges huddled in the narrow streets just south of the Taj. Services on Taj Road link the two. On the eastern bank lies the peaceful, inlaid marble tomb of **Itimad-ud-Daulah▶▶** and north of here, the **Ram Bagh▶**, (*Open* daily dawn–dusk. *Admission: inexpensive*), Babur's ruined pleasure gardens, now being restored. Agra's tongas, cycle- and auto-rickshaws need extra-hard bargaining, but bicycles are rented in the Taj Ganj area. Delhi trains stop at Agra Cantonment station, trains to Rajasthan use both Cantonment and Agra Fort station.

Marble inlay on Itimad-ud-Daulah's tomb in Agra (above)
A back street in Agra (right)

The fort Surrounded by high red sandstone walls, **Agra Fort▶▶▶** (see panel) is entered from the south through Amar Singh gate. From here a long elephant-ramp leads through a garden to the main section open to the public. It was built by successive emperors from the 1570s throughout the 17th century, and combines Akbar's walls and tiled gates with Shah Jahan's delicate Moti Masjid (Pearl Mosque) and once-elegant palaces.

Start in the south, at the solid red sandstone Jahangiri Mahal, the women's palace, incorporating numerous Hindu features, with a more modest palace to the south. North lies the Anguri Bagh, a symmetrical garden edged to the east by two golden pavilions with curved roofs. These flank the central Khas Mahal, a partly restored marble pavilion that was probably a breezy retiring-room. Beyond this is the Musamman Burj, an octagonal tower crowned by an exquisitely decorated open pavilion where, legend has it, Shah Jahan lay on his death-bed, gazing at the Taj Mahal. Next door are the *hammams* (bathing rooms), with complex water-channels. From the tower a staircase leads to the Diwan-i-Khas, the private audience hall, with finely inlaid pillars opening onto a wide terrace dominated by a black marble throne. West of the ruined Macchi Bhawan is the beautiful Diwan-i-Am (public audience hall). Finally, stop at the pretty marble Nagina Masjid and Mina Bazar, both built for the women of the harem.

TO SHOP OR NOT?
Agra has a fine selection of locally made jewellery, carpets, inlaid marble and soapstone objects, but it is also a hotbed for con-men who deal ably with naive tourists. Prices are high and include hidden commissions, and many salesmen are dishonest. Try to save your rupees for less touristy towns.

The North

Taj Mahal►►► However many images you may have
seen of the Taj Mahal (for entry tips, see panel page 120)
the reality is still breathtaking, its scale stupendous and its
surface ever changing with the light. Favourite visiting
times are sunrise and sunset, when the translucent white
marble seems to float in a soft, often misty glow, its reflection shimmering in the long, rectangular water-channel
that leads through the gardens. At any time of day it is
thronged with visitors, from foreign tour-groups to
picnicking families and young Indian couples.

Ultimate balance The gardens were designed in typical
Mughal style to evoke an Islamic paradise of peace and
tranquility. They are cut into quadrants by waterways and
lined with flowering shrubs and shade-giving trees. Their
symmetry is reflected in the two buildings flanking the
tomb: to the west, a sandstone and marble mosque, and to
the east, the *jawab* (answer) which exists purely for visual
balance. This symmetrical purity continues in the four
slender minarets that rise more than 40m (131ft) at each
corner of the enormous square platform, and the four
domes surrounding the central 'pearl'.

Sumptuous handiwork Access to the vast platform is by a
central staircase, where shoes must be removed. From here
you enter the domain of superlative craftsmanship and
design, embodied in beautifully engraved Koranic calligra-
phy and floral motifs, niches, carved balustrades and

immaculate stone inlay. Views across the Yamuna are particularly atmospheric at sunset. Inside, the real tombs are housed in the crypt, while the lavishly inlaid public tombs stand beneath the lofty dome. Perfectly aligned with the main entrance gate, Mumtaz's tomb is joined to one side by the larger one of Shah Jahan. Surrounding them is another masterpiece, a magnificent lace-like marble *jali* screen studded with precious stones. A small **museum** (*Open* Sat–Thu 10–5. *Admission: free*) displays portraits of Mughal emperors, architectural drawings and models of the Taj, porcelain and photographs.

Excursion

Fatehpur Sikri►► (see panel page 120) Some 37km (23 miles) west of Agra lie the remains of the ambitious city built by Akbar *c*1570–85 but virtually abandoned within twenty years, for reasons of state, and not as legend has it, because of lack of water. The delicate, red sandstone palaces have been carefully restored and the city is an atmospheric destination, easily covered in half a day.

Palaces As you approach from Agra Gate past the Mint, the Diwan-i-Am (public audience hall) opens onto a courtyard with the emperor's throne-room to the west. Behind this is one of Fatehpur's most intriguing structures, the Pachisi board, a gigantic stone board-game for which Akbar is said to have used slave-girls as pieces. Rising to the north is the Diwan-i-Khas (private audience hall) where decorative features combine Hindu, Muslim, Christian and Buddhist symbols. At its centre is the throne pillar topped by a circular platform from which radiate four bridges used for Akbar's theological discussions. In the southeast corner stands the intricately decorated Anup Talao pavilion, once the palace of Akbar's favourite wife.

South of this are the emperor's own quarters, the Daulat Khana, arranged on two storeys. Beyond the *zenana* is Fatehpur's most arresting sight, the Panch Mahal. This five-storeyed palace tapering to a single *chhatri* and bordered by broad overhanging eaves is a feast of pillars, each one an individually decorated symbol. Other palaces include the lovely Hawa Mahal and the elaborate palace of Raja Birba.

Mosque The imposing Jami Masjid is fronted by a massive gateway opening onto a vast courtyard that seethes with hawkers. Inside are several royal tombs but it is the *dargah* (tomb) of the Sufi saint, Salim Chishti, that is the most elaborate. Gleaming white marble is carved with masterly delicacy beneath a canopy inlaid with mother-of-pearl, a fitting tribute to the man who inspired Fatehpur (see panel).

SHEIKH SALIM CHISTI
The Sufi saint buried in glory at Fatehpur Sikri was behind the misjudged selection of this site for a city. Akbar, finding himself childless, did the rounds of the holy men to gain spiritual support and encouragement for the production of an heir. Chisti, who lived in the village of Sikri, foretold that Akbar would have three sons. This prophecy was borne out, and when the saint died in 1571, the emperor decided to build a new city on the site of Chisti's village in his honour. Fatehpur ('town of victory') was added to the name of the village, but by the end of the 16th century the city lay deserted.

123

The Taj Mahal (above and left), is Shah Jahan's monument to love, and India's most enduring icon

Spotted deer, or chital, are a common sight at Corbett National Park

TIGER JIM

Jim Corbett, the instigator of the national park which bears his name, was a local man born in Naini Tal of Anglo-Irish parents in 1875. His upbringing brought him into close contact with nature and above all with the jungle. He became an excellent shot, and disposed of numerous man-eating tigers and leopards that had terrorized local villagers. When he became an army officer, his interest in wildlife took a more protective turn and he spent years photographing his former quarry and later writing several books. After Independence, he left India for Africa where he died in 1955.

TOURIST OFFICES

MP Tourism, Hotel Tansen, 6a Gandhi Marg, Gwalior (*Open* all day; tel: 0751 2340370, fax: 0751 2340371; email: mptgwalior@sify.com). Also at rail station Permits and bookings for accommodation within Corbett National Park are obtainable from the Main Reception Centre, Ramnagar (*Open* daily 8–1, 3–5; tel: 05947 251489, fax: 05947 251376).

▶▶ **Amritsar** 116A4

The sight here is the Golden Temple, the striking repository of the Sikhs' original holy book, the Granth. Every morning (5am) and evening (9pm) it is ceremonially moved through the temple in a fervent procession well worth witnessing. The 16th-century temple itself is vast, its glittering gold dome rising over a huge tank of holy water, and includes pilgrim hostels and a huge kitchen which feeds all visitors (up to 10,000 daily) for free. An information office at the main entrance is very helpful.

▶▶▶ **Corbett National Park** 116B3

Open: mid-Nov–mid-Jun dawn–dusk. Admission: expensive

Often considered to be India's finest wildlife reserve, Corbett National Park lies in the Kumaun foothills of the Himalayas, 290km (180 miles) northeast of Delhi. Famed for its tigers (it was among the first participants of Project Tiger in 1973), it also offers contrasting landscapes and flora, as it rises from 400m (1,312ft) to 1,200m (3,936ft) within an area of 1,318sq km (509sq miles). This is India's classic safari destination, with comfortable hotels in beautiful locations and rudimentary bungalows (no electricity or food) within the park. Park headquarters (with a library, wildlife film shows and a restaurant) is in the scenic heart of the park, at Dhikala.

Access from Delhi to Ramnagar is by bus via Naini Tal or Ranikhet, or train via Moradabad: count on seven to eight hours. In winter nights can be very cold, so come prepared.

Natural gift India's first national park came into being in 1936 thanks to Jim Corbett (see panel). Today it is a rare patch of true wilderness, incorporating dense jungle (dominated by sal trees), grasslands and bamboo groves. Most of the streams and ravines become waterless during the dry season. Altogether the park has over 100 tree species and around 130 tigers. Leopards are rare here. Corbett is nevertheless rich in wild elephants, jackal, wild boar, chital (spotted deer), sambar, hog deer, langurs and rhesus monkeys. Waterbirds, birds of prey and woodland birds, make up Corbett's total bird-count of over 600 different species.

▶▶ Gwalior 116B2

Madhya Pradesh's northernmost city inspired Emperor Babur's epithet, 'the pearl among the fortresses of Sind'. Rising abruptly on a rocky outcrop from the surrounding plains, the fort's bastions and delicately fretted domes were a majestic backdrop to a momentous history that saw Rajput, Afghan Muslim, Mughal, Maratha and British rulers. Below, the city has developed into a typically characterless sprawl of concrete, relieved only by the mosque and the elegant 16th-century **tombs of Ghaus Mohammed and Tansen▶**. Tansen was a singer, who was one of the 'nine jewels' of Akbar's court. To the south is the ostentatious **Jai Vilas Palace and Museum▶▶** (*Open* Thu–Tue 9.30–5. *Admission: expensive*), containing a mindboggling collection of kitsch treasures belonging to Gwalior's last rulers (see panel).

Past glory The imposing **fort▶▶▶** (*Open* daily 8–6. *Admission: moderate*) has a wealth of Indian architecture covering seven centuries. Much of the work was done under the Rajput Man Singh. At the fort's heart is his four-storeyed Man Mandir, a masterpiece of ornate, stonework faced with decorative mosaics. The more sober interior has vast chambers divided by *jali* screens. To the north stand the Vikram Mandir, the Karam Mandir and, in the north-eastern corner, the Gujuri Mahal, built by Man Singh to win a peasant girl. This now houses a museum (*Open* Sat–Thu 10–5). The southern end of the fort has its oldest monuments. The 8th-century Teli Ka Mandir, towering over 30m (98ft), was a Vishnu temple that the British used as a soda-water factory. To the east, is the graceful Sas-Bahu Ka Mandir, two 11th-century Vishnu temples with beautifully carved interiors. West is a huge *tank*, the Suraj Kund. Jain sculptures (7th–15th centuries) carved into the cliffs are best seen at the western entrance, Urwahi Gate.

Jain sculptures at Gwalior depicting the incarnations of Mahavir (above)
Mosaic detail, Gwalior fort (inset)

SCINDIA EXCESS
In 1875, Jayaji Rao Scindia installed some extra fixtures in his palace to prepare it for a visit by the Prince of Wales and his retinue of 1,000. Having learnt the size of Buckingham Palace's largest chandeliers, he placed an order in Venice for two bigger ones for his Durbar Hall. They weighed over 3.5 tonnes each, so the Maharaja tested the ceiling strength with eight (or 10) elephants, using a 500m (1,640ft) ramp (or a crane). He also had a silver toy train that chugged around the table dispensing post-prandial cigars and brandy.

The Ganga, or Ganges, is India's most revered river. It flows from the chilly heights of the Himalayas and across the scorching plains to its delta on the Bay of Bengal. Along this winding course lie India's most sacred pilgrimage spots, from Gangotri to Varanasi. However, the river's spiritual purity is far from matched by its increasingly polluted waters.

LIQUID ARMS
'...There the Ganga reached out and enfolded me in its enormous liquid arms, just as my mother had drawn me into her arms and painted for me a word-picture of the Ganga flowing through the celestial world, the terrestrial world and the nether world.'
Raghubir Singh, *The Ganges*, 1992

Crowds on Mir Ghat, Varanasi (below)
Hindu faithful in meditation and prayer by the Ganges (right)

126

Central to Hindu and Buddhist cosmology is mythical Mount Meru, the cosmic mountain and axis connecting heaven and earth, from which flow four rivers. Meru has an earthly incarnation in Mount Kailas, rising 6,714m (22,022ft) between two lakes. It was here, in the Trans-Himalaya of Tibet, that the source of the Ganges was long considered to lie. Kailas' majestic domed shape became the inspiration for ancient Hindu and Buddhist temples, and a divine enclosure around the mountain was said to be the abode of the gods, presided over by Brahma. Encircling this heavenly domain three times over was Ganga, the elder daughter of Himalaya, who was eventually persuaded to flow through the tangled hair of Siva to descend to earth (see panel page 235).

The source In reality the Ganges emerges at the Gangotri glacier, due west of Kailas. Here, a swift crystalline stream flows through a desolate landscape of snow and rocks, its freezing waters already crowded with thousands of bathing

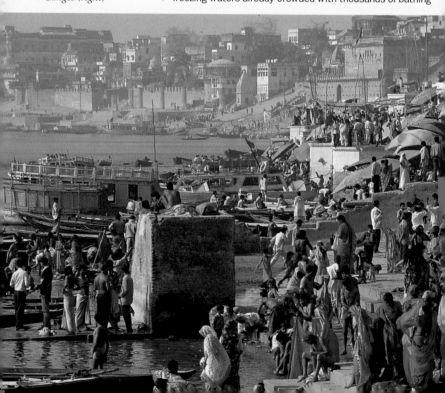

pilgrims who rub themselves with oil to mitigate the extreme cold. People used to trek for weeks from their villages in the plains to realize their lifetime's ambition: a dip in the Ganges as it flows through the abode of the gods. It is the Hindu equivalent of Mecca. Today, most arrive by bus or car, but the highest reaches are still the preserve of determined sadhus. Global warming brings another recent scourge: Himalayan glacier meltdown is causing the rivers of northern India to dry up. The Gangotri glacier, for example, is retreating by 630–720m (700–800yd) a year; eventually the Ganges will be waterless.

Black spot Gushing through the Siwalik hills, which form the last humps of the Himalayas, the Ganges arrives at Haridwar, one of the seven sacred cities of Hindu India. From here it courses through Uttar Pradesh to Kanpur, the state's largest industrial centre and the river's first source of major pollution: 80 per cent of the city's sewage is dumped, untreated, into the Ganges to join toxic industrial effluents from textile, leather and chemical factories.

Confluence Halfway between Kanpur and Varanasi lies Allahabad, exceptionally sacred as it lies at the prayag (confluence) of the Ganges and Yamuna rivers. Hindu mythology multiplies Allahabad's purifying powers by conjuring up the emergence of the underground river of enlightenment, the Sarasvati. In the Vedas, Sarasvati was a water goddess flowing west of the Himalayas through the first Aryan settlements. She was later identified with the holy rituals performed on her banks, and gradually became perceived as Brahma's wife, inventor of Sanskrit and goddess of all creative arts. A spit of land at Allahabad's confluence receives millions of pilgrims, particularly during the auspicious Magh Mela, (lasting a fortnight every January–February) and even greater numbers during the 12-yearly Kumbh Mela.

River of death? Eastwards from here, the increasingly overloaded Ganges traverses Varanasi (Benares), Patna and Calcutta, receiving human corpses, sewage and industrial effluents on a seemingly unstoppable scale. Approximately 45,000 bodies are cremated yearly at Varanasi, while at Kanpur over 200 tanneries discharge chromium-rich effluents. Around Kolkata (Calcutta) some 150 factories pour untreated waste into the brown waters of the Hugli, a Ganga tributary. In 1985, India launched the Ganga Action Plan, which has been ineffectual. Meanwhile, fish die and river-water laced with toxins irrigates farmland, eventually seeping into food and village borewells to cause untold disease and numerous skin complaints. Ganga water, once the only liquid thought fit for orthodox Brahmins, is undrinkable. The river of benediction has been transformed into a river of blight.

Hari ki Pairi, at Haridwar—one of India's seven sacred cities—is much revered by Hindus

► **Haridwar**   *116B3*

Lying at the base of the Siwalik hills on the edge of the Himalayas, Haridwar is one of India's seven sacred cities, for it is here that the holy Ganga (Ganges) leaves the mountains to start its lengthy course eastwards across the plains. Every 12 years Haridwar hosts the incredible festival of Kumbh Mela, drawing millions of pilgrims to its *ghats*. The Dikhanti festival each spring also draws crowds, but at any time this mini-Varanasi exudes fervour and displays the entire gamut of sadhus and beggars—so be prepared. The bazaars offer colourful wares, especially Moti Bazar along Railway Road and Bara Bazar in the north of town.

Heavy worship The centre lies on the west bank of an area sliced by canals into a network of islands and bridges. *Ghats, ashrams,* temples and the hovels of *sadhus* culminate at Hari Ki Pairi, the site of Vishnu's footprint (not accessible to non-Hindus). Every evening at dusk a moving ceremony takes place here, orchestrated by priests and accompanied by musicians. None of the temples is particularly memorable, despite the *Mahabharata's* numerous references to the spot, but it is worth taking the cable-car to the hilltop **Mansa Devi temple►** for good views.

Ashram-land 25km (16 miles) north in the newly created state of Uttranchal lies **Rishikesh►►**, associated with the Beatles and their guru, the Maharishi. This more placid spiritual centre, where meat and alcohol are strictly prohibited, is a real eye-opener on the immensely varied rituals and fervent nature of *sadhus* and yogis. Many stop in Rishikesh before continuing their lengthy pilgrimage northwards to the source of the Ganges (Bhagirathi) at Gangotri, where the goddess Ganga is believed to have descended to earth. This small ramshackle town is almost completely monopolized by *ashrams*, offering courses in yoga, meditation, Sanskrit, natural medicine and countless spiritual paths. Not all is holy however: many loin-clothed *sadhus* are adept at the age-old art of trickery, particularly where visitors are concerned.

Evening worship with floating offerings (*aarti*) takes place at Triveni ghat, near the main concentration of low-key hotels. To the north, at the much frequented Swarg Ashram, *sadhus* wander out of forest caves to worship at modern temples lining the river.

► **Jhansi**   *116B1*

Situated in a remote finger of Uttar Pradesh that dips into Madhya Pradesh, Jhansi holds little interest apart from being a stopover on the way to Orchha. It does have a crumbling 17th-century fort (*Open* daily dawn–dusk. *Admission: inexpensive*), but this is less exciting than the legends of the mid-19th century Rani who fought tooth and nail against the British to regain it (see panel). Her palace, the **Rani Lakshmi Mahal**▶ (*Open* Tue–Sun 9.30–5.30. *Admission: inexpensive*) can be visited.

Orchha From Jhansi, it takes half an hour to cross the Madhya Pradesh border to reach the abandoned Bundela capital of **Orchha**▶▶, partly set on an island in the Betwa river in beautiful forested surroundings. It was founded in the 16th century by the Bundela Rajput ruler, Rudra Pratap, and then abandoned in the 18th century. Evocative palaces, temples and *chhatri* cenotaphs stand next to a sleepy yet functioning village with a busy bazaar and a good selection of accommodation. Other structures emerge scenically from the surrounding scrub.

Decorative riches The fort complex (*Open* daily 10–5. *Admission: inexpensive*) is approached by an arched bridge that leads to the Raj Mahal built by the devout Madhukar Shah. It has sober façades crowned by *chhatris*, and contains an extraordinary interior with striking decorative murals depicting Hindu myths and court life, many still in remarkable condition.

Richer still in its ornamentation is the later Jehangir Mahal, built to commemorate the visit of the Mughal emperor in the 17th century. Strong lines are counter-balanced by delicate *chhatris*, trellis work, *jali* screens and tiles, all introduced by two stone elephants at the main gateway. Other memorable monuments include the still-functioning Ram Raja temple, a former palace, the massive, vaulted Chaturbhuj temple and the Lakshminarayan temple, which is richly painted with murals and lies not far from the village.

The Rani of Jhansi is fêted as one of India's great heroines, for putting up a determined fight against the British. In 1853 her husband died, leaving a kingdom without a male heir, whereupon the British seized the town and fort. After recouping in Gwalior, the Rani launched a massive attack on the fort during the Uprising (Indian Mutiny) of 1857, and in a lengthy bout of bloody fighting some 5,000 of her soldiers died. The Rani, who had by then adopted a baby son who was strapped to her back, managed to escape through the British troops but eventually met her end 'dressed as a man, holding her sword with both hands and her reins gripped between her teeth'.

129

The Lakshman Jhula bridge over the Ganges at Rishikesh

The North

TOURIST OFFICES

Government of India, opposite Western Group (*Open* Mon–Fri 9–4.30, Sat 8–12.30; tel: 07686 272347/8, email: goito@sancharnet.in). Basic map and information on nearby sights, cultural shows and the Khajuraho Dance Festival held in the temple precinct in mid-March. Car- and guide-hire.

MP Tourism, Chandela Cultural Centre, Tourist Village, north of Western Group (*Open* Mon–Sat 10–5; tel: 07686 274051, fax: 272330, email: mail @mptourism.com). Also counter at bus-stand. Sound and light shows take place daily at dusk.

PURSUIT OF PLEASURE

'In a country where the linga cult is the source of religious belief and its manifestations are to be seen in very early periods of civilization the erotic sculptures are but a continuation of that tradition which accepts procreation as a major function of life. The presence of erotic sculptures show that there were no taboos or inhibitions against sex as we have now. *Kama*, or pursuit of pleasure, was deemed to be one of the four *purusharthas* or legitimate aims of life for a Grahast as it was regarded as a stepping stone to *moksha* (deliverance).'
Anonymous author, *Khajuraho*

Ancient erotica—carved pillars at Devi Jagadambi temple, in the Western Group, Khajuraho

▶▶▶ Khajuraho 117C1

Khajuraho is one of the highlights of the northern trail, offering a feast of intricately carved 'erotic' temples scattered over a rural landscape rather marred by heightened commercialism. Although daily flights ferry tour-groups in and out from Delhi, Agra and Varanasi (Benares), it is well worth escaping them to tour the lovely environs perfumed with *mahua* trees.

Background The creators of this stupendous legacy were the Chandellas, thought to be of Rajput origin, who became a powerful dynasty during the 9th century. Forgotten for centuries and engulfed by vegetation, the temples were rediscovered by a British engineer in 1835. Of the original total of over 80 temples, only 22 survive and the once thriving city has been reduced to a sprawling village highly dependent on the tourist trade.

Shakti style Although Siva dominates, some Khajuraho temples are dedicated to Vishnu and there are also traces of Buddhism, Jainism, sun-worship and animistic cults. All are carved in sandstone and were once coated in white gesso, their multiple towers clustered around the lofty main *shikhara* suggesting the holy mountain and strongly reminiscent of the Orissan style. Below is the sanctum enshrining the deity of the temple with a passage leading around side-porches and a front *mandapa* (hall), all alive with sculpted figures and friezes. Each temple is on a high platform, allowing worshippers to circle the edifice and gain close views of the staggeringly complex carvings.

Khajuraho is famed above all for its erotica, but this constitutes only about a tenth of the total. It is thought that the temples were built to celebrate episodes from the marriage of Siva and Parvati (or *shakti*, the divine female force). From this stems the Tantric cult, worshipping the activation of male forces by sexual union with *shakti*.

Priorities The seven temples of the **Western Group▶▶▶** (*Open daily dawn–dusk. Admission: expensive, includes museum*) stand in a beautifully landscaped garden, their lace-like towers aligned in two rows. These are the city's most accomplished structures. The Lakshamana, Viswanath and Kandariya Mahadeva temples are outstanding. South of the enclosure is the unusually plain Matangesvara temple, containing a magnificent *lingam*, more than 2m (6.5ft) high and still worshipped today. Opposite, the museum (*Open Sat–Thu 10–5. Admission: free*) exhibits related fragments and sculptures. Huddled around old Khajuraho is the **Eastern Group▶▶**, composed of three richly carved Jain temples within an enclosure and four scattered Hindu temples. The remote **Southern Group▶**, near the airport, has only two, later temples, one displaying a massive statue combining the head of Siva, the body of Vishnu and the legs of Krishna.

Excursions

Khajuraho is well placed for trips to Panna National Park (25km/15 miles), Pandav Falls (34km/21 miles), the Majhgaon Diamond Mines (56km/35 miles) and, closest of all, the Rajgarh Palace, an atmospheric, isolated palace said to be connected by a tunnel to Khajuraho.

132

▶ Shivpuri 116B1

Once the summer capital of the Scindia rulers of Gwalior, Shivpuri has palaces, hunting lodges and marble-turreted cenotaphs in a landscape of wooded hills, grasslands and a lake, now designated the Mandhav National Park. It lies about 100km (62 miles) from both Gwalior and Jhansi, and includes a complex of ornate *chhatris*▶▶ set in a formal Mughal garden: the stone inlay is particularly striking on the Madho Rao Scindia cenotaph. Crowning a hilltop is the **Madhav Vilas palace**▶, a rose-coloured, colonial-inspired building with marble floors, cast-iron pillars and wide terraces.

▶▶▶ Varanasi (Benares) 117D1

The holiest of holy places in India is Varanasi, a city with a virtually unrivalled status in Hindu mythology. For Mark Twain 'Benaras is older than history, older than tradition, older even than legend and looks twice as old as all of them put together'. Even today, congested with thousands of visitors and pilgrims, Varanasi feels like this. More than any other Indian town, it incarnates the incomparable complexities of Hindu rituals and worship. Around two million inhabitants include an estimated 50,000 Brahmins, and each year the number of pilgrims easily rivals the resident population.

The holy city of Varanasi attracts sadhus *and pilgrims from all over India*

Intensity The extraordinary activity on the *ghats* starts before dawn (see pages 134–135). As the sun rises opposite over Mother Ganges, yogis plunge into meditation and pilgrims dip in the water. Varanasi's mysticism comes hand-in-hand with the less elevated life of hustlers, commissions and drugs, and the city can be deeply unpleasant for independent travellers, who make obvious targets for con-men. To escape unwelcome harassment, it is best to stay in the tree-lined avenues of the Cantonment area, about 4km (2.5 miles) from the vibrant but exhausting *chowk* and *ghats*.

South Varanasi Varanasi is also an important centre of learning and the arts. **Banaras Hindu University►** occupies a huge landscaped campus to the south and includes an outstanding museum of sculpture and textiles, **Bharat Kala Bhavan►** (*Open* Jul–Apr Mon–Sat 11–4.30; May–Jun 7.30–12.30. *Admission: moderate*). Here too is the imposing New Vishwanath temple (1966), a cool marble edifice designed for all castes. Opposite the campus on the strangely empty east bank of the Ganga (Ganges) is only one sight, the dilapidated **Ramnagar Fort►►** (*Open* daily 9–12, 2–5. *Admission: inexpensive*) where inlaid silver *howdahs*, dusty carriages, vintage cars, exquisitely carved ivory and superb Rajput weapons are exhibited in a potent atmosphere of neglect. Along Durga Kund Road, linking this southern area with the centre, stand two significant temples: the Tulsi Manas Mandir, built in 1964 to commemorate the medieval poet, Goswami Tulsidas, and then the red-spired 18th-century Durga Temple (the inner sanctum is closed to non-Hindus).

ANCIENT REFERENCES
The earliest descriptions of Varanasi are found in Buddhist scriptures and in the Hindu epic, the *Mahabharata*. According to Sanskrit puranas, the Varuna and Assi rivers (running along the city's north and south perimeters respectively) originated from the body of the first man at the beginning of time. The sacred Ganga is the eastern perimeter. Varanasi was also known as Kashi (from *kas*, meaning 'to shine') and is the 'city of light', standing on the original ground created by Siva and Parvati.

133

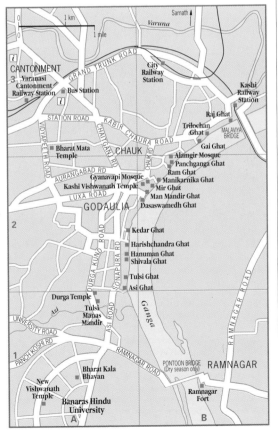

The back streets of Varanasi are a maze of narrow alleyways

The North

Holy cows are as much a part of Varanasi as pilgrims and tourists

POLLUTED WATERS

The sacred waters of the Ganga (Ganges) are visibly polluted. In 1985 the Ganga Action Plan was intended to achieve India's largest-ever clean-up, but poor monitoring, overspending, slow progress and corruption have combined to produce abysmal results. In Varanasi, over 28,000 turtles were introduced into the Ganges to feed on the polluting corpses. Most were poached and the turtle farm is now without a single inmate. A specially designed *dhobi* (laundry) *ghat* lies empty, apart from being used as a public toilet. Sewage was diverted and discharged into the Varuna river, and now causes a rash of water-borne diseases such as jaundice, malaria and skin diseases among local villagers.

SNAP-HAPPY

Varanasi is a sacred place so do be sensitive with who and what you photograph or film. It is forbidden at cremations, but respect should be shown elsewhere too.

Ghat-land Along the edge of the Ganga (Ganges) are over 100 *ghats* (steps leading down to the river), a focus for living, dying and dead Hindus alike. Some *ghats* have a social function, and are places where locals chat while performing their ablutions. Others are the sites for specific religious rituals. Old people are numerous, as anyone who dies in Varanasi on the banks of the Ganges achieves *moksha* (deliverance). A 4am start is the rule if you want to join the pre-dawn hordes of devotees and locals, bathing, performing *puja*, meditating, washing clothes or, in the case of a few, striking out to the opposite bank.

Boat-loads of visitors snap away at these images in the soft, pink light of dawn while hundreds of leaf-born candles drift over the water. Boat-tariffs are lower later in the morning, but rise again towards sunset. Whatever time you visit, bargain hard.

Magnetic forces A good starting-point is the central Dasaswamedh Ghat, named after 10 horses sacrificed by Brahma and considered one of the holiest spots for bathing. Its confluence position has given it specific magnetic forces. To the south is Harishchandra Ghat, Varanasi's second crematorium. Walking or boating north from here brings you to the Man Mandir Ghat. Looming above the riverbank is the Man Singh observatory (*Open* daily 8–5. *Admission: free*), housed in a palatial 1600s building containing frescoes and astronomical instruments. Immediately north of this is the tiger-fronted mansion belonging to the DomRajas, the 'untouchable' family that runs Varanasi's lucrative crematoriums. Goats, buffaloes, *chai*-sellers, postcard-hawkers, boatmen, beggars, *sadhus* and pilgrims all mix in a mesmerizing atmosphere that continues north to Panchganga Ghat.

Cremations Manikarnika Ghat, Varanasi's main crematorium and first stone *ghat*, was built in 1302 to replace earlier sand and clay versions. On the steps is a large *lingam* and behind is stacked the wood that is carefully weighed out for each pyre. Before cremation, the shrouded corpse experiences its last dip in the Ganges. If you arrive during a cremation, remember that photos are strictly forbidden. Beyond the *ghat* is a stepped *tank* supposedly created from a divine earring and, in front, a lop-sided, sinking temple, believed to have been cursed by the builder's mother some 150 years ago. This main stretch ends beyond Ram Ghat at Panchganga Ghat, overlooked by a crumbling Maratha palace.

Seasonal flooding creates an annual need for repairs to the ghats

Heart of the past From Panchganga Ghat, wide steps lead up to the Alamgir mosque, built in 1669 by Aurangzeb from the debris of a Hindu temple. From here a fascinating maze of winding lanes lined with tiny shops, some mere cubicles on two storeys, plunges you back into the Middle Ages. Jewellers, barbers, cobblers, and sellers of curd, spice, oils, herb and betel are all packed in, while cows and bicycles filter through the crowds. Wider streets and more ornate buildings take over at the main *chowk* with its flower-market and its tourist-shops displaying a glittering show of silks, sitars, brass and copperware.

Sectarian rivalry Near the clock tower, along a heavily policed lane, are the Kashi Vishwanath (Golden) Temple and the Gyanavapi Mosque. These epitomize India's ongoing Hindu–Muslim tensions, the armed guards protecting the mosque against Hindu extremists. Their visible presence is a response to threats against it. Muslims make up over 20 per cent of Varanasi's population and this, set against Hindu orthodoxy, does not bode well for peaceful coexistence. The original Vishwanath temple was demolished by Aurangzeb to build his mosque but in 1776 the present Siva temple arose. In 1835 it acquired gold-plated spires and a dome (using one tonne of gold leaf) that shelters the *lingam* below. The original *lingam* is said

SILKS
Varanasi produces many stunning silks and brocades. Although much of the city's output is sold in Delhi, the shops of Varanasi have a huge range of high-quality scarves, saris and bolts of cloth with gold borders or finely woven patterns that create shimmering brocades. The small shop units on the upper floors opposite the Golden Temple deal mainly in well-priced scarves. You can watch the weavers at work at the Government Weaving Centre at Chauka Ghat. Shop without guides or drivers, as commissions may boost the price by 40 per cent. Good deals for silk, scarves and saris can be obtained at Ali Handicrafts, C19, A-5 Lallapura, which is a wholesale shop that welcomes retail buyers.

FESTIVALS
Sarnath celebrates
Buddha's birthday
(Buddha Purnima) at full
moon every May, when
processions and a fair
surround the display of his
relics. The five-day music
festival of Dhrupad Mela
in March–April, brings top
Indian musicians to
perform at Tulsi Ghat.
Ramlila is a month-long
literary festival held at
Ramnagar during
October–November. It is
one of several that feature
the Hindu classics. For
foreign visitors, the most
spectacular event is the
Ganga Festival, held
during Deepavali in
October–November.

136

*Pilgrims often follow a
purifying dip in the
Ganges with a ritual
shave*

to lie in the well that stands between the two rivals. Only Hindus and Muslims are admitted to the temple and mosque respectively, but good views can be had, for a tip, from the upper floors of the shops opposite.

Excursion

Sarnath►► Buddha preached his first sermon at Sarnath, 10km (6 miles) north of Varanasi, and it became a major religious and study centre in the 4th–9th centuries. Excavations were carried out in 1905–10 when the museum was built, and since then the site has acquired Buddhist temples funded from China, Japan, Tibet, Myanmar (Burma) and South Korea, though these are of little interest.

The first monument encountered on the road from Varanasi is the 5th-century Chaukhandi *stupa*, crowned by an octagonal tower (1588) to commemorate the Mughal emperor Akbar's victory. The caretaker will unlock this for a tip.

The next stop is the excellent **Archaeological Museum** (*Open* Sat–Thu 10–5. *Admission: inexpensive*) containing abundant Buddhist statues, among them Ashoka's Lion capital, famed as the national emblem of India. Four lions crown a 24-spoked wheel representing dynamism and continuity—the Buddhist wheel of law. The base is a lotus, a recurring symbol in Buddhism, Hinduism and Jainism. Other marvels include a 1st-century Bodhisattva from Madura and a superb preaching Buddha (5th-century) from Sarnath.

Main site The grounds opposite the museum are dominated by the magnificent Dhamekh *stupa*, elaborately carved by the 5th-century Guptas and marking the place where Buddha's first sermon was delivered. East of the *stupa*, by Sri Lanka's Mulagandhakuti Vihara—the temple of the Maha Bodhi Society—is a symbolic bodhi tree. It was planted in 1931, having been brought from Sri Lanka as a sapling. To the west, beyond the Jain temple, stand the remains of Ashoka's Dharmarajika *stupa* and, behind this, the base of the pillar of the Lion capital displayed in the museum. The main temple opposite, where Buddha used to meditate, is another Ashoka-Gupta relic leading to a succession of votive *stupas*. North of the main temple stretch the ruins of what were once 30 monasteries (according to 7th-century traveller Hsuan Tsang), rising to the Deer Park. This is all part of the mythological belief that saw Buddha as the King of Deer in a former life.

China invaded Tibet in 1950, and began a brutal campaign against Tibetan Buddhism in 1959. The Chinese occupation has driven some 200,000 refugees to live in the Indian Himalayas, including farmers, weavers, monks, and their spiritual leader, the Dalai Lama.

When China invaded Tibet, its ownership claim was based on Mongol imperial expansion throughout Central Asia in the 13th century, and on China's similar expansionism under the Manchu emperors in the 18th century. Buddhism had flourished in Tibet from the 7th century onwards, absorbing characteristics of the earliest religion, Bön. It was finally blended with politics when the first Dalai Lama assumed power, in 1578. Tibetan national identity became indistinguishable from Buddhism, and by the 1950s there were over 6,200 monasteries inhabited by 590,000 monks and nuns in a total population of six million people.

Cultural annihilation In 1959, the Chinese government began their systematic destruction of Buddhism, desecrating monasteries and persecuting monks. The national uprising that followed was brutally crushed, forcing the Dalai Lama and his government into exile. Ever since, their base has been Dharmsala (see page 139), where Tibetans now outnumber local inhabitants, a source of some tension. Tibetan resistance groups, trained by the CIA, attacked the Chinese from bases in Nepal throughout the 1960s but in 1971 the warming of US–China relations ended this support.

Refugees continue to make the arduous journey over the mountains, seeking asylum in Nepal and India, while about 10,000 live in the West. Most still hope to return to a free Tibet with the Dalai Lama as their spiritual leader in a reformed democratic state, but little headway has been made since dialogue with China was initiated in 1979. Meanwhile, over one million Tibetans have died and there are regular purges of the religious community.

WORLD ATTENTION
Although criticized by some Tibetans for his conciliatory attitude towards China, the indefatigable Dalai Lama has been highly successful in gaining international, high-profile support for Tibet's cause. Constantly jetting around the world and being fêted by luminaries such as Richard Gere, Björk, Harrison Ford and Oliver Stone, he has helped inspire a number of films such as Martin Scorsese's *Kundun*, recounting the Dalai Lama's travails, and Jean-Jacques Annaud's *Seven Years in Tibet*, based on Heinrich Harrer's book.

137

Thousands of worshippers attending prayers in Tibet

Rice terraces near Chamba

Western Himalayas

▶▶ Chamba

116A4

Perched in the northwestern corner of Himachal, Chamba is well off the beaten track but offers an array of superbly carved temples in a setting of terraced meadows, oak and pine-clad slopes, lakes and the Ravi river valley. Its isolation encouraged unique forms of painting, sculpture and handicrafts, including delicate, finely worked *rumal* (double-sided embroidered panels). At barely 1,000m (3,280ft), it is considerably warmer than Dalhousie, the main access point via the higher, more scenic road. Khajiar▶, about 20km (12 miles) before Chamba, is an attractively sheltered lake with an island temple.

Temples Dominating the elongated *maidan* or *chaugan* (open grassy space) is the Mughal-influenced Rang Mahal palace, now a college. Chamba's main legacy is its cluster of 10th-century **Lakshmi Narayana temples▶▶**, whose curved, ribbed stone towers have slate-tiled eaves and porches. Bas-reliefs and sculptures, some inlaid with brass, copper and silver, depict the Hindu pantheon. High up at the northern end of town is the 10th-century Chamunda Devi, a timber construction with illustrative carved wood panels. South of the *chaugan* stands the Bhuri Singh museum (*Open* Mon–Sat 10–5. *Admission: free*), displaying an intriguing selection of Kangra miniatures, palace murals, temple statues and some beautiful *rumal*. A scenic drive 65km (40 miles) east reaches **Brahmaur▶**, the idyllic ancient capital, with 8th- to 10th-century temples built in the classic Pahari style of these hills.

▶ Dalhousie

116A4

The erstwhile Marquis of Dalhousie, Governor-General (1848–56), retreated here for his health, and gave his name to this quiet town. It became a popular colonial sanatorium and hill-station that, by the 1920s, rivalled Shimla. It commands imposing views from a lofty 2,000m (6,560ft) site, with rugged mountains to the west and the gentle valley of Chamba to the east. Although there are no specific

TOURIST OFFICES
HP Tourism, near bus-stand, The Mall, Dalhousie (*Open*, in theory, Mon–Sat 10–5, plus (in season) Sun 10–1; tel: 01899 242136).
HP Tourism, Kotwali Bazar, Dharmsala (*Open* Mon–Sat 10–1.30, 2–5; tel: 01892 224212).
HP Tourism, Scandal Point, The Mall, Shimla (*Open* daily in season 8am–8pm, at other times 9–6; tel: 0177 2252561; email: hptdc@sancharnet .in.com). Maps, tours, buses.
HP Tourism, near the Maidan, Dhalpur, Kullu (*Open* Mon–Sat summer 9–7, winter 10–5; tel: 01902 222349; www.hptdc.nic.in). Maps, information.
Jammu & Kashmir Tourism, Airport Road, Leh (*Open* Mon–Sat 10–4; tel: 01982 252297).
Leh Tourist Information counter, Fort Road (bazaar), Leh (*Open* Mon–Sat 10–4). Helpful.

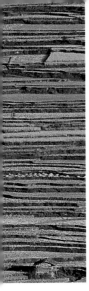

sights, the fresh mountain air attracts an increasing flow of visitors who use it as a base for trekking and horseriding. English bungalows dot the town, but the foreign population today consists mainly of Tibetans, who make and sell a variety of handicrafts and woollen garments.

▶▶ Dharmasala 116A4

Site of the Dalai Lama's residence and monastery ('Little Lhasa'), Dharmasala is a magnet for Western Buddhophiles, backpackers and New Agers, whose presence has spawned countless meditation, yoga and music courses. There are about 7,500 Tibetans here, forming half the population. The main concentration of hotels, 'travellers' restaurants, temples and Tibetans is in Mcleodganj, a sprawling village tucked dramatically into the shadow of snowy peaks and about 600m (1,968ft) higher than Dharmasala. Between the villages are two steep, twisting roads used by buses, jeep-taxis, hikers, Tibetans and maroon-robed Buddhist monks and nuns. Dharmasala itself is useful only for the large Kotwali bazaar and transport facilities.

Mcleodganj The commercial centre of Mcleodganj, dominated by Tibetan culture and shops, clusters around the bus-stand, bazaar and prayer-wheels of the Namgyalma temple. From here Temple Road runs downhill past shops, tour agencies and craft workshops to the **Namgyal monastery▶**, a modern replica of the one in Lhasa and standing opposite the Dalai Lama's residence. Inside the elevated temple (*tsuglagkhang*), the main altar is flanked by 100 volumes of the Tibetan translations of Buddha's teachings, surveyed by a fearsome Guru Padma Sambhava, the 8th-century Indian who propagated Buddhism in Tibet. The peaceful atmosphere of wind-chimes, flags and pine-trees is interrupted every afternoon by the vociferous 'one-hand-clapping' of debating monks, well worth observing. The monastery bookshop and canteen are open to everyone. The road continues downhill to the **Tibetan Library▶▶** (*Open* daily 9–5 with an hour for lunch. *Admission: free*), containing a wealth of archives, manuscripts, books and old photos as well as a small museum. Lectures and courses on Tibetan Buddhism and language are held here.

Peace and wildlife From Mcleodganj's bus-stand, another rough road runs a short distance (2km/1 mile) northeast to **Bhagsu▶▶**. This makes a beautiful walk that finishes at a walled Siva temple with a waterfall plunging into a deep valley just beyond. Kites, eagles, butterflies and monkeys are constant companions on the way.

GLIMPSING THE DALAI LAMA
This spiritual leader and king-in-exile has become quite a globe-trotter and so is not always in Dharmasala. When he is, his residence is heavily guarded. The Dalai Lama receives thousands of requests for private audiences but very few are actually granted. Far more common are his public audiences, when several hundred acolytes are individually greeted. Information and registration for these is available at the Tibetan Welfare Office on Bhagsu Road.

Tibetans in Dharmsala (below)

Tripura Sundri Devi Temple at Naggar in the Kullu Valley

BEYOND LEH

A day-trip south by car or jeep with a local guide can cover the following sights: the royal palace at Stok (10km/6 miles); an older one at Shey (15km/9 miles); the huge monastery complex of Tiske (25km/15.5 miles); the immaculate little monastery at Stakna (30km/18 miles), and the spectacular 17th-century monastery of Hemis (45km/28 miles). Other monasteries lie along the road west towards Srinagar, notably Spituk (8km/5 miles), Phyang (16km/10 miles), which hosts a compelling festival in July, and the richly decorated Akhi (70km/43 miles), a huge monastery complex founded in the 11th century at the same time as neighbouring Lekir. Countless trekking destinations include Changthang and the Hemis sanctuary across the Zanskar range.

BUSES

Buses from Delhi operated by HPTDC go to Dharamasala, Manali and Leh (Jul–Aug only).

▶▶ **Kullu Valley**   *116B4*

Celebrated with the epithet 'Valley of the Gods' and mentioned in the *Mahabharata* and *Ramayana*, Kullu is one of Himachal's most delightful regions. In spring, this narrow valley (80km/50 miles) blossoms between pines and cedars while snow tops the peaks. Mountain villages, terraced apple orchards, hot springs and forests invite endless trekking, and there are numerous Hindu temples to visit. Despite centuries of being exposed to outside influences, due to its position on a Central Asian trade-route, and more recent influxes of Tibetans and tourists, local traditions remain strong among the *paharis* (hill-people) and nomadic shepherds who roam the hills.

A smoke? Among the crops are cannabis (*charas*) plantations, that have made the valley, especially **Manali▶**, a favourite haunt for Westerners wanting cheap and abundant dope. This over-subscribed resort at the foot of the Rohtang Pass is definitely past its best, (most of the Westerners on a permanent high who once monopolized the place have moved on, to be replaced by Indian holiday-makers) but offers a wide range of accommodation, beautiful surroundings and buses that cover the gruelling 25–30-hour trip to Leh.

To the castle In the south, the market town of Kullu itself is hardly inspiring, having succumbed to the glories of concrete. It is, however, a transport hub and a necessary stopover en route to better things. Far more interesting is **Naggar▶▶** 28km (17 miles) north, the local capital for 1,400 years. Beautifully situated on wooded slopes and commanding sweeping valley views, the town has several ancient temples and, on a high outcrop, a castle that is now partly a hotel and museum. Naggar's most illustrious foreign resident was Nicholas Roerich, a Russian artist and mystic who died in 1947 and is commemorated by the Nicholas Roerich Gallery (*Open* daily 10–1, 2–5. *Admission: inexpensive*). Paintings and photographs in the gallery give a taste of his wide-ranging interests.

▶▶▶ Leh   *116B5*

The remote, bleak and dramatic moonscapes of Ladakh, sharpened by their unusual crystalline light, centre on Leh. The fortunes of this once flourishing market town on the Silk Road into China plummeted in the 1950s when the Chinese border was closed, but revived in 1974 when Ladakh was opened to tourism. The brevity of the warm season means that in summer visitors far outnumber the local mixture of Muslims, diminutive Ladakhis, Tibetans, Baltis and mercantile Kashmiris.

Despite this invasion, Leh's infrastructure is appalling: power-cuts, dirt, sewage and notoriously unhygienic food add to the problems of altitude sickness. Yet this unique and perceptibly isolated region captivates most visitors, whether they are investing in fabulous Ladakhi and Tibetan handicrafts, trekking or tracking down remote *gompas* (monasteries).

Above Overlooking the northern town is the ramshackle nine-storey **palace▶** (*Open* daily 7–6. *Admission: inexpensive*), built in the 16th century with jutting wooden balconies, buttresses and a roof-terrace with amazing views. Badly deteriorated, with perilous holes in some floors and flaking murals, it is rather a sad testimony to Leh's royal family, though a small museum exhibits a few heirlooms. Rising high above the palace is the 15th-century **Namgyal Tsemo gompa▶▶** (*Open* daily 7–9am. *Admission: moderate*), comprising two temples. The first, with repainted murals, houses a gigantic Buddha, the second preserves beautiful wall-paintings.

Below Huddled at the base of this hill is the **old town▶▶**, an atmospheric maze of narrow lanes that ends at the Jama Masjid and the main bazaar. You can buy Tibetan, Ladakhi and Kashmiri handicrafts here. Beyond the church is the **Ladakh Ecology Centre▶** (*Open* daily 10–5. *Admission: free*), dedicated to encouraging sustainable local crafts, agriculture and small industries. In an idyllic rural setting 3km (2 miles) north is the **Sankar Gompa▶▶** (*Open* daily 7–9am, 5–7pm. *Admission: inexpensive*), a monastery dating from the 17th century and rimmed by *chortens*. This is Ladakh's centre for the 'yellow hat' sect (a branch of Buddhism). The large prayer-hall is a riot of colours, gilded statues and murals.

Ladakhi women selling vegetables on the streets of Leh

▶ **Shimla** *116B4*

Shimla, at 2,200m (7,216ft), is the capital of Himachal. Until 1819, when the British uncovered its charms, Shimla was a mere village. From 1865 to 1939, it was the summer seat of government, which would move here each year from Calcutta and later Delhi. This British presence has left a wealth of old hotels, bungalows and municipal buildings strung along a ridge overlooking the 'Indian' maze of twisting lanes, weathered corrugated iron and **bazaar▶** below. The Mall, once banned to most Indians, is the main promenade. It runs from the canary-yellow Christ Church (1844) and the Library (1910) at its eastern end to join The Ridge at Scandal Corner (a name derived from the elopement of a British official's daughter with an Indian prince). Just before this much-frequented crossroads is the Gaiety Theatre (1887), which is still in use.

A half-hour walk west is the **state museum▶** (*Open* Tue–Sun 10–5. *Admission: inexpensive*) in an elegant mansion. Exhibits range from miniatures to colonial water-colours, Kullu masks and bronzes. A short walk up Observatory Hill leads to Rashtrapati Niwas **▶▶**, once the Viceregal Lodge and now the Indian Institute of Advanced Studies (*Open* Tue–Sun 10–5. *Admission: inexpensive*), an impressive neo-Elizabethan mansion, built in a luxurious fashion in 1888. It is well worth seeing, but permission is needed from the officer in charge. Shimla also offers some rewarding walks, to the elevated Jakhu temple, high on the ridge with superb views (2km/1 mile), the Glen (4km/2.5 miles), and Prospect Hill with its Kamna Devi temple (5km/3 miles).

Cultural diversity in northern India; an English church in Shimla (top) and a Ladakhi woman

▶ **Srinagar** *116A5*

What was once the paradisical playground of the Mughals and the British is now an army encampment, plunged into militancy and turmoil since the late 1980s. Tourists have been replaced by soldiers, armed police and paramilitary groups, while the more enterprising Kashmiris have fled to safer pastures. The line of control betwen Pakistan and India-occupied Kashmir is home to one million troops. Much of the trouble originated with militants belonging to JKLF (Jammu and Kashmir Liberation Front) seeking *azadi* (independence), and from other factions supporting integration with Pakistan, which has actively trained and armed them. Islamic fundamentalists and the Hindu majority of Jammu are other contributors to the unease.

Terrorism Kashmir's historical complexities are many, not least the paradox of a fervently Muslim population that in 1846 was sold by the British to a Hindu ruler. In 1947, the last maharaja, an autocratic hedonist vacillated between joining India or Pakistan. Wars and the drawing of new borders followed, but the promised referendum was never held, and today the rest of the world can only hope that nuclear tests by both countries continue to be no more than sabre-rattling. Since 1988, bombs and assassinations have killed tens of thousands of people, and Kashmir underwent seven years of direct rule (and military control) from Delhi, which imposed curfews, brutality and imprisonment without trial. The reintroduction of state elections in 1996 brought marginal improvement. But in 2001 world events such as 9/11 and, three months later, a terrorist attack on the Indian parliament created increased tension, bringing renewed threats of nuclear war between India and Pakistan. Another glimmer of hope came in 2002 when the new state government offered compensation to victims and released long-term prisoners. Military presence has been reduced in the Vale of Kashmir as violence is concentrated in the border zones.

With caution As a result of this calming of the situation in Srinagar, tourism is slowly returning. If reliable advice is sought before going, visitors will find a warm welcome from a population that has been virtually ostracized over the last decade or so. The legendary houseboats on Lake Dal await business, as do the many traders whose astuteness also demands caution. Pashmina (in multiple guises), embroidery and lacquerware are still churned out by villagers in difficult conditions. Visitors should remain within Srinagar itself, where military presence assures relative safety, and avoid moving around after dark. If booking a trip to Kashmir from Delhi use only tour operators recommended by the tourist office. Countless scams have been carried out by desparate Kashmiri touts.

KASHMIR SHAWLS

Shawls were first produced in Kashmir around 1450 by weavers from Turkestan, and a century later were being used by Akbar as valuable diplomatic gifts. Through the Portuguese and the British, Kashmir shawls became fashionable in Europe: Empress Josephine, wife of Napoleon, is said to have owned some 400. The simple floral motifs of 18th-century shawls developed into the heavy, swirling patterns popular in Georgian Britain, where the manufacture of copies began. By 1870, Jacquard-woven paisley shawls (made in Paisley, Scotland, and elsewhere in Britain) had swamped the market, leaving work only for Kashmir's deft embroiderers. Pashmina wool comes from the soft underbelly fur of mountain-goats and produces feather-weight shawls fine enough to be pulled through a ring. The best quality of all, more common in Ladakh, is *shahtush* from the Tibetan gazelle and endangered species. Trade in *shahtush* is prohibited.

Dal Lake at Srinagar is deceptively tranquil in this troubled land

The Northeast

145

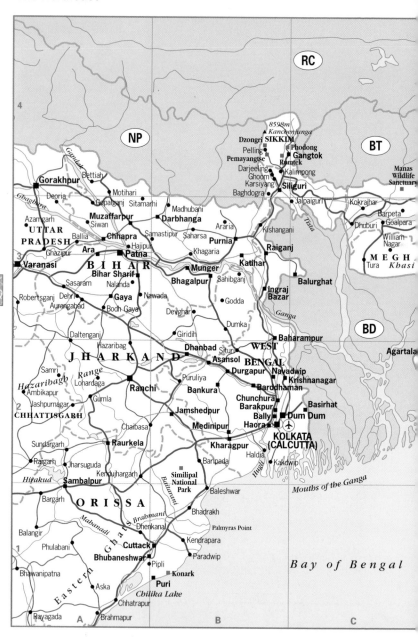

Northeast For all the difficulty of making comparisons in India's kaleidoscope of cultures and landscapes, the northeast is arguably the most diverse and certainly the least frequented region of all. Sweeping through the parched plains of Bihar and West Bengal, the increasingly polluted Ganga (Ganges) finally ends in the flood-prone delta of Bangladesh, just east of Kolkata (Calcutta). To the south lies verdant Orissa, a prosperous state whose unique temples culminate at Konark's superlative Sun

ARUNACHAL PRADESH

• Anini

5108m

Dibang

Lohit

Along •

Pasighat•

Daporijo•

Tezu

7089m▲

Ziro•

Dibrugarh• Tinsukia

Tawang•

Bomdila•

Seppa

Itanagar•

Sibsagar•

• Khonsa

Tezpur•

Jorhat•

Mon•

Brahmaputra

Kaziranga

Wildlife

Sanctuary

Golaghat•

Mokokchung•

langaldai•

Nagaon•

Wokha•

• Tuensang

Guwahati•

A S S A M

• Zunheboto

Dispur•

Diphu•

NAGALAND ▲ 3826m

Dimapur• Kohima•

Shillong•

Jowai•

A Y A

Hills

Haflong•

Karong•

Cherrapunji•

Ukhrul•

Tamenglong•

Silchar•

Imphal•

Thoubal•

Bishnupur•

MANIPUR

Dharmanagar•

Churachandpur•

Chandel•

TRIPURA

Aizawl•

MIZORAM

Mizo

Hills

Jdaipur•

BUR

Lunglei•

Lawngtlai•

0   100   200   300 km

0   100   200 miles

D   E

147

*An Orissan fisherwoman
carries fish in a turtle
shell*

temple. Following the Bangladeshi border due north to the
Himalayas, the trail leads to the beautiful state of Sikkim,
where snowy peaks tower over Buddhist monasteries.
Finally, on India's easternmost frontier, there are the
troubled states around Assam, which can suffer from
insurgency—take local advice before visiting.

The magnificent The logical starting-point and base
for visiting this region is the city of Kolkata (Calcutta),

The Northeast

148

RAILWAY HAZARDS

'At Sukhna station in the winter of 1900 the staff was held up one bright morning by a tiger which had spent the early hours lying on the cool, cemented surface facing the booking office. Needless to say, its days were numbered, for a soldier happened to be at the Forest bungalow, and at the earnest solicitations of the staff came across and dispatched it. Again, early in 1915, the rumble of an incoming train awoke a tiger which had been asleep under the first railway culvert outside the station limit, which in its mad rush out knocked over an Indian wayfarer who just managed to crawl into the station, shaking like an aspen leaf...On another occasion, a herd of wild elephants caused a little flutter among the station staff and also compelled the driver of a train to back right into Sukhna...'
E. C. Dozey, *A Concise History of the Darjeeling District since 1835*

Kolkata still has hand-pulled rickshaws

'the many-sided, the smoky, the magnificent' in Rudyard Kipling's words. Kolkata is bursting at the seams with a ceaseless influx of impoverished peasants from Bangladesh and from West Bengal itself, and is best known in the West for its extreme misery, yet it has an incomparable spirit of survival. This was British India's first capital, the greatest colonial city of the East, whose cosmopolitan middle class experienced a socio-cultural boom unique in India. Bengali intellectuals set the example, from the prolific Rabindranath Tagore (see pages 150–151) to, more recently, the film-maker Satyajit Ray. From the 1930s onwards, many turned to Communism, and West Bengal is now governed by a Marxist party. Despite the chaos, the straining infrastructure and the poverty, Kolkata is full of surprises, boasting, for example, India's first underground train and a cricket stadium whose scale reflects the Bengalis' greatest passion.

Hindu might From the 8th to the 13th centuries, when Kolkata was a mere cluster of mud-flat villages, glorious temples were being built in Orissa, a strikingly fertile, subtropical region rich in tribal people and with a strong crafts tradition. Its beautiful, unspoilt sandy beaches were discovered long ago by Pacific ridley turtles. Bhubaneshwar, Puri and Konark are the temple centres, and are dominated by superbly carved beehive-shaped structures rising to celestial heights; in some cases they are behind walls that restrict entry to Hindus only (notably in Puri). Earlier still, in the 3rd century BC, Orissa's powerful Kalinga dynasty was routed by Ashoka in a battle so ferocious that it led to his conversion to Buddhism. Many of Ashoka's rock edicts survive here, particularly at Dhauli, near Bhubaneshwar.

Nirvana? The heart of Buddhism, ironically, lies in Bihar, an uninspiring, near-destitute state whose main claims to fame are its caste-wars, uncontrolled crime, slums, widespread poverty and corruption. If you can brave the *dacoits* who sporadically attack trains, your destination should be Bodh Gaya, the site of Buddha's enlightenment and now a major Buddhist pilgrimage centre.

Rising higher Far more welcoming are the delightful, atmospheric hill-stations of the Himalayas: Darjiling and Kalimpong, where remnants of colonial days mix with a cross-section of Lepchas, Nepalese, Bhutanese and Tibetans in idyllic, undulating landscapes carpeted with tea-plantations or pine-forests. To the north rises the rugged emptiness of Sikkim, watched over by the awesome peak of Kanchenjunga. Buddhism and commerce coexist easily in the bustling capital of Gangtok, where red-robed monks drop into cafés to eat *momo* (dumplings) beside newly thriving entrepreneurs. Beyond this unfolds pristine nature, now only partly restricted for trekking or visiting the western mountains, where the jewel is the monastery of Pemayangste. Restrictions are more necessary in the turbulent states of the far-flung northeast. This is a region of great ethnic diversity where dance, music and crafts traditions have been preserved in isolation from the rest of India.

Above: Bodh Gaya, a place of pilgrimage for Buddhists from around the world
Below: Buddhist monks

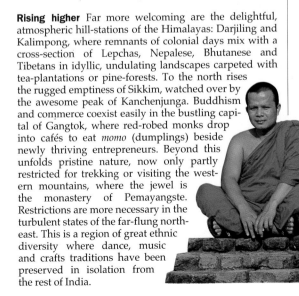

Three generations of the Tagore family left an indelible mark on Bengali society and, eventually, on India. The last and most famous was Rabindranath who attained international readership and esteem. The Tagores' lives and philosophies represented a renewed dynamism of spirit after centuries of dynastic, Mughal, then British control.

150

The Tagore Museum in Kolkata

Bengal in the 19th century was a hothouse of reformist and progressive movements that culminated in the humanist approach of the poet-philosopher Rabindranath Tagore (1861–1941). His ideas subsequently inspired the leaders of the Indian independence movement, Gandhi and Nehru, and his experimental, international university at Santiniketan still functions today.

Eclectic role-model Rabindranath's grandfather, 'Prince' Dwarkanath Tagore (1794–1846), was a Kolkata merchant who lived in opulent style thanks to his extensive business, agricultural and shipping interests. True to his time, he lived a double life, following Hindu traditions at home (now the Tagore Museum) and, in his entertainment annexe, laying on lavish receptions. Dwarkanath was also a philanthropist: the first Indian member and patron of the Asiatic Society, he helped found the National Library. He was also involved in the creation of India's first centre of modern education, the Hindu College, and its first medical college and hospital, in 1835.

This extraordinarily astute and generous man supported the progressive movements of his day, whether religious, social or political, and was much inspired by his friend Rammohun Roy (see panel), the visionary social and religious reformer. Dwarkanath twice broke the Hindu taboo against sea-voyages by crossing the ocean to visit Europe and England, where he died prematurely.

The saint and sage Born in 1817, Dwarkanath's eldest son, Debendraneth, was no less remarkable. Brought up in a cocoon of luxury, he went through an existential crisis at the age of 18, experiencing a sudden aversion to wealth and its trappings. From then on, he spent his life searching for a spiritual truth. He studied the Vedas, Sanskrit texts and Western philosophy, and

The Tagores

AFTER THE CATACLYSM
'The wheels of Fate will one day compel the British to give up their Indian empire. But what kind of India will they leave behind, what stark misery? When the stream of the last two centuries' administration runs dry at last, what a waste of mud and filth they will leave behind them!...As I look around I see the crumbling ruins of a proud civilization strewn like a vast heap of futility. And yet I shall not commit the grievous sin of losing faith in Man. I would rather look forward to the opening of a new chapter in his history after the cataclysm is over and the atmosphere rendered clean with the spirit of service and sacrifice.'
From *Crisis in Civilisation*, Tagore's last public address, in April 1941.

151

finally united his ideas in a new religion dedicated to the worship of a universal and formless divinity. On his father's death, Debendraneth was played a strange card by fate: it was discovered that the debts of the family firm far exceeded its assets and so, with great joy, he found his inheritance reduced to zero. Yet he was shrewd enough, over the years, to rebuild a material base for his large family and integrate his peripatetic spiritual leanings. His favourite destinations were the Himalayas and Santiniketan ('abode of peace'), where he contemplated nature as a mystic and came to be known as the Maharshi (saint and sage).

Universal man In 1861 the Maharshi's 14th child, Rabindranath, was born. This child prodigy who wrote his first verse at the age of eight was nurtured by his father and never obstructed: freedom and truth were the guiding ethics. Over the years, his poetry, songs, lyrical drama, novels and social comedies won him international recognition but he was also deeply concerned by the plight of the Indian peasant and actively helped rural communities. In 1913, his Nobel Prize cheque went straight to his experimental school and to an agricultural bank that he had set up. His love for India had no room for xenophobia and he held responsible both the oppressors and the oppressed for the ills of the land.

Roving ambassador Although in basic sympathy with Gandhi, with whom a lifelong friendship started in 1915, Tagore had a more humanist, less ascetic approach. The contrast between the two was best described by their mutual English friend, C. F. Andrews: 'Tagore is essentially a modern; Mahatma Gandhi is the St. Francis of Assisi of our own days.' Their differences became more apparent in the 1920s when Tagore became India's roving spiritual ambassador, preaching co-operation between East and West, while Gandhi was advocating non-cooperation. Rabindranath's brilliance sparkled until the very end, as he dictated poetry on his deathbed.

Rabindranath Tagore (below); his study (above)

Monsoon season in Kolkata, when the heavy rains cause floods

▶ ▶ ▶ Kolkata (Calcutta)

Kolkata, India's second metropolis, with over 15 million inhabitants, hits new arrivals with an incomparable blast of fumes, humid heat, dirt, tumbledown buildings, broken pavements and human misery. What must be the world's most decrepit cars manoeuvre and honk past hand-pulled rickshaws and buses fit for the dump, while men clad in *dhotis* soap themselves under roadside water-pumps. This looks like a paralyzed city, abandoned to a strange destiny yet efforts are being made at a clean-up, and Kolkata may surprise you. Among the squalor and neglect are more bookshops, email offices and speakers of English than anywhere else in India. Kolkata's cultural life beats anything that Mumbai (Bombay) or Delhi has to offer and the stately colonial edifices seem, for once, an integral part of this city of paradoxes. Startling decay and rampant overcrowding cannot detract from a specific fascination and excitement found only in Kolkata.

Rise to power Named after the ferocious goddess Kali worshipped by local villagers, the city was founded in 1690 by an English trader, Job Charnock, who chose the Hugli estuary as the site for an East India Company trading post. Bengal's muslin, grain, silk yarn, tobacco and saltpetre gradually created a dual city: the palatial British settlement of Chowringhee, ranged around the huge open space of the Maidan bordering the Hugli river, and the 'native' quarter of filthy lanes and chaotic hovels beyond.

By 1772 Fort William was built and Calcutta had become the capital of the British Empire in India. From then until 1911, when the capital was moved to Delhi, Calcutta boomed. Imposing municipal buildings that earned it the

TOURIST OFFICES
Government of India, 4 Shakespeare Sarani (*Open* Mon–Fri 9–6, Sat 9–1; tel: 033 2282 5813/7731, fax: 033 2282 5321, email: indtour@cal2.vsnl.net.in). Very helpful information. WBTDC, 3/2 BBD Bagh East (*Open* Mon–Fri 10.30–1.30, 2.15–5.30; tel: 033 2248 8271, fax: 033 2248 5168, email: wbtdc@cal2.vsnl.net.in). Tours, boat trips, permits, guides and car hire. Also counters at the airport and Howrah station.

soubriquet 'city of palaces' were erected, and in 1876, even filtered drinking water and drainage systems were installed in the city.

New thinking Parallel to the expanding British infrastructure, a new class had been created, the Babu. These *nouveau riche* merchants built fabulous mansions and became famed for their decadence: one would light his cigars only with ten-rupee notes (twice the monthly earnings of a coolie). Equally important was the development of the Bengali intelligentsia; reformist luminaries such as Rammohun Roy, Vivekananda and Dwarkanath Tagore (see pages 150–151) greatly contributed to the liberal thinking that eventually brought independence and democracy.

Radicalism This overtly cosmopolitan city (its ethnic groups include Armenians, Chinese, northeast tribal people and Gurkhas) has been controversially run since 1977 by the CPIM (Communist Party of India Marxist). Desperate Bangladeshis and Bengali villagers continue to pour in, crowding the city even more, and charitable efforts by Mother Theresa's successors, the Kali temple and individual citizens are mere drops in the vast ocean of poverty. In the mid-1960s Kolkata's problems provoked another extremist movement, the Naxalites, who sought to eradicate social inequality through what eventually became anarchic assassinations.

Lay-out The centre lies east of the Hugli's cantilevered Howrah Bridge, that groans under record-breaking traffic (60,000 vehicles a day) crawling towards the main railway station (Howrah) on the west bank. To the south a newer bridge, the Vivekananda Setu, leads west to the beautiful Indian Botanical Gardens. Crowning the centre is the vast Maidan, edged to the east by J Nehru Road (formerly Chowringhee), whose restored glory is the stunning Oberoi Grand hotel. Halfway down, beside the Indian Museum, is Sudder Street, crammed with budget and some mid-range hotels, travellers' cafés and travel agencies. South of here are more salubrious, modernized streets lined with clubs, embassies, expensive shops, hotels and airline offices. Park Street has the Asiatic Society at one end (No. 1), and at the other the atmospheric Park Street cemetery (dating from 1767).

North of the Maidan sprawls old Kolkata, where British monuments are juxtaposed with mosques and mansions, the university, bazaars and the red-light district. The Parasnath Jain temple is the furthest sight of major interest.

Goats are a common sight in the streets of Kolkata

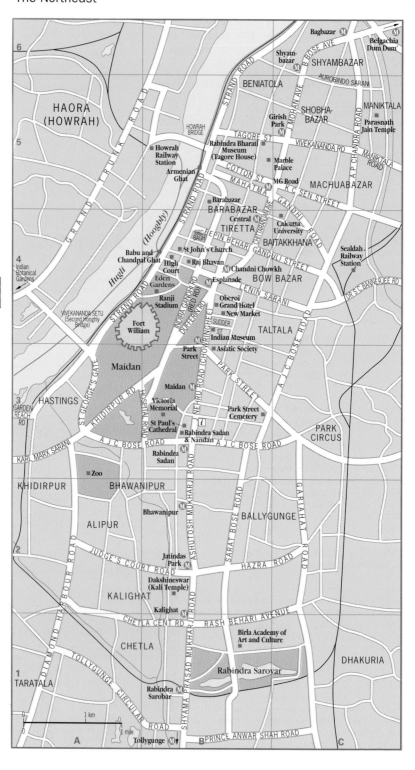

▶▶ BBD Bagh (formerly Dalhousie Square) 154B4

Kolkata's administrative centre was created in the late 18th century and still has the original red brick Writers' Building (1780) on the north side. It was once the headquarters of the East India Company, and is now the State Secretariat. East of here stands St. Andrew's Kirk (1818), evidence of the large Scottish community that once monopolized the trading-houses of the commercial district surrounding the Stock Exchange.

On the west side stands the unusual Customs House, next to the domed white Post Office (1868) and, one block south, St. John's Church (*Open* daily 9–12, 5–6. *Admission: free*) built in 1787 to resemble London's St-Martin-in-the-Fields. The cemetery contains Job Charnock's tomb and a monument to victims of the Black Hole of Calcutta (see panel); inside is *The Last Supper* by Johann Zoffany. South of this is the large walled Raj Bhavan, the magnificent Governor's residence built in 1802 (*Open* only with special permission) and, southwest, the High Court. Beyond are the Eden Gardens in the Maidan, where a pretty landscaped park is crowned by a pagoda. The neighbouring cricket stadium accommodates 100,000 vociferous spectators, and is Kolkata's favourite institution.

▶▶▶ Dakshinieswa (Kali Temple) 154B2

Near Belur Math Metro: Kalighat or Jatindas Park
Open dawn–dusk. Admission: free

Founded in 1602, this temple represents the heart and soul of Kolkata. Some 2,000 poor are fed twice a day by its kitchens, and mothers with newborn babies flock to give thanks to the 'tree of life', an ancient cactus hung about with black stones donated for fertility. At the back of the temple is a shrine dedicated to Brahma, near the slaughter area for black kid goats. Considered representatives of evil, these squealing creatures meet their end with long *pujas* carried out in the main hall facing the sanctum. The statue of Kali herself, fearsome and black-faced with three eyes, is always surrounded by a dense crowd of heavily garlanded worshippers. To escape from this intensity, take the side entrance leading to the peaceful *tank*. The resident Brahmin guides are very informative, but they are extremely insistent in their demand for donations.

▶▶▶ Indian Museum (Jadu Ghar) 154B4

27 Jawaharlal Nehru Road
Metro: Park Street. Open: Tue–Sun 10.15–4.30.
Admission: moderate

India's oldest museum started life in 1814 as part of the Asiatic Society, and in 1875 opened its doors to the public. It houses a stunning collection of archaeological treasures, starting in the lobby with two superb 2nd century BC statues that came from a Buddhist *stupa*. The *stupa* is partly reconstructed in the adjoining Sunga Room. Gandhara, Mathura, Hoysala and Chola (see pages 36–39) sculptures follow and across the verdant courtyard are prehistoric, anthropological and geological exhibits which are very mediocre with bad signage and dusty displays. The courtyard is surrounded by corridors of artefacts and sculptures and is a restful place to sit. The second floor, mainly zoological, leads to a wing that is closed for renovation.

THE BLACK HOLE OF CALCUTTA
This notorious episode in colonial history took place in 1756, apparently on the site of the present Post Office which, at the time, was the first fort. The nascent British community was easily overcome when the forces of Siraj-ud-Daula, the young Nawab of Bengal, mounted an attack. Although most British managed to escape, 146 were captured and imprisoned in a tiny guardroom with little ventilation. Many died in this 'black hole', but the claim that only 23 survived may have been a British exaggeration.

155

Men bathing in the Kali Temple tank

THE OBEROI GRAND

Kolkata's most prestigious hotel, the Oberoi Grand, was raised from the ashes of the old Theatre Royal in 1911 by Arathoon Stephen, an Armenian who started life as a barrow-boy and ended as one of Kolkata's real-estate barons. With additional floors eventually providing 500 rooms, it became India's most luxurious hotel and the city's most fashionable watering-hole. It enjoyed two glorious decades—until polluted water killed six hotel guests. In 1937, the ageing institution was forced to close down. It was resurrected by Rai Bahadur Mohan Singh Oberoi, ebullient from his success with Simla's legendary Cecil Hotel. Within a year, he had renovated and re-opened the hotel. After requisitioning during World War II, it thrived again in the 1950s, Kolkata's last period of brilliance. It is still one of Kolkata's most sumptuous and expensive hotels.

Victoria Memorial, a white-marble masterpiece

►► Marble Palace   154B5

Muktaram Babu Metro: Girish Park. Open: Tue–Wed, Fri–Sun 10–4 with permit from Government of India Tourist Office or WBTDC office. Admission: compulory to have a guide, who will demand a tip

This extraordinary colonnaded edifice crumbles gracefully in a walled garden. It is a relic of a wealthy Muslim landowning family, some of whom still live here, bound by a trust not to sell. Built in 1835 during the city's heyday, it reflects the opulence and Anglophilia of that period: Queen Victoria is honoured with a huge wooden statue. Inlaid Italian marble floors lead past Belgian glass chandeliers, gilt-framed mirrors and French clocks, and the painting gallery (wide open to Kolkata's dust and humidity) displays no lesser artists than Rubens, Murillo, Reynolds and Titian. Dust-sheets and caged birds add to the theatrical atmosphere.

►► Rabindra Bharati Museum   154B5

6/4 Dwarkanath Tagore Lane
Metro: Girish Park. Open: Tues–Sun 10.30–4.30. Admission: inexpensive

Housed in the attractive family home of the Tagores, this fascinating museum covers Bengal's 19th-century progressive movement (spearheaded by Dwarkanath Tagore), and Rabindranath Tagore's life, prolific writings and associations, with paintings, photos and old furniture.

►► Victoria Memorial   154B3

Queen's Way
Metro: Maidan. Open: Tue–Sun 10–5. Admission: moderate

This enormous building (1906) reigns supreme over the southern end of the Maidan, fronted by large ponds and a huge statue of a glowering Queen Victoria. It was Lord Curzon's ode to the then defunct sovereign. Inside, the lofty atriums and upper galleries have changed little, displaying huge Victorian oils, commemorative busts of colonial heroes, colonial water-colours, East India Company documents, arms and diverse British Raj memorabilia. More dynamic in style is the Kolkata Gallery, admirably spelling out the rise (and to a lesser extent the fall), of the city, with superb aquatints of the 1780s, photos and well-presented panels, culminating in a lifesize replica of an old street.

Practical details

Transport Kolkata surprisingly boasts an immaculate 1980s underground metro system, unique in India, that runs Mon–Sat 7am–9.45pm, Sun 3pm–9.45pm from Dum Dum (3km/2 miles from the airport) in the north to Tollygunge in the south. It is by far the best way to reach the city's principal sights, although the empty marble platforms hardly reflect the teeming masses above ground. Keep your ticket as you need it to get out.

Double-decker and mini-buses ply countless routes, but are often crowded and are fertile ground for pickpockets. Unless you can use the women-only carriages, trams are not a comfortable experience for female visitors. A tram heritage tour takes place on Sunday mornings.

Kolkata's cheap, beaten-up taxis actually use their meters, with charts to calculate fare adjustments (which double the fare or more), but it is often quicker to walk.

Auto-rickshaws are available, mostly outside the centre. Kolkata's speciality, human-pulled rickshaws, are used by locals, but many visitors prefer to avoid them.

The Hugli ferry service operates daily from 6am to 8pm between Babu Ghat and Howrah Station, and Armenian Ghat and Howrah Station.

Shopping New Market, one block north of Sudder Street, is the obvious shopping destination. Its 1874 structure shelters a vast, labyrinthine market selling food, household goods, jewellery, handicrafts and clothes, but beware of the numerous touts and pickpockets. Russel Street has auction houses, home decoration shops, jewellery and smart boutiques, while at dusk J Nehru Road's general souvenir and handicrafts shops compete with a mass of street-vendors selling watches, sunglasses and immaculate white shirts. The Central Cottage Industries Emporium at No. 7 and Dakshinapar Shopping Complex at Dhakuria in the south have products from all over India, and Handloom House offers good *khadi* (handwoven, handprinted cloth), at 2 Lindsay Street. Bazaars exist all over Kolkata, such as Jagannath Ghat (flower market), Shyambazar (coconut market) and Bentinck Street (tailors, shoemakers and sweetmeats). The Oxford Bookshop, Park Street, offers a good selection of English-language books.

CULTURAL BONANZA
Kolkata has a lively programme of theatre, music, dance, film and art. Listings and reviews are in the English-language press (*The Telegraph*, *The Statesman*) or pick up the pamphlet *Calcutta: This Fortnight* from the WBTDC office. Venues include the Birla Academy of Art and Culture (concerts, theatre, art exhibitions), Rabindra Sadan (a concert hall and theatre), Kala Mandir (some plays in English) and the Government of India tourist office auditorium ('Dances of India' nights every weekend).

157

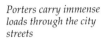

Porters carry immense loads through the city streets

Plum in the middle of the arid, poverty-stricken state of Bihar is Buddhism's holiest site, Bodh Gaya, where Buddha reached enlightenment. Together with nearby Nalanda, this has become a major pilgrimage destination, visited and invested in by East Asian Buddhists, in complete contrast to its miserable environs.

TRANSMITTING THE WORD

Buddha's disciples met at Rajgi to draw up a definitive version of *dharma* and *vinaya* (rules of monastic conduct). They memorized their conclusions, using complex mnemonic devices, but wrote nothing down. The only Buddhist text to have survived in an ancient Indian language is the Pali Canon, produced in Sri Lanka around the 1st century BC.

A depiction of Buddha, Bodh Gaya

The Buddhist monuments of Bihar are redolent with the spirit of Gautama Buddha, born as Prince Siddhartha in the mountains of what is now Nepal, around 560BC. After marrying and fathering a son, at the age of 29 he decided to abandon his life of luxury and search for a more engaging truth. For six years he wandered as an ascetic and beggar, before finally reaching the bodhi tree at Bodh Gaya. Here, at full moon on his 35th birthday in May, he plunged into a night of meditation that was to be his path to enlightenment. According to Buddhists, this involved first examining his previous existences to gain knowledge of himself, then seeing the endless cycle of birth and death that humans were caught in (*kharma*), thirdly understanding the causality and interdependence of the world (the cycle of *samsara*), and finally, with this newly gained perception, transcending the greed, hatred and delusion that had previously tied him to rebirth and suffering.

The truth At the moment of maturing from *Bodhisattva* ('on the path to Buddha-hood') to Buddha ('the awakened one'), his knowledge thus crystallized into the four truths concerning the essence, origin, cessation, and path to the cessation of *dukha* (suffering). These encapsulate the teaching of Buddhism. After spending 49 more days under the tree meditating on this, Buddha set off to teach the world about his discoveries. His first sermon took place at Sarnath, near Varanasi, and from there he built up a group of followers, the *sangha*, a community of monks and nuns who continued to teach after his death around 486BC.

Bodh Gaya Indelibly marked by all this is the village of Bodh Gaya where Buddha not only reached *nirvana* (the extinction of desires) but also spent the rest of his life preaching. A pipal tree which is a descendant of the original bodhi tree stands near the Mahabodhi temple. The temple was built in the 7th century over a 3rd century BC shrine established by Emperor Ashoka (but heavily altered and restored in the 19th century).

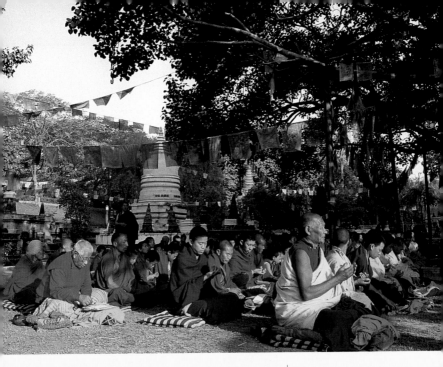

Its soaring pyramidal tower rises more than 50m (164ft) above the sanctuary which contains a large gilded statue of Buddha, in the asana (yogic posture) signifying enlightenment. This temple is now rivalled by numerous others of varying sizes and styles, erected over the last decades by the Buddhist nations of Myanmar (Burma), Thailand, China, Japan, Tibet, Bhutan, Sri Lanka and Vietnam. All are watched over by a gigantic and graceless stone Buddha installed in 1989.

Although most of the year Bodh Gaya sees only a steady trickle of pilgrims joining the resident monks, it springs to life between November and February, when a general forum of international Buddhists takes place, partly led by the Dalai Lama. Commercial concerns flood the village and the environs are invaded by ceremonies, meditation courses and lectures by the different Buddhist schools, activities that create an animation that seems far from *nirvana*—a state of total peace.

Universal university Anyone visiting Bodh Gaya also goes to Nalanda, about 60km (37 miles) northeast. This was the site of one of the world's earliest universities, originally a monastery built during Buddha's lifetime. It developed into a celebrated centre of learning from the 5th to the 12th centuries, attracting students and scholars from Tibet, China, Korea, Japan and Indonesia. The 7th-century Chinese pilgrim-scholar, Hsuan-Tsang, described Nalanda as catering for 10,000 studious monks with 2,000 teachers and 9 million manuscripts—possibly an exaggeration. He praised its 'carved and ornamented, pearl-red pillars, richly adorned balustrades', towers and turrets. Mercilessly sacked by Afghan invaders in the 12th century, Nalanda's *stupas*, temples and monasteries now stand in ruins, and most of the surviving statues are to be found in museums.

Tibetan monks praying under the bodi tree at Mahabodhi temple

BUDDHA'S PROGRESS
With adherents throughout Asia for 2,500 years, Buddhism has survived inroads from Islam and the resurgence of the far older beliefs of Hinduism. It remains the world's most practised religion, whether in Himayana (Lesser Vehicle), Mahayana (Greater Vehicle), Tantric or Zen interpretations. Its widespread influence throughout China, Indochina, Southeast Asia and Japan is directly due to one of Buddhism's fundamental obligations, the need to spread the word or Buddhist law known as *dharma*. It is becoming increasingly popular in the West, partly as a result of the proselytizing of the charismatic Dalai Lama.

TOURIST OFFICES
WBTDC, Hill Cart Road,
Shiliguri (tel: 0353
2431974). Also informa-
tion counters at New
Jaipalguri railway station
and at Baghdora airport.
WBTDC, Bellevue Hotel,
1st floor, 1 Nehru
Road/The Mall, Darjiling
(tel: 0354 2254050).
Basic maps, information
about train, treks. Local
tours.
Darjiling Gurkha Hill
Council, Silver Fir
Building opposite Hotel
Alice Villa, Darjiling (tel:
0354 2254214). Enquire
at either of these offices
about the exceptional
Ropeway Cable Car that
crosses the northern
valley: sometimes it
works, sometimes it
doesn't. Both also give
information about visiting
tea estates.

TOY TRAIN
The train puffs and
zigzags up its narrow-
gauge track from New
Jalpaiguri and Shiliguri
through Karsiyang and
Ghoom to Darjiling, a feat
of 1880s engineering not
to be missed. Taking
8–10 hours to cover the
90km (56 miles) from the
plains to Darjiling's
2,134m (7,000ft)
altitude, it is slow, dirty,
frequently breaks down,
and majestically accom-
plishes a complete circle
at Batasia Loop between
Ghoom and Darjiling. The
rewards are a unique
experience, the tinkering
of the accompanying engi-
neers, and stupendous
views. Rather than
attempt the full-blown
trip, make the four-hour
ride to Karsiyang (twice-
daily) or, even shorter, to
Ghoom at 11.30am then
return by bus or jeep. The
train does not run in
winter or during the
monsoon.

Eastern Himalayas

Rising from the dusty plains of West Bengal and Bihar is a
tiny Indian chunk of the eastern Himalayas, squeezed
between Nepal and Bhutan with Tibet unfolding to the
north. This sparsely populated, captivatingly beautiful
region is dominated by the mighty Kanchenjunga, at
8,500m (27,880ft) the third highest mountain in the world,
with Everest looming to the west. In the foothills, at a lofty
2,100m (6,888ft), lies Darjiling, renowned for its Gurkhas,
tea-estates, narrow-gauge railway (the toy train, see panel)
and enduring Anglo-Indian atmosphere. To the east, in
lush, warmer surroundings, is less well-known
Kalimpong, with strong Bhutanese and Tibetan influences.
To the north lies the magical state of Sikkim, strongly
Buddhist, replete with orchids and rhododendrons, and
requiring a special entry permit.

Power struggles This entire area was once ruled by its own
monarch, but in recent centuries control has been lobbed
between Bhutan, Tibet, Nepal and British India. Britain
obtained Darjiling from Sikkim in 1835 and acquired
control over Sikkim in 1890, through a treaty with China
that defined the nebulous Sikkim–Tibet border.
Kalimpong, originally a strategic Sikkimese trading crossroads, was occupied by Bhutan in 1706, then gained by
British India in 1865. At Indian Independence, Sikkim
remained a protectorate of India, keeping its king, but in
1975 widespread domestic dissatisfaction led it to become
a fully fledged state of India. Darjiling's Nepalese majority
(Gurkhas) is now run by a Gurkh Council, and there are
increasing demands for special, 'Gurkhaland' status, independent of West Bengal.

Access to any of these points is through the unpleasant
little town of Shiliguri. Trains from Delhi or Kolkata
(Calcutta) stop at New Jalpaiguri (5km/3 miles away), and
the only airport in the region, Baghdora,
is 12km (7.5 miles) west. Buses, share-
jeeps and taxis leave from Shiliguri's
Tenzing Norgay bus station, taking three
to four hours to Darjiling or Kalimpong
and six or seven hours to Gangtok, capital of Sikkim. Make sure you arrive in
Shiliguri by early afternoon, or you will
have to stay overnight—something to be
avoided.

▶▶▶ **Darjiling (Darjeeling)** *146B4*
Whether you brave the tortuous railway
or the road with its switchbacks up to
Darjiling, you will be rewarded on
arrival by the sight of a vast pine-clad
valley, with the town tumbling steeply
downhill from Chowrasta, the highest
point, to the bus-stand far below.
Colonial bungalows and newer concrete
edifices line alleys, steps and the main
street (for pedestrians only from halfway up). Nights can be extremely cold
and damp, and early rises are essential if
you want to glimpse Kanchenjunga

before clouds descend. The lively Nehru Road (formerly The Mall), has good retreats for tea, snacks and meals, with abundant handicrafts shops.

From Chowrasta a circular walk leads north, past the delightful Windamere Hotel to Observatory Hill for mountain views at dawn. St. Andrew's, Loreto School and the Gymkhana Club are colonial relics on its western flank. Signposted downhill (west) from Woodland Hotel is the **Natural History Museum►** (*Open* Fri–Wed 10–4. *Admission: inexpensive*), founded in 1903 and now run down. From here, Jawahar Road continues north, downhill to the **Zoo►** (*Open* Fri–Wed 10–4. *Admission: inexpensive*), home to yaks, Siberian tigers, Tibetan wolves and more. Snow leopards and red pandas are housed in a separate Breeding Centre, a 10-minute walk from the zoo. Beyond is the **Himalayan Mountaineering Institute►►** (*Open* daily 9–1, 2–4. *Admission: inexpensive*). Outside stands a hilltop statue of Tenzing Norgay, the sherpa who accompanied Sir Edmund Hillary to the summit of Everest in 1953 and was the Institute adviser until he died in 1986.

► Ghoom   *146B4*

Ghoom, reached from Darjiling by train, bus, taxi or on foot (8km/5 miles), has a 19th-century Buddhist monastery, **Yiga Choling►**, with a lavishly painted interior. The monastery, where yellow-hat Buddhism is practised, is now masked by an ugly resort hotel. **Tiger Hill►►**, 5km (3 miles) beyond Ghoom, is a very popular pre-dawn destination (jeeps leave Darjiling daily at 4am, book in advance) where a tower gives wonderful views from the plains of Bengal to Everest.

TRANSPORT
This mountainous region is easier to get around than almost anywhere else in India, though journey times are long. Share-jeeps carrying up to 15 passengers are the quickest means. When booking numbered seats, canny travellers invest in two each to ease the squeeze. Ask for the front seat whenever possible.

Tea growing in Darjiling Inset: A monk at Ghoom's Yiga Choling monastery

YIGA CHHOLING MONASTERY
GHOOM ESTD. 1850

161

The Northeast

PERMITS AND TOURIST OFFICES
Sikkim Tourist Centre, MG Marg, Gangtok (*Open* Mon–Sat 10–4, closed second Sat of month; tel: 03592 223425, fax: 03592 22647, email: sikkim@sikkim.ren.nic.in).

Fifteen-day permits should be obtained either while applying for your Indian visa or at Sikkim Tourism offices in Delhi (tel: 011 2611 5346), Kolkata (tel: 033 2281 5328) or Siliguri (tel: 0353 2432646). You can also obtain them at the border posts of Rangpo or Melli.

Kalimpong has no tourist office but hotels, particularly Hotel SilverOaks and the Himalayan, have lots of information. Morgan House (tel/fax: 03552 255384) can also be helpful. For information on cultural tours and trekking in the surrounding areas contact Gurudongma Tours and Treks (tel/fax: 03552 255204; email: gurutt@satyam.net.in; w.gurudongma.com).

Sikkimese woman

▶▶ Kalimpong   *146B4*

This is an isolated hill-town, and at 1,250m (6,100ft) considerably warmer than its neighbours and still preserving a relaxed, friendly atmosphere as a crossroads for Tibetans, Bhutanese, Sikkimese and Gurkhas. From Darjiling, a three-hour jeep-ride winds through rolling tea-estates then down to the sub-tropical vegetation of the **Tista river▶▶** before ascending again through forests, bamboo and flower nurseries to Kalimpong.

Sights The main Rishi Road cuts along a ridge, roughly north–south. The large market, bus and jeep-stand, restaurants and a few handicraft shops are midway on the eastern side, monasteries to the northeast and better hotels joining colleges to the south. Like Darjiling, Kalimpong saw many Christian missionaries, including Reverend Macfarlane who by 1873 had founded 25 primary schools, with lessons in Hindi. An attractive church (1881) is named after him. Near here is the Arts and Crafts co-operative, founded in 1897 to promote local handicrafts. Uphill is **Thorpa Choling Gompa▶**, a Tibetan monastery founded in 1937, with an important library of ancient scripts. Below stands the much older **Bhutanese Thongsa Gompa▶** (1692), faced with prayer-wheels and home to around 60 monks. Its beautiful old murals have sadly been repainted in less refined style. Immediately south stands the massive Parnami Mandir, a Hindu temple devoted to Krishna.

Towering to the southeast is Durpin Hill, on which stands Kalimpong's largest monastery, Zong Dog Palri Fo-Brang Gompa, with fabulous Kanchenjunga views. To the north of town is Deolo Hill, site of Dr Graham's Home (1900) which combines an orphanage, school, dairy and bakery.

▶▶ Sikkim   *146B4*

Sikkim's destinations for individual visitors are Gangtok, Rumtek, **Phodong Monastery▶**, Dzongri and Pemayangtse. A minimum of two people can get permits to travel to and trek in specific regions (available through Gangtok travel agents) and still others are completely open. It is, however, never advisable to stray from the designated trekking routes, which provide spectacular scenery dotted with monasteries. Yak treks are Sikkim's latest novelty.

Starting point Sikkim's capital, **Gangtok▶**, sprawls like Darjiling down a high valley at 1,500m (4,920ft), but has more concrete and traffic, a palpably more mercantile attitude and less character. At its commercial heart are the shops, hotels and restaurants of MG Marg, with Lal Bazar at its southern end and the noisy Highway 31A slicing uphill to the north. Furthest up the highway, at zero-point (from where kilometres north of Gangtok are measured), is the Cottage Industries Institute. From here a side road meanders uphill to the **Enchey Monastery▶** (1901), blessed by a Tantric Lama known for his power of flying. (*Open* daily. *Admission: free.*) Visitors can join prayer sessions at 5–7am and 5–7/8pm.

Gangtok's most interesting sights lie to the south. The **Chogyal Royal Palace and Chapel▶** (*Closed* to the public) is about 2km (1 mile) south, on a wooded bluff, the **Namgyal Institute of Tibetology▶▶** (*Open* Mon–Sat 10–4. *Admission: inexpensive*) welcomes visitors. Founded in 1958 to further knowledge of Tibetan and Mahayana Buddhism, it stores the 24 volumes of writings by the 5th Dalai Lama (1617–82). Exhibits also include Buddhist scrolls, statuettes and ritual objects. A short distance along the ridge is the reliquary **Do-Drul Chorten▶** (1960s), a gold-topped *stupa* surrounded by prayer-wheels, flags and young monks from the neighbouring monastery. Far below lies the Chogyal Palden Thondup Memorial Park, in memory of the last king of Sikkim.

Rumtek The majestic **Rumtek Dharma Chakra Centre▶▶** (*Open* daily dawn–dusk. *Admission: free*) lies an accessible 24km (15 miles) away on the opposite hill. It was founded by the head of Kargyugpa Buddhism when he fled Tibet in the 1960s, and built as a replica of the original head-quarters. This huge, terraced, monastery and prayer-hall is part of a self-sufficient community that continues outside the gates. A short distance further on a bluff stands the smaller **Rumtek monastery▶▶** (1730), beautifully reconstructed after a disastrous fire. Zurmang Kagyud Gompa in Lingdum, East Sikkim (20km/12 miles from Gangtok) is also worth a visit.

HANDICRAFTS

Sikkim offers few handicrafts apart from carved wooden *choksees* (tables), hand-woven tableware, beautiful but expensive silverware and Chinese-style tufted-wool carpets. Recent prosperity, much aided by government projects, seems to have relegated traditional crafts to second place. Far more interesting are the goods found in tourist shops in Darjiling and Kalimpong, whose owners net the entire region. *Thangkas* (Buddhist scrolls), Tibetan jewellery, Sikkimese silver, ceremonial robes, Bhutanese weavings, tribal art from Nagaland, local handknitted pullovers and scarves, rabbit-fur gloves…the list is endless. Search out Soni Emporium, Mani Link Road, Kalimpong, which has enticingly unusual selections. Manjusha Emporium, Nehru Road, Darjiling, is West Bengal's fixed-price outlet for all manner of Himalayan handicrafts.

163

Rumtek monastery, a centre for Kargyugpa Buddhism

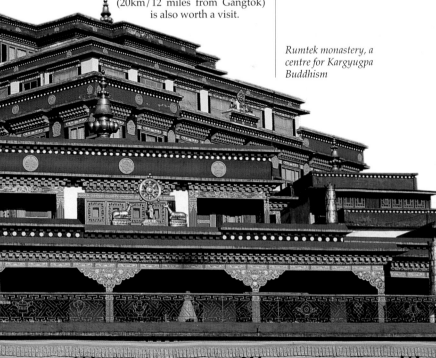

UDAYAGIRI AND KHANDAGIRI CAVES

These much-promoted Buddhist and Jain cave-temples, 8km (5 miles) from town, are in no way comparable to the Ajanta and Ellora Caves of Maharashtra (see pages 178–179), they are best regarded as providing an interesting backdrop to a peaceful ramble enlivened by monkeys and views. Dating from the 2nd century BC, the cave-temples punctuate the sandstone and vegetation in two facing hills. The best preserved are Udayagiri's Cave 1, the Rani Nur; Cave 10, Ganesh Gumpha; and Cave 14, Hathi Gumpha, which contains an inscription of King Kharavela of the 2nd century BC Chedi dynasty. The modern Jain temple crowning Khandagiri has panoramic views of the area.

Orissa

The state of Orissa (also written 'Odisha') nestles on the Bay of Bengal between West Bengal and Andhra Pradesh. This often bypassed gem, protected by the Eastern Ghats, has a heavy rainfall from May to November, and is a beautifully lush, fertile region. Rice fields stand bordered by banana and coconut palms, and the thatched, hand-painted mud-huts are fronted by large ponds. Coal, bauxite and iron ore-mines function profitably here, and there are rich veins of gems and nickel, virtually untapped. Industrial centres have produced Orissa's recent upsurge in prosperity, in contrast to its former status as one of India's poorest states, although in 1999 the state was devastated by a cyclone and floods.

Temples and turtles Orissa's main attractions are its elaborate temples. There are no fewer than 500 in Bhubaneshwar alone, as well as the historical colossi of nearby Puri and Konark. Less well known are the 62 tribes of varying culture, size and dialect, whose traditions can be witnessed only on a guided tour. Handicrafts are much in evidence, as Orissa is renowned for unique techniques, producing metalwork animals, Pipli appliqué (see panel, page 166), *ikat* silk and cottons, and incised palm-leaf manuscripts. Further enticement lies in the crocodiles and birdlife of the coastal mangrove forests, the Pacific ridley turtles at Bhitar Kanika National Park (north of Konark), the white tigers of Similipal National Park in the north and the rich winter birdlife of Chilika, a vast lake in the south. Magnificent, unspoilt beaches sweep down the coast past Konark to Puri, where tacky domestic tourism takes over.

▶▶ Bhubaneshwar   146A1

The modern services centre of Bhubaneshwar is, at first sight, hardly inspiring. Hotels, banks and markets radiate from Rajpath, which crosses the railway to a junction with Jaidev Marg. South from here are the museum, tourist office and a string of handicraft shops. About 2km (1 mile) further on is the temple area and old town. The scattered temples are best visited by rickshaw.

Temple style Orissan temples have a distinctive *deul* that rises from a square base to form a ribbed, bell-shaped structure, crowned with a flat, round stone and surmounted by a *kalasa* ('vase of plenty'). The complex, refined sculpture includes geometric patterns, *chaitya* windows, latticework, scrolls, animals, dancers, dwarves, gods and sometimes erotic figures. The furthest south and the most elaborate and mature in form is the **Lingaraja temple▶▶▶** (11th century) whose multiple towers, the highest reaching 40m (131ft), can be viewed by non-Hindus only from a platform overlooking the wall.

More accessible is the midway group. It includes the **Parasurameshvara temple▶▶** (cAD750), with images of Siva, and elements that reach perfection in later temples, such as the superb 10th-century **Muktesvara temple▶▶▶**. This temple, still in use, represents a transition in South Orissan architecture, and the niches of the compound wall include Buddhist and Jain images alongside Hindu ones. Of note are the richly sculpted archway, shrine and *tank*.

East from here along Tankapani Road is the **Raja Rani temple▶▶▶**, another 11th-century gem standing in a large garden that sets off the lofty main tower. The furthest east is the **Brahmesvara temple▶▶** (1060), isolated in a peaceful, semi-rural setting. It is still frequented by devout worshippers of Lakshmi, whose image is set into the outer wall, and of the Sivalinga inside the shrine. Crowning it is a magnificent, lavishly sculpted tower. Non-Hindus are not particularly welcome here, so be sensitive.

Museums Exhibits at **Orissa State Museum** (*Open* Tue–Sun 10.30–5.30. *Admission: inexpensive*) include reproductions of lovely *chitra muriya* (flourpaste wall-drawings) and 50,000 palm-leaf manuscripts. Tribal crafts are exhibited in traditional huts at the Tribal Research Museum (*Open* Mon–Sat 10–5. *Admission: inexpensive*), northwest of the centre, that were badly damaged in the 1999 cyclone.

Detail from the Parasurameshvara temple at Bhubaneshwar

An idyllic rural route runs 65km (40 miles) southeast of Bhubaneshwar to the outstanding Surya (Sun) temple (*Open* daily dawn–dusk. *Admission: moderate*). This crowning glory of Orissan—or indeed of Indian—medieval art once dominated the coast, but the sea has since retreated behind the white dunes and the temple now stands in a large compound fronted by coconut and *chai*-stands, persistent 'guides' and postcard-vendors, cafés, low-key hotels and a small museum (*Open* Fri–Wed 10.30–5. *Admission: free*).

Erotica fantastica The Surya temple was constructed in 1238–64 out of khondalite and chlorite (sandstone) that together create a remarkable palette of yellow, ochre, green and black. This masterpiece was sacked by Muslim invaders in the 17th century, and was soon buried under sand. It was not excavated until the early 1900s, whereupon its gigantic representation of the Sun God's chariot was revealed in all its glory, with 12 pairs of intricately carved wheels pulled by seven horses. Equally astonishing was the abundance of erotic sculptures that peppered the façade, which are more realistic and visible than at Khajuraho (see pages 130–131). In 1903, the *jagamohana* (antechamber) was bricked up to prevent further collapse, but the exterior walls have been superbly restored, displaying a profusion of groups and couples engaged in explicit, acrobatic performances straight from the *Kama Sutra*. Ecstatic bliss is linked to the Tantric concept of the female force or *shakti*, and Konark may have been a centre for this particular cult that was later suppressed by Hindu orthodoxy.

Pilgrims and tourists visit the Surya temple at Konark

ORISSAN HANDICRAFTS
Brilliantly coloured appliqué parasols, bedspreads, bags and other items are made at Pipli, a large crafts village on the road between Bhubaneshwar and Konark. Other Orissan specialities are palm-leaf miniatures and scrolls (including erotica), *tarakashi* (woven wire), used to create beautiful little ornaments and filigree jewellery, and *dhokra*, a lost-wax casting method that produces delightful figures. Orissan textiles, both silk and cotton, have strong, bold colours and designs. There are textile shops near Puri's temple which have wide selections.

Structures The first structure encountered is the Nata Mandir, a raised, colonnaded platform probably used for dance and music performances. Carved into the plinth are dancers, musicians and erotic couples. West of this is the main temple, fronted by the magnificent Jagamohana, whose pyramidal roof rises nearly 40m (131ft) above a lavishly carved platform. This incorporates the famous wheels beside friezes of elephants, battles, human figures, scrollwork, *chaitya* windows and *nagas* with human heads. At the back are the ruins of the sanctuary tower, where three statues of Surya survive; the most striking stands, life-

size, in a shrine on the south side. The deity was spirited away to Puri long ago, but the sanctum preserves a profusely carved platform with a kneeling figure thought to be King Narashimadeva, the temple-founder. It is worth walking round twice, once at the lower, platform level and again above, in order to appreciate the structure and sculptures. In the grounds stand the raised colossi: elephants to the north and rearing chargers to the south. The Dance Festival every February is well worth targeting.

▶ **Puri** *146B1*

Sadly, the great Jagannath temple of Puri, one of India's most visited pilgrim-centres, is out of bounds to non-Hindus. Built in the early 12th century, inspired by Bhubaneshwar's Lingaraj temple, it is the abode of Lord Jagannath, the Lord of the Universe. The main *deul* rises 65m (213ft) above numerous surrounding *mandapas*, together creating an impressive sea of towered roofs. To the left is a vast kitchen and restaurant area, easily the largest in the world, said to feed 25,000 people daily. Prepared according to strict Brahmin rules, the food is distributed to pilgrims and to the 6,000 temple administrators and priests. To glimpse the animated life within the walls, visit the Raghunandan Library (*Open* Mon–Sat 8–12, 4–7. *Admission: free*) opposite the eastern gateway. A guardian will accompany you to the rooftop for a tip.

Puri's grand market street is lined with incongruously ornate buildings that act as a backdrop to armies of beggars and polio or leprosy victims. To the south lies the endless white-sand beach, whose central stretch has pony and camel-rides, cheek-by-jowl hotels, restaurants and rubbish. The currents can be dangerous.

THE LORD'S ANNUAL OUTING
At full moon each July, the three statues of Lord Jagannath, his brother and his sister are wheeled out of the temple on huge canopied chariots and dragged by thousands of devotees to their summer residence which is just over 1km (0.5 mile) away. This *Rath Yatra* ('car festival') is the high point of the year, and the procession is accompanied by musicians, elephants and teeming millions. At the gods' summer temple, new attires are donned daily, and eight days later the whole proceedure is reversed as the procession moves the statues back again. About half a million devotees visit Puri annually, many during this extraordinary festival.

167

Jagannath temple, a prominent feature of Puri's skyline

Striking east out of West Bengal brings you to a remote corner of India that exists in a state of flux between insurgency and traditional tribal life. Immensely scenic, sometimes dangerous, the far northeast does not make for easy travelling, but the rewards can be great.

PERMITS AND TOURIST OFFICES

Entry restrictions for the seven states change so make enquiries at Indian consulates before making any travel arrangements. At the time of writing, Assam, Meghalaya and Tripura are completely open. Arunachal Pradesh, Mizoram, Manipur and Nagaland require Restricted Area Permits, which means travel in minimum groups of four, following specific itineraries and with a maximum stay of ten days. Apply to the Ministry of Home Affairs, Foreigner Division, Lok Nayak Bhavan, Khan Market, New Delhi 110003 (tel: 011 2469 3334). Allow about two weeks. Government of India, B K Kakati Road, Guwahati, Assam (tel: 0361 2547407; e-mail: indtour@asm.nic.in) provides information.

India's isolated and politically sensitive far northeast consists of seven states clustered around Assam; all one state until the 1960s. This is a wildly beautiful region of mountains, tropical rainforests and plains of rice fields bisected by the mighty Brahmaputra river. Among its many extremes, it has astonishing amounts of rain, enjoyed by a fantastic patchwork of ethnic groups more closely related to peoples in Tibet and Southeast Asia than the rest of India. Of the seven states, only five enjoy relative normalcy: Assam, Tripura, Mizoram, Meghalaya and Arunachal Pradesh. The others, Nagaland and Manipur are in a state of constant insurgency, with governments that are neither competent nor powerful enough to maintain order. Corruption is endemic and there is still violence, extortion and murders, often related to inter-ethnic conflicts and separatists.

Not just tea At the heart of this northeast region is Assam, home of high-grade tea, wild elephants and two of India's finest wildlife sanctuaries, Kaziranga and Manas. The latter should, at present, be avoided for security. Guwahati, the capital, has fascinating old temples and tea-auctions, besides a good tourist infrastructure. A one-off here is Majuli, a huge riverine island home to tribal peoples, Assamese monasteries, a unique culture and great birdlife. Access is from Jorhat. North of Assam is a botanist's dreamland, the mountainous, often cloud-shrouded state of Arunachal Pradesh, where dense tropical jungle gradually gives way to alpine flora at altitudes of over 5,000m (16,400ft), on the border with Bhutan and China. These mountains are where you can visit Asia's second largest monastery, Tawang, home to 500 Buddhist Lamas.

Waterlands Meghalaya and Tripura lie to the south of Assam, bordering Bangladesh. Both are open to visitors. Tiny Tripura, picturesque, hilly, and full of lakes and bamboo groves that produce interesting cane handicrafts, was once a princely state, and the capital, Agartala, has a wonderful Indo-Saracenic palace set in Mughal gardens. There is tension in Tripura between the Bengali (Bangladeshi) majority and tribal minority who are attempting to regain their power. Dubbed the 'abode of clouds', Meghalaya has the world's highest rainfall, and decades ago drew many Scots to inhabit its lush, rolling hills. Former colonial hill-resorts include fantastically wet Cherrapunji and the 1,500m (4,920ft) lakeside capital, Shillong, now well past its best. This is another region for naturalists, favoured by hundreds of butterfly species, where orchids, ferns, bamboos and palms sprout exuberantly. Militants from neighbouring states frequent Meghalaya for rest and recreation purposes.

Side-step Snaking down the border with Myanmar (Burma) are the states of Mizoram, Manipur and Nagaland, the latter being the thorniest point of the far northeast. Mizoram's friendly, peaceful and colourful capital, Aizawl, rises like a citadel over pastoral valleys inhabited by the Christianized Mizos. Originally from Myanmar the Mizos preserve strong egalitarian, agricultural and musical traditions. In the Mizo Hills lies the Dampa Sanctuary; its bamboo and semi-deciduous forest contain swamp deer, tigers, leopards, elephants and gibbons. Mysterious Manipur and its capital, Imphal, has an isolated, independent past. The Meithei inhabitants invented polo and developed their own form of Hinduism as well as impressive dance, music and weaving traditions. In the last few years underground organizations have multiplied, and massacres of Kuki and Naga minorities occur.

Land of the Nagas Most fascinating of all is the state of Nagaland. This fertile strip of hills is home to 16 ethnic groups, which were described in ancient Sanskrit literature as 'hillpeople living on nature's gifts, warlike and possessing formidable weapons'. Their deep-rooted craft traditions still survive, making this an enticing destination but all border areas should be avoided.

Opposite page: Aizawl in Mizoram
Above: Mosmai waterfall in Meghalaya
Below: The high landscape of Arunachal Pradesh

The Centre

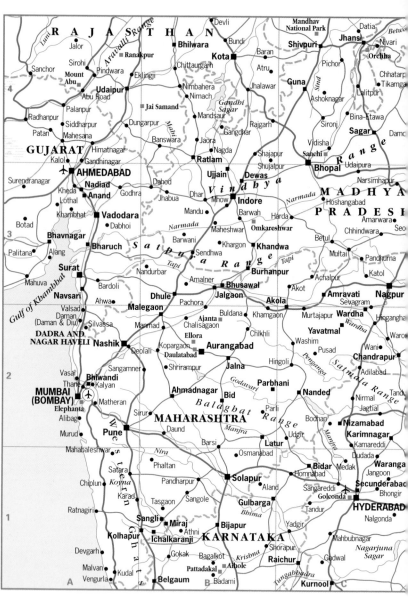

Previous pages:
Women selling brightly
coloured rugs, textiles
and saris at Delhi market

CENTRE For many visitors, this region is the stepping-stone into the subcontinent. India's largest city, Mumbai (Bombay), arrogantly and dynamically occupies a west coast isthmus, protected by the Western Ghats. These mountains unfold into the arid Deccan plateau, comprising the states of Maharashtra, Andhra Pradesh and the south of Madhya Pradesh. Bijapur, though just inside Karnataka, has been included here as its Mughal history and architecture relate to this region. To the east lies the sprawl of Hyderabad, rich in the relics of its outrageously wealthy Nizam rulers and to the north the ghost-town of Mandu, with a wealth of Mughal monuments. The fabulous

172

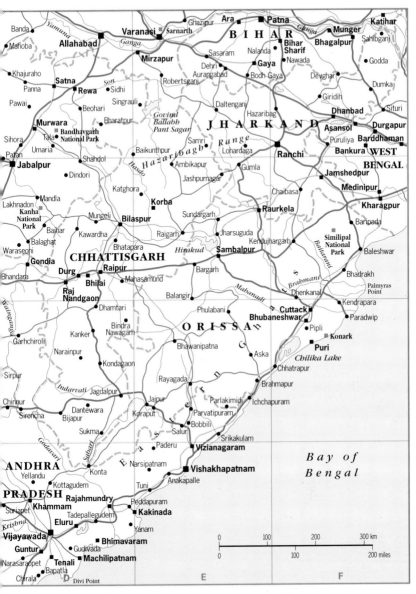

national parks of Kanha and Bandhavgarh, in the remote east of Madhya Pradesh, offer a slim chance of glimpsing a tiger, and a much better one of seeing plenty of other mammals and exotic birds in rewarding wildernesses

SPIRITUAL GLORIES The glories of the centre are undoubtedly its ancient spiritual sites, including the Buddhist *stupas* of Sanchi, dating back to Ashoka (3rd century BC), the rock-cut temples of Ajanta and Ellora, and, not quite in the same league, Mumbai's Elephanta. The cave-temples were chiselled directly out of the rock (usually basalt) to create massive monoliths, reliefs, friezes, towers and

The Centre

MUMBAI'S FIRST INHABITANTS

'And where are they now, the first inhabitants? Coconuts have done best of all. Coconuts are still beheaded daily on Chowpatty beach; while on Juhu beach, under the languid gaze of film stars at the Sun 'n' Sand hotel, small boys still shin up palms and bring down the bearded fruit....Rice has not been so lucky; rice-paddies lie under concrete now; tenement towers where once rice wallowed within sight of the sea... Of all the first inhabitants, the Koli fishermen have come off worst of all. Squashed now into a tiny village in the thumb of the handlike peninsula, they have admittedly given their name to a district—Colaba. But follow Colaba Causeway to its tip—past cheap clothes shops and Irani restaurants and the second-rate flats of teachers, journalists and clerks—and you'll find them, trapped between the naval base and the sea.'
Salman Rushdie,
Midnight's Children, 1981

Mumbai (Bombay) is still a busy seaport

arches; some are more than 2,000 years old. At Ajanta, superb sculptures share their glory with a wealth of frescoes depicting not only Buddha and his life but also courtly and monastic customs and characters. At Ellora the caves were initiated by Buddhist monks in the 7th century then developed by Hindu and Jain priests over the following three centuries. The result is one of the world's greatest sights, Cave 16, the Kailasanath temple. The base for visiting these caves is Aurangabad, which has several other major sights, not least the fiendishly labyrinthine fortress of Daulatabad, and the Bibi-ka-Maqbara, like a less grand Taj Mahal. Aurangabad, Bijapur, Hyderabad and Mandu were all Muslim-controlled cities, where Islamic architecture reached its zenith.

OLD BATTLES Today, Maharashtra is India's most industrialized state, but its past is rife with battles and opposition to the reigning Mughals. The greatest Maratha warrior, Shivaji (1627–80), was renowned for his astute guerrilla tactics and for decades terrorized the Mughal emperor Aurangzeb. At the same time Shivaji created unity and pride among the Marathi-speaking population, whose control gradually extended east to Orissa. By the time the British arrived, Maratha power was diminishing but it was Mumbai (Bombay) that, in 1885, saw the birth of the Indian National Congress, subsequently a forceful influence in the move towards Independence.

NEW BATTLES Since 1966 the Marathas have launched another crusade, this time under the banner of 'Maharashtra for the Maharashtrians'. Using the hero Shivaji as a figurehead and the tiger as its emblem, the Shiv Sena ('Shivaji's army') has been guided by newspaper-owner Bal Thackeray. Its neo-fascist net now encourages Hindu fundamentalism throughout the nation, and appeals especially to the poorly educated lower Hindu castes. In the 1996 Maharashtra state elections, Shiv Sena swept to power in coalition with the

right-wing Hindu BJP (Bharatiya Janata Party), a socially divisive result. However, in 1999 the tables were turned and a Congress coalition resumed power in Maharashtra, although Mumbai is still under the Shiv Sena. The leader of Shiv Sena, Bal Thackeray, resigned in 2005 after a string of poor election results for his party.

DECCAN HEARTLAND Southeast of Mumbai, beyond the popular hill-station of Matheran high in the forested Ghats, lies the heavily industrialized city of Pune. Car factories and engineering companies co-exist with the bizarre Osho Commune, an internationally renowned *ashram* that has more to do with creature comforts than the benefits of the spirit.

From here the dry Deccan plateau of central India takes over, where villagers eke out meagre livings cultivating sugarcane, cotton, wheat and millet. In some areas tribal people provide a splash of colour, and rocky outcrops and boulders give shape to the otherwise monotonous, flat landscape, but it is essentially the cities that are of interest to visitors.

The Kailasnath temple at Ellora represents Siva's Himalayan home

WORSHIPPING THE LAND
Rural India formed the basis for Gandhi's political philosophy, and it was in the northeast corner of Maharashtra, at Sevagram, near Nagpur, that he chose to set up a model village and *ashram* in 1933. Today men and women still sit on the verandas of their huts, spinning and singing in memory of the Mahatma, and the hospital continues to offer low-price treatment to local farmers.

The Centre

TOURIST SERVICES
India Tourism, Krishna
Villas, Station Road East
J180 (*Open* Mon–Fri
8.30–6, Sat 8.30–1.30;
tel: 0240 2331217;
email: gitoaur@vsnl.com).
Also counter at airport.
Helpful.
MTDC, Holiday Camp,
Station Road East (*Open*
Mon–Fri 9.45–5.30; tel:
0240 2331513).
Information and daily
tours of city sights.
Classic Travel shares
MTDC office (tel: 0240
2335598). Private travel
company operating in
conjunction with MTDC
(Open Tue–Sat
7am–10pm). Ticketing,
tours, car rental.

*Chand Minar at
Daulatabad Fort (right)
Bibi-ka-Maqbara
(below), reminiscent of
the Taj Mahal*

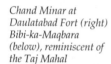

▶ **Aurangabad**   *172B2*

This sprawling industrial city still feels like a village, with
unsealed, unlit streets and quarters that are distinctly
medieval in atmosphere. Investment is now pouring in
thanks to a Japanese mining company and the infrastructure (including the road to Ajanta) should be vastly
improved in the next few years. Aurangabad is mainly of
interest as a base for Ajanta and Ellora but it, too, has its
own cave-temples, as well as relics of Aurangzeb, the last
of the six great Mughal emperors, who gave his name to
the town. There are good air connections with Mumbai
(Bombay), Delhi and Rajasthan, and trains to Mumbai and
Hyderabad. Accommodation, scattered around the 'new'
town, spans the full range.

City sights Aurangabad's atmospheric old centre is well
worth a half-day's exploration. Fourteen gates surround
its walled perimeter and ox-carts trundle along narrow
streets, some lined with *mahari* (traditional carved wooden
façades). The city is still home to a substantial Muslim
population and veiled women flit past domed mosques
(closed to non-Muslims). In the main square stands the
early 18th-century Shahganj mosque, partly concealed by
shops and a market, with the main City Chowk (market)
immediately to the west. Beyond this is the Kali Masjid,
dating from the founding of Aurangabad in the early
1600s. Just north is the Jama Masjid, whose 55 domes rise
above a delicately worked stucco façade.

Over the river Northwest of the old city, across the Kham
river, are Aurangabad's main monuments. **Panchakki▶**
(*Open* daily 8am–8pm. *Admission: inexpensive*) is an ingenious Mughal mill whose large grinding stones were
powered by water channelled underground from a spring
6km (4 miles) away, then raised by siphon to a reservoir.

The pretty gardens at the back contain the tomb of Baba Shah Musafir, the *Sufi* adviser to Aurangzeb (Muslims only). Another 3km (2 miles) north is the **Bibi-ka-Maqbara►►** (*Open* daily dawn–10pm. *Admission: moderate*), a Taj Mahal lookalike built in the late 17th century as the mausoleum for Aurangzeb's wife and now considered the finest Mughal monument in the Deccan. Gleaming white domes and minarets crown a high platform in beautiful walled Mughal gardens that are bisected by a long water-channel spouting fountains. Although it is beautifully laid out, superbly situated against a backdrop of hills, and at a distance looks as grand as the Taj Mahal, its materials, details, finish and even proportions are in no way comparable with the original.

Rock temples From here the road crosses undulating scrubland to the **Aurangabad Caves►►** (*Open* Tue–Sun dawn–6pm. *Admission: inexpensive*). These are divided into two main Buddhist groups and date mainly from the 4th to the 8th centuries. The most interesting are in the eastern group, where the lavish colonnaded shrines of Cave 7 include a preaching Buddha flanked by high-relief carvings of voluptuous *apsaras* (dancers) and musicians. In Cave 6, one Buddha is surrounded by kneeling disciples and another meets Ganesa.

Military might The magnificent **Daulatabad Fort►►** (*Open* daily dawn–6pm. *Admission: moderate*) stands 13km (8 miles) northwest of Aurangabad, on the road to the Ellora Caves. It crowns a seemingly impregnable volcanic hilltop rising dramatically out of farmland. One of India's oldest forts, it was built by Bhilam Raja of the Yadava dynasty in 1187, when it was known as Deogiri. In 1327, Emperor Mohammed-bin-Tughluq attempted to transfer his capital here from Delhi. During this tragic experiment thousands of Delhi migrants perished on the march that was 1,100km (682 miles) long, or, if they survived the journey, succumbed to famine and drought later. The formidable fort itself was continuously occupied by Muslim rulers until Independence, and Mughal tombs dot the surrounding countryside. At the base of the sheer rock walls stands the victory tower, the **Chand Minar**, opposite the Jama Masjid (1318). From here bastions, walls and moats end at the Chini Mahal, beyond which dark, maze-like passageways finally emerge into daylight at the Baradari, a royal pavilion used by Shah Jahan. The citadel is reached by more steep stairways, worth climbing for the views.

Excursions

Ajanta▶▶▶ (*Open* Tue–Sun 9–5.30.
Admission: moderate). The Ajanta caves
are a landmark in Indian art and
culture, illustrating the evolution of
Buddhism from the 2nd century BC to
the 7th century AD. In all, 27 caves were
sculpted and chiselled out of the
layered granite rock of a spectacular
semi-circular ravine in the Sahyadri
hills, 110km (68 miles) northeast of
Aurangabad. These are India's earliest
surviving shrines, whose structures,
whether *viharas* or *chaityas*, inspired
numerous later dynasties. They clearly
reflect the two schools of Buddhism
that emerged in the 2nd century AD:
Himayana (the original purist faith)
and Mahayana (the more liberal
version aimed at the masses). The
colours, concepts and designs of their
murals are unique. During its heyday,
Ajanta is thought to have been home to
more than 200 monks and numerous
artists and craftsmen. The caves were
forgotten after the 7th century, until a

party of British officers hunting tigers discovered them in 1819. A major 21st-century clean-up has now taken place, much reducing the former chaos of hawkers and touts.

Highlights Cave 1, a huge late 5th-century *vihara*, combines magnificent *Jatakas* (illustrations of the life of Buddha and social and court life) with monks' cells and several sculptural masterpieces. Cave 2, a more intimately scaled *vihara*, has superbly decorated shrines, and ornate, 6th-century columns. Ajanta's fragmented earliest paintings (2nd century BC to 2nd century AD), are in the *chaityas* of Caves 9 and 10, with their magnificent *stupas* and rows of octagonal pillars. The 5th-century *vihara* style can be seen again in Cave 16, where a giant statue of the teaching Buddha dominates the 20m-long (22ft) hall and its murals of the 'Dying Princess' and Siddhartha (Buddha pre-enlightenment). Cave 17, slightly later and showing the transition to Mahayana Buddhism, contains some of Ajanta's liveliest murals, depicting *apsaras* and spirits floating across the sky, a royal procession, blissful lovers, animals and vegetation. Ajanta's most elaborate façade is at Cave 19, a Mahayana *chaitya* rich in paintings and sculptures surrounding a huge central *stupa*. The lofty window of Cave 26, flanked by high relief statues, fronts an enormous *chaitya*, remarkable for a 9m (30ft) 'sleeping Buddha'.

Ellora▶▶ (*Open Wed–Mon 9–5.30. Admission: expensive*). Equally inspiring are the 34 cave-shrines of Ellora, created between the 7th and 10th centuries AD to honour Buddhist, Hindu and Jain beliefs. They stud a granite escarpment about 30km (19 miles) from Aurangabad, on an old trading route and so, unlike the more remote Ajanta, were much used by travellers. The highlight here is the 8th-century Cave 16, the extraordinary Kailasnath temple, conceived as a temple mountain dedicated to Siva. Measuring 50m (164ft) in length and 30m (99ft) high, this unique creation incorporates a *gopuram*, pavilion, courtyard, assembly hall, sanctum and towers, all lavishly carved but blending with the natural shape of the rock. To the right of the entrance, a path leads up to the clifftop, offering a clear and remarkable view of the ambitious structure. Most interesting among the other Hindu temples (Nos 13–29) are Cave 14, with statues of Vishnu, Lakshmi and Siva; Cave 21, with sophisticated figures of Ganga and a dancing Siva; and Cave 29, with superb bas-reliefs depicting Siva legends.

Back to Buddha South of here are the 7th- to 8th-century Buddhist caves (Nos 1–12). Outstanding are Cave 5, with a superb trio of statues, and Cave 10, a *chaitya* with a spectacularly ribbed 'ship's hull' ceiling and a Buddha emerging from the shadows of the ambulatory around the stupa. Overlooking the main hall is an upper gallery decorated with amorous couples and offering close views of the lively friezes of dwarves and *naga* queens below. Cave 12 has rows of Buddhas in three storeys.

The Jain Caves (Nos 30–34) are some distance north of the Hindu Caves but should not be overlooked. Here, the finest is undoubtedly the early 9th-century Cave 32, dominated by a pot-bellied Mahavir. On the gallery above, there are rich wall carvings and traces of murals.

VISITING THE CAVES
The original way into the Ajanta caves was from the river-bed at the base of the cliffs, whence stairs lead up at intervals to the cave-temples above. This route can still be followed but the main entrance is up a long flight of stairs that reaches the level of the caves. Bring adequate water and a powerful torch so, although some caves are now lit with fibre optic lights, others remain unlit. Remember that in order to preserve the priceless murals, flash photography is forbidden. Some cave-guardians offer to turn a blind eye for a tip—ignore them.

179

Inside Cave 26 (left) and (inset) a mural depicting Buddha in Cave 1, Ajanta

MURAL TECHNIQUES
The rock was chiselled to roughen it, then a layer of clay mixed with cow dung and powdered rice husk was applied. This was left to dry before being given a coat of smooth white lime plaster. The surface was then smoothed with a trowel, ready for the artists, who sketched their pictures using cinnabar (a bright red mineral). The paint was made with pigments from the mineral-rich surroundings, and the brushes were generally of squirrels' hair. A last burnishing left a lustrous surface. Mistakes have been made in restoration, but now UNESCO and the Archaeological Survey of India appear to have devised a suitable modern technique.

▶▶ Bandhavgarh National Park   *173D4*

Open: Nov–Jun, daily dawn–noon, 3–dusk with seasonal variations. Admission: moderate.

This park offers the best chance in India of spotting a tiger, (there are round 50 plus 27 leopards), among massive rocky hills that rise abruptly from swamp and thick forest. The most striking outcrop is Bandhavgarh, crowned by a fort thought to be some 2,000 years old, according to ancient texts and Sanskrit inscriptions etched into the sandstone of surrounding cave-shrines. The dynasties that inhabited it included the Chandellas, creators of the fabulous temples of Khajuraho. The 16th century Rewa dynasty moved north, leaving the fort to be engulfed by vegetation.

A leopard at Bandhavgarh National Park

Splendid isolation Bandhavgarh's relative isolation makes access difficult, but trips can be arranged from Khajuraho, Varanasi or Jabalpur to the park headquarters at Tala, where accommodation is located. Even here, outside the park perimeter, it is common to see elephants and monkeys, and great gaur (Indian bison), sambar, barking deer and nilgai often graze in the grasslands at dusk. The elusive white tiger of Rewa was discovered here, but none have been seen in the park since one was captured by a maharaja in 1951. Birdwatchers may spot hornbills, drongos, flycatchers, parakeets and eagles among the 150-odd known species. Jeeps are the only way to get around and can be hired through a hotel or at the park headquarters. The luxury alternative is to ramble through the outer edge of the park on an elephant.

▶▶ Bijapur   *172B1*

Nudging the Maharashtra border from Karnataka, the small town of Bijapur has superlative 15th- to 17th-century Islamic architecture. Mosques, mausoleums, palaces and forts, built with wealth gained from conquering the Vijayanagar at Hampi, fill the skyline within a compact walled centre punctuated by five gates and 100 bastions. Muslim orthodoxy is the rule here, so behave respectfully.

Big dome The star of Bijapur is the **Gol Gumbaz**▶▶ (*Open daily 6–6. Admission: inexpensive, free on Fri*) containing the tomb of Mohammed Adil Shah under one of the world's largest domes. Left unfinished in 1660 when the Adil Shah dynasty was in serious decline, the squat stone structure lacks majesty, but the spacious 'whispering gallery' preserves startling acoustics, best experimented with early in the morning before the crowds arrive. Access is by stairs in a corner tower that gives sweeping views over the town. A gatehouse museum (*Open Tue–Sat 10–5*) displays some exceptional Chinese porcelain, Deccani miniatures and Bijapur carpets.

Facing Mecca Far more restrained is the **Jama Masjid**▶▶, one of the Deccan's most beautiful mosques. This dates

Gol Gumbaz, in Bijapur

from the mid-16th century, when Bijapur flowered under Ali Adil Shah; he was also responsible for the city walls and water-systems. The elegant, colonnaded prayer hall features a marble floor decorated with a grid representing a prayer space for each of the 2,000 or so worshippers. The mosque roof covers the entire courtyard and is crowned by a series of domes, the largest located over the central *mihrab* (prayer niche facing Mecca).

Other sights The modestly scaled but delightful **Mehtar Mahal and mosque▶** (*c*1620) has delicate minarets of carved stone. Also worth a look are the dilapidated Asar Mahal (1646) and the central citadel. The **Ibrahim Rauza▶▶** was designed by a Persian architect in the early 17th century as the tomb of Ibrahim Adil Shah and was possibly the inspiration for the Taj Mahal. Again, exquisite stonecarving skill is exploited to its utmost in the minarets, domes and screens that decorate the mausoleum and mosque opposite.

TOURIST OFFICE
KSTDC tourist office, Hotel Mayura Adil Shahi, Anandamahal Road, Annexe Bijapur (*Open* Mon–Sat 10.30–1.30, 2.15–5.30; tel: 08352 20934).

The best way to get around the compact centre of Bijapur is by bicycle, available for hire at several places near the bus-station or from the Mayura Adil Shahi hotel. Auto-rickshaws are also easily available.

For four centuries the state of Hyderabad was the hub of Muslim power in the Deccan. From the 18th century until Independence it was governed by a succession of fabulously wealthy rulers, named the Nizams of Hyderabad. The seventh and last in line was one of the world's richest men, but also one of its most miserly.

The interior of the lavish Italianate Falaknuma Palace, home of the Nizams of Hyderabad

FALAKNUMA PALACE
The last Nizam never lived in Hyderabad's magnificent Falaknuma Palace (1883) after his father met his death there. From then on it functioned as a guest-house for state visitors and royalty, from George V and Queen Mary to India's first President, but the days of dinners for 100 people, eaten off gold plates, were over. Its Italian marble, stained glass, chandeliers, interior fountains, murals, case-ment ceilings, gilded cornices and embossed camel-hide upholstery are all still pristine and it is being converted into a luxury hotel.

The last days of the British Raj also constituted the death throes of power for India's 565 princely rulers. Renowned for their exotic ways of life, their hunting, palaces, Rolls Royces, elephants and concubines, they had become an anachronism in a world reeling from the shock of World War II. Not all lived up to this image: some held sway over only a few cow pastures, others ruled efficiently in the interests of their subjects. Others still, notably the Nizam of Hyderabad and the Maharaja of Kashmir, headed states that easily rivalled European countries in size and popula-tion. They both enjoyed the privilege of the 21-gun salute (as did the rulers of Gwalior, Mysore and Baroda), an accolade directly related to the ruler's loyalty to, and funds expended for, the British.

Last call Mir Osman Ali Khan (1886–1967) was the seventh in line of a dynasty that emerged in 1724 during the chaotic period of Mughal decline. In 1800, after decades of divided loyalties, the second Nizam was finally persuaded to allow British forces a garrison in Secunderabad, so opening the gates to the influence of the British. In 1911, the young Osman came to the throne unexpectedly when his gregarious and alcoholic father toppled off a veranda of the fabled Falaknuma Palace, went into a coma and died. Raised in an atmosphere of palace intrigue and sycophancy, Osman paraded in magnificent costumes and jewellery, and used one of the world's largest diamonds as a paperweight. He rapidly entered the good books of the British by contributing US$100 million to their World War I coffers. He also appealed to India's Muslims to support the British rather than Ottoman Turkey, allied to Germany. As a result he was given the title 'His Exalted Highness', unique among India's princes.

Mr Avarice Osman's character became ever more volatile, partly due to an opium habit that he had adopted to calm his violent temper. 'His Exalted Highness' suffered from pyorrhoea, had decaying teeth and became increasingly oblivious to his scruffy appearance, wearing the same dirty fez for 35 years. Holed up in his palace, where garages were filled with unused cars and cellars were stuffed with bins of priceless emeralds, diamonds and rubies, the Nizam lived in a filthy bedroom where he ate off a tin plate, squatting on a mat. He was in constant dread of being poisoned, and obliged a food-taster to share his unvarying diet of cream, sweets, fruit, betel-nuts and nightly opium. He smoked cigarette butts left by his guests, and cut back the electric current in the palace to save on bills. Meanwhile, some 10 million dollars in cash were stuffed away in his dusty attics, and eventually chewed up by rats. His early prudence in financial matters had developed into an all-consuming obsession.

The end At Independence, in 1947, the last Nizam presided over India's most populous state, composed of 20 million Hindus and 3 million Muslims. Reluctant to read the writing on the wall, this frail, diminutive old man dreamed of an independent sovereign state and for a full two months resisted signing any agreement with the new Indian government. Finally, under great pressure, he capitulated, but filed a case with the UN Security Council against India for intervening in the internal affairs of Hyderabad. The Indian army was put into action, and from 1948 to 1956 the Nizam played the role of constitutional ruler, preserving his fortune and privy purse (see panel). In 1956, the state of Hyderabad ceased to exist and the city became capital of Andhra Pradesh. Until his death in 1967, Osman Ali Khan lived on in the crumbling King Kothi palace.

PRINCELY PRIVILEGES

When India became independant in 1947, its princes gave up power in return for privileges such as free medical treatment and exemption from paying water and electricity rates. In 1971 Indira Gandhi introduced a bill abolishing these privileges, but the Supreme Court declared it illegal. As a result, she was forced to call new elections. She was overwhelmingly returned to power, and the princes' last privileges were lost forever.

His Exalted Highness, the Nizam of Hyderabad

Mughal gateway in Hyderabad

BUYING TEXTILES
A good place to snap up superb textiles and saris, in particular beautiful Andhra *ikats*, is Kalanjali, a large air-conditioned emporium opposite the Public Gardens on Hill Fort Road.

▶▶ Hyderabad/Secunderabad   *172C1*

Burgeoning, buzzing and polluted, the capital of Andhra Pradesh is rich in Islamic monuments. As a bonus, it offers a delicious non-vegetarian cuisine that may come as a relief for some emerging from the vegetarian south. Known for its Bidri-ware (engraved or inlaid metalwork), pearls, diamonds and highly coloured glass bangles, Hyderabad is also developing high-tech industries to rival Bangalore. The population of 5 million, mainly Telugu-speaking, has a large proportion of Muslims, reflecting the city's importance from the 16th century onwards, when it replaced nearby Golconda as a seat of Muslim power.

Layout The old city lies south of the Musi river, spreading out in a grid pattern from the Charminar, the magnificent arch that has become a symbol of Hyderabad. Under Asaf Jahi in the 18th century, the increasingly wealthy town expanded north of the river, then in the early 1900s gained the administrative and residential settlement of Secunderabad that lies north-east of the immense Hussain Sagar lake. Today, wealthier residents prefer the airy hills scattered with stark boulders on the western side of the city towards Golconda Fort; this too is where the better hotels are located. The airport is at the northern end of the lake close to the railway stations.

Old city Hyderabad's Islamic heart beats in the narrow lanes of the Lad Bazar and the arcaded streets leading to the imposing **Charminar▶▶**. This square arch with a fourth-floor mosque, corner minarets and a small Hindu shrine below, was built in 1591, probably to celebrate the end of a plague epidemic. Immediately southwest looms the **Mecca Masjid▶▶**, where construction started in 1614 but was not completed until 80 years later, by Aurangzeb. Accommodating 10,000 worshippers, with huge arches and pillars made from single slabs of black granite, and bricks from Mecca embedded in its red-brick gateway, it is a potent religious and architectural symbol. An open-sided structure to the left contains the tombs of the Nizams of Hyderabad (see pages 182–183). The city's oldest mosque, the **Jama Masjid▶** (1597), lies northeast of the Charminar. Running west from the arch is the fabulous **Lad Bazar▶▶**, strongly reminiscent of an Arab *soukh*, with stalls full of glittering glass bangles, cut-glass bottles, perfumes, wedding outfits, water-pipes and other wonders. Alleyways around Mitti Ka Sher and Charkaman specialize in antique silver filigree, Bidri-ware and crystal, while Japanese cultured pearls, graded and finely strung in Hyderabad, are sold by dealers on Sadar Patel.

Museums The rambling **Salar Jung Museum▶▶** (*Open* Sat–Thu 10–5. *Admission: expensive*) stands north of this area on the riverbank and houses the extravagant collection of Salar Jung III (1889–1949), the Nizams' Prime Minister. Its 35,000 *objets d'art* range from the sublime to the ridiculous, and among the paintings, jewellery, textiles, swords, glass, South Indian bronzes, Italian marbles and Indian miniatures are some extraordinary items, including jade, ivory and Marie-Antoinette's dressing-table. Across the Afzal bridge are the broad avenues of the commercial district, with jewels of 1920s and 1930s architecture, including the State Library and the General Hospital. In the Public Gardens stands the **State Archaeological Museum▶** (*Open* Sat–Thu 10.30–5. *Admission: inexpensive*), converted from one of the Nizams' mansions and displaying some superb early bronzes, reproductions of the Ajanta frescoes and stone sculptures.

Golconda It is 11km (7 miles) west of Hyderabad at **Golconda Fort▶▶** (*Open* Tue–Sun 8–6.30. *Admission: expensive*) that the might of the city's founders resounds. The fort, which dates from the 13th century, was expanded under the Qutb Shahi kings (*c*1512–1687) until three tiers of walls stretched 7km (4 miles) around it. The city of Golconda inside was famed for its diamond trade, mosques, harems, royal palaces, dungeons, and the vault that contained the coveted Koh-i-noor diamond. Much is now ruined but the fort's scale, complexity and military might remain apparent. Immediately north lie lovely gardens containing the impressive tombs of the **Qutb Shahi▶▶** (*Open* Sat–Thu 10–4.30. *Admission: expensive*), with stuccoed arches and minarets.

TOURIST OFFICES
India Tourism, Sandozi Building, 2nd floor, 26 Himayat Nagar (*Open* Mon–Fri 6am–7pm; tel: 040 2763 8338).
AP Travel & Tourism Development, Tankbund Road, Hyderabad (*Open* Mon–Sat 10.30–5, closed 2nd Sat each month; tel: 040 2345 3036; email: aptdc@satyam.net.in; www.aptourism.com). Information on tours, and the sound and light show at Golconda Fort (in English daily Nov–Feb 6.30pm, Mar–Oct 7pm. *Admission: moderate*). Information counters at airport and railway.

185

Inscription on a cannon at Golconda Fort

The Centre

AROUND INDORE

Indore, at the heart of the Malwa plateau, was the seat of the Holkars and later became a major textile trading centre. Cricket heroes rather than kings are idolized now, and the town itself is smothered in a blanket of industrialization. Avoid it if you can, but it may be a necessary stopover on the way to Mandu or to Ujjain (see page 197). Indore is regularly thronged with pilgrims heading for the sacred shrines that surround it, at Ujjain, Maheshwar and the holy island of Omkareshwar. The last two are situated 70–90km (43–59 miles) south of Indore. An intriguing offbeat circuit can be made by car, combining these major temple sites with Mandu.

▶▶▶ **Kanha National Park**   *173D3*

Open: Nov–Jun, dawn–dusk. Visitors' centres daily 8–11am, 3–5pm. Admission: expensive.

This fabulous reserve is Rudyard Kipling country, encapsulated in his *Jungle Book*, written a century ago. Already protected in the 1930s, Kanha achieved national park status in 1955 and in 1974 became one of the first participants in Project Tiger (see page 100). Today, there are few tigers in this park of 2,000sq km (772sq miles), but it is densely inhabited by 22 other species of mammal. Palm squirrels, langurs, jackal, wild pigs, spotted and swamp deer (the latter unique to this park), sambar and black buck are all easily spotted. More elusive are the Indian hare, wild dog, barking deer, Indian bison, fox, sloth bear, striped hyena, jungle cat, panther, four-horned antelope and Indian porcupine. Over 200 bird species also inhabit the deciduous forest and savannah that clothe hills and meadows crossed by streams. These include bee-eaters, golden orioles, paradise flycatchers, egrets, grey hornbills, kingfishers, minas, parakeets and Indian rollers.

Practicalities Isolated Kanha is best reached from Jabalpur (a bumpy five-hour drive), which has train connections with Varanasi (Benares) and Bhopal. The nearest airport is at Nagpur, about 220km (136 miles) southwest. Park headquarters are at Kisli, with visitors' centres at Khatia (tel: 07649 277242) and Mukki, where there is also accommodation. All hotels organize jeeps with guides in conjunction with the Forest Department, as this is the only way to explore the park. Observation towers are judiciously placed along the main circuit. The only drawback is the number of visitors, particularly in the early months of the year. In winter, night temperatures descend to just over zero, so come prepared with warm clothing for dawn forays.

▶▶ **Mandu**   *172B3*

This deserted hill town 100km (62 miles) southwest of Indore once inspired the Mughal emperor Jehangir to write, 'I know of no place so pleasant in climate and so pretty in scenery as Mandu during the rains'. This by no means precludes a visit during the dry season, as it offers a refreshing escape from the plains, being 600m (1,968ft) up in the rugged Vindhya hills. The 45km (28 miles) of parapets and walls are entered by 12 gates (the Delhi Gate is the most impressive), and surround ruined palaces, pavilions, mosques, *tanks* and gardens. Lodging is limited but perfectly adequate, and bicycles are on hire to get you around the sights of the fort.

Crumbling glory As the fort capital of the Parmar rulers of Malwa it was called Mandapa-Durga ('hall of the goddess Durga', a name that became Man-du). Towards the end of the 13th century the town fell to the Muslims. A century later it was promoted from a mere pleasure resort to royal capital of the Sultans of Malwa. Renamed Shadiabad (the original 'city of joy'), it nurtured the arts and tolerated Hindu, Jain and Muslim beliefs. Mandu's heyday came in the late 15th century when Sultan Ghiyas-ud-din built the Jahaz Mahal for his harem of 15,000 women, creating a highly influential style of Islamic architecture. From then on Mandu shuttled between various rulers before being abandoned in the early 18th century, the time of the demise of the Mughals.

187

Jahaz Mahal at Mandu (above)
Roopmati Pavilion at Rewa Kund (below)

Sights Numerous and fascinating to explore, Mandu's monuments are dominated by the magnificent Jahaz Mahal, that is 120m (130yd) long, two-storey palace with balconies and open pavilions that rises between two lakes and resembles a floating ship. Close by are the sloping walls of the Hindola Mahal (Swing Palace), also built by Ghiyas-ud-din, who would enter astride an elephant up a long ramp. Towering over the village group on a high platform is the domed Jami Masjid, inspired by the great mosque of Damascus. Original tiles, Koranic inscriptions and *jali* screens remain intact. Hoshang Shah's spectacular Afghani marble tomb stands just behind this. Other, much earlier, sights can be found at the sacred Hindu site of Rewa Kund, where Baz Nahadur's palace and the lovely Roopmati Pavilion overlook an ancient reservoir.

TOURIST OFFICES
For Kanha, contact MPSTDC, Regional Office, Railway Station, Jabalpur (*Open* Mon–Fri 10–5; tel: 0761 2677690, fax: 0761 2677590; email: mptroijbp@sancharnet.in). Car hire, runs bus to Kanha Park daily—ring to check times and to book. Mandu can be reached by bus or taxi from Indore. MPSTDC Regional Office, Tourist Bungalow, behind Ravindra Natya Griha, Rabindranath Tagore Road, Indore (*Open* daily 10–5; tel: 0731 2528653). Organizes car trips to Mandu. Information in Mandu itself at MP Tourism's Tourist Cottages and Travellers' Lodge (tel: 07292 263235; email: tcmandav@sancharnet.in).

Mumbai Chhatrapati Shivaji, formerly known as Victoria Terminus, is an outstanding hybrid of Victorian Gothic and Indo-Saracenic style

▶▶▶ Mumbai (Bombay)

The capital of Maharashtra is India's brashest, most confident and most populous city, displaying all the contrasts spawned by rampant corruption, social chasms and political extremism. This cosmopolitan metropolis of 16 million people sprawls some 40km (25 miles) down a narrow peninsula and encompasses both the flashy villas of the nouveaux riches and the pathetic encampments of the indigent, strung out between the airport and the high-rises of Juhu and Bandra. In the historical heart of Mumbai are colonial buildings, exclusive clubs and the modern blocks of India's largest commercial centre. They line broad avenues choked with beaten-up double-decker buses beside the latest Japanese cars. A few streets away, prostitutes drape themselves in doorways, while in

Colaba, well-heeled visitors flock to the venerable Taj Mahal Hotel with its unbeatable view of Mumbai's emblem, the Gateway of India.

Waterfront magnificence—Gateway of India and the luxurious, red-tiled Taj Mahal Hotel

Slow start This cosmopolitan city started life as seven islands inhabited by Koli fishermen who worshipped the goddess Mumbadevi (hence 'Mumbai'). When the Portuguese assumed the reins in 1534 they changed the name to Bom Bahia (Beautiful Bay) but little else changed in this backwater. In 1661, Charles II of England received the islands as part of a royal dowry; unimpressed, he sold them for a pittance to the East India Company. Reclamation work commenced and within a short time Mumbai was offering a large protected harbour for trading ships ducking the monsoon. Commerce blossomed along with ship-building (a Parsi undertaking), and was boosted in 1853 by the opening of India's first railway line, which started in Mumbai. The subsequent opening of the Suez Canal in 1870 assured Mumbai's pivotal role in trade across the Arabian Sea.

Stars and strikes Traders, merchants and entrepreneurs flocked to the booming city, and in the 20th century it embraced the movie business, creating Bollywood and a star-struck following of millions. In the last few decades, Mumbai has repeatedly hit the headlines with frauds, gang wars, violent strikes and deadly sectarian violence, including bombings and massacres at various moments in the 1990s. The Shiv Sena, an extreme right-wing Maharashtran political movement emerged (see pages 174–175), and although its political power has since been reduced, it remains a strong social force.

Strung out Love it or hate it, Mumbai does not care. India's largest economic power, materialist and westernized, is not particularly concerned with nurturing its

END OF AN ERA
On 28 February 1948, Bombay witnessed the departure of the last British troops, who ceremonially left the newly independent subcontinent through the Gateway of India. Saluted by a guard of honour of Sikhs and Gurkhas to the tune of an Indian Navy band, the soldiers of the Somerset Light Infantry slow-marched through the arch to the barges moored below. Centuries of collaboration, confrontation, tragedy and, finally, negotiation were wrapped up in that emotion-charged moment. And then, unexpectedly, from the huge crowd amassed along the waterfront emerged the strains of *Auld Lang Syne*.

The Centre

190

TOURIST OFFICES
India Tourism, 123 M
Karve Road, opposite
Churchgate Station
(*Open* Mon–Fri 8.30–6,
Sat and holidays 8.30–2;
tel: 022 2207 4333, fax:
022 22014496, email:
gitobest@bom5.
vsnl.net.in). Will arrange
city tours and trips. Also
counters at the airports
(international open 24
hours, domestic manned
7am–last flight),
MTDC, Opposite L.I.C.
Building, Madame Cama
Road, near Nariman Point
(*Open* daily 9–7; tel: 022
2202 6713, fax: 2285
2812,www.
maharashtratourism.gov.
in). Counters at airports
and railways. Tourist
police have now been
introduced in Mumbai to
relieve the pressure on
visitors.

*Red double-decker buses
complement the British
building styles that still
dominate the city*

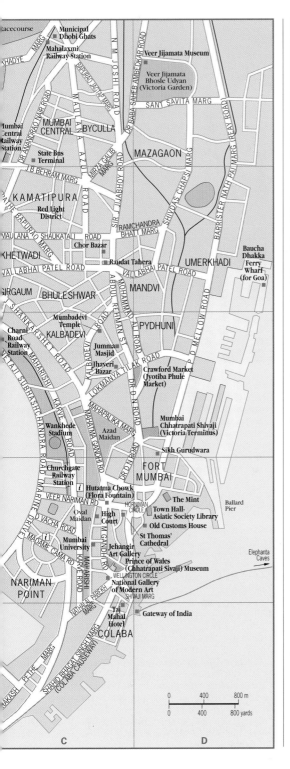

Statue of King George V outside the Prince of Wales Museum (Chhatrapati Sivaji)

THUS SPAKE ZARATHUSTRA

Zoroastrians, or Parsis, originated in Persia as followers of the prophet Zoroaster (Zarathustra, c800BC), who taught of the opposing forces of good and evil and an afterlife in heaven or hell. After the Islamic conquest of Persia in the 10th century, many Parsis went to Gujarat, from where they later moved to Mumbai for its entrepreneurial potential. Parsis contributed greatly to the city's economic momentum and education but their numbers have fallen, to less than 60,000 today. Foremost among them is the Tata family (with interests in watches, hotels, trucks, pharmaceuticals, and more). Their ancestors Sir Ratan Tata and Sir Dorab Tata donated valuable art collections to the Prince of Wales Museum.

An artisan at Chor Bazar, the city's principal antiques and junk market

visitors (helpful tourist offices apart), and historical sights are hardly numerous. The main concentrations of hotels, restaurants and tourist-shops are in the pretty, tree-lined streets of Colaba and along Marine Drive, respectively the east and west of the southern peninsula. Immediately to the north, west of a string of *maidans*, are Fort Mumbai's neo-Gothic and Byzantine buildings. These include Churchgate Station, Victoria Terminus (now renamed Mumbai Chhatrapati Shivaji) and Crawford Market, (now Jyotiba Phule Market), all Victorian relics. North of Marine Drive and Chowpatty Beach is the exclusive Malabar Hill, beyond which lie Haji Ali's offshore tomb and, east of the race course, the municipal *dhobi ghats* (see panel, page 194) the northernmost point of interest before the suburban sprawl.

▶▶ Fort Mumbai   *191D2*

The historical heart of Mumbai has a wealth of idiosyncratic Indo-Saracenic and neo-Gothic monuments, though few are open to the public. Notable façades are the High Court (1879), the Secretariat (1874) and Mumbai University (1857), the last partly financed by Parsi and Jewish businessmen. Horniman Circle is the place for neoclassical architecture, exemplified in the Doric Town Hall (1823) which houses the Asiatic Society Library, the Old Customs House (incorporating a Portuguese section) and the Mint (1829). At Fort Mumbai's southeastern point looms the **Gateway of India▶**, a massive stone arch built in 1924 to commemorate a visit by George V and Queen Mary. It is now used principally as the embarkation-point for ferries to Elephanta, and well frequented by hustlers.

▶ Malabar Hill   190A3

Rising on a headland overlooking the popular evening haunt of Chowpatty Beach, this exclusive residential area is best visited by taxi. At the less salubrious southern tip is an ancient Hindu site marked by the Walkeshwar Temple, rebuilt in 1715, with the **Banganga tank▶** below. Further up the promontory is the **Jain temple▶**, between film stars' mansions and businessmen's apartment blocks. Although relatively new, it gives a good idea of the strict rituals and prosperity of its masked worshippers, seen crossing marble floors and passing through silver-plated doors to the central sanctum to honour Adinath, the first teacher-saint. Further north and higher up the hill are the Hanging Gardens, a park built over a reservoir. Opposite this is the Kamala Nehru Children's Park, interesting only for fine views over the city.

Bone-cleaners Most visitors to the hill come to stare at the Towers of Silence—though hidden inside a walled enclosure they are hardly a spectacle. This is where the Parsis dispose of their dead by leaving the corpses to vultures; men lie atop the black tower, women on the yellow tower and children on the green tower. Only pall-bearers are allowed inside, though the odd toe has apparently found its way onto the balconies of nearby flats.

▶▶ Mani Bhavan (Gandhi Museum)   190B4

19 Laburum Road, Gamdevi
Open: daily 10–6. Admission: inexpensive

It may not be the first Gandhi Museum on your itinerary, but this one has a special atmosphere that justifies a visit. It lies in an attractive residential area northeast of Malabar Hill and is where Gandhi lived sporadically between 1917 and 1934. The house has barely changed since then, and its simple furniture makes a peaceful setting for a comprehensive display of photographs, letters, the Mahatma's spinning-wheel and an antiquated phone. An extensive library is used by researchers.

▶▶ National Gallery of Modern Art   191C2

SP Mukharji Chowk (Wellington Circle),
opposite Prince of Wales
Open: Tue–Sat 11–6, Sun 11–4. Admission: inexpensive

Airy museum offering an overview of Indian post-Independence art, with emphasis on the Progressive Artists Group that included Husain, Souza, Raza and Ara. The upper floors complete the display with self-assured images from the 1990s, and an auditorium shows related films. There are more contemporary art exhibitions, of varying quality, at the Jehangir Art Gallery (*Open* daily 9–7. *Admission: free*), next to the Prince of Wales Museum.

▶▶▶ Prince of Wales Museum (Chhatrapati Sivaji)   191C2

159–61 Mahatma Gandhi Road, Fort
Open: Tue–Sun 10.15–5.30. Admission: expensive

This impressive, domed structure set in lovely gardens is the highlight of Mumbai's historic and cultural sights. Inaugurated in 1923, it houses a vast collection acquired through public and private donations. Indus Valley relics (2500BC) and Assyrian palace reliefs (9–8th century BC) are

193

The dhobi-wallahs
provide a manual laundry
service for the city

the earliest exhibits, followed by Gandhara, Gupta and Maharashtran sculptures. On the first floor over 200 superb miniatures are displayed next to a decorative arts section, and other halls cover Nepal and Tibet. Top floor exhibits include jade, ivory, European glass and china.

Excursion

Elephanta▶▶▶ (*Boats with guide* half-hourly 9–2, last return 6pm. Faster catamarans: depart at 10.30, return at 2. Private boats only during monsoon. *Boat and admission: expensive*). The magnificent cave-temple of Elephanta lies less than an hour from the Gateway of India by 'luxury' boat. It offers a foretaste of Ajanta and Ellora (see pages 178–179) plus a unique image of Siva in his triple form. The island, originally Gharapuri, was named Elephanta by the Portuguese after the huge elephant sculpture that now stands in the Victoria Garden. There are several rock-cut shrines here but only the most elaborate is open. This dates from the early 8th century and is ascribed to the Rashtrakutas, who artfully combined late Gupta and Chalukyan styles. It lies at the top of a long, steep climb from the jetty that entails dodging vendors before you arrive at your goal. These, and the island girls who for a small fee will pose for photographs with copper pitchers, tend to dissipate one's sense of the divine. Tourist police presence should now improve matters.

Multi-faceted Siva Just inside the main entrance porch are two images of Siva; on the left he appears as Yogishwara (Great Ascetic) and on the right as Nataraj (Lord of the Dance). Beyond stretches the gloomy, pillared interior, with reliefs of other incarnations of Siva along the back walls. Side courtyards contain subsidiary shrines. The focal point is the platform of the *lingam* shrine, round which devotees walk seven times clockwise. Remove shoes before entering this shrine. At the centre of the back wall is Elephanta's most remarkable sight, the triple-headed Siva Mahesamurti. This superb 6m-high (20ft) relief depicts the god as destroyer (left), protector (centre) and creator (right). To the left of this masterful depiction of moods is Ardhanarishvara (Siva in languid style as the embodiment of male and female). To the right is Gangadhara (the descent of the Ganga (Ganges) to earth through Siva).

DHOBIS AND TIFFIN-WALLAHS
In the warren of municipal dhobi ghats next to Mahalakshmi station, some 4,000 *dhobi wallahs* (washermen) work in shifts starting at 4am, thwacking and pounding the city's dirty laundry in low walled areas connected by water-channels. Behind, steam billows from sheds containing huge boiling vats. Another Mumbai speciality are the 3,500 or so *tiffin-wallahs* who daily handle 100,000 lunch-boxes collected from dutiful suburban wives, transported by train, then whisked from the central stations to the desks of the individual office-workers. An organizational *tour de force*.

Practical details

Transport If arriving at Mumbai's domestic or international airport, use the prepaid taxi service to go downtown. For travellers making a connection, airport hotels are plentiful and span the full price range. There are regular shuttles between the two airports.

In the city, black and yellow cabs are easy to find; drivers are compelled by law to use meters but may need to be reminded of this. Auto-rickshaws function only in the suburbs. Horsedrawn carriages operate around the Taj Mahal Hotel and along Marine Drive; again, bargain hard.

Mumbai also has efficient though overloaded suburban train services from Mumbai Chhatrapati Shivaji/CST (formerly Victoria Terminus/VT), Mumbai Central and Churchgate Station. Go to the latter for trains to the Buddhist Kanheri Caves, which are about 50 minutes away. Long-distance train journeys can be booked at the Foreigners' Counter at CST (*Open* 8.30–4); go early.

Shopping Food and traditional goods are sold at the riveting Jyotiba Phule (Crawford) Market, just north of the railway station, Mumbai Chhatrapati Shivaji. Opposite this Victorian complex, *kurtas* (traditional loose tunics), saris, Kashmir shawls and embroidered textiles fill the labyrinthine network of stalls in Mangaldas Lane. Here too is the Jhaveri Bazar, full of dazzling new gold and diamond jewellery, and much frequented by young brides-to-be. Antiques, fakes and dusty junk are the speciality of the legendary Chor Bazar in Maulana Shaukat Ali Road. The best day to go shopping is Friday, when the streets fill with 'antique' vendors, though shops are open daily except Sunday.

The city's other shopping hubs are the Oberoi shopping arcade and the Taj Mahal Hotel, where prices are more obviously geared to plump western purses. The widest selection of regional handicrafts is to be found at the Central Cottages Industries Emporium, 34 Shivaji Marg, which stocks furniture, textiles, miniatures and many other products in between. The Taj itself has the excellent Nalanda Bookshop, with a vast selection of art books and fiction.

The city's tiffin-wallahs take home-cooked lunches to office-workers

OSHO AND RAJNEESH

The main attraction for young westerners in Pune is Osho Commune International. It was founded in 1974 by the now legendary Bhagwan Rajneesh, known for his predilection for Rolls Royces. Rajneesh was at one point accused of crimes that included tax evasion, drug abuse and fraud, all apparently committed while he was setting up an eccentric utopian project in Oregon, USA. His teaching combined *Sufism*, Buddhism, meditation techniques and yoga with more west-inspired sexual liberation and computer technology. Rajneesh's spirit lives on, and Pune's luxury lair continues to attract followers—at a price and on production of an HIV-negative certificate.

TOURIST OFFICE

MTDC (Central Office Building, I-Block, Pune, tel: 020 2612 6867/ 8169; fax: 020 2611 9434). Counter at railway station and airport.

Parvati Hindu Temple at Pune, Maharashtra

▶ Pune
172A2

Pune was for a long time the heart of Maharashtra and this history, together with its altitude and closeness to Mumbai (Bombay) made it a favourite hill-station in colonial days. Industrialization has taken its toll but there are enough sights to justify a short visit. Foremost is the **Raja Dinkar Kelkar Museum**▶▶ (*Open* daily 8.30–6. *Admission: moderate*), a mansion housing an unusual, idiosyncratic collection of functional objects amassed over several decades by its late founder, who was also a poet. Carved wooden doors, inkpots, nutcrackers, textiles, toys and brass lamps are displayed, and there is a section on the role of Indian women. The Gandhi National Memorial, in what was the **Aga Khan Palace**▶ (*Open* daily 9–12.30, 1.30–5.30. *Admission: inexpensive*) was once the residence of the Muslim Bohra leader and was subsequently used by the British as a prison for dissidents. These included Gandhi and his wife Kasturba, who died here. Her memorial stands in the garden, and a photo-exhibition is devoted to him. His Hindu assassin came from Pune.

It is well worth touring the **Osho Commune International**▶▶ (Tours start at 10.30 and 2.30. *Admission: moderate*; tel: 020 5601 9999, fax: 020 6501 9990, www.osho.com, email: commune@osho.net). This New Age community offers endless esoteric courses and a vast residential complex with facilities worthy of a luxury hotel.

▶▶▶ Sanchi
172C4

One of India's most significant Buddhist sites lies 47km (30 miles) northeast of Bhopal. It encompasses *stupas*, monasteries, temples and pillars dating from the 3rd century BC to the 11th century AD. Like many of Madhya Pradesh's spiritual centres, it is well off the main tourist circuit. A museum (*Open* Sat–Thu 10–5. *Admission: expensive*) at the entrance displays exceptional sculptures and fragments, and sells useful guidebooks. Allow a half-day to explore this superb World Heritage site.

Heavenly structures Dominating the main walled precinct is the 40m (131ft) diameter Great Stupa. It was built by Ashoka, as was the nearby pillar inscribed with his edict

Eastern gateway of the Great Stupa at Sanchi

warning against a schism among Buddhists. Additions to the *stupa* were made by subsequent rulers, notably the Andhras (1st century BC); these include the outstanding and gloriously carved sandstone *toranas* at the four cardinal points. Their magnificent carvings (some now in foreign museums) illustrate the lives of Buddha and inspired many subsequent Indian art forms. Devotees would enter at the eastern *torana* and walk clockwise, following the passage of the sun. Crowning the *stupa* itself is the three-tiered umbrella (*chattra*), the sacred tree to heaven above the holy reliquary buried in the mound.

▶ Ujjain   *172B3*

Ujjain, one of India's most sacred cities, lies 55km (34 miles) north of Indore. Its origins go back to the ancient Sanskrit texts of the *Upanishads* (the philosophical basis of Hinduism) and the Puranas and attracts thousands of pilgrims. They come to bathe in the sacred River Shipra or perform *puja*, and numbers reach around 15 million during the 12-yearly Kumbh Mela. Sadly the **Mahakaleshwara temple▶** is a modern (though traditionally designed) replacement of the original, one of India's 12 *jyotirlingas*, but its extensive and colourfully populated complex of shrines, courtyards and *tanks* compensates for this.

Other attractions include the **Gopal Mandir▶**, a 19th-century temple devoted to Ganesa and the still-functioning 18th-century observatory, the Vedha Shala. On the outskirts is the Kaliadeh Palace (1458), superbly located on a river island but closed to the public. The **Bhartrihari Caves▶▶** are favoured by *sadhus* and a sect of yogis who honour the 5th-century scholar-poet, Bhartrihari.

STUPA SYMBOLISM
Stupas are dome-shaped Buddhist monuments, said to take their shape from an upturned begging-bowl used by the Buddha to symbolize the sacred mountain. Some 84,000 were allegedly erected by Emperor Ashoka to spread *dharma* throughout his empire. Sanchi's Great Stupa, when doubled in size by the Andhras in the 2nd century, became India's largest Buddhist monument. These early stone *stupas* were burial mounds and contained a reliquary. At Sanchi, Stupa 3 has revealed caskets containing the bones of some of Buddha's disciples. The three tiers of the *chattra* represent the Buddha himself, the Law and the community of monks.

Entire families encamped in lean-tos beside Mumbai's highways, legless beggars, sleeping bodies on streets, child labour: Poverty is the unavoidable face of India. Despite visible progress in recent years, India remains handicapped by a web of socio-religious conflicts and a population that is multiplying fast.

Shanty towns are a feature of every Indian city

TROUBLE FOR THE COUNTRY

'Our newspapers, for instance, are very much class-oriented. When we say we want to remove poverty it is not simply because poverty is bad—it is bad, evil and ugly and a very big human problem— but also because it will create trouble for the country: if poverty and richness co-exist there will be social tension. Either you kill off the poor people, or you learn to live together, and you can only learn to live together if the poor feel there is some amount of sharing...Everyone is conscious of his rights, whether he is brown-skinned, black-skinned, a woman, a youth or a poor person.'
Indira Gandhi, *My Truth*, 1981

'Poverty and uttermost misery have long been the inseparable companions of our people', wrote Jawaharlal Nehru, who felt much of the blame could be laid on the colonizing British. By forcing India to import British-made products such as textiles, and keeping monopolies on necessities such as salt, the British Raj had prevented the development of local industries. In the post-Independence years, Nehruvian socialism built up domestic industry and technology through protectionism and five-year plans. The aim was to eradicate illiteracy, disease and poverty. Today it is estimated that more than 70 per cent of the workforce is illiterate or little educated and 60 per cent are self employed as anything from a shoe-shiner to a farmer, neither of whom receive any benefits and often live in inhuman conditions.

Manipulation The reasons for this are many and complex. Corruption is high on the list, as are enduring caste divisions. India is one of the ten fastest-growing economies in the world, yet members of low castes still toil their lives away in bondage to a landowner. Add to these factors a deep antipathy between Hindus and Muslims, and the incendiary nature of the situation is apparent. In 1992–93, some 1,400 Mumbai citizens died as a result of bitter clashes following the destruction of the Ayodhya mosque by Hindu extremists. Both Muslims and Hindus were involved, but the victims were all from the lower levels of society, in a city that soon after registered the world's highest real-estate prices. Such paradoxes lead to movements spearheaded by politicians who, whatever their beliefs, are often sucked into the vortex of corruption.

Caste system Gandhi and the Indian constitution demanded that caste discrimination be outlawed. The untouchables were renamed *harijans* ('children of God'), and quotas were set to aid their integration into society. The constitution was drafted by India's first Minister of Law, Dr Ambedkhar, a great supporter of the *harijan* cause who later took the radical step of encouraging them to abandon the caste-ridden system of Hinduism in favour of Buddhism. He died in 1956, before this policy could be developed, but is still a figurehead.

Today the *harijans*, who prefer the label of *dalit* ('oppressed'), are a fast-growing force. The government, previously dominated by Brahmins (the educated, priestly caste) has, since 1995, seen a huge influx of *dalits*, and in 1996 only one cabinet member was a Brahmin. This has led to a backlash as Brahmins demand their own quotas. In Bihar, India's poorest and most lawless state, marauding caste armies wage war against Brahmins. They were encouraged by their Chief Minister, Laloo Prasad Yasav, until his imprisonment for corruption in 1997. In true nepotistic style, he was replaced by his wife, while he enjoys heroic status. In neighbouring Uttar Pradesh, the *dalit* Chief Minister Mayawati is breaking all records in nouveau-riche-style excess.

Moving forwards Famine is now relegated to the past, thanks to the Green Revolution instigated in the mid-1960s by Prime Minister Indira Gandhi. This policy introduced new high-yield grain and expanded irrigation projects. Now farmers feed the nation and also export their produce. The wealth of India's new middle class (estimated at around 350 million) does seem to be trickling down. Plump women in saris and trainers jog along Marine Drive or visit diet clinics while others live 10 to a room in tenements. It seems that extreme poverty is retreating, but rising prosperity is offset by a growing population. While the percentage of the population suffering from poverty decreases, the number of individuals affected remains almost the same.

THE DREGS
'In the villages, the untouchables were virtually helpless; almost none of them owned that eventual guarantor of dignity and status, land. Few worked it as tenants, and of those tenants fewer still would be able to make use of the paper guarantees of the forthcoming land reforms. In the cities too they were the dregs of society. Even Gandhi, for all his reforming concern, for all his hatred of the concept that any human being was intrinsically so loathsome and polluting as to be untouchable, had believed that people should continue in their hereditarily ordained professions: a cobbler should remain a cobbler, a sweeper a sweeper.'
Vikram Seth, *A Suitable Boy*, 1993 (referring here to the early 1950s).

▶▶▶ REGION HIGHLIGHTS

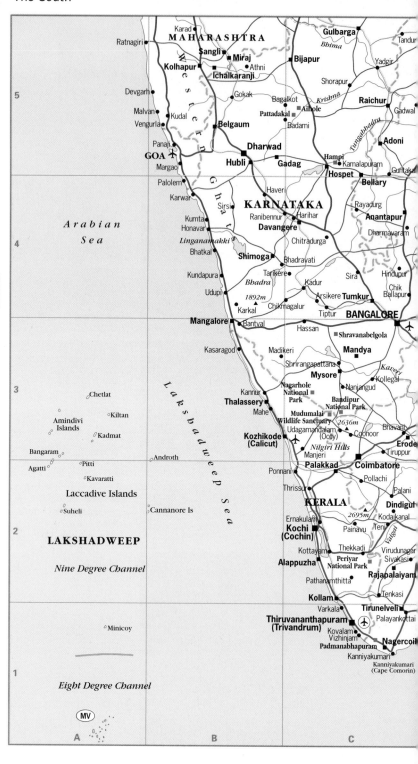

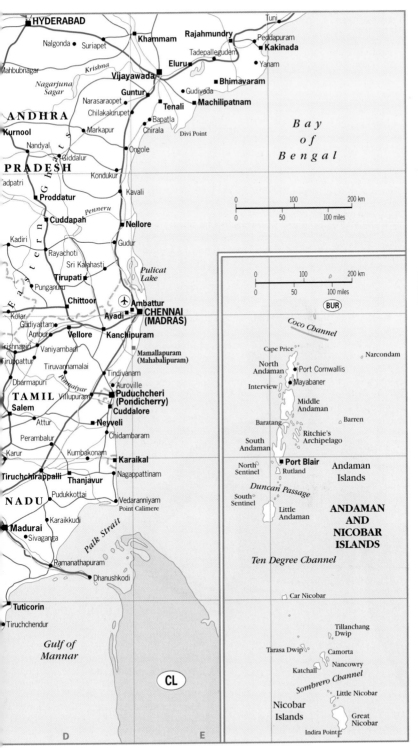

HYDERABAD

Nalgonda • Suriapet

Khammam

Rajahmundry

Tuni

Peddapuram

Kakinada

Mahbubnagar

Krishna

Tadepallegudem

Yanam

Eluru

Vijayawada

Bhimavaram

Nagarjuna
Sagar

Guntur

Gudivada

Narasaraopet

Tenali

Machilipatnam

ANDHRA

Chilakalurupet

Bapatla

Kurnool

Markapur

Chirala

Divi Point

Nandyal

Ongole

Bay
of
Bengal

Biddalur

PRADESH

Kondukur

adpatri

Proddatur

Penneru

Kavali

0   100   200 km

0   50   100 miles

Cuddapah

Nellore

Kadiri

Gudur

Rayachoti

Sri Kalahasti

Tirupati

Pulicat
Lake

Punganuru

Chittoor

0   100   200 km

0   50   100 miles

BUR

Kolar

Ambattur

Gudiyattam

Avadi

CHENNAI
(MADRAS)

Coco Channel

Ambur

Vellore

Kanchipuram

Cape Price

Narcondam

Krishnagiri

Vaniyambadi

North
Andaman

Port Cornwallis

Tiruppattur

Tiruvannamalai

Mamallapuram
(Mahabalipuram)

Mayabaner

Dharmapuri

Tindivanam

Interview

Ponnaiyar

Auroville

Middle
Andaman

TAMIL

Villupuram

Puduchcheri
(Pondicherry)

Barren

Salem

Cuddalore

Baratang

Attur

Neyveli

Ritchie's
Archipelago

Perambalur

Chidambaram

South
Andaman

Karur

Kumbakonam

North
Sentinel

Port Blair

Andaman
Islands

Karaikal

Rutland

Tiruchchirappalli

Thanjavur

Nagappattinam

Duncan Passage

NADU

Pudukkottai

South
Sentinel

Vedaranniyam
Point Calimere

Little
Andaman

ANDAMAN
AND
NICOBAR
ISLANDS

Madurai

Karaikkudi

Sivaganga

Palk Strait

Ten Degree Channel

Ramanathapuram

Dhanushkodi

Car Nicobar

Tuticorin

Tiruchchendur

Tillanchang
Dwip

Gulf of
Mannar

Tarasa Dwip

Camorta

Katchall

Nancowry

CL

Sombrero Channel

Little Nicobar

Nicobar
Islands

Great
Nicobar

Indira Point

D   E   F

The South

ESCAPING THE MONSOON

When the long-awaited monsoon finally breaks over India in early June, it is Thiruvananthapuram that sees it first. The downpours slowly move north from Kerala to reach Rajasthan in July, by which time rainfall has greatly diminished. Meanwhile, to the east, a separate branch sets in from the Bay of Bengal, sweeping across Calcutta and the Gangetic plain to Delhi. Tamil Nadu is different. Unlike the rest of India, this southeastern state receives its highest rainfall in October–December, during a tempestuous season of often destructive cyclones.

SOUTH As it narrows to its final point at Cape Comorin (Kanniyakumari), southern India traverses an incredible diversity of landscapes, cultures and architectural styles. This is India's gentle half, where hours can be spent in temples watching fervent devotees or flower-sellers stringing garlands. Or you can pass the time stretched out on glistening white sands, meandering in a boat through the Keralan backwaters, walking in the refreshing Nilgiri Hills or riding astride an elephant in a wildlife sanctuary. Women in bright saris with jasmine in their hair and men in white dhotis invariably bear the sign of the gods in ash or yellow sandal-paste on their foreheads, a sign of their strong Hindu beliefs. The bewitching and intriguing people of the south speak Tamil, Malayalam, Kannada or Konkani. They are generally open in spirit, making most interactions a pleasure illuminated by smiles.

RURAL SOCIETY This section covers the states of Tamil Nadu, Karnataka, smaller Kerala and tiny Goa. There are few large towns, Chennai (Madras) and booming Bangalore being the exceptions. Kochi (Cochin), Mysore, Madurai and Thiruvananthapuram (Trivandrum) remain small-scale, rewarding stopovers between the rural wilds. Unlike the north, this region was hardly touched by Muslim invaders until the 16th century, and preserves a wealth of Hindu temples and traditions. The dark-skinned Dravidians of Tamil Nadu are descended from India's original inhabitants and perpetuate 3,000-year-old beliefs. The Keralans claim India's highest literacy rate and these standards of education encourage a sense of professionalism that permeates society. Karnataka has a fascinating mixture of hill-tribes and stretches of unspoilt coast that continue into Goa. In the former Portuguese colony of Goa Catholicism comes into conflict with partying Western youth and haphazard tourist developments.

A temple guard at Padmanabha Swami temple in Thiruvanantha-puram

AGES PAST The south is rich in the relics of a string of powerful Hindu dynasties whose influence spread throughout Southeast Asia: the Pallavas (at Mamallapuram and Kanchipuram), Chalukyas (Badami), Cholas (Thanjavur), Nayaks (Madurai), Hoysalas (around Mysore) and Vijayanagar (at the sublime Hampi). Karnataka has a circuit of Jain sites, including the unforgettable high point of the shrines and towering statue at Shravana Belgola. The labyrinthine recesses of the major and still-functioning temples at Madurai, Thanjavur and Tiruchchirappalli provide mesmerizing sights, even though their inner sanctums are inaccessible to non-Hindus.

A devout attitude extends to food and drink as the south is predominantly vegetarian and *thalis* are the rule. Alcohol is not easily available in religious towns, although tea and excellent locally grown coffee are accepted stimulants.

COLONIAL IMPRINTS The Malabar Coast (from Goa to Kochi) was the stepping-stone into India. Spices, ivory and silk drew traders from the 16th century onwards, and major ports arose such as Portuguese Goa and Kochi (later Dutch), British Chennai (Madras) and French Pondicherry. Catholic and Protestant missionaries arrived but did not introduce Christianity—Syrian-Christian communities had been here from the 5th century, and the Apostle Thomas is reputed to have made converts and been martyred here. The British developed Chennai, and hill-stations such as Udagamandalam (Ooty) and Kodaikanal.

ON THE WILD SIDE There are several national parks and sanctuaries in the Western Ghats, with tigers at Bandipur and Periyar. These reserves harbour elephants, sambar, sloth bears and langurs, also found at Nagarhole, Mudumalai and in the tropical jungles of the Silent Valley. The reserves are easily accessible from the coast and are generally well run with good accommodation and guide services. Their popularity mounts in the dry season, so advance booking is advisable. Then there are the highly developed resorts at Goa, less so at Kovalam and beach-side pilgrimage sites such as Varkala and Mamallapuram (Mahabalipuram), where sybaritic pursuits combine with a backdrop of temples and swaying coconut-palms.

Temple guardian on the Brihadeshwara temple at Thanjavur (left) Maharaja's Palace, Mysore (above)

PECULIARLY INDIAN
'The chain of the Ghats... divides the west from the plains; a dark violet colour, it stands out with unbelievable clarity against the red strip of sunset that still lingers on the horizon; its granite peaks have shapes that are peculiarly Indian and exist nowhere else, simulating towers, pyramids, domes of pagodas. And the spindly palm-trees which are, besides a few cruel-looking aloes, the only plants here, rise from the ground in hard lines, silhouetted against what is left of the light, scratching the pale gold of the sky with their dark sticks.'
Pierre Loti, *India (Without the English)*, 1903.

Carved stone figure at Malegitti Sivalaya temple

CHALUKYAN TEMPLES
Although Vishnuites, the Chalukyans (see page 38) encouraged Jain and Siva worship and supported the artisans who laboured over the centres of worship. Under them, a wealth of architectural experiments took temple-building from the simplicity of Buddhist rock-cut *chaityas* and *viharas* to a more sophisticated style. This became the prototype of southern temple structures under the Pallavas.

▶▶ **Badami**   *202C5*

In the fertile heart of the Deccan, over 150 temples were erected by the Chalukyan dynasty in the 5th–8th centuries. Their most dramatic setting is at Badami, where steep red sandstone cliffs are studded with cave-temples and freestanding structures. The main accommodation is here, making it an ideal base for exploring the environs. For the moment it remains low-key and well off the main tourist circuit, a peaceful stopover between Hampi and Bijapur, or an excursion from Goa.

To the lake This small town curls around a lake that is said to have healing properties and has a dramatic backdrop of striking rock formations. From the utilitarian main road, with bank, post office, bus station, hotels, restaurants and funkily decorated *tongas* (pony-carts), narrow lanes lead through a maze of whitewashed houses with ornately carved doors, packed between Hindu temples, mosques and Chalukyan ruins. At the back of the village is the **Medieval Sculpture Gallery**▶ (*Open* Sat–Thu 10–5. *Admission: free*), which houses items recovered from

Aihole, Pattadakal, and Badami, including exhibits connected with an ancient fertility cult. Following the path eastwards round the lake, you pass the **Nagamma shrine▶**, devoted to the serpent goddess, before reaching the two beautiful **Bhuthanatha temples▶▶**, where Siva is worshipped as the God of Souls. The temples become magical towards sunset when watery reflections invade the sanctuary.

Woman with laundry at Badami

Rock sights Far above loom the ruins of the fort built by the later Vijayanagar empire. This can be reached through a gateway next to the museum. From here a steep climb through dramatic rock fissures eventually reaches the clifftop 'gun point', with fabulous views. At the far western end is the 7th-century **Malegitti Sivalaya temple▶▶**, magnificently carved with figures of Siva and Vishnu. A long but scenic walk overlooking the lake or a *tonga* ride along the main road brings you to the South Fort. Immediately below are Badami's **cave temples▶▶▶**, the oldest of which date from the 6th century. Cave 3 is outstanding, with carved statues of Siva, Hanuman and Vishnu reaching 5m (16ft) in height, and fragmented frescoes. Cave 4, Badami's only Jain temple, houses several statues of Mahavir, and Cave 1 has a statue of Siva as the 18-armed Natarja. Sweeping views over the lake and town are usually enlivened by monkeys.

Excursions

At least half a day should be spent exploring the idyllic rural surroundings of Badami for other Chalukyan experiments in temple-building. **Aihole▶▶▶**, about 40km (24 miles) away, was the first Chalukyan capital and has some 125 scattered structures. The exceptional Durga Temple (named after the nearby fort wall, not the goddess) lies within a landscaped area (*Open* dawn–dusk. *Admission: inexpensive*) at the centre of the village. Its unusual semi-circular apse and colonnaded ambulatory have superb sculptures dating from the late 7th century. Older still is the Lad Khan Temple (named after a Muslim prince who lived here), with a *shikhara*, a common feature of later Hindu temples. Here too is a small archaeological museum (*Open* Sat–Thu 10–5. *Admission: free*). Aihole's oldest structure is thought to be the severe Meguti Temple (AD634), a Jain temple on a hilltop above a simple Buddhist temple. Both temples afford excellent views of the surroundings.

World Heritage Site Halfway between Badami and Aihole is **Pattadakal▶▶▶**, the Chalukyan capital during the 7th–8th centuries and now a World Heritage Site. Enclosed in the archaeological park (*Open* dawn–dusk. *Admission: free*) is a succession of intricately carved sandstone temples; some have gently curved towers crowned by lotuses and all are inhabited by agile monkeys. The Virupaksha Temple (AD740) is exceptional, with its lively carvings and beautiful green stone *nandi*.

Closest to Badami is **Mahakut▶▶**, a temple compound built around a *tank* and dotted with shrines and statues, all shaded by huge banyans. The whitewashed 7th-century Mahakuteswara temple dominates, and the activities of swimmers and devotees create a unique atmosphere.

207

BANGALORE TOURIST OFFICES

India Tourism, KFC Building, 48 Church Street (Open Mon–Fri 10–6, Sat 9–1; tel: 080 2558 3030, fax: 080 2558 5417, email: indtour@kar.nic.in).
KSTDC information booths at the airport and railway station and two downtown offices: Badami House, N R Square (Open daily 6.30am–10pm; tel: 080 2227 5883) and Karnataka Tourism, 49 Khanija Bhaven, 2nd floor, Race Course Road, Bangalore (tel: 080 2235288; fax: 080 22352626; email: discoverkornataka@ vsnl.net; www. karnatakatourism.org

A painted statue of Krishna (opposite) at the Parthasarathy Temple at Triplicane in Chennai (Madras)

CHENNAI TOURIST OFFICES

India Tourism, 154 Anna Salai (Open Mon–Fri 9.15–5.45, Sat 9.15–1; tel: 044 2846 1459; email: indtour@vsnl.com). Helpful.
TTDC, T N Tourism Complex, Wallajab Road (Open Mon–Fri 10–5.30; tel: 044 2538 3333; fax: 044 2536 1385; email: ttdc@vsnl.com).
ITDC, 29 Victoria Crescent, C-in-C Road (Open Mon–Sat 6am–8pm, Sun 6–2; tel: 044 2846 0285).

▶ Bangalore
202C3

Karnataka's capital is a crossroads for connections between Mysore, Chennai (Madras) or Hampi, and few travellers will escape a transit here, whether travelling by plane, train or bus. Bangalore is rated as India's (if not Asia's) fastest developing city thanks to its booming computer and software industries, but in the process has become westernized and unpleasantly polluted. Once dubbed a 'garden city', it now has only a few historical green spaces: Cubbon Park (1864), with a rather mediocre museum (*Open* Thu–Tue 10–5. *Admission: inexpensive*) and the **Lalbagh Gardens**▶ (*Open* daily 8–8. *Admission: free*), laid out in 1760 by Hyder Ali. The latter has a copy of London's Crystal Palace brought by the British together with gardeners from Kew Gardens. Sightseeing diehards can dodge traffic to reach the southern side of the city and **Tipu Sultan's Summer Palace**▶ (*Open* daily 9–5. *Admission: inexpensive*), but this is a pale shadow of his main palace in Shrirangapattana (see page 238).

▶▶ Chennai (Madras)
203E4

The recent transformation of the name Madras into Chennai has left many of the city's admirers dismayed. This stately old port nevertheless retains a distinct atmosphere that combines Tamil traditions with a long and still visible British legacy. Its airport may be international and its one-way systems highly regulated, but cows frequent the highway into town and water buffaloes with bells on their painted horns stop at traffic-lights. Despite the disadvantages of a sprawling city with a population of around six million, Chennai's rich past makes it interesting enough to fill a couple of days.

History Founded in 1639 by the East India Company, the capital of Tamil Nadu stretches along the Bay of Bengal. When the British arrived, they found a community of Portuguese Jesuits around San Thome (there since around 1520), a few Armenian traders and a weavers' colony at Chennapatnam. Lured by the cheap local cloth but wary of a Dutch trading post at Pulicut to the north, the British established themselves at Madrasapatnam, a settlement which expanded around Fort St. George. Over the centuries Madras gradually absorbed surrounding villages, survived partial destruction when it was captured by the French in 1746–48, and grew to become a key commercial city of colonial days, generously endowed with striking Indo-Saracenic public buildings. Today its commercial services are located along Anna Salai (formerly Mount Road), a broad avenue that cuts diagonally across the city southwest of the Fort, while the sights generally lie on or just off the 12km (7 mile) beach road.

Spiritual sights At the southern end of Marina Beach is Mylapore, one of the busiest quarters of the city, full of traditional housing. Mylapore is dominated by the **Kapaleswarar temple**▶▶, a Dravidian temple with a huge *tank*, dating from 1250 but rebuilt in the 16th century. Though non-Hindus may not enter the main sanctuary, they are allowed through the colourful *gopuram* into the compound to join the peacocks after which the district of Mylapore is named. Countless festivals are held here, the

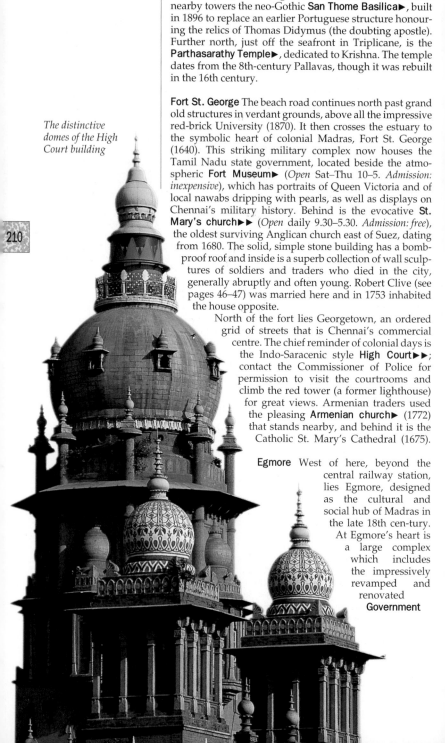

greatest being the annual temple celebration in March–April. Surrounding streets, packed with fruit- and flower-sellers, are a delight to wander in. On the seafront nearby towers the neo-Gothic **San Thome Basilica▶**, built in 1896 to replace an earlier Portuguese structure honouring the relics of Thomas Didymus (the doubting apostle). Further north, just off the seafront in Triplicane, is the **Parthasarathy Temple▶**, dedicated to Krishna. The temple dates from the 8th-century Pallavas, though it was rebuilt in the 16th century.

Fort St. George The beach road continues north past grand old structures in verdant grounds, above all the impressive red-brick University (1870). It then crosses the estuary to the symbolic heart of colonial Madras, Fort St. George (1640). This striking military complex now houses the Tamil Nadu state government, located beside the atmospheric **Fort Museum▶** (*Open* Sat–Thu 10–5. *Admission: inexpensive*), which has portraits of Queen Victoria and of local nawabs dripping with pearls, as well as displays on Chennai's military history. Behind is the evocative **St. Mary's church▶▶** (*Open* daily 9.30–5.30. *Admission: free*), the oldest surviving Anglican church east of Suez, dating from 1680. The solid, simple stone building has a bomb-proof roof and inside is a superb collection of wall sculptures of soldiers and traders who died in the city, generally abruptly and often young. Robert Clive (see pages 46–47) was married here and in 1753 inhabited the house opposite.

North of the fort lies Georgetown, an ordered grid of streets that is Chennai's commercial centre. The chief reminder of colonial days is the Indo-Saracenic style **High Court▶▶**; contact the Commissioner of Police for permission to visit the courtrooms and climb the red tower (a former lighthouse) for great views. Armenian traders used the pleasing **Armenian church▶** (1772) that stands nearby, and behind it is the Catholic St. Mary's Cathedral (1675).

Egmore West of here, beyond the central railway station, lies Egmore, designed as the cultural and social hub of Madras in the late 18th cen-tury. At Egmore's heart is a large complex which includes the impressively revamped and renovated **Government**

The distinctive domes of the High Court building

Museum►►► (*Open* Sat–Thu 9.30–5. *Admission: inexpensive*). The museum (1851) has an exceptional collection of more than 2,000 South Indian bronzes, Hindu sculpture, Buddhist marble sculptures from Amaravati, some dating from the 2nd century BC, folk art, a notable natural history section and a lively performing arts programme. The architectural highlight of Pantheon Road is the **National Art Gallery**►► (*Open* Sat–Thu 9–5. *Admission: inexpensive*), another of Chennai's Indo-Saracenic gems. Designed by Henry Irwin in the early 1900s as the Victoria Memorial, it now houses 10th- to 13th-century bronzes, Mughal miniatures, Deccani painting and handicrafts. Also here are sections on botany, archaeology, anthropology and art, the Connemara Public Library and a Children's Museum.

South of the Adyar Chennai's two rivers give the city an easily comprehensible layout. To the north, the Cooum River divides the Fort area from Chepauk and Triplicane, while to the south the Adyar River fringes a more verdant residential area where some important institutions are located. Most prominent is the **Theosophical Society**►► (*Open* Mon–Sat 8.30–10, 2–4. *Admission: inexpensive*), set in magnificent gardens shaded by banyan trees and dotted with shrines. This world headquarters was founded in 1882 by Annie Besant and includes a school, museum, library and meditation centre. Immediately east is Elliots Beach, quieter than Marina Beach but still not advisable for swimming. Another important cultural complex, the **Kalakshetra**► ('Home of Arts') lies south of here, again in a lovely garden. Dedicated to reviving the traditional arts of dance, music and painting, it has an unusual theatre where a festival is held every December.

West of here lies Guindy National Park, with a race course, the Raj Bhavan (Government House, built in 1817) and Snake Park (*Open* Wed–Mon 8.30–5. *Admission: inexpensive*). By the Armenian Bridge, in the cave where St. Thomas lived, is the Little Mount shrine (Chinnamalai). Nearby are two commemorative churches to 'Doubting Thomas'; one built in 1551 by the Portuguese and the other erected in 1971. Further southwest, on the airport road, is **St. Thomas Mount**►, considered to be the site of the apostle's martyrdom. Crowning this hillock is another 16th-century Portuguese church with a much-venerated cross (reputed to have bled) inserted into a wall.

Across the sea Far into the Bay of Bengal about 1,400km (868 miles) east of Chennai are the **Andaman Islands**►►►, a slice of Eden in an emerald sea. These, and the off-limits Nicobar Islands to the south, are home to some of the world's oldest and most isolated tribal peoples, who are largely protected from outside influences. Watersports and unspoiled beaches are big attractions, as are the rich forest wildlife and nearly 250 bird species. Port Blair, the capital, was established by the British in 1789, became a penal colony the following century and is now the entry point, with the bulk of accommodation and services. A 30-day permit is required, obtainable at the same time as your Indian visa, or on arrival at Port Blair airport. The Immigration Officer also can grant permission for short visits to other Andaman islands (www.and.nic.in). Access to the islands by ship is from Chennai or Kolkata.

211

SHOPPING
Parrys Corner in Georgetown and the entire length of Anna Salai offer the main concentration of shopping centres and emporia for fabrics, handicrafts and jewellery. The India Silk House, 846 Anna Salai, and Handloom House, 7 Rattan Bazar, George Town, have a wide selection of silks and cottons. Gem Palace, in Hotel Adyar Park, is great for traditional South Indian jewellery. Poompuhar, 818 Anna Salai, is the place if you're after good-quality bronze items.

The South

TOURIST OFFICES
India Tourism,
Communidade Building,
Church Square, Panaji
(*Open* Mon–Fri 10–6, Sat
10–2; tel: 0832 2223412;
email: goatour@ sanchar-
net.in). GTDC, Trionora
Apartments, Dr Alvares
Costa Rd, Panaji (*Open*
Mon–Fri 10–5; tel: 0832
2226515, fax: 0832
2223926, email:
indiatourismgoa
@sancharnet.in). Desks at
the bus station, airport and
railway station.

▶▶ Goa
202B5

Goa is a package-holiday paradise, squeezed between the
sea and the lush forested hills. It offers a classic tropical
cocktail of glistening sands, swaying coconut palms and
ultra-fresh seafood. Luxury hotels and budget guesthouses
overlook fishermen mending their nets, and beer comes
cheap and chilled. Some visitors feel that Goa is over-west-
ernized, and even its proud, Konkani-speaking inhabitants
tend to agree. 'Discovered' by pioneering hippies looking
for peace and love, Goa's beaches are now filled with
persistent hawkers during the day and rave parties at night,
and hotel prices are soaring. For those intent on discovering
the 'real' India, Goa is best treated as a relaxing break on the
southern trail, or even as a charter-flight gateway to the
subcontinent, but certainly not as an end in itself.

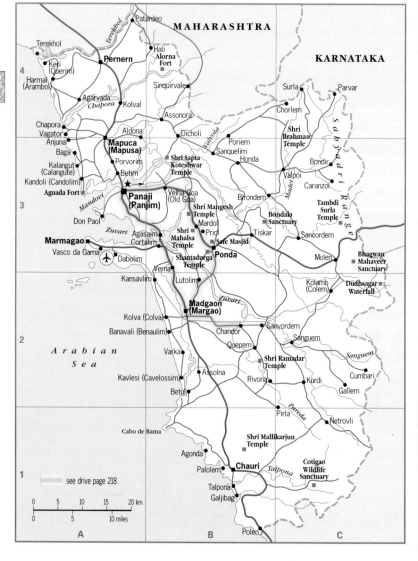

Past glory It is hardly surprising that the Portuguese who came in search of spices in the 16th century decided to put down roots in this tropical paradise. Goa's natural boundaries, the Arabian Sea and the Sahyadri mountains, had sheltered it from much of India's inland turmoil, while its strategic location on the newly discovered trade route to the East made it even more attractive. Goa had long flourished as a port, particularly under the military protection of the Vijayanagar commander Madhav Mantri, who managed to protect Goa from the acquisitive Muslim sultans. In the 1470s, however, Goa finally succumbed to the Muslims and was ruled by Adil Shah of Bijapur. Then in 1508 Alfonso de Albuquerque arrived from Portugal and captured the port, a victory that led to 450 years of Portuguese rule (see pages 214–215).

Many of Goa's street vendors (inset) come from tribal families in Karnataka
Net repairs on Kalangut Beach (below)

Panaji (Panjim) The capital divides the developed northern beaches from the more relaxed southern Goa. It has ramshackle old buildings with picturesquely decaying walls, tiled roofs and overhanging balconies, standing beside modern concrete structures and shady bars. Gloomy Portuguese shops still have their late-19th-century wooden fittings. Crowning the central plaza on a small hill is the whitewashed **Church of Immaculate Conception**▶▶, dating from 1541. The cobbled back streets bordering Ourem Creek in the quarters of Fontainahas and Sao Tomé are particularly atmospheric.

In Goa, Latin influences fuse with Indian colour to produce an enchanting hybrid. Goa's traditions of language, religion, food, music and dance have remained firmly entrenched despite the end of Portuguese rule in 1961. Goans may be Indian, but they are Goan first.

FESTIVALS

Fireworks, floats, parades and dancing regularly fill the streets of Goa, as both Hindu and Christian festivals are celebrated with enthusiastic abandon. Carnival in February or March is a major festival; Easter and Christmas are welcomed with religious reverence and family gatherings. The festival of Goa's patron saint on 3 December, St. Francis, is marked by processions around his tomb at the Bom Jesus Basilica; in August, at the Novidades harvest festival, sheaves of paddy rice are blessed at churches.

214

Goa, originally founded to dominate the lucrative spice trade, was Portugal's first foothold in Asia and came to rival Lisbon in its magnificent churches and thriving port. It was from their Goan base that Portuguese merchants headed further east in the 16th century, founding major trading ports at Malacca (Malaysia), in Indonesia's Spice Islands and East Timor, and building up important trading networks. This was their golden century before other European powers caught up with them.

Settling in After naming the tropical paradise Dourada ('golden'), soon corrupted to Goa, the Portuguese appropriated other territories along the Malabar coast. Daman, Diu, Salcete, Bassein and, not least, Bom Bahia ('beautiful bay'), better known as Bombay (now Mumbai) all fell to their flag. The Portuguese were initially on good terms with local Hindus and the nearby Vijayanagar kingdom, with whom they set up trading links, and they appointed local officials, built forts and employed Indian troops. A notable new law prohibited *sati*, where widows threw

themselves on their husband's funeral pyre. Other laws relating to property gave a woman the right to half the estate of her husband, unlike the rest of India. This has no doubt contributed to the easy confidence of Goan women. Above all, uniquely among all the colonizing nations, Portugal encouraged intermarriage, a policy designed to preserve the unity and multiply the offspring of settlers. As a result, Portuguese names such as Pereira, Alvares and Braganza are still prominent and Goans have Latin features. Portuguese is spoken by the older generation and a few landowners, but Konkani (Goa's own language) and Marathi (from Maharashtra) are more general.

Catholicism The most visible legacy of the Portuguese is their churches, not only the imposing monuments of Old Goa but also the more typical whitewashed façades nestling among palm trees elsewhere. Christians form a third of the population, but the introduction of Christianity was not painless. Franciscans, Dominicans and Jesuits arrived in the 1540s, all intent on

Portuguese influences pervade all aspects of life in Goa, from church architecture and religious festivities (left) to its cuisine

converting the 'heathens'. Despite the more compassionate influence of Francis Xavier (see panel page 216), persecution and violence were used by the Portuguese Inquisition. Permission was obtained from the Portuguese Viceroy to criminalize Hinduism and raze temples. These actions resulted in thousands fleeing from their homes to more tolerant Muslim areas inland, and building temples near Ponda, just outside Portuguese jurisdiction.

Pork and plantains A happier meeting of cultures produced Goan cuisine. Alongside tandoori, rice and dal, Goan restaurants offer *chourisso* (a spicy pork sausage), *sarpotel* (pickled pig's liver cooked in vinegar with tamarind), and *vindalho* (spicy pork or beef marinated in garlic, chillies and vinegar). Chillies and cashew nuts were introduced by the Portuguese, as were plantains brought from their African colonies; Goans also use coconut sauces. *Pomfret* (a local flat fish) and *bangra* (mackerel) abound, while lobsters, clams, prawns or kingfish may be smothered in *balchao*, a hot curry and onion sauce. Bread is usually excellent; sweets are made with coconut, rice, nuts and jaggery (palm sugar). You will also find India's best choice of beers and local wines (port being the most palatable), local rum and *feni* or toddy (made either from fermented cashew apples or from the sap of palm trees).

RHYTHMS
Music flows in the Goan blood and most Goans can pluck at a guitar or pick out a tune on the piano. Old-time taverns in Panaji will invariably have background music, traditional or otherwise. Much Goan music is derived from haunting and lyrical Portuguese love songs, but young musicians have also taken to hard rock and many work the nightclub circuit of India's big cities.

ST. FRANCIS XAVIER
The 'Apostle of the East' is largely the reason why there are millions of Christians throughout India and Southeast Asia. He was born in 1506 in Spain, studied in Paris, was ordained in Venice and joined the fledgling Jesuit order. In 1541 the Portuguese king sent him to bring some morality to the newly founded diocese in the east, and he was soon building churches, healing and converting. From Goa he travelled on to Sri Lanka, Malacca, Ambon in the Spice Islands, China and Japan, proselytizing and founding churches. After dying prematurely at sea he was buried on an island off China. Malaccan Christians brought his body back to bury in their church, from where it was dug up again and removed to Goa.

GETTING AROUND
Kadamba Transport runs buses throughout the state from the main bus-stands at Panaji, Mapuca and Madgaon (also called Margao). Auto-rickshaws are easily available, as are normal taxis, though rates are well above the average for India. Goa's unique motor-bike taxis take pillion passengers, and are recognizable by their yellow mudguards and white number-plates. Better still is another Goan speciality—motor-bike rental, with models ranging from a standard 50cc machine to a 350cc Enfield Bullet, suitable for Easy Rider clones breezing up into the Ghats. An international driving licence is required though not always demanded.

Velha Goa (Old Goa)   212B3

Velha Goa, about 8km (5 miles) east of Panaji (Panjim), was the original walled town built as the bastion of Portuguese Catholicism in Asia, and at the time dubbed the Rome of the Orient. Abandoned in the 17th century due to repeated cholera outbreaks, this town of grandiose churches, wide avenues, gardens and stately mansions is now populated only by busloads of tourists and pilgrims. Towering beside the main road is the **Basilica of Bom Jesus▶▶** (*Open* Mon–Sat 9–6.30, Sun 10.30–6.30. *Admission: free*), a red laterite edifice completed in 1605—and now a World Heritage monument—that houses the tomb of the Jesuit missionary, St. Francis Xavier. This is located to the right of the heavily gilded, baroque altar with its figures of Jesus and Ignatius Loyola, the founder of the Jesuit order. The ornate chapel and tomb made of marble and jasper were donated by the Medici ruler, Cosimo III, in 1696, and come to life every decade when the severely decaying corpse is ceremonially carried to the **Se Cathedral▶▶▶** opposite.

Se Cathedral The cathedral was the fruit of lengthy construction, 1562–1640, in a purist Tuscan style, and is staggering in proportions (*Open* Mon–Fri 7.30–6, Sun Mass 7.15, 10, 4. *Admission: free*). Only one of the twin towers remains; the other was struck by lightning in 1776. Within the flaky, white-washed walls, massive pillars divide the nave from side aisles and numerous chapels where the main decoration is concentrated. In one chapel is kept the Cross of Miracles, which is said to grow in size and have healing properties. The heavily gilded central altar depicts the martyrdom of Saint Catherine, to whom the cathedral is dedicated.

More crosses At the back is the **Church of St. Francis of Assisi▶▶**. Its convent section is now the Archaeological Museum (*Open* Sat–Thu 10–5. *Admission: inexpensive*), housing a rich collection of Goan antiquities. The beautiful church (1521), now under restoration, displays superb decorative paintwork and woodcarving, and the floor is inlaid with elaborately engraved tombstones. Of Velha Goa's many other monuments, the most interesting are opposite the cathedral: the domed Church of St. Cajetan (1651), modelled on St. Peter's in Rome and, nearer the ferry landing, the Viceroys' Arch, which commemorates Vasco da Gama (1597, rebuilt in 1954). A rare relic of pre-Portuguese Goa, the Adil Shah Gate, stands on the site of the Bijapur Sultans' fortress. The now ruined palace was later occupied by the Portuguese Viceroys.

North Goa
This is Goa's most developed coast, increasingly spoiled by uncontrolled hotel and villa developments, characterless

The magnificent altar in
Se Cathedral, Velha Goa

restaurants and endless tourist-stalls. The 8km (5 miles) stretch of golden sand between Aguada Fort and Baga includes Kalangut (Calangute), a rapidly built package-tour destination. This said, it's ideal for those looking for lively nightlife combined with a quick dip beside the fishing-boats. Baga itself is popular with budget travellers both for techno music-bars and for safe swimming. Beyond the cliffs to the north are the beaches at Anjuna and Vagator. At Anjuna the 'alternative' lifestyle of the 1970s continues unabated, complete with beach parties; Vagator is more sedate and popular with day-trippers.

Rave time Despite witnessing years of rave-parties and hosting a Wednesday 'hippie' market, **Anjuna▶** beach retains its natural beauty thanks to its classic palm-lined curve. Little Vagator cove, just a short walk south of the main beach, is more secluded and less populated than both Vagator and Anjuna beaches. It is a favourite with youthful sybarites. Both resorts can be reached from Mapuca (Mapusa), a dilapidated inland town which comes to life only for its colourful Friday market. For a really untouched setting, head north of the Chapora river to the fishing village of **Harmol (Arambol)▶▶**. Here, two beaches offer low-key café-bars and, behind the smaller beach, a sulphurous lake with therapeutic mud-baths.

Last of the northern beaches at 44km (27 miles) from Panaji is **Terekhol▶**, reached by an antiquated car-ferry from the village of Keri after a circuitous but scenic drive through paddy-fields and palm-groves. Tiracol Fort, now a hotel with river views, dominates this last tip of Goa.

BEACH ETIQUETTE
There is a long-running battle over nudism in Goa, and sadly many tourists hot off the plane blatantly flout local sensibilities. Despite years of hippie freedom tolerated by some Portuguese Goans, nudism is still distinctly offensive to the Hindu population. Signs on the main beaches clearly state 'No nudism' and there are sporadic police efforts to enforce this. Apart from anything else, a nude sunbather soon attracts a crowd of oglers, which somehow lessens the pleasure. Otherwise, the main drawback to beach life is the steady flow of vendors and masseurs. You cannot escape them, but be polite about your refusals.

Drive

Goa

This full day's drive takes in Goa's Christian, Hindu and Muslim past, visiting historic temples, a mosque and a 17th-century church. The route passes through stunningly beautiful, lush hills, surrounded by plantations and paddy-fields.

From Panaji, drive east to Velha Goa and its wonderful churches, then follow the NH4 southeast through Priol towards Mardol. It is worth stopping

A stately Portuguese mansion

here to visit the popular and ornate 18th-century Shri Mangesh temple, Goa's main Sivaite shrine. The Sri Mahalsa temple, 2km (1 mile) south of here, is where carvings depict the incarnations of Vishnu. A few kilometres further are the peaceful gardens of the Safe Masjid, a modest white-washed mosque built in 1560 by the Bijapuri sultan. This is one of only two Goan mosques to have survived the ferocious Portuguese Inquisition.

Continue to the chaotic, unattractive administrative town of Ponda with its ruined fort. A cluster of Hindu temples was built here because Ponda was outside Portuguese territory. Take a rigth turn at Pharmagiudi to the outstanding Shantadurga temple (1738) that rises out of the forest about 3km (2 miles) west at Kavalem. Follow the road to Madgaon south-west past plantations of cinnamon, turmeric and lemongrass, cross the Zuvari river and reach Lutolim, a pretty, typically Portuguese town just off the main road 3km (2 mikles) after crossing Borim Bridge. Lush gardens surround grand old mansions, some of which can be visited by appointment; Casa Arajao Alvarez (daily 9–6.30). Continue south, stopping to see the baroque Church of the Holy Spirit (1675) on the square. Nearby are the sumptuous De Joao Figueiredo House and Da Silva House and the labyrinthine covered market. Lutolim is also home to Ancestral Goa, a model village depicting Goan life.

If you still have energy, strike out 13km (8 miles) east to Chandor to visit the star of Goa's mansions, the magnificent Menezes-Braganza house (*Open* daily 10–5, but check. *Admission: free*; but moderate donations expected). It is stuffed with antique furnishings and Chinese porcelain, and exudes an air of faded grandeur. Return to Panaji via Madgaon and the fast NH17.

South Goa

From Panaji a highway runs due south, crossing the wide, traffic-choked Zuvari estuary to reach **Madgaon (Margao)▶**, a market town with a baroque church and some fine Portuguese mansions. This is the main stop for all trains from Mumbai (Bombay) or Mangalore before Vasco da Gama, so many people overnight here—but Madgaon's main role is as a transport hub.

To the west is a string of beaches whose powdery white sand and undeveloped hinterland offer a much more rewarding experience of Goa than the beaches in the north. Traffic goes slower and back roads meander through paddy-fields, passing hamlets with proud churches and pretty Portuguese houses.

Relax Due west of Madgaon is Kolva (Colva), which has more facilities than any other beach along this stretch and is the most popular with domestic tourists. Far more peaceful is **Benavali (Benaulim)▶▶**, a tiny, relaxed resort to the south. This has several budget hotels, excellent seafood restaurants and a verdant village inland. Next south is Goa's pricey paradise, Varka, continuing into **Kavlesi (Cavelossim)▶▶**, also known as Leela Beach. The international hotels here are self-sufficient luxury havens, but less expensive options do exist.

Paradise Beyond the idyllic fishing village of **Betul▶** and Cabo de Rama, the landscape changes dramatically. Roads twist through the jungle-clad Sahyadri Hills past stark black laterite headlands and secluded coves. This is where Goa becomes the stuff of dreams, and **Palolem▶▶▶** is there to fulfil them. Its beach has safe swimming, while village life merges harmoniously with growing tourism, but weekends can be crowded. Further south still are magnificent, pristine beaches. The **Cotigao Wildlife Sanctuary▶** lies 10km (6 miles) east of Chauri. This remote tract of forest harbours gazelles, panthers and hyenas, but visitors are more likely to spot the usual monkeys or wild boar.

TO THE FALLS

One of Goa's most stunning natural sights is the Dudhsagar waterfall, said to be India's highest at 600m (1,968ft). This torrent of water is hidden deep in the 240sq km (93sq miles) of the Bhagwan Mahaveer Sanctuary on the edge of the Western Ghats close to the Karnataka border, and access is easiest by train from Colem (Kolamb), which gets you to a rocky, slippery access route. Alternatively, take a GTDC waterfall tour. You can swim in the pools. The falls are at their best following the monsoon, which is between October and December. By April their glory is fading.

219

Sunset at Palolem beach, South Goa

Hampi reached its zenith during the reign of Krishna Deva Raya, when it was described by the Portuguese traveller, Domingo Paes, in 1520 as being as large as Rome with a king's palace that was more spacious than the castles of Lisbon. Chariot Street was '...a very beautiful street full of very beautiful houses with balconies and arcades in which are sheltered pilgrims...there are also houses for the upper classes and the king has a palace in the same street where he resides when he visits the temple.'

By the Tungabhadra river at Hampi, where huge granite boulders characterize the landscape

▶▶▶ Hampi   202C5

This star of the Deccan spreads its drama and magic over 26sq km (10sq miles) of low hills, wild vegetation and sculptural granite boulders, integrating nature with ruins to extraordinary and captivating effect. When choosing the site for their 14th-century capital, the Vijayanagar kings (see page 43) were drawn by Hampi's legendary significance as much as by its strategic qualities as it was thought to have been the site of the monkey kingdom that features in the Ramayana (descendants of the mythical monkeys still bound around the ruins). The Vijayanagar founders were two brothers, officers of the declining Hoysala kingdom, who broke away to set up a new order on the banks of the Tungabhadra river. As the Vijayanagar dynasty grew in strength so did the splendour of Hampi (known at the time as Vijayanagar), but in 1565 it succumbed to a combined onslaught by Muslim rulers, who sacked much of the city and massacred over 100,000 inhabitants.

Practicalities Hampi is one of India's greatest sights, but its isolation has so far saved it from excessive tourist invasion. Other than by road, the only access is by overnight train from Bangalore to Hospet, where accommodation remains pleasantly low-key. The village of Hampi itself has a few guest-houses, which are much in favour with backpackers taking a break from Goa. They contend with malarial mosquitoes drawn to the open sewers. From Hospet there are regular buses covering the 14km (9 miles) to Hampi Bazar or to Kamalapuram, a village on

the south side of the site where the **Archaeological Museum** (*Open Sat–Thu 10–5. Admission: inexpensive*) and one hotel are located. Cyclerickshaws and auto-rickshaws are also easily available.

Spiritual centre Along the south bank of the Tungabhadra river, starting from Hampi Bazar, is the sacred centre, announced by the *mandapas* of Hemakuta Hill. In the village itself looms the 50m (164ft) *gopuram* of the **Virupaksha Temple▶▶** (*Open daily dawn–dusk. Admission: free*), which dates from the 9th century and is still in use. The highlight of the courtyards is the ceiling outside the main shrine, which is richly decorated with frescoes depicting mythological scenes. Running east from here is a broad, avenue that was once the Chariot Street of the Vijayanagar kings, but is now lined with tourist cafés, stalls and village houses.

Carved stone chariot at the Vithala Temple in Hampi

Just before the avenue ends at Matanga Hill, a turn-off to the left, thronged with pilgrims, follows a circuitous riverside path. This passes many temples, including a small and much visited Siva shrine at a beautiful bend of the river where locals gather to wash and fish. Giant boulders and idyllic rural landscapes continue to the **Vithala Temple▶▶▶** (*Open daily dawn–dusk. Admission: expensive*). This well-preserved complex displays remarkable sculptural skill in a variety of styles, not least in the 56 pillars of the main pavilion, each of which was carved out of a single block of granite to depict mythical animals and figures. In the courtyard stands an intricately carved stone chariot, the vehicle for Garuda, Vishnu's steed. Green parrots and frangipani trees add to the atmosphere, while outside stands the King's Balance. On this, the story goes, rulers would weigh themselves against gold and jewels which were then distributed to the population.

Palatial relics Another generous half-day can be spent exploring the royal urban site, that lies about 2km (1 mile) south of Hampi Bazar and ends at Kamalapuram. The main **palace buildings▶▶** here betray a gradual influx of Islamic styles. They include the graceful domed two-storey pavilion called the **Lotus Mahal**, inside the walled *zenana*, and the striking **Elephant Stables**. South of here is the small but superbly carved **Hazara Rama temple**, with its rare depictions of Vishnu as Buddha inside the sanctum and prolific friezes outside. Grouped with it are the **Mahanavami Dibba**, a high platform used for watching festivities and faced in bas-reliefs of animals, and the **Pushkarini**, a stepped *tank*. Finally, the **Queen's Bath** is a large square bath area surrounded by a delicately decorated arched corridor and projecting balconies. Hampi is now a World Heritage Site.

HOSPET
When the night-train from Bangalore creaks into Hospet bringing a flurry of new travellers, a rickshaw race for accommodation follows. Hospet's hotels are limited in number and many visitors end up staying longer than they intended, so demand is intense. The small, friendly town has a reasonable choice of restaurants, the best being attached to hotels, and a lively market area at its southern end. Halfway along the main street, Station Road, is the bus station which provides connections (albeit circuitous) with Bangalore, Hubli (for Goa), Badami, Mysore, Bijapur and Hassan. Money can be changed at the State Bank of India.

Varadarajaperumal temple and temple tank at Kanchipuram

▶▶ Kanchipuram   203D3

This major pilgrimage centre, one of India's seven sacred cities, lies in the hot, dusty interior of Tamil Nadu, 70km (43 miles) southwest of Chennai (Madras). It is renowned for its wealth of sculptural styles reflecting the maturity of Pallava art (see page 38) but its importance stretches back to the pre-Christian era when it was a great centre of Buddhist learning. Ashoka built *stupas* here and over 100 Buddhist monasteries existed. After the Pallavas (4th to 9th century AD) came the Cholas, who retained Kanchipuram as their capital, and then Chalukyan and Vijayanagar rulers. Decline came in the 18th century when Madras emerged under the British as the foremost city in the region and Kanchipuram became a backwater. It remains a fairly small town, little touched by the 20th century. There are three main areas, each devoted to a particular belief (Siva, Vishnu or Jain), and altogether over 100 temples are still used by the faithful. Remember that non-Hindus cannot enter the main sanctuaries. The easiest way to get around is by rickshaw, alternatively you can hire bicycles near the bus station.

The greats The earliest surviving temple, and one of the most impressive, is **Kailasanatha▶▶▶** (*Open* daily dawn–noon, 4pm–dusk. *Admission: inexpensive*), west of the centre. This relatively small 7th- to early-8th-century structure is laid out according to canonical texts with eight small shrines aligned from the entrance, ending at a beautiful courtyard overlooked by a pyramidal tower. Images of Siva and Parvati abound as do traces of frescoes. The largest and most important of the Sivaite temples, the **Ekambaresvara▶▶** (*Open* daily dawn–noon, 4pm–dusk.

Admission: inexpensive) lies northeast. Most of it dates from the 16th–17th centuries. Five granite *prakarams* are introduced by a towering *gopuram* and lead to the 'hall of a thousand pillars' (in fact, numbering about half that). Behind the sanctum, inaccessible to non-Hindus, that contains an earth *lingam,* and through gloomy hallways lies another open courtyard dominated by a mango tree, estimated to be over 2,000 years old.

Back towards the centre, the **Kamakshi Aman temple►** (*Open* daily 6–noon, 4–8.30pm. *Admission: inexpensive*) displays a variety of styles covering a span of about eight centuries. The riotously coloured *gopurams* are the most recent addition. The temple is dedicated to Siva's wife Parvati in her form as Shakti, representing cosmic energy. In Kanchipuram she becomes Kamakshi, the ruling deity of the town.

Closest to the railway is the **Vaikuntha Perumal temple►►**, an 8th-century Pallava structure that has three vertically rising sanctums dedicated to Vishnu and crowned by a superb carved *vimana*. Bas-reliefs narrate the history of the Pallava dynasty, including their battles against the Chalukyas, and the entrance hall has pillars sculpted with lions, which is a Vijayanagar addition.

► Kanniyakumari
202C1

Also known as Cape Comorin, this is the extreme tip of India and a pilgrimage town, now irredeemably devoted to commercial concerns. The island **Vivekananda temple►** (*Open* daily 8–midday, 2–4pm. *Admission: inexpensive*), just offshore, honours a 19th-century Bengali theologian and monk who once meditated on the rocks. He preached religious tolerance and later founded the Ramakrishna Mission in Chennai (*Ferries* Wed–Mon every half-hour 7–11, 2–5). The rocks also attract hundreds of pilgrims to see the 'footprint' of the Devi Kanya, an incarnation of Parvati as an eternal virgin, and the protector of India's coast. She is also worshipped on the mainland opposite, at the Kumari Amman temple.

Close by stands the **Gandhi Mandapam** (*Open* daily 7–12.30, 3–7. *Admission: free*), where the Mahatma's ashes were displayed before being immersed in the sea.

SEA, SUN, MOON AND WIND
Kanniyakumari is the point where the Bay of Bengal meets the Arabian Sea, and both mingle in the great sweep of the Indian Ocean. During the April full moon, the horizon offers the spectacle of the sun setting and the moon rising simultaneously—for a brief moment that invariably draws crowds. North of here is a vast field of wind turbines—a striking experiment in new sources of energy. The winds of the cape create the perfect natural motor.

ASHRAMS
Ashrams are places for renewing the spirit, with the help of a guru (or his followers). South India's most traditional *ashram* is probably the Sankaracharya *math* (monastery) at Kanchipuram. Since Adi Sankara (7th–8th century) founded it, there has been an unbroken line of *sanyasins* (ascetics nearing spiritual perfection) serving at its head.

223

Vivekananda temple lies on an island just off Kanniyakumari

It is easy to lose all sense of time on the Keralan backwaters as you drift through silent lagoons, watching swooping kingfishers and flying fish. People have been using this vast network of rivers and canals in the same ways for centuries, and even today, they act as the only link between more remote villages and the town.

224

CHRISTIANITY
Pretty little whitewashed churches are a common sight in the backwaters. This reflects the fact that the south, and Kerala in particular, is home to a large proportion of India's 23 million or so Christians. The first Christian converts in the Keralan region may have been those who followed the teachings of the apostle Thomas Didymus (Doubting Thomas), martyred in Madras in the 1st century. From the 5th to the 6th centuries, Syrian Christians came from the Middle East to the Keralan coast, full of missionary zeal.

SNAKE BOAT RACES
January, July, August and September are the months of Alappuzha's snake boat races, with boats manned by crews of over 100 men flying through the backwaters at breakneck speed. The most famous is the Nehru Trophy Race on the second Sunday of August, when some 40 highly decorated boats compete in front of enthusiastic crowds. They are joined by naval helicopters showing off their prowess.

Transport boat in the backwaters (above)
Coconut cutter (right)

From north to south the dreamlike, watery expanse known as Kuttanad extends 75km (46 miles), from Kochi (Cochin) through Allapuzha (Allepey) to Kollam (Quilon), and inland to Kottayam. This 'Venice of the East' boasts 1,500km (930 miles) of waterways, once used by merchant ships laden with ivory, gold, silver, rubber and spices heading for the Cochin, and by maharajas with their royal court in tow. Meandering channels edged by lush vegetation, groves of coconut or banana-palms and rice-fields connect with wide open rivers and lagoons in an succession of idyllic images. Life moves slowly, a pace matched by local transport—it takes up to 12 hours from Allaphuzha to Kollam using the motorized public ferry.

Daily life Apart from their undeniable tropical beauty, the backwaters offer a fascinating insight into the rural lifestyle of their inhabitants. Colourful thatched or tiled houses (*nalukettu*) pop up between the palms or cluster together in communities complete with whitewashed Portuguese church, Hindu temple, mosque, bank and the occasional hospital (with ambulances that go by water). Most houses are built close to the banks to make use of the unending water supply, and some inhabitants, despite living on a narrow spit of land, manage to pack in cows, pigs, chickens and ducks alongside vegetable plots.

Children with satchels trot over log bridges on their way to school or are paddled in canoes. Utensils and clothes are washed from the banks and huge loads of coconuts or bananas are moved in precarious dug-outs. Larger boats made of seasoned wood bound with coir rope transport heavier cargoes, sometimes shaded with woven bamboo roofs, while fishermen and nets pile into longboats with sides that swoop into curved prows.

Tourist cruises There are numerous choices for visitors. The easiest budget options are the boats operated by DTPC (District Tourism Promotion Council) between Kollam and Alappuzha, with daily departures in both directions at 10.30am, to arrive 6.30pm—meal stops en route. The full-day trip can be monotonous, so it's worth considering an overnight break at Coir Village Lake Resorts (where you can watch the coir being processed), or leaving the boat halfway and continuing by bus.

To check schedules and book, contact DTPC, Government Guest House, Kollam (*Open* Mon–Sat 10–5; tel: 0474 2743620 and the DTPC centre at the bus stand (tel: 2745625). In Alappuzha contact either ATDC, Komala Road (tel/fax: 0477 2243462, email: info@ atdcalleppey.com; www.dtpckollam.com).

Local transport The frequent local ferries are cheaper and bring you closer to the locals. Many have flat roofs, which give more space and wider views—but take a hat, plenty of water and a supply of cashew nuts. Particularly recommended is the route from Alappuzha to Kottayam, taking under three hours, time to capture the atmosphere.

Luxury specials For more expansive budgets, Kumarakom is a lagoon about 50km (31 miles) south of Kochi, reached by speedboat in just over an hour. Here on a private island stands the Coconut Lagoon, a sumptuous heritage resort displaying the best of traditional Keralan architecture. Nearby, in a grand old colonial house that once belonged to a British estate-owner, is the Taj Garden Retreat. Both establishments offer comfortable accommodation and organize sunset cruises in kettuvallom (converted cargo boats) or overnight trips in houseboats, by far the best way to experience the backwaters from dawn to dusk.

TOURIST OFFICES

India Tourism, Willingdon Island, next to Malabar Hotel (*Open* Mon–Sat 9–5.30; tel: 0484 2668352). Helpful with information and guides. KTDC Reception Centre, Shanmugham Road; Ernakulam (*Open* Mon–Sat 8am–7pm; tel: 0484 2353234, email: ktdccok@sancharnet.in). KTDC hotel-booking, tours.

Tourist Desk, Main Boat Jetty, Ernakulam (*Open* Mon–Sat variable hours; tel: 0484 2371761, email: touristdesk@satyam.net.in). This enthusiastic private operation offers good information on buses, ferries and back-water trips.

*Chinese-style fishing nets (below) at the mouth of Kochi harbour.
Kathakali performer (right)*

►► Kochi (Cochin) 202C2

With a history stretching back to the time of King Solomon, when it was known as the 'Queen of the Arabian Sea', Kochi has long been the most cosmopolitan of India's cities. Arab, Phoenician and Chinese traders all stopped here in search of the precious pepper, cardamom and coriander that still grow profusely in the nearby Nilgiri Hills. Ivory, silks and fragrant sandalwood were further enticements. Marco Polo and Vasco da Gama followed, as did the Dutch East India Company and later the British. Today, Christians, Jews, Muslims and Hindus still live side by side, and Chinese fishing-nets, introduced by merchants from the court of Kublai Khan, continue to haul in fish. The adjoining backwaters make a popular tourist destination (see pages 224–225).

Layout Curling around the water, Kochi is made up of several islands and two main centres: Ernakulam, the modern town, and Fort Cochin/Mattancherry, the historical settlement on the peninsula. In between lies Willingdon Island, created by the British to improve deep-water harbour facilities. To the north is Bolgatty Island. Bridges and ferries connect the various parts of this water-bound city. At the same time as promoting its rich cultural past, Kochi continues to function as a major port, giving it a rough edge that is not always enjoyable. Services and hotels are situated in Ernakulam, the airport and railway terminus is on Willingdon Island, and the sights are all concentrated in Mattancherry and Fort Cochin. Ferries run very frequently and there are plenty of auto-rickshaws to take you around each area.

Fort Cochin This sleepy enclave is the original Portuguese settlement on the tip of the peninsula, but its architecture came to be dominated by Dutch and British styles. India's

oldest European church, **St. Francis▶▶** (*Open* Mon–Sat 9.30–5.30, Sun afternoon. Sunday service in English at 8am), was built here in 1503 by Portuguese Franciscans, originally in wood, later in stone. It was subsequently taken over and modified by both Dutch Protestants and British Anglicans. Vasco da Gama, the Portuguese explorer and the first to sail around Africa to reach Asia, was buried here in 1524 but his body was later transferred to Lisbon. It is a charming, simple structure with a vaulted timber ceiling, *punkah* fans and a tropical façade. Just south is the rather more kitsch, 20th-century Santa Cruz Cathedral. A short walk to the north reveals one of Kochi's picture-postcard images, the cantilevered **Chinese fishing-nets▶▶**. At high tide, levers and weights are operated by teams of fishermen to lift piles of silvery fish from water. Identical structures line the backwaters further inland. Fish are also caught from trawlers, and there is a fish-market on the beach on the west of the peninsula, teeming with porters bearing head-baskets.

Painted palace Due east of Santa Cruz is the **Mattancherry Palace Museum▶▶▶** (*Open* Sat–Thu 10–5. *Admission: free, but donations expected*), entered from Moulana Azad Road. The palace was origi-

nally built in 1557 by the Portuguese to placate the Raja of Kochi. It was later extensively renovated by the Dutch, who gave it a massive square tiled roof, and it is often referred to as the 'Dutch Palace'. In traditional Keralan style, two whitewashed storeys surround a central courtyard and temple. The outstanding feature of the palace is the wealth of frescoes that decorate the walls of the royal bedrooms and private chambers, depicting lively scenes from the *Ramayana* and the *Mahabharata*. They were painted in a Keralan technique using vegetable and mineral pigments finished with a coat of oil and pine resin. Similar painting techniques can also to be seen at Padmanabhapuram (see page 248) and at the Siva temple in Ettumanur. The oldest frescoes, dating from the late 16th century, face the royal bedroom next to the Coronation Hall, and 19th-century versions cover the walls of the women's bedrooms. The palace also houses some wonderful regal relics and old Dutch maps of Kochi.

(see page 248)

KATHAKALI
Kochi has four major venues for Kathakali, but Art Kerala gives preference to groups. Dancer-actors enact stories from the Hindu epics, preceded by a public make-up period, when you can watch the symbolic make-up being applied. At Kochi Cultural Centre, Souhardham, Manikath Road, Ravipuram (tel: 0484 2368153), make-up 5.30, the performance at 7pm. Kerala Kathakali Centre, Cochin Aquatic Club, River Road, Fort Kochi (tel: 0484 2215827), starts with make-up at 5 and performance at 6.30. The city's oldest show is at the See India Foundation, Devan Gurukalam, Kalathip-arambil Lane, near Ernakulam Junction station (tel: 0484 2376471). Make-up at 6, performance at 6.45.

The tropical climate ensures an abundance of fruit

Jew Town South of the palace lies the neat quarter locally known as Jew Town, a community dating back to the 2nd century AD when Palestinian Jews fled persecution by Romans. Long before, 'black' Jews had come from Babylon and Persia, then in 1492 another wave arrived after being expelled from Spain. Today, only a handful of families remain and their traditional spice shops and trading agencies have given way to shops targeting the luxury tourist trade, mainly dealing in antiques—some genuine, some reproductions, and worth investigating. At the heart of Jew Town stands the **Pardesi Synagogue**▶▶ (*Open* Sun–Fri 10–12, 3–5. *Admission: inexpensive*), built in 1568 for the white Jewish community. It had to be completely rebuilt in the 1660s after Portuguese–Dutch battles had destroyed it. Of particular and curious interest are the floor-tiles: 18th-century Cantonese hand-painted ceramics depicting a love-story between a Chinese princess and a commoner (evidence of the vast and flourishing trade network of the time). Crowning the synagogue is a clock-tower erected by Ezekiel Rahabi, who was also responsible for importing the tiles (see panel).

CHANGING PICTURES
'No two are identical. The tiles from Canton, 30cm x 30cm (12" x 12") approx., imported by Ezekiel Rahabi in the year 1100BC, covered the floors, walls and ceilings of the little synagogue. Legends had begun to stick to them. Some said that if you explored for long enough you'd find your own story in one of the blue-and-white squares, because the pictures on the tiles could change, were changing, generation by generation, to tell the story of the Cochin Jews. Still others were convinced that the tiles were prophecies, the keys to whose meanings had been lost with the passing years.'
Salman Rushdie, *The Moor's Last Sigh*, 1995

Ernakulam Apart from the atmospheric palace hotels of Willingdon Island (the Taj Malabar Hotel) and Bolgatty Island (Bolghatty Palace), the rest of Kochi's interest is centred on Ernakulam. Shops and banks are concentrated along MG Road. It is worth taking a taxi or bus 12km (7 miles) southeast to the **Hill Palace Museum**▶▶, Chottanikkara Road, Thripunitra (*Open* Tue–Sun 9–12.30, 2–4.30. *Admission: inexpensive*), a Keralan-style palace in beautiful grounds. As well as some exceptional Hindu ritual artefacts, bronzes and paintings, it now contains the royal memorabilia that was in Kochi's Parishath Thamburan Museum.

Lakshadweep Islands Kochi is the base for flying to these idyllic islands, scattered some 200km (124 miles) away over the coral reefs. Lakshadweep remains an ultra-exclusive haven apart from local fishing communities, who also make coir products from coconut. Only one island, Bangaram, is open to foreign visitors with expensive twice-weekly flights operated by NEPC. The tiny airport is on the island of Agatti and from there a boat or helicopter (during the monsoon) connects with **Bangaram**▶▶▶, where stunning beaches and mesmerising coral reefs are well served by the Island Resort hotel. Kadmat island's beach resort is also open. Individuals should contact Casino Hotel, Willingdon Island, Kochi (tel: 0484 2668421, fax: 0484 2668001, email: contact@cghearth.com), or Sports, Lakshadweep Office, Indira Gandhi Road, Willingdon Island, Kochi (tel: 0484 2668387, fax: 2668647, email: laksports@vsnl.net).

▶ Kodaikanal   *202C2*

Kodaikanal, founded in the 19th century by the British, lies at over 2,300m (7,544ft) on the southern ridge of the Palani Hills, about 120km (74 miles) northwest of Madurai from where it is a four-hour bus-ride. Although very popular with Indians during April–June, this hill-station is not of major interest except for walks. Nights can be very cold and damp October to December, while in summer it suffers from sweltering heat.

Flower-power There are beautiful forest walks and water-falls in the hills and the town itself has several parks. At its centre is a large octopus-shaped lake. Bicycles, boats and horses can all be hired here. The main services, including a tourist office, are along Anna Salai. Immediately south is Bryant's Park and the scenic **Coaker's Walk▶** which, on a clear day, offers stunning views. At the northern tip of the lake is Observatory Road, leading up to the Observatory (*Museum:* tel: 04542 240214. *Open* for visits by prior appointment Sat–Thu, Fri 10–noon, 3–5. *Admission: free*). Several kilometres south are the **Pillar Rocks▶**, rising dramatically above the hillside. North of the town is **Chettiar Park▶**, home to the curious Kurinji flower that blossoms once every 12 years.

KOCHI FERRIES
Much faster, cheaper and more scenic than buses, ferries are the ideal form of transport for this waterbound city. The most popular route runs from Ernakulam's main jetty to Fort Kochi Customs (the stop for all Fort Kochi's sights), then continues to Mattancherry Jetty. The first runs at 7am the last around 9.30pm. Frequent ferries connect Ernakulam main jetty with Willingdon Island's Embarkation Jetty (close to the tourist office) and others between Fort Kochi's Customs Jetty and Willingdon's Terminus Jetty. Ferry timetables are posted at ticket offices beside every jetty.

229

TOURIST INFORMATION
TTDC, Bus stand, Resthouse, Kodaikanal (tel: 04542 241675).

An idyllic, palm-fringed beach in the Lakshadweep Islands

Gopurams of the Sri Meenakshi, the vast temple complex that lies at the heart of Madurai

TOURIST OFFICE
The very helpful Tamil Nadu Tourist office is in the Hotel Tamil Nadu, West Veli Street, near the Periyar bus-stand (*Open* Mon–Fri 10–5.45; tel: 0452 2334757, www. tamilnadutourism.org). Also tourist information counters at the railway station and the airport.

ELEPHANT CITY
Elephants crop up everywhere in Madurai, but one place where you are certain to meet one is at the temple. Alongside dozens of priests working full-time to keep the cogs of Hinduism turning, there is an elephant 'blessing' visitors. No marriage, political function or religious feast takes place in Madurai without an elephant, and banks are known to give loans for their purchase. Feeding them or giving them money is considered a religious action.

▶▶▶ **Madurai** *203D2*

This extremely sacred city, Tamil Nadu's oldest, was originally designed in a lotus motif but has since expanded into a cacophonous labyrinth of temples, bazaars and narrow streets packed with stalls, squatting vendors, rickshaws, cows, buffaloes and the odd ambling elephant. It is a perfect size, small enough for easy orientation and large enough for interest to spread over several days. Garlands of scented jasmine, graceful Tamil women, vegetarian specialities and friendly people make it a quintessential southern town, not to be missed.

Heart of the matter The vast walled complex of the **Sri Meenakshi temple**▶▶▶ (*Open* daily 5am–12.30, 4–9.30pm. *Admission: inexpensive*) with its shadowy chambers, *tank*, carved columns, shrines and courtyards built between twelve towering *gopurams*, is considered south India's finest example of Dravidian architecture, and is Madurai's spiritual and geographical heart. Certainly it has one of the most powerful and revealing atmospheres of any Hindu temple. Most of the structure dates from the Nayak dynasty (16th–18th centuries) but certain individual shrines date back earlier, to the Pandiyas (see page 39). The inner sanctums containing the stone images of the goddess Meenakshi (a form of Parvati) and that of Siva (Sundareswarar) are closed to non-Hindus but there is plenty to see outside.

The main entrance is through the East Gate, leading to a corridor lined with temple-souvenir stands. In the northeast corner is the Temple Museum in the Ayirrakal Mandapa ('Hall of 1,000 Pillars', in fact 985). The magnificent hall is flanked by prancing lions and other creatures superbly sculpted round the columns. Stone carvings mingle with curious drawings of 'thought forms' as perceived by yogis, but display panels detract from the structural splendour and scale. In a courtyard outside stands a *nandi*, symbolically guarding the Siva shrine.

Closer to the south entrance is the magical pool of the Golden Lotus Tank, always crowded with worshippers, some bathing before *puja* to remove guilt, others just sitting and chatting. West of here is the Meenakshi shrine where, every evening at 9pm, Siva's statue is ceremonially brought 'to sleep', accompanied by the elephant, priests, musicians and devotees. North of this area a maze of dark corridors contains countless statues splattered with *ghee* and pigment, both being traditional offerings. It is well worth hiring a guide to explore the highlights, but the temple is also fascinating just for the sight of worshippers hurling *ghee*, circling statues or applying *tikkas* (the dots painted on the forehead by Hindus).

Palatial sights The streets surrounding the temple are a hive of tailors' shops, jewellers and general souvenir shops. The Pudu Mandapa is an extraordinary tailors' market inside a crumbling palace that opens onto East Chitrai Street. On the northern side, hustlers spirit visitors to rooftops for sweeping views over the temple and especially the gold-topped *gopuram* that is above the central sanctuary. A short walk or rickshaw-ride southeast takes you to the **Thirumalai Nayaka Palace▶▶** (*Open daily 9–1, 2–5. Admission: inexpensive*), built in 1636 and partially renovated. Intricately stuccoed domes rise above an open quadrangle edged by lofty arcades, all that remains of the original palace. An excellent museum recounts the history of the palace and various entertainments are staged in the courtyard. A sound and light show in English is at 6.45pm.

Educational tour A few kilometres northeast of the centre, beyond the Vaigai river on the Tammukam Road, is a landscaped complex that includes the **Gandhi Museum▶▶** (*Open daily 10–1, 2–5.30. Admission: free*), in a lovely 17th-century palace. It gives a fascinating photographic account of the freedom struggle and Gandhi's role. The *dhoti* that he was wearing when he was assassinated is preserved in a dark room, still bloodstained, like a religious relic.

TEPPAM FESTIVAL
The Teppam Festival is held at full moon in late January–February, to commemorate the birth of King Thirumalai Nayak. The normally empty pool of the Teppakulam *tank*, about 5km (3 miles) southeast of the centre of Madurai, is filled for the occasion. Statues of Siva and Meenakshi are brought to the central island temple, from where they circle round the vast *tank* on floats. Thousands of pilgrims line the banks watching the progress of their gods, while the full moon hangs above.

231

Golden Gopuram, Sri Meenakshi temple

Ayurvedic medicine has been practised in India for over 2,000 years. Its complex principles are based on the use of natural ingredients to restore the balance of mind and body. Medication can be purely herbal or use minerals and metals, while treatments involve specially prescribed diets, elixirs, yoga, steam-baths and massage.

Ayurvedic cures for sale in the Kodaikanal bazaar

No visitor to India's south can escape mention of Ayurveda, usually applied to bogus massages that are offered at every tourist centre, but also associated more seriously with certain health resorts. Ayurveda is Sanskrit for 'laws of health' and is one of the four *Vedas,* or Hindu sacred texts. Over the centuries, this traditional Indian medicine became modified by contact with foreign systems but is now enjoying a resurgence in popularity. Ayurvedic products include toothpaste and shampoo, and the system has been adopted and extensively researched in Russia and China.

Air, water, fire Many of Ayurveda's more extraordinary practices, such as vaccination, anaesthesia by inhalation and dietetics, have been adopted in the West in the last century or so, but the system is in principle holistic as it aims to treat people's physical, psychological and spiritual attributes together. At its basis is *Tridosha*, the theory that there are three elements: fire, water and air. All human functions are located in one of these three *doshas* (cosmic forces) that, in turn, are divided into two aspects: the matter and the essence. Further complex sub-divisions identify specific organs, and take into consideration temperature, emotions, physical alertness and personality. All are examined in the context of the patient's age and family circumstances and all these interconnected factors form the basis of the doctor's diagnosis and therapy.

Ayurvedic therapy Body functions are divided according to the three characteristics of the doshas. *Vayu* (wind or air) incorporates respiratory and sound-producing apparatus, the digestive tract, bladder, and substance-retaining organs as well as wind and flatus. *Pitta* (sun or fire) is related to the liver, spleen, heart and eyes. *Kaph* (moon or water) controls the flow of moisture in the body from the brain to salivary and gastric juices, cardiac fluids and those in joints.

The physician's formidable task is to maintain the balance of these three forces and, since the same three classifications are identifiable in foods, choose the appropriate remedy. Asthma, for example, is thought to indicate that the air element is over-dominant. A diet is prescribed to exclude any *vayu* foods such as rice and spices, and

PULSE-READING
A major diagnostic tool for Ayurvedic practitioners is pulse-reading. They claim that by placing three fingers on the pulse and pressing it, they can tell within seconds what is wrong. The problem might be constipation or cancer, or a psychological condition such as anxiety or depression. They also say they can tell if you live on junk food (your pulse will be muted) or take the contraceptive pill. Above all, they claim to predict the onset of diseases, as these have six definable stages.

therapies are practised to stimulate the other two elements. Surgery was a highly developed science in the early days of Ayurveda but an organ was removed only if it was considered a threat to the proper functioning of the rest of the body.

Positive relationship Ayurveda is based on a positive interaction between doctor and patient that extends to the latter's spiritual welfare. Even in times of good health, an Ayurvedic doctor advises on diet, the regulation of personal habits, the choice of marital partner and sexual behaviour. Seeing the patient as more than a passive biological system, Ayurveda emphasizes the patient's responsibility in developing well-being.

Therapies Ayurvedic health resorts offer a variety of therapies, best experienced on a daily basis for two weeks. These include massages with herbal oils, good for rheumatic problems and stress; *njavarakizhy*, a treatment that induces perspiration by the application of medicated rice compresses, good for joint pains, arthritis and some skin diseases; *dhara*, a mental relaxant of herbal oils and buttermilk poured on then massaged into the forehead and upper body to help insomnia, mental tension and skin problems; *pathrasweda*, a massage with bunches of boiled medicinal herbs, used to improve circulation and tone muscles; and *udvarthanam*, a massage with herbal powders designed to help obesity, paralysis and rheumatism. Medicated steam baths are another favourite treatment for eliminating toxins, reducing fat tissues and helping skin disorders.

AYURVEDIC STRESS-BREAKERS
- Eat at regular times.
- Sip hot water thoughout the day, or lukewarm water in summer.
- Use a stainless-steel tongue-scraper or the back of a spoon to remove impurities every morning.
- Make lunch your biggest meal.
- Eat dinner by 8pm.
- Get to bed by 10pm.
- Never use an alarm-clock.
- Practise meditation.

Ayurvedic potions (above) and massage (below)

TOURIST OFFICE
Tamil Nadu Government
Tourist Office, Covelong
Road, at entrance to town
on Chennai road (*Open*
Mon–Fri 9.45–5.45, tel:
04114 242232). On hire
are guides, useful for
understanding temple
intricacies, bicycles,
essential for getting round
the scattered sights, and
cars. Bicycles can also be
hired in the centre. A
dance festival is held
every December–January.

BEACH LIFE
The waters of the Bay of
Bengal are relatively safe
to swim in but female
swimmers in particular
will find they attract
appreciative crowds of
spectators. The best bet
is to use the beaches
north of the village in
front of the more expen-
sive hotels. These can be
reached either by the
inland road or by walking
up the sand.

*Sculptor in
Mamallapuram*

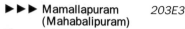

▶▶▶ Mamallapuram   *203E3*
(Mahabalipuram)

The sculptural extravaganza of Mamallapuram is yet another highlight of south India and has been designated a World Heritage Site. Under the Pallava dynasty (4th–9th centuries) this flour-ishing port became the place where the art of temple construction was rede-fined. Although only one of the seven shore temples remains, the rock-cut temples nearby incorporate superb bas-reliefs. To this day Mamallapuram thrives as a major stone-carving centre—the dawn call here is the rhyth-mical sound of chisel chipping stone. All this, along with local fishing activities, an unspoilt palm-lined beach and a wide range of accommodation, provide the ingredients for deserved popularity.

Continuing enigma Before the reign of Narasimha Varman I (AD630–668), Indian shrines had been built of wood or carved into caves. Narasimha Varman and his architects used the rocky outcrops of the local landscape to carve scale replicas of temples or *rathas* (chari-ots of the gods), but their purpose is still a mystery as they were never used for worship and many remained unfinished. It is possible that they were to show off the talents of local sculptors, and their influence certainly spread, from Ellora to Java.

Tumultuous tale The Pallavas' greatest work is an immense relief depicting the **Descent of the Ganga▶▶▶**, or 'Arjuna's Penance' (*Open: daily dawn–dusk. Admission: expensive*). The name depends on whether the central figure is Siva's ancestor, Bhaghiratha, the holy ascetic responsible for persuading the gods to release the heavenly Ganga (Ganges) onto earth or Arjuna, the warrior from the *Mahabharatha*. Measuring about 27m (88ft) long and 9m (30ft) high, it is a work of art as tumultuous as Indian life itself. A wealth of animals and gods interact with the protago-nist. In the central cleft where water once flowed from a cistern above, sculpted *nagas* swim upstream watched by two monumental elephants to the right.

To the lighthouse West, north and south are several notable *rathas* and *mandapas* (pillared halls). Carved into the boulders and fronted by pillars with squatting lions are bas-reliefs illustrating Hindu mythology. They include Vishnu as Varaha (the cosmic boar), Vishnu asleep on the giant serpent experiencing the cosmic nightmare (Vishnu Anantasayin), and Krishna lifting Mount Govardhana. Furthest

The Descent of the Ganga, or 'Arjuna's Penance', carved in stone

north are the **Trimurti cave-temples▶**; before this looms **Krishna's Butterball▶▶**, a gigantic boulder that sits poised on a sloping rock face, apparently ready to roll. From here a path winds southwards and uphill towards the Old Lighthouse that once doubled as a Siva temple. It now stands beside the New Lighthouse, and both have panoramic views. Just below is the mid 7th-century **Mahishasura Mardini temple▶▶**, which shows the buffalo demon being slain by a masterfully sculpted, eight-armed Durga, a feminine aspect of Siva, sitting astride her lion in supremely confident and regal style.

Five rathas About 3km (2 miles) south of the village is an outstanding group of *rathas* from the 7th–8th centuries known as the **Pancha Pandava▶▶▶**. Four of them are carved from a long granite boulder running north–south, while the fifth stands just out of line. There are also a gigantic elephant, lion and bull. The architectural styles show a marked Buddhist influence. Every wall and level is profusely sculpted (some are more complete than others).

On the shore Whipped by the wind and eroded by the thundering waves, the stunning **Shore Temple▶▶▶** (*Open*: daily dawn–dusk. *Admission: expensive* includes five *rathas*) is majestic and somewhat melancholy, standing in isolation on the beach. It is thought to be India's oldest freestanding temple, and was built in the early 8th century. The approach is through an enclosure surmounted by small *nandis*, behind which rises the main *vimana* on six richly carved levels beside a smaller one. There are two shrines dedicated to Siva, one each side of another devoted to Vishnu, entered from the south.

DESCENT OF THE GANGA
The great relief at Mamallapuram (Mahabalipuram) probably depicts the descent of the the goddess Ganga to earth, one of Hinduism's greatest tales. For a thousand years (a mere drop in time for Hindu myths), Siva's ancestor Bhagiratha performed great acts of austerity and penance in order to persuade the gods to release the heavenly Ganga (Ganges). When he finally succeeded, the next challenge was to prevent the impact of the falling water from destroying the earth. In stepped Siva himself, who stoically agreed to receive the river on his head where it meandered for further aeons through his tangled hair before flowing gently onto the earth from the Himalayas.

The Maharaja's Palace illuminated by thousands of light bulbs

ROYAL TRAINS
Mysore's regal sights continue at the railway station, where the royal retiring rooms were favourites with the former Maharani. A long colonnaded veranda leads to the Rani's room with its floor-length curtains and regal bed, and the public waiting-room has a fountain. Beside the station is the Rail Museum (*Open* Tue–Sun 10–1, 3–5. *Admission: inexpensive*); where old locomotives and special coaches for the royal family are displayed.

►►► Mysore   202C3

Few Indian cities can rival the stately charm and easy-going atmosphere of Mysore, a former princely capital 140km (87 miles) southwest of Bangalore. With a population of around three quarters of million, it remains a manageable size with tree-lined streets and well-maintained historic buildings, and makes an excellent base for this region's numerous cultural relics and wildlife sanctuaries. Often dubbed the 'city of palaces', it in fact has five, and several mansions as well, some of which have been converted into attractive, atmospheric hotels. Jasmine, incense, silk, carved sandalwood and rosewood are the main local products, bringing fragrance to the Devaraja market. *Mallige* is Mysore's jasmine speciality and its heady scent permeates the air when it blossoms in spring. Mysore is fairly westernized, though. You will not see many people in loincloths, and auto-rickshaw drivers ruthlessly raise their fares for visitors.

Palaces and more palaces Hard to miss at the heart of town is the massive **Maharaja's Palace►►►**, standing within walled gardens (*Open* daily 10–5.30. *Admission: moderate*. No cameras or shoes inside but free lockers available at northern entrance). Built in 1897–1912 to replace a palace that burned down, it was designed by the prolific Henry Irwin in typical Indo-Saracenic style, sprouting turrets, arches and columns at every opportunity. Every Sunday night and during festivals the palace is lit by 50,000 bulbs—a dazzling sight.

Inside, flashy decoration takes over. Though it borders on kitsch it is still remarkable for its state of conservation and craftsmanship. The central octagonal Peacock Pavilion is a riot of colourful art nouveau tiles and stained glass, with walls lined with paintings of Mysore festivities. Doors of fabulously carved Myanmar teak lead to a portrait gallery before you reach the first floor eye-stopper, the public Durbar Hall. This vast colonnaded turquoise and gold hall, open to the front, incongruously combines paintings of Hindu divinities with royalty;

while chandeliers and a 'Durbar lift' add a western touch. From here solid silver doors inlaid with ivory lead to the private Durbar Hall, harbouring more stained glass, chandeliers and a carved wood ceiling. Visitors shuffle through the palace along a clearly marked route; palace guards throughout are always willing to give information.

On the western flank of the palace, beyond a small temple and camel-rides, is the **Maharaja's Residential Museum►►** (*Open* daily 10.30–5.30. *Admission: inexpensive*). This idiosyncratic collection is well worth the visit, giving a far more human picture of Mysore's royalty than the grandiose palace. Broken chairs, toy cars, paintings, palanquins, sepia photos, brocade costumes and even a day-bed with crystal legs are all jumbled together, and the guardroom has a collection of weapons.

Sensuous sights West of the Maharaja's Palace stands another palatial abode, the Jaganmohan Palace now used as the **Jayachamarajendra Art Gallery►►** (*Open* daily 8.30–5. *Admission: inexpensive*), with more regal relics, including portraits of the royal family, miniatures, furniture, glass, porcelain, musical instruments and Western and Indian *objets d'art*. A short stroll north to KR Circle, with its ornate clock tower (not to be confused with another one near Gandhi Square) leads to the hectic activity and sound of the **Devaraja market►**. This maze of narrow medieval alleys is lined with booths selling neat piles of brilliantly coloured textile dyes, sandalwood incense, piles of jasmine and marigolds, antiquated tools and utensils, and much more besides, altogether creating a very magical atmosphere at nightfall.

The avenue running north from KR Circle, Sayyaji Rao Road, is the main shopping street and includes the Cauvery Arts and Crafts Emporium. To see Mysore specialities being made, take a rickshaw 2km (1 mile) southwest to the Government Silk Factory, Manathandy Road (*Open* Mon–Sat 8–11, 12.30–5. *Admission: inexpensive*; tel: 0821 521803).

TOURIST OFFICE
Regional Tourist Office, Old Exhibition Buildings, Irwin Road, Mysore (*Open* Mon–Sat 10–5.30; tel: 0821 2422096, fax: 0821 2421833). Also counters at the railway station and bus-stand. Information also available at the Hotel Mayura Hoysala, 2 JLB Road (tel: 0821 2425349).

237

Marigolds are sold in Devaraja market—the demand for them is such that they are sold by weight

*Statue of Gommata at
Shravanabelgola*

THE WORLD COLOSSUS?
The monolithic Gommata
is the largest statue
carved from a single block
of stone in India, but is it
the biggest in the world?
The Buddha images at
Bamiyan in Afghanistan
are at least twice as high
but are not carved out of
a single block as is
Gommata. Egypt's image
of Ramses II is bigger, but
is not free-standing.
Memnon's two colossi are
at least 3m (10ft) taller
than Gommata and about
two millenniums older, but
they are not monolithic.

Excursions

Chamundi Hill▶ A drive 13km (8 miles)
south of Mysore leads to this symbolic
hill crowned by the 12th-century
Chamundeshwari temple (*Open* daily
7–2, 4–7.30. *Admission: free*; or pay to
jump the queue). The temple is
dedicated to Mysore's ruling goddess,
Chamundi, better known as Durga.
There are special worship days on
Tuesdays and Fridays, when it is nearly
impossible to see the goddess's solid
gold statue. True pilgrims reach the
temple by climbing 1,000 odd steps
from the base, passing the superb black
granite **nandi▶▶** (made in 1659) about
two-thirds of the way up. Sweeping
views show the Lalitha Mahal Palace
(1931), with a dome copied from St.
Paul's in London, and the Rajendra
Vilas Palace (1939), both now converted
into luxury hotels.

Shrirangapattana▶▶ This island town
is inextricably linked to the history of
Mysore and its rulers. It sits in the
Kaveri (Cauvery) river 16km (10 miles)
to the north, and was once the headquarters of Hyder Ali and his son, Tipu
Sultan, the Muslim conquerors of
Mysore's Wodeyar family. 'Better to
live one day as a tiger than a thousand
years as a sheep' said Tipu (*c*1750–99)
who, after allying himself with the
French to defeat the British invaders,
died in a bloody battle against Arthur
Wellesley, later the Duke of Wellington.
Tipu's summer palace, the Daria Daulat
Bagh (*Open* Sat–Thu 9–5. *Admission: inexpensive*), is an
exquisitely decorated 1784 teak structure that was occupied after his death by his English conqueror. Superb frescoes in naive style illustrate various battles, and upstairs
a collection of paintings and memorabilia overlooks the
lovely Mughal gardens. At the eastern end of the island
town stands the Gumbaz, a mausoleum with doors of
ebony inlaid with ivory, where father and son are buried.
   Long before the arrival of its Muslim conquerors,
Shrirangapattana was famous for the Sri Ranganatha
Temple, an imposing 10th-century Vishnuite edifice that
still attracts throngs of pilgrims. This stands near a
mosque within the walled fort that dates from the
Vijayanagar dynasty in 1454; when Vijayanagar power
waned in the early 1600s they gave way to the Wodeyars.

Shravanabelgola▶▶▶ This extraordinary Jain pilgrimage
site, 93km (58 miles) north of Mysore, spreads over two
hills, several *tanks* and a village. Its highlight is the main
temple (*Open* daily 6–6. *Admission: free*) on Indragiri Hill.
Inside its precincts is a monolithic statue of Gommata, that
is 17m (56ft) in height. Long-armed and with legs
entwined with creepers, he is wonderfully serene and

oblivious to the crowds of prostrate pilgrims below. This fantastic feat of engineering dates from cAD980 and makes a fitting climax to the long climb up the granite hill that goes up nearly 700 steps, passing numerous rock inscriptions and intermediary *basadis* (shrines). Take water and socks to protect your feet—no shoes allowed. Every 12 years a major anointing ceremony takes place to honour Gommata: devotees pour holy water, *ghee*, coconut milk, turmeric and honey liquids over the head from specially erected platforms while crowds watch in complete silence. Sculptures of Jain *tirthankaras* (prophets) and *yaksas* (demigods), as well as 9th–19th-century reliefs carved into boulders, continue on Ghandragiri, the small hill to the north.

Wildlife sanctuaries (*Admission: expensive*; to both parks) There are panthers, elephants, chital, sambhar and barking deer together with numerous bird and reptile species at **Nagarhole (Rajiv Gandhi) National Park▶▶**, 96km (60 miles) southwest of Mysore. The state-run Kabini River Lodge has excellent amenities and guides, and is the best place from which to explore the park. Otherwise the Forest Department at Kutta organizes tours. Due south of Mysore is the **Bandipur National Park▶▶**, set up by the Maharaja of Mysore in 1931 and one of 23 national parks in India selected to participate in Project Tiger in 1973 (see page 100). You may not see a tiger, but other wild elephants, mammals and birds are plentiful among the teak, rosewood and bamboo that borders the Mudumalai Wildlife Sanctuary.

DASARA FESTIVAL

This 10-day event takes place every September–October, transforming Mysore into a centre of non-stop pomp and pageantry as the city celebrates the victory of the goddess Chamundeswari over the demon. The jewel-encrusted gold throne is brought out of the Maharaja's Palace, and the palace façade is illuminated nightly as a backdrop to countless cultural events. The climax comes on the 10th day, when an elephant carrying a statue of the goddess in the maharaja's golden *howdah* leads a procession from the palace to Bannimantap on the outskirts, accompanied by soldiers and royal chariots.

239

National parks like Nagarhole employ working elephants

The Hoysala dynasty built three quite magnificent temples within easy striking distance of Mysore, at Somnathpur, Halebid and Belur. Each one has its own remarkable features, but all three temples have outstandingly ornate filigree stonework that is a tribute to the prowess of the sculptors and stonemasons.

JAIN EXTENSIONS
The Parsvanatha Jain temple (12th century) stands south of Halebid's main temple. It consists of three *bastis* (sanctuaries). In the first stands an impressive monolithic statue of the 23rd *Tirthankara* (prophet), the last manifestation before Mahavir, surrounded by lathe-turned pillars. The second, smaller temple is of little interest, but the third reveals a superbly worked interior dome and a statue of the 16th *Tirthankara*, Santinatha. Outside stands a Jain dovecot raised high on a pillar, and said to enclose a statue of Brahma as protector.

Kesava temple at Somnathpur

For about two centuries the Hoysalas remained within the feudal domain of the Chalukyas, who ruled from successive capitals around Badami. By the mid-13th century, the Hoysalas had attained power and at their zenith they controlled most of Karnataka and parts of Tamil Nadu. By then they had already built over 100 temples, making prolific use of the local soapstone (chloritic schist). When first quarried, this is soft enough to allow intricate carving before slowly hardening and darkening in colour on exposure to the air. The Hoysala dynasty supported Siva, Vishnu and also Jain beliefs; their fall came in the mid-14th century with the rise of the Vijayanagar dynasty at Hampi.

To the temples The three main examples of Hoysala art are the well preserved temples at Somnathpur (35km/22 miles east of Mysore) and at Belur and Halebid, both near Hassan, 157km (97 miles) northwest of Mysore. The latter two are best visited on a day-trip that can also take in Shravanabelgola (see page 238). Somnathpur can be included on a half-day trip to Shrirangapattana (see page 238). The tourist office in Mysore organizes a day tour to Belur and Halebid.

Style The compact sanctuaries of all three temples share a unique star-shaped form raised on a layered platform—originally within a colonnaded cloister (most evident at Somnathpur). These platforms allow for walking around the temple (always in the sacred, clockwise direction), and show off bands of finely carved gods, goddesses, warriors, musicians, animals, birds and foliage, alongside brackets carved as supple feminine figures.

Somnathpur The temple here is often considered the highlight of the three. It was constructed in 1268 by a Hoysala general with three shrines devoted to Vishnu in different forms: Kesava, Janardana and Venugopal. The façade sculptures are raised on a platform flanked by crouching elephants. From the base upwards they show elephants, galloping horses ridden by soldiers and, at eye-level, heavily bejewelled deities in flowing garments. Scrollwork above works its way around the jutting angles

240

Ornate sculpture, typical of Hoysala structures, at Belur temple

of the star-shape before culminating in three profusely carved tapered towers. Inside are lathe-turned pillars, another hallmark of the Hoysala style. These horizontally ridged columns reappear at the Hassan temples, as do the spectacular domed ceilings carved with banana buds and lotus-flowers. The shrine figure of Venugopal is particularly lively, showing Vishnu with inclined head and flute (unfortunately broken) raised to lips. Unusually for Indian temples, these ones bear the sculptors' signatures.

Belur The Chennakesava temple (1117) stands within a huge compound and contains a single shrine. This is filled with lathe-turned pillars and columns with a jagged-edged symmetry, all barely visible in a gloom penetrated only by shafts of light through the jali walls. The Narasimha pillar is profusely carved on the capital, shaft and base with niches containing images. Outside, as well as friezes of animals and deities, the Hoysala sculptors created 42 bracket figures of voluptuous women. Everything is carved with incredible detail, including a fly on a lizard.

Halebid More complex and fluid in style, the Hoysaleswara temple at Halebid stands in open gardens next to a small museum (*Open* Sat–Thu 10–5. *Admission: free*). The shrines, probably for Siva and his consort, now contain lingams. The elaborate carvings over the porches show makaras (mythical creatures symbolizing the Ganges) with a few erotic couples. Inside, the colossal statues include Ganesa, legendary ancestor of the Hoysalas.

MORE HOYSALA
The Hoysaleswara temple was not the only one at Halebid. Over a dozen temples are mentioned in records and others still exist, less well preserved but obviously carved by the same team of artists. Among these are the Manikeswara temple (1136) and the Kedareswara temple on the western bank of the Dvarasamudra Tank. The latter had a tower as recently as the 19th century, but rampant vegetation and general neglect eventually destroyed it.

**BLUE MOUNTAIN
RAILWAY**
The twisting narrow-gauge
track of the Nilgiri toy train
climbs up through magnificent dense forest and
tea-plantations, crossing
250 bridges and crawling
through 16 tunnels over
a total distance of 45km
(28 miles). This short
distance can take over
four hours, but the train
is comfortable and views
are superb. If you
miss the train, there
are frequent buses cover-
ing the Coimbatore–
Mettuppalaiyam–Coonoor–
Ooty route.

▶▶ Nilgiri Hills   *202C3*

Tamil Nadu's Nilgiris (meaning 'blue mountains') occupy
the junction of the Eastern and Western ghats and are an
obvious destination for cooling off from the heat of the
plains. The highest peak, Doda Betta, rises to 2,636m
(8,646ft), while Udagamandalam lies at 2,240m (7,347ft)
and Coonoor at 1,860m (6,100ft). Temperatures rarely rise
above 25°C (77°F) in summer, and during winter nights
drop to zero. As a result, landscapes are spectacularly
green, carpeted in the tea estates that brought local prosperity, or in spices such as cinnamon, cardamom and
cloves. On the northern flanks, the road descends through
the **Mudumalai Wildlife Sanctuary▶▶** with its popular
Elephant Camp before entering Karnataka through the
Bandipur National Park to Mysore. To the south access is
from Coimbatore town. From here trains connect with the
Nilgiri Blue Mountain Railway, a scenic narrow-gauge toy
train service that twists slowly through the hills from
Mettuppalaiyam through Coonoor to Ooty (see panel).

Coonoor▶ Smaller, less popular
and less commercialized than Ooty,
Coonoor (divided into Lower and
Upper) has managed to preserve an
old-fashioned, peaceful feel. There
is little to do here except indulge in
long walks, taking in the tea-plantations, Sim's Park (*Open daily
8–6.30. Admission: inexpensive*) and
its well-tended botanical garden
with hundreds of rose varieties, or
Lamb's Rock, a sheer precipice
commanding wonderful views of
the plains, about 8km (5 miles)
from town. A good area for seeing
wildlife is around Dolphin's Nose,
which about 7km (4 miles) south of
Coonoor, Law's Falls is worth
the trip to see it thunder some
60m (197ft) through the forest.

Kothagiri▶ The oldest of the Nilgiris' three hill-stations lies at 1,980m (6,450ft), northeast of Coonoor, and is shielded from the monsoons by the Doda Betta range. From here it is about 20km (12 miles) to Kodanad View Point, along a precipitous road with fabulous views of the tea-estates and the Moyar river. Accommodation in Kothagiri remains limited and fairly basic, so it is best visited on a day-trip.

Udagamandalam (Ooty)▶ Most visitors are disappointed by this once fashionable hill-station, now a characterless concrete sprawl with endless souvenir shops and hotels aimed at the flocks of domestic tourists escaping the heat. At the base of the town is a large racecourse (the season is in March–April), with the bus-station and artificial lake (boating available daily 8–6) to the west and the market flanking it to the north. Hotels and guest-houses are gradually filling the slopes to the south, while the very British colonial relics lie uphill and north of the bazaar, beyond the crossroads of Charing Cross.

Local interest It is easy to explore the commercial centre on foot, stopping to sample local confectionery, countless natural oils (eucalyptus, geranium, lemon-grass), honey, tea or coffee, all products of the Nilgiris. Other sights of interest are fairly scattered but auto-rickshaws are always plentiful. At the **Botanical Gardens** (*Open daily 8–6. Admission: inexpensive*), laid out in 1847 by the Marquis of Tweeddale, over 1,000 exotic and ornamental plants and flowers blanket the beautiful grounds, and there is an ancient fossilized tree trunk. Next door stands the elegant Raj Bhavan, built in 1877 by the Governor of Madras to resemble his family seat at Stowe in England. Only the well-tended grounds are open to the public. The neo-Gothic St. Stephen's Church (1820s), with an evocative interior and graveyard, is thought to have been built using timber from Tipu Sultan's palace at Shrirangapattana, hauled up to Ooty by elephants. West and uphill again from here is the once snooty Ooty Club (1830), which is still functioning as a club. Further along the Mysore Road is the Government Museum (*Open Mon–Thu 9–1, 2–5. Admission: inexpensive*) with displays on the indigenous Toda people and their crafts. There are also lovely walks in the area, to the Elk Hills (5km/3 miles), Wenlock Downs (8km/5 miles), and around Avalanche Lake (28km/17 miles) and the Mukurthi National Park (40km/25 miles).

TOURIST SERVICES
Tamil Nadu TDC, Tamil Nadu Hotel Charing Cross, Wenlock Road, Ooty (*Open* Mon–Fri 10–1, 2–5.45; tel: 0423 2443977; fax: 2444369). Well disposed but often lacking essential maps. Daily tours whisking visitors round the main sights of the Nilgiris are also available from a number of travel agents.
There are numerous private bus-services to destinations beyond Ooty as far as Mysore. To arrange elephant rides and accommodation at Mudumalai contact the Wildlife Wardens office, Mahalingam Building, Coonoor Road (*Open* Mon–Fri 10–5.30; tel: 0423 2444098).

243

Opposite: Nilgiri steam train at Coonoor (top) and a Toda village hut Below: Tribal woman

The South

TOURIST OFFICES

Pondicherry TDC,
40 Goubert Salai (*Open*
Mon–Fri 8.45–1, 2–5; tel:
0413 2334575; email:
tourism@pondy.pon.nic.in;
www.tourisminpondicherry.
com).
Auroville Information
Centre/La Boutique
d'Auroville, Ambur Salai,
12 Jawarhalal Nehru
Street. (*Open* Mon–Fri
9.30–5.30; tel: 0413
2339497).

▶▶ Periyar National Park   *202C2*

At the southern end of the Western Ghats on the
Kerala–Tamil Nadu border lies a 26sq km (10sq miles)
stretch of water whose thickly forested banks are reputed
to be among the best in India for wildlife. Elephants,
langurs, wild boar, bison, sloth bear, sambar deer, porcu-
pines, flying squirrels, leopards and the increasingly
elusive tiger all inhabit the depths of this sanctuary, and
herons, egrets, darters, kingfishers and the great Malabar
grey hornbill are among the 260 or so bird species sighted.
Apart from this, the sanctuary is stunningly beautiful and
its best hotels (former royal hunting lodges) occupy prime
lakeside spots with lovely early morning views.

*Periyar National Park
is one of India's most
popular national parks*

PERIYAR

There are three major
sources for accommoda-
tion and activities in the
Park (which include boat
trips, elephant rides and
treks). These are: the
Wildlife Warden, Thekkadi
(tel: 04869 2322027),
the Forest Department
(tel: 04869 322028) and
Kerala Tourist
Development
(tel: 04869 2322023).
Tours of the local spice
and tribal villages are run
by the District Tourism
Office at Kumily
(tel: 04869 222620).

Timing Periyar's high season is December–March, but
hotels fill up at any weekend or public holiday, making
advance booking essential. It is not worth visiting during
and just after the monsoon, when lakeside sightings
become rare as the wildlife has no need of water from the
lake and the high humidity also encourages leeches.

On the trail The nearest access town is Kumily, which has
good bus connections with Kottayam, in the Keralan backwaters, and Madurai. Between Kumily and Thekkadi,
where budget and mid-range accommodation is concentrated, seemingly endless plantations of cardamom,
pepper, coffee, bananas and tapioca eventually give way to
evergreen and semi-deciduous forest, typical of this altitude (between 750/2,460ft and 1,500m/4,920ft). The best
way to observe wildlife is from a boat in the early morning
or late afternoon, when animals and birds are most active
and wild elephants come to the lake. Unfortunately
Periyar's growing popularity has led to a parallel increase
in boats, some large and noisy enough to scare away even
the most fearless of mammals. A better bet is to hire a guide
and trek through the surrounding forest or, better still, stay
overnight in one of the viewing towers run by the Forest
Department in Thekkadi.

▶▶ Puduchcheri (Pondicherry)

The most famous of France's four trading posts in India was, until recently, a sleepy backwater with little evidence of its former status. The opening of a new coastal highway has now reduced the bus journey from Chennai (Madras) to less than 4 hours and, inevitably, the number of visitors and facilities is growing. It now offers surprising pockets of sophistication and a burgeoning antiques trade.

Established in the early 18th century by the French, it finally entered independent India in 1954. It still has some ornate Catholic churches (including the neo-Gothic Sacred Heart). A grid layout is split north–south by a canal that once divided the French quarter (edging the sea), from the Indian quarter inland.

Breezy stroll Goubert Salai is the main beach promenade, dominated at its northern end by a gigantic statue of Gandhi. The Hôtel de Ville is also here. The Raj Nivas, an elegant 18th-century building, was built for the French governor and fronts the shady Government Park. Immediately south is the **Pondicherry Museum▶** (*Open Tue–Sun 10–1, 2–5. Admission: inexpensive*), with artefacts from Pondicherry's original prehistoric settlement and Pallava, Chola and Vijayanagar sculptures, alongside French bourgeois furniture and other items. Far livelier than these relics is the large, colourful **central bazaar▶▶** that lies inland on MG Road, just north of the Cathedral.

Market-seller in Puduchcheri

Aurobindo The mystically inclined flock to the **Aurobindo Ashram** (*Open daily 8–noon, 2–6. Admission: free,* but donations are requested), in rue de la Marine. It includes educational facilities, countless commercial outlets for *ashram* products and several guest-houses. Though the principal concern may be spiritual welfare, it is also one of India's wealthiest *ashrams* (see page 223). The tombs of Aurobindo and his faithful follower, Mirra Alfassa, are here. Alfassa founded the splinter-group experiment in international utopia at **Auroville▶▶**, 10km (6 miles) away, a fascinating, half-hippy, half-New Age community, whose inhabitants seem far more fulfilled than the poker-faced ashramites in town. There were bitter disputes at the *ashram* and Auroville when Alfassa died in 1973, which were resolved only when the government stepped in. Despite this, Auroville has over 1,200 inhabitants occupying over 80 settlements. Followers are international, with a high proportion of Indians, as well as Americans, Europeans, Russians and Japanese. Auroville products, such as fine paper and silk, are sold all over India.

SRI AUROBINDO

Aurobindo (1872–1950), a Bengali philosopher, originally came to Pondicherry in 1910 to escape persecution by the British authorities, who had already imprisoned him for supporting the independence movement. The *ashram* that he set up combined his own yogic systems with modern science and ideals of community living. Among its disciples was Mirra Alfassa, a Parisian of Arab origin, who came to be known as *la Mère* (mother). On Aurobindo's death, this much revered woman took over.

Faded splendour at the Royal Palace, Thanjavur

►►► Thanjavur (Tanjore)   203D2

The architectural star of the Chola dynasty (late 9th to mid-12th centuries), the **Brihadeshwara temple**►►► (*Open daily 6–1, 3–8. Admission: free*), rises above the small town of Thanjavur in splendid perfection. Its audacious conception and scale, perfect symmetry and incredible sculptural finesse make it one of India's greatest temples. It has been designated a World Heritage monument. The temple was built by King Rajaraja I in around AD1000 to honour Siva and also to project his own great power. Inscriptions record that 400 dancers were employed, as well as 200 other temple functionaries. The lofty 62m (38ft) *vimana* is India's tallest.

Temple prowess The main entrance is from the east, leading through two successive *gopurams*, both of them lavishly carved, to the enormous central courtyard whose walls display beautiful Chola frescoes. Here, a pavilion containing the obligatory *nandi*, at 6m (20ft) long monolithic masterpiece, faces the main temple. A colonnaded *mandapa* leads to the sanctuary containing a massive granite platform profusely carved with god-images and inscriptions. Above this rises the awesome *vimana*, with the sacred Siva-*lingam* below its dome. Theories abound as to how this 80-tonne block was raised to the apex: the most probable method was a ramp similar to those used by the ancient Egyptians. Steps rise to the inner sanctum, open only to Hindus. The surrounding ambulatory passages contain huge sculptures of Siva and more impressive frescoes.

Museums The **Archaeological Museum**► (*Open daily 9–1, 3–6. Admission free*), in the southwest corner of the temple courtyard, illustrates restoration work and displays some sculptures. A more interesting collection is housed in the dilapidated but impressive **Royal Palace**►► (*Open daily 9–6. Admission: inexpensive*). This 16th- to 17th-century complex lies northeast of the temple. Inside are the

TOURIST OFFICE (THANJAVUR)
Tamil Nadu TDC, Hotel Tamilnadu Complex, Jawan Bhawan, opposite main post-office (*open* Mon–Fri 10–5.45; tel: 04362 230984). Counter at Hotel Tamil Nadu, Gandhi Road. The TTDC organizes a daily-tour of Thanjavur's temples. There are over 90 Chola temples.

superbly renovated **Durbar Hall Art Gallery**▶ (*Open* daily 9–6. *Admission: inexpensive*), exhibiting Chola bronzes, the Rajaraja Museum (with more Chola bronzes and stone sculptures) and the Royal Museum (*Open* daily 9–6. *Admission: inexpensive*), displaying the rulers' accessories. It is now possible to climb the restored Bell Tower, for great views (*Admission: inexpensive*).

▶▶ Thiruvananthapuram (Trivandrum)   202C1
Now that it has an international airport receiving charter flights directly from Europe, Kerala's state capital has recently awoken to the potential of tourism and some inhabitants have become very demanding. The town's undulating layout remains attractive and, as the capital of Travancore from 1750 to 1956, it offers a good introduction to Keralan culture. The leafy town centre slopes uphill along MG Road, from the fort, railway, bus terminals and bazaar to the museums and luxury hotels that dominate the northern hill.

Museum and park complex At the centre of a park stands the **Arts and Crafts Museum**▶▶ (formerly the Napier Museum), an extraordinary architectural hybrid of geometric brickwork, Keralan roofs, stained glass and arabesque windows designed by R. F. Chisholm in the 1870s. Inside is a no less striking collection of Chola bronzes, Keralan woodcarvings, ivories, Buddhist sculptures and Southeast Asian objects. To the east, through the frangipani trees, is the **Natural History Museum**▶, with a classic display of stuffed birds and animals, including kangaroo and porcupine embryos. North of the Napier is the **Sri Chitra Gallery**▶ devoted to Asian art, with works by Raja Ravivarma figuring strongly, his earlier out-put more successful than the later. The three museums (*Open* Tue–Sun 10–4, but closed Wed morning. *Admission: inexpensive*) are covered by a single ticket, obtainable at the Natural History Museum. North of the museums are a zoo and botanical gardens, attractively laid out along shady paths.

Fort At the bustling southern end of town, a large walled fort contains the Padmanabha Swami temple, open only to Hindus, whose *gopuram* rises behind a large *tank*. Built in 1733 by a Tranvancore raja, the temple contains a large statue of Vishnu reclining on the serpent, Anantha, after whom the town is named ('the abode of the sacred serpent'). Flanking the west side of the *tank* is the **Kuthiramalika Palace Museum**▶▶ (*Open* Tue–Sun 8.30–12.30, 3.30–5.30. *Admission: moderate*). This has been the Travancore royal family's main palace since the late 18th century and is a fine example of Keralan wood architecture, with verandas, screens, shutters and superbly carved pillars surrounding a motley collection of regal paraphernalia.

TOURIST OFFICES
Tourist Information Centre, Park View, Thiruvananthapuram, opposite park. Helpful. (*Open* Mon–Sat 10–5; tel: 0471 2321132; email: info@keralatourism.org). India Tourism at airport is also very helpful. KTDC, Mascot Square (*Open* Mon–Sat 10–5; tel: 0471 2316736). Also at railway and Thampanor bus station. KTDC tours include a marathon bus-ride to Kanniyakumari.

A participant in Thiruvananthapuram's Elephant March

Lighthouse on the head-
land at Kovalam

Colourful temple,
Varkala

Excursions

Kovalam►► Although its popularity overstretches the facilities of this low-key beach resort, Kovalam offers an idyllic sweep of palm-lined beaches, a hedonistic atmosphere and a beautiful hinterland of lagoons, coconut groves and paddy-fields. The main concentration of budget guest-houses, bars and restaurants is squeezed into the southern Lighthouse Beach, with some better accommodation on the headland dominated by the lighthouse. Adjoining it to the north is Eve's Beach (or Hawah Beach). For the moment, this remains relatively unspoilt, as most of the hotels are on the verdant slopes and main road behind the coconut-palms. Beyond the headland is the private Ashok Hotel beach, continuing into Samudra Beach,

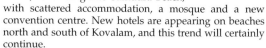

with scattered accommodation, a mosque and a new convention centre. New hotels are appearing on beaches north and south of Kovalam, and this trend will certainly continue.

Marking time Swimming is dangerous due to rip-tides, and drownings occur frequently despite the presence of numerous lifeguards. Oblivious to the dangers and the prostrate bodies of Western sun-worshippers, fishermen sing as they haul in their nets. Other locals offer Ayurvedic massages (see pages 232–233), run up cheap clothes on clacking sewing-machines, or harass tourists with endless piles of sarongs and fruit. Beachside restaurants offer excellent fresh seafood, with dazzling sunsets thrown in. There are some pleasant walks through the rice-fields behind the beach or south of the lighthouse to Vizhinjam, a busy fishing-village dominated by a large mosque.

Padmanabhapuram►► (*Open* Tue–Sun 9–5. *Admission: inexpensive*; includes tour but tip expected); Southeast of Thiruvananthapuram (56km/35 miles) on the road to Kanniyakumari, is the former palace of the Rajas of Travancore. It was the raja's seat of government from around 1550 to the 1750s. The palace typifies traditional Keralan architecture, with tiled, gabled roofs, carved wooden screens, slatted windows, trapdoors and stone pillars surrounding verdant courtyards, all very well maintained. A small museum at the entrance displays sculptures and copies of the beautiful murals in the upstairs rooms closed to the public.

Fishermen at the resort of Kovalam

Throughout the palace tropical hardwoods are used to stunning effect: superbly crafted items include the four-poster bed carved out of Ayurvedic woods in the raja's bedroom, elaborate Belgian mirrors, Thanjavur miniatures and suspended beds in the women's bedrooms. There are shrines to the goddesses Durga and Saraswati, but best of all is the bedroom designed for Vishnu, the official Travancore deity, where brass lamps and superb frescoes honour his name (*Padmanabha* refers to the lotus in Vishnu's navel).

Varkala▶▶ When Kovalam was discovered by the charter-flight operators, backpackers moved on to this idyllic village. It lies about 55km (34 miles) northwest of Thiruvananthapuram, is easily reached by train and is rather like Bali with its magical combination of temples, palms, rice-paddies and beach. From the temple crossroads a lower access road (Beach Road) connects a handful of hotels with the beach while, immediately north, a clifftop road leads to the main cluster of budget accommodation. On the way it passes a Taj Hotel that blocks the view of a former Travancore palace, now a government guesthouse. Mineral springs gush out of the dramatic red laterite cliff-face at the northern end of the beach, an added bonus for thirsty beach-bums. The springs were also inspiration for the clifftop Nature Cure Hospital where patients are treated with natural therapies.

Spiritual concerns Thought to be about 500 years old, the hilltop Janardhana Swami temple overlooks the temple lake. Behind the Keralan gable-roofed entrance gates is a fervent world of worshippers (although the temple is dedicated to Vishnu, there is a major Siva shrine by a massive banyan tree). The worshippers circle round the various shrines, throwing *ghee* for *puja*. Down at the crossroads are a Hanuman temple and a colourful Anyappan temple. The low wooden building beside the *tank* is sometimes used for Kathakali performances (see panel page 227) and hotels often stage their own. Pilgrims also flock to the *ashram* and shrine of Sri Narayana, a guru whose egalitarian teachings brought Mahatma Gandhi to Varkala.

(see panel page 227)

TOURIST SERVICES (KOVALAM)

Several hotels organize boat-trips around the local lagoons. The Western Travel Service (*Open* 8am–midnight; tel: 0471 2481334) opposite the bus stand (up the slip-road from Eve's Beach) organizes tours to Kollam's backwaters, Periyar, Kanniyakumari and Ponmudi. The KTDC in Thiruvananthapuram organize a range of tours (tel: 0471 2321132).

CULTURE AND CRAFTS

Thiruvananthapuram is a lively centre for the performing arts, including the Keralan martial art of Kalaripay, and Kuttiyattam (9th-century Sanskrit drama). Enquire at the tourist office about venues and dates. The town also sells local handicrafts, best seen at the government emporium SMSM (Kairali) Handicrafts, behind the Secretariat, and at numerous shops along MG Road.

▶▶ Tiruchchirappalli 203D2

More easily known as 'Trichy', this sprawling town is a stopover between Chennai (Madras) and Madurai, whether travelling by air or by road. It also serves as a base for visiting Thanjavur, 55km (34 miles) to the east. Ruled successively by the Pallavas, the Cholas, Vijayanagar and the Nayaks of Madurai, Trichy is now a thriving commercial town, known particularly for its *bidis* (Indian cigarettes) and artificial gemstones.

Trichy's main showstopper is some distance north at the temple town of Srirangam, on an island in the Kaveri river. Here looms the **Sri Ranganatha Swami temple▶▶▶** (*Open* daily 6.15–1, 3.15–8.45. *Admission: free*), a labyrinthine Vishnuite monument that encloses courtyards, homes, shops and shrines. Founded in the 5th century, the temple has continued to expand over the centuries, gradually acquiring seven concentric enclosures and 21 *gopurams* the most recent of which, the garishly painted southern gatehouse, is late 20th century.

The oldest and most beautiful buildings start at the fourth *prakaram* (enclosure) where shoes must be removed before you enter the superb Kalyan Mandapa (thousand-pillar hall). The Sheshagiriraya Mandapa (horse court), is a Vijayanagar creation of rearing horses and hunters formed as massive and elaborate pillars. Opposite is the earlier, 13th-century shrine to Krishna as Venugopala, displaying more superb stone-carving and brightly painted frescoes. The last section open to non-Hindus is the fifth *prakaram*, but you can get a ticket (*inexpensive*) to climb to the top of the wall for an overall view of the bristling *gopurams* and gilded *vimana*

Tiruchchirappalli, a thriving commercial town

Painted rock sculpture in Tiruchchirappalli

topping Vishnu's inner sanctum. Before leaving Sriranagam, it is worth walking through to the river banks to the north, where the daily business of body- or sari-washing continues in exactly the same way that it has done through the centuries.

▶▶ Tirupati   203D4

Beautifully located at the foot of forested hills studded with red-ochre rocks, Tirupati is renowned for its Vishnuite **Sri Venkateswara temple▶▶** (*Open* daily dawn–midnight. *Admission: free)* 15km (9 miles) away up the Tirumalai hill (identified as the mythical Mount Meru). Thousands of pilgrims climb the wooded slopes daily to see the fearsome image of Vishnu at the heart of the complex; alternative access is by hair-raising taxis and buses from Tirupati. To escape waiting for hours in long queues, it is worth paying extra for a special viewing—in fact an official form of queue-jumping. Avoid visiting the temple on any festival day, when the flood of humanity is overwhelming. It is nevertheless a highly organized place that copes admirably with pilgrim-control, and its astute hair-cutting industry (see panel) is a lucrative sideline.

The temple dates from the Pallavas and later Cholas but it was the Vijayanagar kings who poured in their wealth and craftsmen, as well as arranging the details of festivals and worship that continue to this day. Three *prakarams* lead to the inner sanctuary with its gilded *vimana* and gates surrounding the striking 2m (6.5ft), black-faced and jewel-studded statue of Vishnu. Outside the sanctum is a small museum (*Open* daily 8–6. *Admission: inexpensive)* displaying the various temple sculptures.

▶▶ Tiruvannamalai   203D3

Arunachala Hill, which rises above Tiruvannamalai, has an almost mythical status in Indian culture, as it is reputed to be the place where Siva appeared to Brahma and Vishnu as a fiery column (see page 17). Inspired by this, Tiruvannamalai's most important temple, the **Arunachaleswara temple▶▶** (*Open* daily 6–1, 5.30–10. *Admission: free)*, is dedicated to Siva in the form of Agni, the god of fire. The fire festival which is in November–December attracts thousands of devotees who watch ritual flames on the hilltop and worship at the *agni-lingam* inside the temple.

Dating back to the 11th-century Chola dynasty, this enormous temple complex was much extended by later Vijayanagar rulers. Four *prakarams* surmounted by lofty *gopurams* surround the central sanctum (open to non-Hindus) containing the sacred *lingam*, which is ceremonially bathed six times a day in a special ceremony. Access is through the eastern gateway and a long, incongruous covered bazaar specialising in metalware. In the first, highly populated courtyard a large *tank* stands opposite the thousand-pillar hall, and in the next stands the shrine to Parvati, Siva's consort, faced by his steed, Nandi. The final courtyard is rimmed by superbly carved pillars and images of numerous gods, and encloses the central Siva sanctum.

The town itself is a peaceful little place, and site of the Ramanashram, founded by a local sage who died a few decades ago. The *ashram* is open to day visitors.

251

Lurking behind the male-dominated Hindu pantheon is the Mother Goddess (Devi), an archetype imprinted on the Indian psyche. This is the most powerful and complex of the goddesses, a multiple personality who is as closely linked to nurturing as to destruction.

CELLULOID DEVI
Indian film-makers find Devi a rich source of metaphors and symbols. Satyajit Ray's *Devi* (1960) shows an image of the goddess taking shape in clay and straw, before entering a narrative about myth and religious belief. Mainstream Hindi cinema is full of references to the maternal rather than wifely aspects of Devi, representing her as outside sexuality and therefore not threatening to man.

Statues of Hindu deities in a courtyard at Chettiar Hindu Temple

252

Devi, or Mahadevi (Great Goddess) owes her strength to her ancestry in the great mother goddess of pre-Aryan times and to her role as Siva's consort, when she embodies *shakti* or female energy and reflects the multiple natures of her husband. Her identities range from the mild-mannered, self-sacrificial Sati, through seductive Parvati and destructive Durga, to the homicidal Kali.

Sweetness and light The ultra-feminine Sati married Siva against her father's wishes and later burned herself to death in defence of Siva's honour. While Siva was giving her his last embrace, creating the cosmic dance of destruction, Sati's body was dismembered by Vishnu, its 50 pieces creating 50 sacred sites. This is the origin of the Tantric worship of the *yoni*, the female organ that balances the male *lingam*. Sati's self-immolation was the example for widows who threw themselves on their husband's funeral pyres, a tradition that was banned by both British and Portuguese. Parvati, the voluptuous reincarnation of Sati, was the daughter of the Himalayas and sister of Ganga, the goddess of the River Ganga (Ganges). In order to seduce Siva, who had turned to asceticism, she underwent severe penance. Their subsequent marriage was far from har-monious, despite Parvati's ability to calm the volatile temper of her husband.

Destruction and death At the other extreme, the mother goddess rides into battle. Swinging her ten arms astride her tiger, Devi was born to kill demons, above all the buffalo demon and later Durga, whose name she adopted.
To conquer this demon, Devi grew one thousand arms and produced nine million beings from her body to form an invincible army. More terrifying still is Kali ('conqueror of time'), the black-faced earth mother who is associated with demonic rites and even human sacrifice.

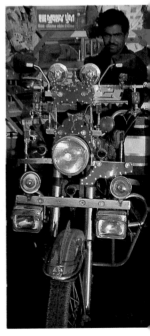

Arriving

By air Most visitors arrive at India's international airports of Delhi or Mumbai (Bombay), and less commonly at Chennai (Madras), Bangalore and Kolkata (Calcutta). Goa and Thiruvananthapuram (Trivandrum) are for charter flights. European flights generally land and depart in the dead of the night. Arrival in the nocturnal streets of the big cities is quite an experience, but airports are well prepared, with exchange facilities, hotel-booking and prepaid taxi-counters as well as official tourist offices that are all open to cater for international flights. For peace of mind and particularly in Delhi, which fills up with business travellers, it is worth booking a hotel in advance through your travel agent. Immigration procedures can last over an hour, so be prepared.

In Delhi, the Indira Gandhi International Airport (tel: 011 2565 2011) is about 25km (16 miles) south-west of the centre, a distance rapidly covered by taxis (see page 69) at night but taking much longer in daytime traffic. Terminal One handles domestic flights and is linked to Indira Gandhi by frequent shuttles.

The busy Sahar International Airport (tel: 022 2682 9000)in Mumbai (Bombay) is 30km (17 miles) north of the centre, with the Santa Cruz domestic terminal slightly closer. There are free shuttles between the two. In total and surprising contrast, the airports at Kolkata (Calcutta, tel: 033 2511 8787) and Chennai (Madras, tel: 044 2256 0551) are well organized, modern and clean, although Kolkata's little-used Dum Dum international and domestic terminal, 20km (15 miles) northeast of the centre, is quite modest. Prepaid taxis are bargains, with the alternatives of an airport bus or Kolkata's state-of-the-art metro. Chennai (Madras) has its terminals in the same building at Meenambakkan airport, 16km (10 miles) southwest of the centre, and organizes prepaid taxis and express buses. And Bangalore is emerging as a new international gateway to central and southern India. The airport is 10km (6 miles) east of the city.

By sea The only sea-routes into India are ferries from Sri Lanka and ships between Penang and Madras. Cruise-ships dock at certain Indian ports: enquire at your local travel agent.

By land Road access to India is from Nepal by bus (through four border-points), from Lahore (Pakistan) to Amritsar by bus (the actual border-crossing being on foot) or by train (it takes hours to clear customs), from Bangladesh via the Jessore–Kolkata (Calcutta) road or from Bhutan by road to Darjiling or Gangtok (this requires a special permit). Make sure your visa is multiple-entry if you are considering an excursion out of India and want to return. For all these crossings, check on requirements and political developments in advance at the relevant embassies.

Customs regulations
Duty-free allowances of one litre of spirits and 200 cigarettes (or 50 cigars) apply. Anyone bringing over US$10,000 in cash or travellers' cheques should theoretically complete a currency declaration form. Small items such as perfume, binoculars, a camera and five rolls of film are allowed, but more valuable items such as special camera or video equipment and lap-tops should be declared on a Tourist Baggage Re-export (TBRE) form that is submitted to customs on departure.

Wildlife souvenirs sourced from rare or endangered species may be either illegal or require a special permit. Before purchase, check your home country's regulations.

Travel insurance
It is essential to take out good travel insurance that covers you for repatriation if necessary. Make sure your policy has a 24-hour emergency number in the region. If paying for your ticket by a credit card that includes travel insurance, check to see exactly what this covers.

Visas and permits
Visas are necessary for all nationalities to visit India. Tourist visas are valid for 90 or 180 days from the date of issue and are either single-entry or

multiple-entry. Two photos, a completed application form and a valid passport are needed, together with a fee in cash. Visa-processing has speeded up; in some places, such as the Indian High Commission, London, tourist applications take only a few hours. Postal visas take much longer. Special permits for restricted areas are best applied for at the same time; allow two weeks. Visas are also issued at Foreigners' Regional Registration Offices in Delhi, Mumbai, Kolkata and

Taxi outside the magnificent City Palace, in Jaipur

by the Chief Immigration Officer, Chennai but this will be testing.

Departing
Reconfirm your international flight at least 72 hours before departure. India's international departure tax should be included in your ticket—but check with your travel agent.

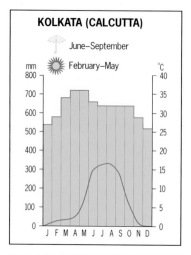

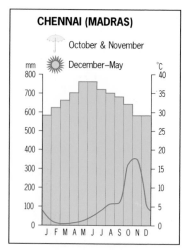

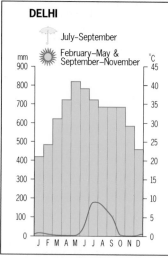

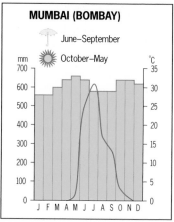

Essential facts

Climate

India's climate varies enormously, from the parched northwest to the lush, sub-tropical south and snow-capped Himalayas. Above all, it is determined by the monsoon. One arm of the monsoon generally hits the southwest coast in early June, spreading up the Western Ghats to reach the northwest about two weeks later, by which time rainfall is much lighter. In the last few years, it has even been non-existent in parts of Gujarat and the desert of Rajasthan. The other

arm swoops across the Bay of Bengal to unleash its torrents on Kolkata (Calcutta) and the northeast, before moving westwards towards Delhi. During this period, June–September, landslides and floods can be disruptive, if not fatal. The southeast sees a dry summer and a rainy season with destructive cyclones from mid-October to December.

The build-up to the monsoon in mid-April to May produces stifling, humid heat, rising to well over 40°C (104°F) in the plains: visitors should head for the Himalayan hill stations or Western Ghats. When the monsoon madness ends in October, the clear skies of Indian winter set in. By December–January temperatures are quite low in the northern plains, but the south remains warm.

When to go

For deserts and beaches, the high season in Rajasthan, Kerala and Goa is December–February. Hill-resorts have a huge influx of visitors in April–May, sending prices rocketing. The Himalayan region is extremely cold in winter, and Ladakh is accessible only in June–September. Most national parks are closed in the monsoon season. The best times for nearly every region are March–April and October–November.

National holidays

Strictly speaking there are only four national holidays: 26 January (Republic Day); 15 August (Independence Day); 2 October (Mahatma Gandhi's birthday); and 25 December (Christmas). However each region and each religion celebrates a string of festivals: on one official list they amount to 87. Muslim holidays vary according to the Islamic calendar, while Hindu, Jain and Buddhist festivities follow the lunar calendar. See pages 24–25.

Time differences

India is 5.5 hours ahead of GMT and 8.5 ahead of EST. The half-hour was invented at Independence to differentiate from Pakistan's 5 hours. As India is a tropical region, sunrise and sunset hardly vary throughout the year.

Opening times

Banks generally open Mon–Fri 10.30–2.30, Sat 10.30–12.30 (except in big cities whre hours are longer); post offices Mon–Fri 10–5, Sat 10–12; and government offices Mon–Fri 9.30–5, Sat 9.30–1. Shops open Mon–Sat 9.30–6 or sometimes later. Even in the big cities and bazaars, Sunday is very much a day of rest. Closing days for museums vary according to regions, but most close on Mondays.

Money matters

Indian currency is the rupee, with notes ranging from Rs2 to Rs500. (those under 10 are coins). There are 100 paise to a rupee, although these are almost obsolete. Always keep low-denomination notes handy for beggars, tips and small purchases. Your main supply of money should preferably be a balance of travellers' cheques and cash. Most major currencies are changed in larger city banks, with US dollars and pound sterling the most popular. On unexpected public holidays there is always a shop that will change cash at a reasonable rate. Hotels generally cash travellers' cheques only for guests. Airport exchange-counters offer good rates and also efficient service.

Credit cards including Visa, Diners, Mastercard and Amex are widely accepted at more expensive establishments, airlines and in tourist areas, but not in remote areas. When you make purchases by credit card, the vendor will raise the price to cover the bank's percentage. Beware that card fraud exists. Cash against cards can be obtained at a number of banks and ATMs are proliferating.

Tipping

Be liberal, and bear in mind that the price of a box of matches in the West is regarded as a very reasonable tip in India. Keep a stash of Rs10 notes handy. In hotels tip anyone from the porter to the *dhobi-wallah*, and add 5–10 per cent to your bill if service is not already included. In restaurants, it is always appreciated if you round up the bill. As rickshaws and taxis usually require advance negotiation, tips are not necessary, but tip if you feel it is merited. Drivers and guides appreciate tips of Rs50–100 a day.

Getting around

By air

Air travel in India changed dramatically in 2005 with the arrival of India's first low-cost airlines: Spice Jet, Kingfisher and Air Deccan. These carriers offer fares at a fraction of the cost of Air India's domestic services, although fierce competition means that not all will survive. At the moment, however, the prospect of a 1-hour flight instead of a 12-hour train journey, for around 2,000 rupees, is proving attractive to local and foreign travellers alike. Jet Airways (www.jetairways.com), bridging the gap between the low-cost airlines and the national airlines, has the most wide-ranging domestic routes and is professionally run. Similarly, Saraha Airlines (www.airsahara.net) is a mid-range domestic airline. Spice (www.spicejet.com) offers services to many major cities. Kingfisher (www.flykingfisher.com) currently has flights to Bangalore, Delhi, Kolkata and Mumbai,while Air Deccan (www.airdeccan.net) has extensive services to 34 cities. All new airline allow online ticket purchases. Some airlines are more unreliable than others, and are known to cancel less-than-full aircraft. State-run Indian Airlines serves the majorityof routes but has an appalling record of delays and cancellations.

The monthly publication *Excel*, available at major airports and city bookstores, lists the routes, times and prices of India's main airlines.

Always use a hard currency (in cash, travellers' cheques or credit cards) when buying passes/tickets, it not only exempts you from domestic airport tax (currently 10 per cent of basic fare), but also means no charges for either cancellations or reservation changes, subject to availability.

Overbooking is a perennial problem. If you are a victim, ask to see the manager and try gentle persuasion. If all else fails, a healthy tip might help.

By car and motorbike

Self-drive It is very rare for Westerners to rent self-drive cars in India, although it is possible through international companies such as Europcar or Budget. There are lower rates if you book in India and you will need an international driving licence.

Self-drive is not advisable. It means confronting the chaos of Indian traffic with cows, bullock-carts, bicycles, rickshaws, trucks and buses. People always use their car horn and the bigger vehicle always wins. Accident rates are high, road-signs are rare, roads are often in bad condition, and night-driving is very dangerous.

Motorbikes The main places for renting motorbikes are Goa and Kovalam. Insurance is compulsory but crash-helmets are not obligatory in India, so bring one from home or buy one locally. Again, avoid night-driving and if you have an accident, go straight to the local police.

Chauffeur-driven Although this has connotations of extreme luxury in the West, in India it is quite usual and by far the best option. Drivers generally know their region and, if hired through a reputable agency (local tourist offices will advise), can also be excellent guides. Daily rates vary considerably but expect $25–50 per day, depending on distance. There is a kilometre charge above a basic allowance, and overnight trips cost more. Drivers usually sleep in the car, but passengers pay for meals, a minimal cost. The most common vehicle is the Ambassador (*c*1950), although Japanese cars are slowly encroaching in more affluent areas. Remember to tip at the end of your trip.

By Jeep

Jeeps come into their own in the Himalayan region, offering fast transport. Save money by using share-jeeps where available, as around Darjeeling and Sikkim.

By train

The mysteries of Indian railways (www.indianrail.gov.in) leave many first-time visitors bemused, but it is the most sociable, cost-efficient, and illuminating way of getting around the country. Some 12 million passengers are transported daily over a vast network of 'up' and 'down' trains. These were once proudly run by the Anglo-Indian community, and many

of the Raj-era habits survive, from Ladies' Retiring-rooms to red-jacketed porters. Many metre-gauge tracks have been converted to faster broad-gauge, notably around Goa, but this does not mean your locomotive will be speeding along. Train-journeys are slow affairs, allowing time to enjoy the landscape, get to know your fellow-travellers and buy endless cups of *chai*. Food-vendors are omnipresent but official railway meals are safest (can be ordered in advance) or take your own. Steam trains, known as toy-trains, still run on the stupendous Darjeeling and Nilgiri Hills narrow-gauge tracks.

For night-trains, take your own mineral water, toilet-paper and a padlock and chain to attach your bag to the bunk. This is usual and an effective though not infallible deterrent to thieves. Keep your money and all documents on your body.

Porters at Mumbai Chhatrapati Shivaji (Victoria Terminus), Mumbai (Bombay)

Carriages, in descending order of cost and ascending order of crowdedness, are: AC first class (air-conditioned, two- or four-berth cabins with lockable doors); standard first class (non-air-conditioned, two- or four-berth curtained cubicles—being phased out); ACII tier (air-conditioned carriage, with two- or four-berth curtained cubicles); ACIII tier (air-conditioned open carriage with three-berth cubicles); AC chaircar (air-conditioned carriage with reclining seats—great for day travel) and second class (non-air-conditioned seats/berths, some wooden). Not all routes have first-class or air-conditioned carriages. Some luxury air-conditioned trains, such as the Shatabdi Express (day-time journeys) and the Rajdhani Express (overnight journeys), link the major cities and impose surcharges, but meals, mineral water and hot drinks are included in the cost. Air-conditioned chair-cars with reclining seats or Executive Class are the ultimate for day-travel.

Reservations on night-trains should be made as far in advance as possible. Booking through tourist counters at city railway stations gives you access to special tourist quotas (berths reserved for foreigners and non-resident Indians). Otherwise you join the general queues for Indian travellers and are allocated berths according to availability through an efficient computerized system. For both, you need to complete a form with the train identification number, date of departure, your name, age, nationality and sex. When you finally board the train, passenger-lists will be on each carriage and you will be grouped with other foreigners or, if female, with other women or families. Bookings made abroad must be

reconfirmed, in person, at the official office/counter of a major terminal. Deal only with people at the designated counter. Anyone else, however respectable or plausible, is a tout. Railway employees are not issued with identity cards, so any you are shown are fakes and the office is always within the station itself.

Bedding can be ordered in advance for second-class travel—it's included for the other classes. Indrail passes are available from half a day to 90 days. There are three types: a) AC first class, b) second class, and c) valid for all the in-between categories. Passes give booking priority, allow easy cancellations, and waive reservation fees, sleeper charges and supplements but do not necessarily offer savings on the already low fares. They can be purchased at major railway offices or through appointed agents abroad. See the appointed agents at www.indianrail.gov.in or

Late-comers on a public bus

visit www.indiarail.co.uk. Luxury tourist trains in Rajasthan and Gujarat are booked through separate offices (see page 74). If you are travelling extensively by train, buy a copy of *Travel Links* or *Trains at a Glance*, for train timetables.

By bus

Long-distance bus-travel is sometimes unavoidable, particularly in mountainous areas or regions where railway tracks are still narrow-gauge and extremely slow. Numerous private 'luxury' buses operate much-visited routes (as popular with domestic tourists as foreigners) and offer marginally more comfort than the state-run equivalent. Local tourist offices will advise on the best option. Private buses generally require advance bookings for their numbered seats, as do some state-run express routes, but many public buses are first in, first served—often a scrum—with the last ones hanging on the roof.

By taxi/rickshaw

Taxis are easy to find; negotiating the fare is harder as few drivers use

On-street repairs being made to an auto-rickshaw or 'auto'

meters—except in Kolkata (Calcutta).

Motorized three-wheeler taxis are called auto-rickshaws (shortened to 'autos') as opposed to cycle-rickshaws, the human-propelled variety. Kolkata is the only city that still transports people by human-pulled rickshaws. Autos are an excellent way to buzz through heavy traffic, if you can bear the fumes. Negotiate a price for several hours if you plan intensive sight-seeing. Meters are used in smaller towns, but rarely in tourist areas and cities. You will inevitably be overcharged at first, but will soon get a clear idea of average fares. Avoid the haggling syndrome: the foreigner's compulsion to barter over prices that are negligible at home. Official meter fares were raised in Delhi in 2003 in an attempt to stop this practice.

Student and youth travel

For those aged 12–30 years, there is a 25 per cent discount on standard air fares and on some late-night flights.

Communications

An STD/ISD phone-booth, Delhi

Media

India has a thriving, outspoken press, a result of its many regional languages and identities. National newspapers and weekly news-magazines in English are readily available, making it easy to keep abreast of internal and external affairs, though the accent is usually on the former. *The Hindu* and *The Asian Age* are probably the best, closely followed by the *Statesman*, *Times of India*, *Indian Express*, *Independent*, *Economic Times* and the Calcutta-based *Telegraph*. Many have special Sunday editions with extra supplements. Of the weekly magazines, *Outlook* gives good in-depth reporting; next best is the more sensationalist *India Today* while more analytical *Frontline* is fortnightly. *Business India* concentrates on financial news. Each state also has its own English-language daily, as well as newspapers in the local language.

Television was transformed in the 1990s, with over 80 satellite and cable TV channels reaching India. Indians now watch BBC World, CNN, sports and entertainment channels, and tend to give the government-run Doordarshan the cold shoulder. They have, however, remained ultra-faithful to their own cinema—Bollywood.

Post offices

The postal service functions far more efficiently for international than for internal mail. Postcards and letters abroad take 7–10 days, while air-mail parcels may surprise you by their speed (one week to Europe is common) and surface-mail by its slowness (six months on average). Parcels should be wrapped by professionals, who can usually be found outside large post offices and are artists in the use of cloth and sealing-wax. Shops will also send your purchases home but make sure they are sent by registered post (costing a minimal extra) and use your own judgement as to whether the shopkeeper is honest or not. When possible obtain the registered-post receipt or make sure your shop receipt itemizes the cost of freight or postage. Large cities are the worst for conning gullible tourists. Speedpost and other air-courier services are also available.

Telephone, fax and internet
STD/ISD phone-booths are found everywhere and operate long opening hours. Call-charges are calculated by the second, shown on an automatic screen as you speak, and rates vary little between rival booths. Trunk-calls become cheaper after 9pm, when you can expect crowds, but international rates are the same whatever the hour.

In larger towns, some phone-booths double up as fax offices, and internet offices are now widespread. Mobile phones can be rented at large hotels or through private mobile phone outlets. Several million new telephone lines are being installed in India resulting in temporary confusion.

- **International code** 00 + country code
- **Directory enquiries** 197
- **Dialling code for India** 91

Language
Over 550 million people speak Hindi, which is India's official language, though in some areas, particularly the south, English can prove to be more useful. When using the latter, roll the 'r' in exaggerated fashion. The 'a' in Hindi is long, the 'i' as in 'me'.

Hello/goodbye	**Namaste** (to a Hindu: while saying this, hold your palms together at chest level)
	Aslam alequm (to a Muslim)
Yes/no	**Ji han/ji nahin**
That's all right	**Koi bat nahin/ Thik hai**
What's your name?	**Apka nam kya hai?**
My name is…	**Mera nam… hai**
Do you speak English?	**Ap ko angrezi ati hai?**
I don't understand	**Samaj nahin aya**
What is this?	**Yeh kya hai?**
How much is this?	**Iska kya dam hai?**
Where is…?	**…kahan hai?**
How far?	**Kitna dur?**
Which is the Jaipur bus/train?	**Jaipur ka bas/train kahan hai?**
When does the Jaipur bus leave?	**Jaipur bas kab jaegi?**

Morning/afternoon	Suba/dopahar
Evening/night	Sham/Rat
Straight on	Sidha
Wait	Thero
Stop	Ruko
A room/bathroom	kamra/bathroom
Fan/air-conditioning	pankha/air-conditioning
Clean sheets/ blanket	saf chadaren/ kambal
Laundry-man	dhobi-wallah
The menu please	Menu dikhaiye
The bill please	Bill dijiye

1	ek
2	do
3	tin
4	char
5	panch
6	chhai
7	sat
8	ath
9	nau
10	das
11	gyara
12	barah
13	terah
14	chaudah
15	pandrah
16	solah
17	satrah
18	atharah
19	unnis
20	bis
100/200	sau/do sau
1,000/2,000	hazar/do hazar
100,000	lakh

tea	chai
chicken	murg
prawns/fish	jhinga/macchli
mutton	gosht
diced curd	panir
potato	aloo
boiled rice	bhat/sada chawal
seasoned fried rice	pulau
lentils/with garlic	dal/tarka dal
unleavened bread	roti/chapati
leavened bread	nan
deep-fried bread puff	puri
curd/yoghurt	dahi
scrambled eggs	keema
cauliflower	gobi
chickpeas	chana/chana dal
spinach	sag
okra/ladies' fingers	bhindi
onions	piaz

263

Emergencies

Crime, safety and police

Apart from banditry in the state of Bihar, India is generally a safe destination. Use your common sense: keep passport, travellers' cheques, credit cards and money in a money-belt or on your body, particularly when using public transport, and don't flourish wads of large-denomination notes. If using mid-range to expensive hotels, lock valuables in your bag in your hotel room or, better still, leave them in a safe-deposit box. Budget-travellers should be extra careful, particularly if sleeping in dormitories. Buy a padlock and chain to secure your bag on night-trains and don't put any valuable items into your checked-in luggage on flights: X-ray machines reveal all, and bags can be slit open.

Goa is the black-spot for muggings but police are cracking down on this. The most common crime in India is confidence-trickery. Touts abound in touristy areas and are adept at deceiving visitors. Beware of anyone approaching you in large railway stations such as Delhi or Mumbai (Bombay) and be extra careful in surrounding streets. Unofficial money-changers are not to be trusted. When using a credit card, do not let it out of your sight, as duplicate forms can easily be made and signed.

If you are the victim of a crime, report it to the police immediately. They are unlikely to resolve anything, but for insurance claims you will need a copy of the police report. Travellers' cheques take time to replace (keep serial numbers separate), as do passports. For the former, contact the issuing bank and for the latter, your embassy or consulate.

Embassies and consulates

Australia 1/50G Shantipath, Diplomatic Enclave, New Delhi (tel: 011 4139 9900)
Canada 7–8 Shantipath, Diplomatic Enclave, New Delhi (tel: 011 5178 2000, fax: 011 5178 2020)
New Zealand 50–N Nyaya Marg, Diplomatic Enclave, New Delhi (tel: 011 2688 3170, fax: 011 2687 3165)
UK 50 Shantipath, Diplomatic Enclave, New Delhi (tel: 011 2687 2161, fax: 011 2611 6094)
USA Shantipath, Diplomatic Enclave, New Delhi (tel: 011 2419 8000)
Germany 6/509 Shantipath, Diplomatic Enclave, New Delhi (tel: 011 011 2687 1831)

Health, vaccinations and pharmacies

There are no vaccination requirements for entering India unless you have been in an area infected with yellow fever. It is strongly advisable to check your tetanus, polio and typhoid jabs are up to date (boosters are needed every few years). Inoculations against meningitis and Hepatitis A (contracted from contaminated food and water) are also strongly recommended. Consult your doctor several weeks before your trip as some courses of action need to be started well in advance of your departure. Cholera epidemics occur periodically, but the vaccine is not effective.

Malaria is widespread during the rainy season, except at higher altitudes. Preventative treatment needs to be started at least one week before departure and continued several weeks after leaving. The side-effects of the pills can be strong, so avoid taking them for very long periods (several months). Use mosquito repellent liberally, above all at night-fall, and burn mosquito-coils at night. These can be purchased locally.

India's worst health hazard is bacteria-ridden water, which also affects uncooked fruit and vegetables. Do not eat the latter and only ever drink mineral water (some visitors to India brush their teeth with it). Avoid ice and cold or reheated food (be wary of buffets). It is almost inevitable that you will get some form of 'Delhi-belly' (upset stomach, diarrhoea). If you do, drink lots of fluids (not coffee or fruit-juices, although flat cola drinks are beneficial), and take water mixed with oral rehydration salts. Avoid eating until you feel hungry, then start with dried toast, boiled rice, yoghurt or bananas. Anti-diarrhoea medication can relieve stomach cramps or in an emergency but do not cure the problem. If symptoms persist for several days, consult a doctor as you may have dysentery.

Dehydration and sunburn can be seriously debilitating. Always drink lots of water, use sunscreen liberally, wear a hat if trekking or visiting large temple sites, and keep up your salt intake. Another illness that is easy to pick up and hard to get rid of is the common cold, usually caused by air-conditioning or rapid changes in altitude. Always dress in layers that you can add to or take off easily.

While it is advisable to have a small medical-kit with you (including antiseptic ointment, antihistamine cream for insect bites, anti-diarrhoea tablets, aspirin or other pain reliever, a general antibiotic and a roll of plaster for cuts), pharmacies stock all basic medication. Sunscreen and tampons are rarities, so bring them with you. Premoistened towelettes and antibacterial hand lotion can also be indispensable. Emergency treatment and consultations are offered at Indian clinics and hospitals, where doctors are usually very competent and speak good English.

Simple precautions with food and drink can help to prevent illness

Other information

Alcohol

Prohibition is now in force only in Gujarat, Manipur and Mizoram. Some other states operate 'dry days' or impose high taxes on alcohol, or apply both measures. In Goa, on the other hand, beer and spirits (Indian-made whisky, rum or gin) flow like water and are extremely cheap.

Begging

Beggars are everywhere in India and visitors have to learn to deal with them at their own discretion. Alms-giving at temples or to mutilated beggars is common practice, but many so-called *sadhus* are quite simply con-men. Kolkata (Calcutta) presents the most difficult situations, but the pleading women and babies pursuing visitors in Sudder Street are actually part of an organized syndicate. Keep a stock of rupee coins handy, but don't let yourself be pressurized if a crowd of beggars suddenly materializes. Children are adept at asking for rupees or pens and many visitors are a soft touch, but it is not a good idea to encourage them. It is far better to give money or items such as pens to their parents.

Camping

As budget accommodation is already extremely cheap, camping is not common in India, except in certain hotel grounds and on organized treks when all facilities will be laid on. Some states are developing campsites with youth-groups in mind, and regional tourist offices will advise on these. The Indian YMCA has information on their own camping facilities: contact the YMCA Tourist Hotel, Sansad Marg, New Delhi.

Clothing

The mainly tropical climate of India demands loose cotton, linen or silk clothing, with a pullover and wind-jacket for higher altitudes and for northern India during the winter months. Women especially should dress modestly: avoid cropped tops, shorts, above-the-knee skirts and tight clothing. Local clothing is the best, from *kurta-pajamas* (cotton tunics

266

CONVERSION CHART

FROM	TO	MULTIPLY BY
Inches	Centimetres	2.54
Centimetres	Inches	0.3937
Feet	Metres	0.3048
Metres	Feet	3.2810
Yards	Metres	0.9144
Metres	Yards	1.0940
Miles	Kilometres	1.6090
Kilometres	Miles	0.6214
Acres	Hectares	0.4047
Hectares	Acres	2.4710
Gallons	Litres	4.5460
Litres	Gallons	0.2200
Ounces	Grams	28.35
Grams	Ounces	0.0353
Pounds	Grams	453.6
Grams	Pounds	0.0022
Pounds	Kilograms	0.4536
Kilograms	Pounds	2.205
Tons	Tonnes	1.0160
Tonnes	Tons	0.9842

MEN'S SUITS							
UK	36	38	40	42	44	46	48
Rest of Europe	46	48	50	52	54	56	58
US	36	38	40	42	44	46	48

DRESS SIZES						
UK	8	10	12	14	16	18
France	36	38	40	42	44	46
Italy	38	40	42	44	46	48
Rest of Europe	34	36	38	40	42	44
US	6	8	10	12	14	16

MEN'S SHIRTS						
UK	14	14.5	15	15.5	16	16.5	17
Rest of Europe	36	37	38	39/40	41	42	43
US	14	14.5	15	15.5	16	16.5	17

MEN'S SHOES						
UK	7	7.5	8.5	9.5	10.5	11
Rest of Europe	41	42	43	44	45	46
US	8	8.5	9.5	10.5	11.5	12

WOMEN'S SHOES						
UK	4.5	5	5.5	6	6.5	7
Rest of Europe	38	38	39	39	40	41
US	6	6.5	7	7.5	8	8.5

and pants) to *salwar kameez* (long-sleeved dress and trousers for women) or heavy woollen pullovers, scarves and shawls in the Himalayas. Beach resorts such as Goa and Kovalam offer endless 'travellers' clothes' at rock-bottom prices. Bring little with you, and supplement as necessary on the way. If you are travelling during the rainy season, an umbrella is vital and easily found locally. The main item to choose carefully before departure is footwear: bring good, comfortable walking shoes and leather sandals. Although the latter are available in some areas, quality is variable. Multiple changes of clothing are not necessary. *Dhobi-wallahs* will pick up your laundry in the morning and return it, impeccably washed, in the evening, at an absurdly low cost.

Electricity
This is run at 220–240V. Socket sizes vary, so take a universal adaptor with you. Power-cuts are common in many areas. Make sure you have a good torch.

Etiquette and local customs
Indians, whether Hindu, Muslim or Buddhist, have a strong code of conduct and are polite when addressing strangers. Long train and bus journeys are often punctuated with inquisitive grillings by fellow-travellers. Diplomacy is needed: for example if travelling as a heterosexual couple, say you are married.

Hindus and Muslims traditionally use the left hand for performing ablutions, so it is never used for eating or touching others. If eating with your fingers, use only your right hand. Body-contact in public is not accepted except in very Westernized places where hand-shaking may be practised. Very often the most you will see is men holding hands—a common sign of comradeship. Feet should be kept on the ground (not stretched out on tables or over car-seats), as they too are perceived as 'unclean'. When entering any home, temple or mosque, always remove your footwear. If necessary carry a clean pair of socks with you to protect your feet.

Remember above all to respect worshippers (in some inner sanctuaries non-Hindus are forbidden entry; the same applies to mosques for non-Muslims). Jain temples post strict rules outside (banning menstruating women, any items made of leather and often cameras). Give donations when appropriate but not under duress. If a temple guardian or priest takes time to explain the history or significance of a site, he will appreciate a small tip.

Women should not sunbathe topless as this is highly offensive to Indians.

Photography and video
Colour-print and slide film (check expiry), as well as memory cards are easily and cheaply available in large tourist towns; avoid buying from street-hawkers. Have spare batteries when visiting more obscure places. Many monuments and wildlife sanctuaries charge photographic and video fees which can mount up exorbitantly, particularly in Rajasthan. Photography is prohibited, or limited,

267

Photography and video fees at some monuments can mount up

in some Jain temples and this should be respected.

Places of worship
As well as Hindu temples, Muslim mosques and Sikh gurudwaras, India is well provided with Christian churches, especially in the big cities, the south, the once Portuguese areas and former colonial hill-stations.

Toilets
Airports, large museums and decent restaurants have reasonable public toilets but standards plunge at roadside bus-halts and railway stations. Keep a supply of toilet-paper with you, and expect to use squatters often.

Visitors with disabilities
India's potholed pavements, high kerbs and crowds do not make life easy for visitors with disabilities. It is not suitable for people in wheelchairs except for some hotels in Goa, Delhi and Mumbai (Bombay). Enquire at an organization for disabled people at home, or ask your Indian tourist office about specialist tour-operators.

Hall of Victory in Amer Palace, Rajasthan

Women travellers
India is ideal for women travellers, although they will experience a lot of curiosity and sometimes unwelcome attention. This can become annoying, but sexual attacks are very rare.

Use common sense: avoid dark streets at night, ignore any persistent attention, and keep to mid- or upper-range hotels if possible. Indian women have a great sense of solidarity, so stick with other women while travelling. Curiosity about marital status and number of offspring can be dealt with by inventing an absent or imminently arriving husband.

Tourist services
Indian tourist offices overseas
- **Australia** Level 2, 210 Pitt Street, Sydney, NSW 2000 (tel: 02 9264 4855, fax: 02 9264 4860, email: goitosyd@nextcentury.com.au)
- **Canada** 60 Bloor Street West, Suite 1003, Toronto, Ont. M4 W3 B8 (tel: 416 962 3787, fax: 416 962 6279, email: indiatourism@bellnet.ca)

- **UK** 7 Cork Street, London W1X 2LN (tel: 020 7437 3677, fax: 020 7494 1048, email: info@indiatouristoffice.org)
- **USA** 3550 Wilshire Boulevard, Room 204, Los Angeles, CA 90010 (tel: 213/380-8855, fax: 213/380 6111, email: goitola@aol.com); 1270 Avenue of the Americas, Suite 1808, New York, NY 10020/1700 (tel: 212/586-4901, fax: 212/582-3274, email: ny@itonyc.com)

Andaman and Nicobar Islands VIP Road, 189 Junglighat, Port Blair (tel: 03192 233006; email: goitoph@hotmail.com).
Andhra Pradesh 3–60, 2nd floor, Netaji Bhawan Liberty Road, Himayat Nagar, Hyderabad (tel: 040 2326 1360; email: hyd2_indtour@sancharnet.in).
Arunachal Pradesh C-Sector Barapani Police Point, Naharlagun (tel: 0360 244328).
Assam GL Publication Complex, GS Road, Guwahati (tel: 0361 2547407; email: indtour@asm.nic.in).
Bihar Sudama Palace, Kankar Bagh Road, Patna (tel: 0612 2345776; email: goitpat@bih.nic.in.
Goa Communidade Building, Church Square, Panaji (tel: 0832 2223412; email: goitogoa@goatelecom.com).
Karnataka KFC Building, 48 Church Street, Bangalore (tel: 080 5585417; email: indtour@kar.nic.in).
Kerala Willingdon Island, Kochi (tel: 0484 2668352; email: indtourismkochi@sify.com).
Madhya Pradesh Near western group of temples, Khajuraho (tel: 07686 272347; email: goito@sanchar-net.in).
Maharashtra Krishna Villas, Station Road, Aurangabad (tel: 0204 2331217; email: goitaur@vsnl.com).
123 M Karve Road, opposite Church gate, Mumbai (tel: 022 2203 3144; email: india-tourism@vsnl.com.) Also at international and domestic airport terminals.
Meghalaya Tirot Singh Sylem Road, Police Bazar, Shillong (tel: 0364 225632; email: goitoslg@shillong.meg.nic.in.

New Delhi 88 Janpath, New Delhi (tel: 011 23320342; email: goitodelhi@tourism.nic.in.
Orissa B/21, BJB Nagar, Bhubaneswar (tel: 0674 2432203; email: itobbs@ori.nic.in).
Rajasthan State Hotel, Khasa Kothi, Jaipur (tel: 0141 2372200; email: indtourjpr@raj.nic.in).
Tamil Nadu 154 Anna Salai, Chennai (tel: 044 28461459; email: indtour@vsnl.com or goitochn@tn.nin.in. Also counters at domestic airline terminal.
Uttar Pradesh 191 The Mall, Agra (tel: 0562 226378; email: goitoagr@sancharnet.in.
15-B The Mall, Varanasi 221002 (tel: 0542 2501784; email: goitovns@satyam.net.in.
West Bengal 4 Shakespeare Sarani, Kolkata (tel: 033 2282 1402; email: indtour@cal2.vsnl.net.in.

269

Glossary

apsara	temple dancer: often depicted in sculpture	Mahavir	founder of Jainism; meaning great leader
ashram	hermitage	Makaras	mythical creatures symbolizing the River Ganga (Ganges)
avatar	incarnation		
bandhani	tie dying		
bastis	sanctuaries	maidan	open grassy space
Bhagavad Gita	philosophical text from the epic poem *Mahabharata*	mandapa	pillared hall
		mihrab	prayer niche
		minar	tower of a mosque
Bodhisattva	person on the path to Buddhahood	muezzin	Muslim crier
		naga	snake; frequently depicted in sculpture
Brahma	one of the Hindu trinity; the creator	Nandi	bull; Siva's steed
chai	tea	nirvana	state of total peace
chaitya	Buddhist worship hall that was originally rock cut	Parvati	Siva's consort
		prakram/prakaram	enclosure
		puja	religious offering or prayer
char-bagh	Islamic-style quartered garden	Ramayana	ancient Hindu epic poem
chhatri	open-sided roof dome	ratha	chariot of a deity
		Rig Veda	oldest and most sacred of the ancient Hindu texts, the Vedas
dacoits	bandits		
dalits	lower castes		
darsha	mystic ecstasy (Buddhist)	sadhu	ascetic
deul	ribbed, bell-shaped structure	sati	Hindu rite, where a widow throws herself on her husband's funeral pyre (banned by the British in 1829)
dharma	abiding by natural law and religious teachings		
dhobi	laundry		
dhooli	carried chair	shakti	female creative force
dhoti	white loincloth	shikhara	tapered tower
dhurri	rug	Siva	Supreme Lord of the Hindu trinity; the destroyer
durbar	public audience hall		
Ganesh	Hindu god; son of Siva and Parvati. The bringer of prosperity; depicted with an elephant's head	stupa	dome; domed building containing Buddhist relics
		Sufism	Muslim mysticism
Garuda	bird-man (steed of the Hindu god Vishnu)	tank	artificial lake
		thali	small servings of several dishes
ghat	steps leading down to a river; mountains	thangka	Buddhist scroll
gopuram	gatehouse	Tirthankar	Jain prophet
gurudwara	Sikh place of worship	tongas	pony-carts
hammam	steam bath	torana	gateway
Hanuman	Hindu monkey-god	Upanishads	ancient texts establishing the philosophical basis of Hinduism
haveli	multi-storey courtyard house		
howdah	seat for riding on an elephant or camel	Vedanta	early Hindu doctrine meaning 'end of Vedas'
huqqa	water-pipe		
jaggery	palm sugar	Vedas	sacred Hindu texts
jali	carved lattice-work	vihara	Buddhist monastery, usually simple and austere
jyotirlinga	twelve sacred sites associated with the Hindu god Siva		
		vimana	sanctuary tower
lingam	phallic symbol of Siva	vinaya	rules of monastic conduct (Buddhism)
lunghi	coloured loincloth	Vishnu	One of the Hindu trinity; embodiment of mercy and goodness; the preserver
Mahabharata	ancient, highly revered Hindu text. An epic poem that recounts a battle between good and evil		
		zenana	women's quarters

Hotels and Restaurants

Hotel price ratings:
- ● **Budget** (£) up to 1,500 Rs per night
- ● **Moderate** (££) 1,500–3,000 Rs per night
- ● **Expensive** (£££) over 3,000 Rs per night

Budget hotels have at least some rooms with en suite showers and air-conditioning (the others have fans). Rooms in mid-range hotels generally have satellite/cable TV and direct-dial phones. The luxury hotels are of international standard and include business facilities, air-conditioning/central heating, room service (often 24-hour), laundry, currency exchange (for residents), a bar and at least one restaurant. Some of the budget and mid-range hotels give off-season discounts (May–September). A variety of taxes is applied to all accommodation and can increase the bill by about 25 per cent, particularly when the basic rate is high enough (currently 1,500 Rs a night) to attract an extra 10 per cent luxury tax.

Restaurant price ratings (excluding drinks):
- ● **Budget** (£) up to 350 Rs
- ● **Moderate** (££) 350–700 Rs
- ● **Expensive** (£££) over 700 Rs

Bills are increased by the addition of various local taxes, but these are usually detailed on menus.

In the listings below, entries preceded by an asterisk (*) are recommended as places to eat. They include both independent restaurants and the better hotel restaurants. The latter are usually the best places for food in smaller towns.

DELHI
(STD code 011)
*Ambassador (£££)
Sujan Singh Park
tel: 2463 2600 fax: 2463 2252/8219
email: ambassador.delhi@tajhotels.com
Taj hotel with 88 comfortable rooms and 12 suites. Pleasant garden, but no pool. Restaurants offer Indian, Chinese and Continental cuisine. Book ahead for the **Yellow Brick Road** (South Indian) restaurant (££).
*Broadway (£/££)
4/15A Asaf Ali Road tel: 2327 3821–5
fax: 2326 9966, www.broadwaydehli.com
Renovated 1950s hotel well placed near Delhi Gate, with 32 clean rooms (spacious doubles, small airless singles). Excellent bar and Kashmiri/Tandoori restaurant, the aptly-named **Chor Bizarre** (£££). Walks organized through Old Delhi.
*Claridges (£££)
12 Aurangzeb Road
tel: 2301 0211 fax: 2301 0625
email: info@claridges.com
162 rooms and suites. Beginning to show signs of age, but still reigning supreme over elegant residential area close to centre. Old-fashioned atmosphere, with amenities including pool, health club, beauty salon, travel agent and four good restaurants covering the gastronomical gamut, including **The Corbett** (££), a jungle mock-up offering authentic North Indian cuisine, and **Pickwicks** (£/££) for Continental food.

*Hyatt Regency (£££)
Bhikaji Cama Place, Ring Road
tel: 2679 1234/1150 www.hyatt.com
The décor and facilities are superb, but it is rather impersonal, with 508 medium-size rooms and suites. Good restaurants offer a range of cuisine and prices: **Delhi Ka Angan** (££) is the world's first restaurant specializing in Delhi cuisine, while **La Piazza** (££) has excellent Italian, including wine. Disco, night club, health club, tennis, pool in garden, beauty parlour.
*Imperial (£££)
Janpath tel: 2334 1234/5678
fax: 3234 2255 www.theimperialindia.com
231 rooms and suites. An old colonial-style favourite uplifted to luxury category while maintaining traditional atmosphere. Relaxing gardens with coffee shop and three restaurants serving Indian and Continental cuisine. The **Spice Route** (£££) offers an interesting mix of Thai and other Asian styles. Good pool, travel agency, beauty parlour, gym, health club, tennis.
*The Manor (£££)
77 Friends Colony (West)
tel: 2692 5151 fax: 2692 2299
www.themanordelhi.com
The city has now spread around this oasis, but this tastefully custom-designed hotel retains an air of exclusivity. 18 bedrooms and suites, with large beds and modem connections. Restaurant (modern European), exchange (at bank rates), health club— but no pool. A peaceful place, with more personal service than at big hotels in the same price bracket.
*Maurya Sheraton Hotel and Towers (£££)
Sardal Patel Marg, Chanakyapuri
tel: 2611 2233 fax: 2611 3333
www.welcomgroup.com
The huge (484-room) flagship of the Welcomgroup is 8km (5 miles) from the centre, with a lobby overlooking ornamental pools. All creature comforts, but get a room well away from the disco. Excellent service. Outdoor pool. Noted for superb food: restaurants (some with dance floors) include **Dum Phukt** (££/£££) for melt-in-the-mouth Nawabi dishes, slowly cooked in traditional Chinese sealed *deghs*, **Bukhara** (£££), one of the best eating-places in Delhi. 1920s-style Jazz Bar with live music and expensive drinks.
*Nirula's (££)
L-Block Connaught Circus tel: 2341 7419
fax: 2332 4669 www.nirula.com
Popular restaurants, including **Potpourri** (££) for good Indian/Continental food, the **Chinese Room** (££) for Szechuan-style, an English-style pub, **Pegasus**, and (take-away) ice cream and pastry shops.
*The Oberoi (£££)
Dr. Zakir Hussain Marg tel: 2436 3030
fax: 2436 0484 www.oberoihotels.com
Delhi's first and most prestigious luxury hotel opened in 1965. There are 300 rooms and suites, 5 restaurants, endless facilities and top service in a convenient, green location.
*Oberoi Maidens (£££)
7 Sham Nath Marg, Old Delhi
tel: 2397 5464 www.oberoihotels.com
Old colonial building with great atmosphere and 54 well-equipped rooms and suites. Less luxurious than other hotels in this up-market chain and prices reflect this. Still very comfortable, with coffee shop overlooking gardens, tennis courts and excellent pool. The **Curzon** (££/£££) restaurant offers Indian and Continental cuisine and there are barbecue nights.

272

*Park Balluchi (££/£££)
Inside the Deer Park, Hauz Khas
tel: 2685 9369/2696 9829 fax: 2685 9085
Frequent winner of restaurant awards, in peaceful
sylvan surroundings. The concentration is on
Mughlai delicacies and special gourmet requests
are possible—with a little notice.

*Rodeo (££)
A-12 Inner Circle, Connaught Place
tel: 011 2372 3780
The first and only Mexican restaurant in Delhi, Rodeo
spices up a repertoire of Mexican meals by screening
classic Western films on Saturday afternoons.

Sunstar Heritage (££)
8A/43 WEA Channa Market, Karol Bagh
tel: 2571 9790;fax: 2584 1367
email: hsunstar@ndb.vsnl.net.in
Fairly new hotel (opened 1998), with 16 air-conditioned, clean and comfortable rooms, each with
different décor. All have fridge and tea/coffee-making
facilities. No restaurant, but there's 24-hour room
service—from the restaurant at **Sunstar Residency**
(££), just down the road at 8A/50 Channa Market
(tel: 5145 1152). This opened in 2000 and has 19
rooms and suites, all with facilities as above, plus a
small but comfortable restaurant (£/££) for Indian,
Chinese and European food, travel desk and net
access. Both hotels have lifts, reliable electricity and
helpful service. Good value.

*Taj Mahal Hotel (£££)
1 Mansingh Road
tel: 2302 6162 fax: 2302 6070
www.tajhotels.com
Large (300 rooms and suites), but manages to retain
a personal feel. Attractive décor includes a lobby
that emulates a Buddhist hall of worship, marble and
chandeliers. Predictably good (and friendly) service.
Well located. Delicious food includes Mughal/
Peshwari cuisine in the **Haveli** restaurant (£££),
seafood in nautical surroundings in the **Captain's
Cabin** (£££), superb French food in **Longchamp** (£££)
and multi-style Chinese in the award-winning **House
of Ming** (££). Several options for live evening entertainment. Large outdoor pool surrounded by sun-deck
and trees.

*Taj Palace (£££)
2 Sardar Patel Marg, Chanakyapuri
tel: 2611 0202 fax: 2611 0808
www.tajhotels.com
Over 400 rooms designed for business travellers,
with excellent facilities. **Orient Express** (£££) restaurant offers superb French nouvelle cuisine (and
matching service), in one of the train's original carriages. Other speciality restaurants with themed
décor provide Chinese and Indian cuisine. Large outdoor pool, beautiful gardens, tennis, golf, disco.

*United Coffee House (£/££)
E-15 Connaught Place
One of Delhi's old favourites, open all day and still
going strong under the chandeliers. Old-fashioned but
relaxed and stylish service, very popular for power-
lunches. Friendly and efficient service. Mezzanine
area for (good) snacks and non-smoking customers.
Continental, Chinese and North Indian food—all with
a reasonable choice, including dishes aimed at the
calorie-conscious.

*Village Bistro (£/££)
12 Hauz Khas Village tel: 2685 2227
This complex of restaurants provides Continental,

Indian and Chinese cuisine. Weekend brunches are
particularly good value. Varied live entertainment and
views over the Deer Park add to the enjoyment.

YMCA Tourist Hotel (£)
Jai Singh Road tel: 2336 1915/1847
fax: 2374 6032
This is where to get general information about the
YMCA. 105 rooms. Restaurant offers Indian and
Western food. Good pool (extra charge). Travel desk
and baggage storage. Neither helpful nor very clean,
but good value—so book ahead.

YWCA International Guest House (£)
10 Parliament Street
tel: 2336 1561; fax: 2334 1763
email: ywcaindigh@vsnl.net
Basic, but good value and central, accommodation in
24 air-conditioned rooms, with showers and, at reasonable cost, a phone. Western breakfast included
and 24-hour room service available until restaurant is
installed. Good laundry service and travel office.

THE NORTHWEST

GUJARAT
Ahmedabad
(STD code 079)

273

*Holiday Inn (£££)
Khanpur Road, near Nehru Bridge, Khanpur
tel: 2550 5505 fax: 2550 5501
email: reservations@holidayinnahmedabad.com
Palatial style for a reasonably priced high-class hotel
with 63 well-appointed rooms. Good multi-cuisine
restaurants. Indoor pool, dance floor, disco, travel
desk, health club. Very helpful staff.

*Inder Residency (£££)
Opposite Gujarat College, Ellisbridge
tel: 2656 5222 fax: 2656 0407
www.inderresidency.com
A modern, comfortable hotel with 79 rooms. Facilities
include a pool, tennis, health club, travel desk, coffee-
shop and multi-cuisine restaurants.

Quality Inn Rivera (££)
Khanpur Road tel: 2560 1111
fax: 1560 1122 www.qualityinnriviera.com
River views in some of the 69 rooms; tea/coffee-
making facilities, fridge and room service. Quiet and
comfortable. Restaurant, travel desk, car hire, free
airport transfer, exchange, lawn. Good value.

*Vishalla (£)
Vasana, on southern edge of city tel: 2660 2422
Eating here is an experience of Gujarati village life. Sit
on the floor and eat all you can of the set vegetarian
meal—live entertainment. The restaurant is only open
8–11 in the evenings.

Bhuj
(STD code 02832)

*Hotel Prince (£/££)
Station Road
tel: 220370–1 fax: 250373
email: princecad1@sancharnet.in
Smart and central (but sometimes noisy) modern
hotel with 42 rooms. Good restaurants; snacks are
available in garden. Exchange service offered. Tours
and free airport transfer can be arranged.

*Toran Rann Resort (£)
Mirzapur tel/fax: 224910
Government-run hotel built after the earthquake. 24
basic air-conditioned or fan-cooled rooms. Restaurant.

Hotels and Restaurants

Diu

*Samrat (£)
Bunder Road tel: 252327
Small, simple establishment offering 12 clean rooms, with TV and balconies. The restaurant serves good food, there's a bar and helpful staff.

Palitana
(Std code 02875)
*Sumeru (£)
Station Road, near bus station tel: 232327
16 comfortable rooms and five dormitories. TCGL tourist information. Restaurant has limited menu, but it's cheap and does English breakfast.

Sasan Gir National Park
(STD code 02877)
Gir Lodge (£££)
Sasan Gir, Junagadh tel: 285521 fax: 285528
This Taj-group lodge offers a variety of comfortable rooms, the upstairs ones with balconies. Dining (at fixed times) can be a slow process. Pool, gardens, library, travel desk, jeep rental, airport/rail pick-ups on demand. Book ahead.
*Maneland Jungle Lodge (££/££££)
On the edge of the sanctuary tel/fax: 285555
email: ssibal@adl.vsnl.net.in
www.marineland.com
Isolated location a few miles north of main village, Bhalchl village. Small complex of bungalows and cottages, with suites and rooms. Well organized, with excellent restaurant and guides. Book ahead.
*Sinh Sadan Forest Lodge (£)
Sasan Gir, Wildlife Division
tel: 285540–1
A large complex with facilities ranging from air-conditioned rooms with bath (in bungalows) to 30-bed dormitories and two-bed tents. Book in advance. Food (excellent) must be pre-booked.

RAJASTHAN
Ajmer
(STD code 0145)
*Mansingh Palace (££/£££)
Ana Sagar Circular Road, Vaishali Nagar
tel: 24258557/702 fax: 2425858
www.mansinghhotel.com
In beautiful grounds northwest of the centre, this is the best in town, though somewhat overpriced. A well-appointed, modern, 50-room hotel. Excellent multi-cuisine restaurant and bar.
Regency (£)
Outside Delhi Gate tel: 2620296
fax: 2621750 www.bahubaligroup.com
29 well-maintained rooms. Lively, central location. TV, phone. Reasonable vegetarian restaurant and bar. One of the town's better options.

Alwar
(STD code 0144)
*Aravali Hotel (£)
Near railway station tel: 2332883 fax: 2332011
www.hotelaravali.com
Run by helpful family and offering a range of accommodation, from dormitory to air-conditioned doubles. Can be noisy, so ask for a quiet room. Decent bar and restaurant. Pool in summer.
Sariska Palace (££/£££)
Jaipur Road, near park entrance

tel: 241322–4 fax: 241323
email: sariska@del2.vsnl.net.in
Large, converted and refurbished royal hunting lodge, now a Heritage hotel (75 rooms) in extensive grounds. Main lodge has atmospheric interior full of memorabilia. Newer facilities include gym, pool, library, restaurant, Ayurvedic and yoga centre. The Forest Reception Centre is across the road.

Bharatpur/Keoladeo
(STD code 05644)
Bharatpur Forest Lodge (££)
Keoladeo National Park tel: 222760
fax: 222864 www.theashokgroup.com
ITDC lodge fabulously located inside park. 17 comfortable rooms, all doubles with balconies. Restaurant (£) with Indian and Continental food, room service, exchange, friendly staff. Facilities (including boats) for touring sanctuary, though birds come to your window and animals enter the compound. Book ahead.
*Laxmi Vilas Palace (££/£££)
Kakaji-ki-Kothi, Raghunath Nivas, Agra Road
tel: 223523 fax: 225259
www.laxmivilas.com
Haveli-style 19th-century lodge which retains some period atmosphere, with 22 comfortable rooms and suites. Good Indian and Continental food, pool, travel desk and friendly service.

Bikaner
(STD code 0151)
*Bhanwar Niwas (££)
Rampuria Street, 500m (550yd) from Kote Gate
tel: 2529323/2201043
fax: 2200880
email: bhanwarnivas@rediffmail.com
Intriguing 20th-century haveli (courtyard house) tucked away in backstreets of Bikaner's old city (if lost, ask for the Rampuria haveli hotel, rather than the Bhanwar Niwas). 26 large rooms with decorative Indian flourishes; best on upper floor. The vegetarian food is very good and there's a bar.Also offers desert trips.
*Gajner Palace Hotel (££/£££)
Gajner, Teh tel: 01534 255061
fax: 01534 255060/2522408
www.hrhindia.com
Beautiful lakeside 44-room palace with bags of atmosphere: an oasis in the desert about 20km (12 miles) west of Bikaner. Great birdwatching, boating, camel and jeep safaris, with antelopes and wild boar in surrounding sanctuary (and game on menu!). Endless maharaja memorabilia, friendly staff. Barbecues, buffets and cultural programmes. Really top-notch.
Harasar Haveli (£)
Opposite stadium tel: 2527318/2209891 fax: 2525150
37 clean rooms, with room service. Veranda and garden. Use of pool across the road. Multi-cuisine restaurant. Good value and service.
Lalgarh Palace (£££)
Ganga Avenue Road tel: 540201 fax: 522253
email: gm.bikaner@itchotels.com
Some 3km (2 miles) north of railway station on Outskirts of town. 38 lavishly-furnished rooms in an attractive, palatial, red sandstone Heritage hotel/museum, built 1902–12 by Sir Swinton Jacob. Lawns, restaurant, billiards, pool.

Jaipur

(STD code 0141)

*Alsisar Haveli (££)
Sansar Chandra Road tel: 2368290/2364685
fax: 2364652 www.alsisar.com
This is an exceptionally well converted 1890s house which is attractive and full of ethnic character. 30 comfortable rooms, some featuring four-poster beds and frescoes. Inviting outdoor pool and courtyards. Good food, both Indian and Continental. Quiet and with superb service. Exchange. Frequent puppet shows and dance evenings in the bird-filled gardens.

*Arya Niwas (££)
Sansar Chandra Road tel: 2372456
fax: 2361871 www.aryaniwas.com
Excellent value modernized 50-room hotel with vegetarian restaurant, yoga lessons and friendly staff.

*Bissau Palace (£/£££)
Outside Chandpol Gate
tel: 2304371/391 fax: 2304628
www.bissaupalace.com
A stately 1920s Heritage palace-cum-museum packed with antiques, art and books. This is a welcome oasis in Jaipur with pool, tennis, travel desk, laundry, large grounds, pleasant staff, excellent atmosphere and 52 rooms. Two multi-cuisine restaurants, one rooftop with good views of the lively area (northwest of city walls). Folk dance and sitar recital on request. Tours arranged, including camel safaris. Exchange. Bookshop.

*Jai Mahal Palace (£££)
Jacob Road, Civil Lines tel: 2223636
fax: 2220707 www.tajhotels.com
100 rooms and suites only 1km (0.5 mile) from the rail station. Very attractive old palace in Taj group, with lovely gardens, multi-cuisine restaurant.

Maharani Palace (££/£££)
Station Road, opposite Polo Victory
tel: 2204702 fax: 2202112
www.maharanihotels.com
Central, with 60 spacious rooms, basement bar and multi-cuisine restaurants (££). Small pool on rooftop terrace where alfresco meals are served in summer. Travel desk, exchange. Live Indian music.

*Niros (£)
MI Road tel: 2374493/371874 fax: 2371746
www.nirosindia.com
A restaurant popular with Indians and Westerners for Chinese, Continental, tandoori and vegetarian dishes, served in an elaborate, air-conditioned interior. They also do take-aways. Open all day.

*Rambagh Palace (£££)
Bhawani Singh Road tel: 2211919
fax: 2385098 www.tajhotels.com
Jaipur's showiest Taj palace hotel, dating from mid-19th century. The 113 rooms vary in size. Large grounds are superb. Outdoor pool, health club, jacuzzi, beauty parlour, travel desk, tennis, squash, badminton, birdwatching, camel riding. Eating options include barbecues (Oct–Jun) and the **Suvarna Mahal** restaurant (££/£££), with a superb multi-cuisine buffet and mouth-watering desserts. Evening Rajasthani dancers and puppet shows.

*Samode Haveli (£/£££)
Gangapol tel: 2631942 fax: 2632370/631397
email: reservations@samode.com
www.samode.com
A 19th-century Heritage *haveli* in northeast of walled city. Secluded garden courtyard with outdoor

Rajasthani buffet lunch and dinner, superbly decorated dining-room, bar, pool, games. 27 tasteful rooms with antique furnishings. Good rooftop views and friendly service. It's very Indian in feel and popular with groups, so book well ahead.

*The Trident (£££)
Opposite Jal Mahal, Amber Fort Road
tel: 2670101 fax: 2670303
email: reservations@tridentjp.com
In a superb location, all rooms have balconies with views of the Aravalli Hills or Man Sagar Lake and the Water Palace. Opened in 1997, purpose-built 137-room hotel with state-of-the-art facilities, including a water-purifying plant. **Jal Mahal** restaurant (££/£££) offers delicious Continental, Asian and Indian food. Outdoor pool. Travel desk.

Jaisalmer

(STD code 02992)

Gorbandh Palace Hotel (££)
No.1 Tourist Complex, Sam Road,
25km (15.5 miles) from town tel: 253801
fax: 253811 www.hrhindia.com
Traditionally-inspired grandiose Heritage hotel, set in gardens with great swimming-pool. 67 rather worn grand rooms and suites around a courtyard, but good amenities. Restaurant (££), coffee shop, bar. Travel desk, camel rides, puppet shows and alfresco traditional song and dance by a campfire.

Hotel Paradise (£)
Jaisalmer Fort, opposite Royal Palace
tel: 252674
email: hotelparadise_jsmzooi@yahoo.com
25-room *haveli* hotel with fabulous rampart and desert views. Most rooms with balconies, room service. Range of budget options, including camping on the roof. Camel safaris.

*The Trio (£)
Gandhi Chowk, Mandir Palace tel: 252733
Jaisalmer's original rooftop restaurant, partly tented and with great evening views of fort. Elegant setting and presentation. Lamb, tandoori and Rajasthani specialities. Live entertainment, pleasant service and very popular.

Jodhpur

(STD code 0291)

*Hotel Kalinga (£/££)
Near railway station
tel: 2615871 fax: 2627314
email: info@kalingahotel.com
Comfortable, with 35 clean spacious rooms, all with TV and fridge. 24-hour check-out. Stylish multi-cuisine restaurant, the **Kalinga** (£) is open all day. Lift, exchange, travel desk.

*Ajit Bhawan (££/£££)
Opposite Circuit House, Airport Road
tel: 2510410/610 fax: 2510674
email: reservations@ajitbhawan.com
Lovely old Heritage palace built in rambling style around well-tended gardens (with cows) and great pool. 74 varied rooms have traditional features. Barbecued Indian food at **On the Rocks** (£) which is popular with locals; delicious bakery items. The Garden restaurant has dancing. Jeep safaris include a Royal Safari with luxury tents in the desert.

*Devi Bhawan (£)
1 Ratanada Road tel/fax: 2511067
Undoubtedly a great-value place, but only eight rooms

Hotels and Restaurants

(with bath, but not air-conditioned), so book ahead. Family-run and friendly, providing an excellent Indian dinner (£). Lovely garden. Tours.

*Taj Hari Mahal (£££)
*5 Residency Road tel: 2439700 fax: 2614451
email: harimahal.jodhpur@tajhotels.com*
Landscaped gardens surround this 93-room luxury hotel, a tasteful blend of traditional and modern. Restaurants offer Indian, Continental and Asian cuisine. Pool, sports facilities and travel desk.

*Umaid Bhawan Palace (£££)
*5km from centre tel: 2510101–4
fax: 2510100
email: ubpresv.jodh@tajhotels.com*
Luxurious accommodation in art-deco palace of Maharaja (still partly a royal residence). 96 palatial rooms and suites, luxury tents in peak season. Marble-lined indoor pool, health club, beauty parlour, library, formal gardens, travel desk and cinema. Four restaurants, including informal **Pillars** (££) and **Marwar Hall** (£££), for sumptuous multi-cuisine buffets. Non-residents may visit on payment of a charge (deducted from food/drink they consume).

Mount Abu
(STD code 02974)
Connaught House (£/££)
*Rajendra Marg, opposite bus stand
tel: 238560 fax: 2542240
email: idchhh@sancharnet.in,
www.welcomheritage.com*
Once the summer residence of the Maharaja of Jodhpur, this atmospheric old Heritage bungalow lies in quiet gardens. 13 rooms, all with quaint furnishings, some with porches. Multi-cuisine restaurant. Book ahead for both rooms and meals.

*Hilltone Hotel (£/££)
*Near bus stand, PO Box 18 tel: 238391–4
fax: 238395 email: hilltone@sancharnet.in
www.hilltone.com*
Good location on edge of town. Modern 68-room hotel with extensive facilities (restaurant, bar, pool, sauna, exchange). Also cottages in grounds.

Pushkar
(STD code 0145)
Payal Guest House (£)
Main Bazar tel: 2772163
Cheap but with 25 pleasant rooms with hot water. Meals available. A shady courtyard and laid-back atmosphere add to its deserved popularity with budget travellers.

*Pushkar Palace (£)
*Near the lake tel: 2772001/2401
fax: 2772226
www.hotel_pushkar_palace@hotmail.com*
Atmospheric Heritage hotel in renovated palace on eastern shore of lake, wide range of rooms, some with lake views. Laundry, travel desk. Pretty gardens, vegetarian restaurant (£), jeeps, camel and horse safaris, birdwatching. Book in advance.

Ranakpur
*Ghanerao Castle Hotel (£/££)
*Ranakpur Road tel: 02934 284035
www.ghaneraoroyalcastle.com*
17-room hotel 18km (11miles) from Ranakpur. The royal family still inhabit part of the castle. Large colourful rooms, lawn, good cheap restaurant.

*Maharani Bagh (££)
*Orchard Retreat, Ranakpur Road
tel: 0291 25771991
email: balsamadad@sify.com
www.welcomheritage.com*
The best accommodation in town is 4km (3 miles) from the centre. In the lovely erstwhile summer garden of Jodhpur's rulers are 15 traditionally-furnished thatched bungalows with verandas. Bougainvillaea and birds add to the joy of substantial outdoor buffets (£).

Ranthambhor
(STD code 07462)
*Sawai Madhopur Lodge (££/£££)
*Ranthambhor Road tel: 220541/220247
fax: 220718
email: sawai.madhopur@tajhotels.com
www.tajhotels.com*
With 32 rooms, two suites and six tents (Oct–Mar), this Heritage palace, very close to the station, retains a colonial feel, with animal heads on the walls and cricket/croquet on the lawn. Other features include a small outdoor pool, multi-cuisine food and langur monkeys in the gardens.

*Vanyavilas (£££)
*Ranthambhor Road, Sawai Madhopur tel: 223999
fax: 223988 www.oberoihotels.com*
Delightful, peaceful location in landscaped wilderness. 25 luxury tents and personalized service. Safaris, transfers.

Shekhawati
*Castle Mandawa (££/£££)
*Mandawa tel: 01592 223124
fax: 01592 223171
email: reservations@castlemandawa.com*
Wonderfully renovated Heritage castle, marble floors, arches, 74 beautiful bedrooms and bathrooms. Imaginative dining area with frescoes, but a bit rundown. Linked with the cheaper and better-maintained **Desert Resort** (££) just outside town (tel/fax: 01592 223151), which is designed in mud-hut style, with all necessary comforts and a pool. Camel rides.

Dera Dundlod Kila (£/££)
*Dundlod Fort tel: 01594 252519/199
fax: 01594 252519
www.dundlod.com*
Heritage hotel with 22 rooms of widely differing quality and 4 suites. Pool, tennis, entertainment and library. Atmospheric, with murals and very pleasant staff. Rambling corridors link rooms with traditional features, tucked into bastions. Cheap restaurant. Camel, jeep and horse safaris ranging from one hour to several days.

Samode Palace (££/£££)
*Samode, c/o Samode House, Jaipur
tel: 01423 240014 fax: 01423 240025
www.samode.com*
Stunning palace converted into 42-room Heritage hotel, 40km (25 miles) from Jaipur. Superlative interior and beautiful hill setting. Restaurant (£/££).

Udaipur
(STD code 0294)
*Fateh Prakash Palace Hotel (£££)
*City Palace
tel: 2528016–9 email: rwww.hrhindia.com*
Sumptuous Heritage accommodation with stunning

lake and island views. Ten suites and 21 de luxe rooms, decorated with Maharaja's antiques. Personalized service plus pool, holistic fitness centre, riding, travel desk, boats, squash, billiards. Two restaurants: **Gallery Restaurant** (£££), serving Continental set meals, including English cream teas; and **Sunset View Terrace** (£), with great snacks and live Indian music in the afternoon.

Jheel Guest House (£)
56 Gangaur Ghat tel: 2421352 fax: 2520008
Two family-run guest houses with 5 rooms each, all with hot water, offer Udaipur's best lakeside budget accommodation. 8 basic rooms, some with balconies over lake. Good restaurant with Indo-World menu.

Kankarwa Haveli (£)
26 Lalghat, 3 minutes from bazaar
tel: 2411457 fax: 2521403
email: kankarwahaveli@hotmail.com
Renovated, family-run, 18th-century lakeside *haveli* offering 15 clean, quiet rooms, some with lake view. Roof terrace with great views provides snacks and breakfast—other meals are on request. Friendly. Car rental, travel help, excursions. Book well ahead.

*Lake Palace Hotel (£££)
PO Box No.5, Lake Pichola
tel: 2527961/2528800 fax: 2528700
email: lakepalace.udaipur@tajhotels.com
In a fabulous location on an island in Lake Pichola, this unique Taj hotel has 83 rooms and suites, good service and extravagant décor. Excellent Indian and Continental food. Outdoor pool, travel desk, car rental. Book in advance. Booking essential for restaurant.

*Shiv Niwas Palace (£££)
City Palace
tel: 2528016–9 www.hrhindia.com
Legendary Heritage palatial residence transformed into 34 rooms and suites at southern end of City Palace complex. Upper floors have de luxe rooms with private terraces and panoramic views. Many have antique fixtures from Mawar royal households. Tennis, squash, badminton, riding, billiards, boats, holistic massage, marble pool, travel desk. Multi-cuisine restaurant. Good and cheap Indian food served poolside with live Indian music in the evening. Book in advance.

*Udaivilas (£££)
Haridasji Ki Magri
tel: 2433300 fax: 2433200
www.oberoihotels.com
Opened in 2002, this spectacular palace hotel with 87 rooms vies with the City Palace hotels across the lake. Vast layout, no expense spared. Spa, pools. Continental and Indian restaurants.

THE NORTH

Agra
(STD code 0562)
*Amarvilas (£££)
Taj East Gate End, Taj Nagri Scheme
tel: 2231515 fax: 2231516
www.oberoihotels.com
Top-end luxury 102-room hotel, grandiose scale and craftsmanship. Some rooms with views of Taj, plentiful restaurants, pool and amentities.

*Clarks Shiraz Restaurant (£££)
Clarks Shiraz Hotel, *54 Taj Road tel:*

2226121/32 fax: 2226128
www.hotelcalrksshiraz.com
Fabulous rooftop restaurant serving in Mughlai dishes, with live Indian music at night. Booking is essential.

*Mughal Sheraton (£££)
Taj Ganj, Fatehabad Road
tel: 2331701 fax: 2331730
www.welcomgroup.com
Spectacularly designed large modern hotel in Mughal tradition, with hammocks in the gardens and courtyards. Very well-appointed rooms (289) and suites (5), excellent service. Rooftop views of the Taj Mahal. Mughlai cuisine and live Indian music at **Pesharwi** restaurant (££). Other restaurants include **Tajbano** (££), for superb multi-cuisine buffet, and a Continental restaurant with a live dance band in the evening.

Amritsar
(STD code 0183)
Mohan International (££)
Albert Road tel: 2227801 fax: 2226520
email: hotel@jla.vsnl.net.in
Fairly characterless but comfortable. 728 rooms, good Punjabi restaurant, pool.

277

Corbett National Park
A variety of very low-grade accommodation (£) is available within the park, but must be booked in advance. Cabins (these have bathrooms), log huts and tourist huts can be arranged by the Tourist Reception Centre at Ramnagar (tel: 05947 251489, fax: 05947 251376). Forest rest houses can be arranged by the Chief Wildlife Warden, 17 Rana Pratap Marg, Lucknow (tel: 0522 2283903).

Claridges Corbett Hideaway (£££)
Zero Garjia, Dhikala tel: 05947 284132
www.leisurehotels.com.in
Luxury in the wilds in the form of 'tribal' cottages in an orchard. Well-appointed rooms (52), full board, pool and good service. Tours arranged; cycle hire.

Infinity Resorts (ex Tiger Tops) (£££)
8km (5 miles) north of Ramnagar tel: 05947 251279 email: infinitydel@touchtelindia.net
www.infinityresorts.com/
www.tigercorbettindia.com
Comfortable with old-world atmosphere, 24 rooms and high-quality full board. Friendly service. Facilities include a pool, elephant rides, jeep safaris and evening wildlife films. Lovely riverside setting.

Khajuraho
(STD code 07686)
*Chandela (££/£££)
Airport Road tel: 272355, fax: 272365
www.tajhotels.com
Taj hotel, reasonably priced for comfort and service. Well-designed; 94 rooms in large grounds, two excellent restaurants, pool, tennis, archery, yoga, health centre, bookshop, puppet shows.

*Usha Bundela (££/£££)
Temple Road tel: 272386 fax: 272385
email: sales@ubkstar.com
www.ushashriramhotels.com
Two-storey hotel with 66 well-appointed rooms opening on to lawns, garden and pool. Sober, classical style. There is also excellent Indian food at **Bhuj Bundela** restaurant (££) and a 24-hour café.

Hotels and Restaurants

Hotel Marble Palace (£)
Opposite Gole Market
tel: 274353 fax: 274131
Outstanding budget address, 200m (218 yards) from Western group. Surprising marble floors throughout, spacious front rooms, smaller cheaper ones at back. All with good bathrooms, insect screens and unexpected comforts. Also a dormitory.

Leh
(STD code 01982)
Bijoo (££)
Library Road tel: 252131
Atmospheric old Ladakhi house close to bazaar. Comfortable rooms, good restaurant (full board), gardens, terrace. Treks and tours, helpful staff.
*Kokonor Tibetan Restaurant (££)
On second floor in alley off Main Bazaar Road.
Despite the name, good Chinese and Western food is available at fair price, as well as Tibetan.

Manali
(STD code 01902)
Ambassador Resort (£££)
Sunny Side, Chadiyan tel: 252235–8 fax: 252173 www.ambassadorresorts.com
Perched on hillside with lovely views over rooftops of old Manali. Strikingly designed, 57 comfortable rooms and suites. Restaurants with multi-cuisine. Gym, jacuzzi, sauna, beauty parlour, watersports, disco, skating rink, squash, travel desk.
*John Banons (£/££)
Manali Orchards, Old Manali Road
tel: 252335/88 fax: 252392
A long-standing Manali classic. Owner John Banon died in 2005, but the hotel opens in 2006 after renovation with more rooms and a swimming pool.

Orchha
(STD code 07680)
*The Orchha Resort (££)
tel: 252222/3/4 fax: 252677
email: orchharresort@sancharnet.in
Peacefully located by River Chhattris outside the village. 11 air-conditioned tents or 34 rooms all in landscaped gardens with pool. Excellent restaurant.
Sheesh Mahal (£)
tel: 252624 email: sheeshmahal@sancharnet.in
Play at being a maharani in this state-run 8-room hotel inside the island palace complex. Somewhat dilapidated but this adds to the atmosphere. Try the Royal Suite.

Rishikesh
(STD code 0135)
*Ganga Kinare (£/££)
16 Virbhadra Road tel: 2431658
email: hotelganga_02@yahoo.com
Quiet location south of the main temples, by the river with its own private *ghat*. 38 carpeted rooms, most of which overlook the Ganga, two decent restaurants (££), a travel desk which arranges activities as well as tours and exchange. In addition, watersports and free boating.

Sanchi
(STD code 07482)
*Gateway Retreat (£)
On the road to Bhopal tel: 266723

MP Tourism hotel in good location near main *stupa* and rail station. Relaxing garden. 17 rooms. Indian and Chinese restaurant. Book in advance.
Himland Hotel East (£)
Circular Road tel: 26222901–4 fax: 26224241
email: himland@sancharnet.in
www.himlandeast.com
16-room modern hotel, clean, some rooms with balconies and views, exchange. Next door is slightly more classy **Himland West** (£/££) (tel: 2624436), with a multi-cuisine restaurant.

Shimla
(STD code 0177)
*Oberoi Clarkes (£££)
The Mall
tel: 2651010 fax: 2611321
www.oberoihotels.com
This was Mohan Singh Oberoi's first hotel, and one of the earliest in Shimla, and is not air-conditioned. Lots of character, very comfortable, good service, and a restaurant. 32 rooms.
*The Cecil (£££)
Chaura Maidan, Ambedkar Chowk
tel: 2804848 email: reservations@thececil.com
www.oberoihotels.com
Classy Oberoi establishment, providing 79 rooms, indoor pool, golf, billiards, steam bath, health club, gym, tea lounge, library, travel desk, multi-cuisine restaurant (£££). Great views of the Himalayas.
*Woodville Palace (££/£££)
Raj Bhawan Road, The Mall
tel: 2623919/2624038 fax: 2623098
www.woodvillepalace.com
Another of Shimla's royal jewels, set in grounds at western end of town. 14 vast 1930s rooms and suites full of antiques. Excellent multi-cuisine restaurant (££), worth visiting for décor alone. Book ahead.

Varanasi (Benares)
(STD code 0542)
*Alka Hotel (£)
D 3/23 Meerghat
tel: 2401681 email: hotelalka@hotmail.com
Semi-modern hotel that opened in 1997. Very basic, but some of the 31 rooms have balconies. In superb position, with terraces overlooking *ghats*. Wide price range, good terrace restaurant. Book ahead.
*Clarks Varanasi (£££)
The Mall
tel: 2501011 email: clarkvns@satyam.r.et.in
Raj-era establishment with pleasantly designed modern extension in well-tended gardens with pool. Three excellent restaurants (multi-cuisine), travel desk, tennis, golf, yoga, meditation, Indian dance and music on request and 104 good rooms.
Hotel Ganges View (££)
B 1/163 Assi Ghat
tel: 2313218
The bedrooms in this stylishly renovated 100-year-old house are crammed with interesting art and antiques. It's the most comfortable option near the *ghats* and the homey restaurant adds further appeal. Book ahead—this is a popular place.
Surya (£)
A-5 The Mall, Varuna Bridge
tel: 2508466 fax: 2502758
www.hotelsuryavns.com
In Cantonment, near the station and tourist office.

Decent rooms, most overlooking the garden. Camping on lawn. Steam-bath, massage, multi-cuisine garden restaurant (average food), exchange, travel counter.

THE NORTHEAST

Bhubaneswar
(STD code 0674)
*The Trident (£££)
Naya Palli tel: 2301010 /2300890
fax: 2301302 email: reservation@oberoibh.com
Near Botanical Gardens, 5km (3 miles) from town, with 62 rooms, garden, jogging track and pool. Tasteful interior reflects Orissan culture. Restaurant with good à la carte menu, health club, tennis, travel desk.
*Swosti Plaza (££)
P1 Jaydev Vihar tel: 2300008
email: splaza@sancharnet.in
106 rooms in comfortable modern hotel with a 24-hour coffe shop, bar, swimming pool, gym, massage parlour and shopping arcade.

Calcutta see Kolkata

Darjeeling
(STD code 0354)
Elgin (£££)
HD Lama Road
tel: 2257226 email: elgin@elginhotels.com
Elegant 22-room hotel in 120-year-old building in the town centre. Open fireplaces, atmospheric interiors with original art and black-and-white photographs. Breakfast room, outdoor gazebo, cosy bar area, landscaped garden.
Cedar Inn (£££)
Jalaphar Road
tel: 2254446/2253598 fax: 2256764
email: cedarinn@satyam.net.in
The highest hotel in town built in Vicorian Gothic style, with an Alpine twist—each of the 29 rooms has a view of the Kanchenjunga mountain range and is lined floor to ceiling with teak wood. Restaurant, gardens,
terrace; fireplaces in most rooms.
*Windamere Hotel (£££)
Observatory Hill tel: 2254041–2
fax: 2254211/2254043
email: reservations @windamerehotel.com
Darjeeling's best, Heritage hotel dating from 1939, with chintzy charm. Timber construction, old photos, comforts (no TV), terrace views on both sides, gardens, tennis, library, travel service. Efficient, friendly staff. Full board only, which includes traditional afternoon tea—non-residents can make bookings for main meals. Absolutely no smoking. 37 rooms.

Gantok
(STD code 03592)
The Oriental (££)
Upper Cart Road tel: 221180
email: info@orientalsikkim.com
Gantok is a good staging post for treks deeper into West Sikkim. It might be a modern high-rise hotel, but the Oriental is a Gantok landmark and offers smart accommodation and good value for money. There are 16 rooms and 4 suites; the top floor has jaw-dropping views of the Himalaya. A restaurant serves multinational cuisine.

Kalimpong
(STD code 03552)
*Himalayan Hotel (££)
Upper Cart Road tel: 255248
fax: 255122 email: himalayanhotel@gmail.com
Atmospheric 1920s colonial house converted by the MacDonald family and now a Heritage hotel. 18 delightful rooms with fireplaces and large suites in new 'cottages'. Good restaurant, gardens and views, car rental. Book in advance in season.
*Hotel Silver Oaks (£££)
Rinkingpong Road tel: 255296
fax: 255368 email:silveroaks@sancharnet.in
www.elginhotels.com
Light, airy hotel with landscaped garden and 23 comfortable spacious rooms. Views of surrounding hills and centrally located.

Kolkata (Calcutta)
(STD code 033)
*Aqua Java (£)
79 Sambhunath Pandit Street
Lively snack bar, excellent for a quick meal.
*Fairlawn Hotel (££)
13A Sudder Street tel: 2252 1510
fax: 2252 1835 email: fairlawn@cal.vsnl.net.in
www.fairlawnhotel.com
Old-fashioned, eccentric relic of the Raj. Outdoor bar and chintzy, green interior. Run by the memorable Violet Smith and her daughter, Jenny. High ceilings, spacious sitting areas, mixed memorabilia. Separate annex with rooftop garden for sunbathing. Full board only, Hefty English breakfasts. 18 rooms.
*The Kenilworth (££)
Little Russell Street tel: 2282 8394
fax: 22825136 email:
priyad@kenilworthhotels.com
Modern but stylish hotel in old, centrally located British-built building. Popular with business people as well as tourists. 105 rooms. Marble floors, gym, good restaurant, 24-hour room service.
*Oberoi Grand (£££)
15 J Nehru Road tel: 2249 2323
fax: 245 3229 email: fo@oberoi-cal.com
www.oberoihotels.com
The cream; a sumptuous hotel dating from 1870s, though much extended since. 250 rooms surround an attractive pool and garden with lofty palms. Superbly appointed rooms and personalized service. Excellent Thai, French and Indian restaurants (£££). Tea lounge, bars, health club, beauty salon, travel desk, car rental.
*Zaranj (££)
26 J Nehru Road tel: 2249 0369
Air-conditioned restaurant, next to Indian Museum. Very good Punjabi and Bengali dishes.

THE CENTRE

Aurangabad
(STD code 0240)
*Ambassador Ajanta (££/£££)
Airport Road, Chikalthana
tel: 2485211–4 fax: 2484367
email: ajanta@ambassadorindia.com
Large (92 rooms and suites) but quiet hotel, with pool in garden, sauna, health club, sports complex, beauty parlour, barber shop, travel desk and car hire. Good service and excellent food (£££).

Hotels and Restaurants

*Printravel Hotel (£)
Dr Ambedkar Marg tel: 235 2448
An old Aurangabad favourite that's seen better days, but is well run. Rock-bottom rates for clean and spacious fan-cooled rooms with showers and nets. Friendly staff. Good vegetarian restaurant and terrace.

Bandhavgarh National Park
Bandhavgarh Jungle Lodge (£££)
tel: 07627 265317 (c/o Tiger Resorts Delhi) bookings: 011 2685 3760 email: tigerresorts@tigerindia.com
Close to the river, off Umaria Road. An attractive complex of well-equipped pseudo-mud huts. Expensive, but the cost covers full board, park fees and safaris with good naturalist guides.
White Tiger Forest Lodge (£)
Umaria Road, Tala tel: 07627 265308 email: wtflmpt@sancharnet.in
Excellent value and well-organized by MP Tourism. Some bungalows by the river (elephants bathe there) and 26 rooms (few are air-conditioned), good restaurant, bar, jeep hire. Advance booking is advisable.

Bombay see Mumbai

Hyderabad/Secunderabad
(STD code 040)
*Grand Kakatiya Hotel & Towers (£££)
Begumpet tel: 2340 0132 fax: 2340 1045 www.welcomgroup.com
Luxury hotel, part of Welcomgroup. Pool, health club, travel desk. 24-hour multi-cuisine food.
Taj Banjara (£££)
Banjara Hills tel: 5566 9999 fax: 5566 1919 www.tajhotels.com
Good location and outdoor activities around lake. Excellent Hyderabadi cuisine and refurbished rooms.

Kanha National Park
Kanha Jungle Lodge (£££)
Mukki tel: 07637 236015 www.adventure-india.com
19 quite spartan rooms but full board offers good Indian meals and guides to park.
Kipling Camp (£££)
In Morcha 4km (2.5 miles) from Khatia at Kanha NP first gate. bookings through Delhi office tel: 011 5519 3778 or cellphone 0931 354 2800 www.kiplingcamp.com
This is the best option, an 18-cottage complex in rustic safari style. Beautiful setting. Rates include full board, guides and jeep tours. Resident elephant. Book well in advance in peak season.

Mumbai (Bombay)
(STD code 022)
Garden Hotel (££/£££)
42 Garden Road, Colaba tel: 2284 1476 fax: 2204 4290
Good, modernized hotel in quiet leafy street one block from sea. 33 air-conditioned rooms. Multi-cuisine restaurant, exchange, travel desk.
*Indigo (£££)
4 Mandlik Road, Colaba tel: 2285 6316
Indian celebrities and media types circulate in Mumbai's most fashionable bar and restaurant. The high-ceilinged rooms are furnished with leather armchairs while an underground cigar lounge is where deals are cut. If you don't get a reservation to sample the European-led menu and wine list, try turning up for an excellent Sunday brunch.
*Jewel of India (££)
Nehru Centre, Dr Annie Besant Road tel: 2494 9435
Elegant, spacious restaurant serving Mughlai and Kashmiri specialities in the evening. The lunch-time buffet branches out, with Continental, Chinese, Italian and Parsi offerings.
*Leela Kempinski (£££)
Sahar, Andheri tel: 5691 1234 fax: 2838 7624 email: reservations@theleela.com
Luxurious (over 400 rooms) airport hotel. Palatial Mughal-style design, with pool, health club, beauty parlour, golf, disco. Five multi-cuisine restaurants (£££).
*Oberoi (£££)
Nariman Point tel: 5632 5757 fax: 5632 4142
Is connected to **Oberoi Towers** (£££) *(tel: 5632 4343, fax: 5632 4142 email: reservations@oberoi-mumbai.com)*
Guests at either can use all the facilities of both, including superb views, two pools and several top-notch restaurants, some with live entertainment. The choice of cuisine includes Mediterranean, Mexican, French and seafood. The scale is vast (getting on for a thousand rooms and incredible suites), and the service is excellent.
*Taj Mahal Hotel (£££)
Apollo Bunder, Colaba tel: 5665 3366 fax: 5665 0323 www.tajhotels.com
The Taj Group's flagship hotel (in unassailable position opposite Gateway of India) has expanded: a new skyscraper joins the original structure to provide a total of 600 rooms, many with sea views. Top prices for wide-ranging amenities including five multi-cuisine restaurants and three bars, pool, gym and travel desk. The reality does not always live up to the reputation.
*Trishna (££)
7 Rope Walk Lane, Fort tel: 2261 4991
Lively seafood restaurant, bringing ultra-fresh lobsters and crabs to the table; also Chinese, Mughlai and South Indian. Extremely popular with the locals, so booking advisable.

THE SOUTH

Badami
(STD code 08357)
Badami Court Hotel (££/£££)
Station Road tel: 220230 fax: 220207 email: rafiqmht@blr.vsnl.net.in
On main road northeast of town, a well-run modern hotel with 25 clean, comfortable rooms and two suites. There are also a garden, exchange, travel desk, restaurants.
*Mookambika Deluxe Lodge (£)
Station Road, opposite bus-stand tel: 220067 fax: 220106
Reasonable budget hotel, clean, but unreliable plumbing. Small fan-cooled rooms (14) with TV. Efficient travel desk offers excellent day tours by car to Aihole, Pattadakal. The attached **Kanchana Restaurant** (£) offers a good range of food, vegetarian and otherwise with Western breakfasts.

Bangalore

(STD code 080)

*Ivory Tower (££)
12th Floor, Barton Centre, 84 MG Road
tel: 2558 9333 fax: 2558 8697
email: ivorytower@vsnl.net
Good value, but strictly for the non-vertiginous, with splendid views over the city. 16 large, very clean rooms, with refrigerator, tea/coffee-making facilities and good room service. Exchange, bar. The **Ebony** multi-cuisine terrace restaurant (££) is a favourite rendezvous for business people.

*Nahar's Heritage (££)
14 St Mark's Road tel: 2227 8731–6
fax: 2227 8737 email: nahar@b.vsnl.net.in
www.naharhotels.com
A friendly 48-room, good-value hotel, with a very good multi-cuisine restaurant.

*The Park Hotel (£££)
14/7 Mahatma Gandi Road
tel: 2559 4666 www.theparkhotels.com
Ultra-contemporary new hotel with 109 rooms. High standards and service aimed at an international market.

*The Rice Bowl (££)
24 Residency Road tel: 2558 7417
A popular Tibetan Chinese restaurant, noteworthy for being run by the Dalai Lama's sister.

Chennai (Madras)

(STD code 044)

*Annalakshmi (£/££)
804 Anna Salai (opposite LIC) tel: 2852 5109
A volunteer-run restaurant which donates the profits to charity. Renowned for delicious vegetarian food, sometimes with unusual dishes of South-east Asian origin. Booking is essential.

*Connemara (£££)
2 Binny Road tel: 5500 0000 fax: 5500 0555
email: tajcon@giasmd01.vsnl.net.in
Huge, central, art deco Taj hotel near Anna Salai, set in large grounds. Very comfortable. Pool, health club, beauty parlour, bookshop, palmist, travel desk. Restaurants include a Chinese, a French and the outdoor **Rain Tree** (££), serving local cuisine, often with live Indian entertainment. Reserve in advance in season (Dec–Mar).

*New Woodlands Hotel (£)
72–5 Radha Krishnan Road, Mylapore
tel: 2811 3111 fax: 2811 0460
email: reserv@newwoodlands.com
Pleasant large hotel on a busy road. Clean, spacious rooms (176) and suites, some in bungalows. Two Indian vegetarian restaurants (£), good *thalis*; small pool, efficient service. Book in advance.

Saravana Bhaven (£)
21 Kennet Lane, Chennai
tel: 2819 2055 www.saravanabhaven.com
A two-minute walk from Chennai's Egmore station, this bakery, restaurant and ice-cream parlour is a convenient and clean place for a bite to eat before catching a train south. Marble tables and chrome chairs give it a modern, café-style appearance.

Goa

(STD code 0832 for whole state)

*Leela Palace (£££)
Mobor, Cavelossim, Salcete
tel: 287 1234 email: info@leelapalace.com
An upgraded resort around artificial lake, offering rooms and villas, with a range of prices.

*The Mandovi (£/£££)
DB Bandodkar Marg, Panaji
tel: 222 4405 fax: 0832 2225451
email: mandovi_goa@sancharnet.in
Established 1940s favourite on banks of Mandovi river. 66 spacious rooms with balconies. Good multi-cuisine restaurant, bar, helpful GTDC staff.

*Palm Grove Cottages (£)
1678 Vasvaddo, Benaulim tel: 2722533
Lush garden setting with chalets and a bar. 14 double rooms. Garden. Outdoor restaurant.

Panjim Inn (££–£££)
31st January Road, Panaji tel: 2226532
This is the most attractive place to stay in the Goan capital, and judging by the upwardly mobile prices, it knows it. The owners have bought up several properties in Panaji's attractive Portuguese quarter, but their first hotel conversion was this 300-year-old mansion. The rooms, of varying sizes and prices, have antique four-poster beds and what they lack in modern appliances they make up for in colonial furnishings. Meals (breakfast, lunch and dinner) are served on the first floor verandah. Book ahead to reserve a room.

*Sher-E-Punjab (£–££)
18th June Road, Panaji tel: 2227204
For tandoori dishes and snacks head to this clean, modern restauarnt (one of a successful chain) in the centre of town. An ever-attentive army of waiters serve the long dining room, bearing platters of tandoori meats and other North Indian specialities. Prices are reasonable and it's a convenient place for a quick lunch break.

*Tamarind Hotel (£–££)
Kumar Vaddo, Anjuna
tel: 2274319/2273363 www.thetamarind.com
Set in a secluded location about 3km (2 miles) inland from Anjuna. Air-conditioned stone cottages in lush gardens with pool. Outstanding restaurant and bar.

*Tansy Cottages (£)
Vasvaddo, Benaulim Beach Road, Benaulim
tel: 2770574
email:tansytouristcottages@yahoo.co.in
Good location halfway between main road and beach. Large, clean rooms in old house, garden annexe. Basic, but adequate, and budget prices for the 4 apartments and 9 rooms. Good outdoor restaurant/bar: wide-ranging menu.

Hampi

(STD code 08539)

*Hampi's Boulders Resort (££–£££)
Narayanpet tel: 265939
This wilderness resort is several kilometres outside Hampi in a protected conservation area. Drivers take guests, who largely arrive through word-of-mouth recommendations, to Hampi or wildlife spotting each morning. 20 cottages are sprinkled across a remarkable, boulder-strewn landscape, while a circular restaurant and bar are the focal point. Don't miss the evening excursion to see birds roosting by the river.

*The Mango Tree Restaurant (£)
Riverside Drive tel: 241944
Follow the river downstream and you'll spot signs for this delightfully secluded restaurant, the best in Hampi. Kick off your shoes before sitting down at the

Hotels and Restaurants

shaded semicircular terrace overlooking the river and water buffalo in the working fields below. Delicious Western and Indian dishes are served; the fruity Mango Tree Special Curry is a favourite.

Hospet
(STD code 08394)
*Malligi Tourist Home (£)
6/143 Jambunatha Road tel: 28101 fax: 227038 email: malligihome@hotmail.com
Large, dilapidated hotel with popular garden restaurant **Waves** (£) by the pool. Better for food than rooms.
*Priyadarshini Hotel (£)
45A Station Road tel: 228838
Modern hotel between railway and bus station. Clean, spacious rooms with balconies and rural views. Garden restaurant/bar (£) and interior restaurant.

Kochi
(STD code 0484)
*Bolgatty Palace (££/£££)
*Mulavukadu, Bolgatty Island
tel: 2750500/2750003 fax: 2750457
email: bolgatty@vsnl.com*
Lovely Dutch palace (1744) with rambling verandas, 26 vast rooms and suites. Landscaped grounds, totally refurbished by KTDC in 1999. Atmospheric location and two good multi-cuisine restaurants. Bar, health club, pool, exchange.
*Casino Hotel (£££)
*Willingdon Island tel: 2668421 fax: 2668001
email: casino@vsnl.com*
Comfortable 68-room hotel with range of facilities. Very convenient for visiting Lakshadweep Islands; it is the centre for information, permits and bookings. Multi-cuisine restaurant (£/££) specializes in seafood. Gardens with pool; poolside snacks.
*Metropolitan (£/££)
*Chavara Road, near railway station
tel: 237 6931 fax: 237 5227
email: metropol@md3.vsnl.net.in*
With 39 clean, modern rooms, this hotel is good value. Two very good multi-cuisine restaurants, bar, exchange, travel desk and friendly service.
*Taj Malabar (£££)
*Willingdon Island tel: 2666811 fax: 2668297
email: malabar.cochin@tajhotels.com*
Superb Taj hotel in fabulous bay-side location. 100 stylish rooms and suites; good views. Restaurants include the **Waterfront Café** (££) with Keralan and Western buffets. Extensive gardens, good pool.

Kottayam (Keralan Backwaters)
(STD code 0481)
Coconut Lagoon (£££)
*Kumarakom or c/o Casino Hotel, Kochi
tel: 2525835 fax: 2524495
email: casino2000@satyam.net.in*
Heritage resort combining traditional architecture with Ayurvedic facilities. Spacious Keralan houses in lush gardens, restaurant in converted temple, good pool, health centre, watersports, fishing, canoeing, birdwatching, travel desk. Friendly.
*Taj Garden Retreat (£££)
*1/404 Kumarakom
tel: 2524377 fax 2524371
email: retreat.kumarakom@tajhotels.com*
Lakeside resort in renovated colonial mansion. 22

rooms and suites. Adjacent bird sanctuary. Pool and watersports and Ayurvedic spa centre. Houseboats available. Good multi-cuisine food, including Keralan specialities.

Kovalam
(STD code 0471)
Blue Sea Hotel (£)
*Beach Road, near telegraph office
tel: 2481401 fax: 2480401
email: hotelbluesea@eth.net*
Traditional Keralan house set back from road leading to Ashok Hotel and beach. 12 tasteful rooms and 18 quaint family cottages, but basic bathrooms. Luxuriant garden, large pool. Breakfast included.
*Hotel Rockholm (£)
*Lighthouse Road tel: 2480306/406
fax: 2480607
email: rockholm@asianetindia.com
www.rockholm.com*
Friendly hotel in dramatic position on rocks beside lighthouse. Good multi-cuisine restaurant. Comfortable rooms (23), some with balconies and sea views. Exchange, Ayurvedic massage, travel desk, library, airport and railway pick-ups. Book ahead.
Hotel Samudra (££/£££)
*GV Road, Samudra Beach Garden
tel: 2480089 fax: 2480242 www.ktdc.com*
Modern hotel geared towards tour groups. Decent accommodation on quiet beach north of Kovalam. KTDC-run, so provides tours and travel help. Rooms with balconies and sea views. Pool, travel desk, Ayurvedic health centre, restaurant, bar, exchange.
Surya Samudra (£££)
*tel: 2480413 fax: 2481124
www.suryasamudra.com*
Beautiful cliff-top resort in gardens overlooking sea, 8km (5 miles) south of Kovalam. Traditional Keralan houses reconstructed and tastefully furnished. Ayurvedic treatment, pool, excellent restaurant.

Madras see Chennai

Madurai
(STD code 0452)
*Hotel Supreme (£/££)
*110 West Perumal Maistry Street
tel: 234 3151 fax: 234 2637
email: hsupreme@sancharnet.in
www.supremehotels.com*
Modern hotel with 69 suites and rooms. The **Surya** (£) is an excellent Indian vegetarian rooftop restaurant (open 4pm daily). Also Indian, Continental and Chinese restaurant. Bar, exchange, 24-hour travel desk, room service, business centre. Book ahead.
Tamil Nadu I (£)
*West Veli Street, opposite TTC bus-stand
tel: 233 7471 fax: 233 1947*
In central location, with varying standards and rates for its 43 rooms . Breezy verandas, good restaurant, bar, exchange. Good value. Tourist information. Can be noisy. Another, pricier, Tamil Nadu Tourism hotel is located several kilometres north across the river.
Mamallapuram (Mahabalipuram)
(STD code 04114)
*Fisherman's Cove (££/£££)
*Covelong Beach tel: 272304–10 fax: 272303
www.tajhotels.com*

Luxury in splendid isolation. A complex on the beach 20 minutes north of Mamallapuram. Multi-cuisine restaurant and beach barbecue. Watersports, pool.

*Mamalla Bhavan Annexe (£)
104 East Raja Street
tel: 242260/242360/242060 fax: 242160
email: mamalla@vsnl.com
www.mamallahotels.com
An old favourite in heart of village. Clean and friendly, with 38 reasonably well maintained rooms, 24-hour room service, TV. Vegetarian restaurant and alfresco dining. Exchange, travel desk.

Tamil Nadu Beach Resort (£/££)
Covelong Road tel: 27442361
fax: 242268 email: ttdcbrc@yahoo.com
Government-run hotel overlooking beach. Spacious two-storey cottages, balconies with sea views. Pool in leafy garden, restaurants, bar, exchange.

Mysore
(STD code 0821)
Hotel Mayura Hoysala (£)
2 Jhansi Lakshmibai Road tel: 2425349
Charming hotel run by KTDC. 21 rooms. Garden, bamboo-style restaurant, bar, travel desk.

The Green Hotel (££)
2270 Vinobha Road tel: 2512536 fax: 2516139
email: greenhotel@sancharnet.in
A little far from the centre but a nice garden and setting in a stately mansion. Annexe rooms (23) are mediocre and there are 7 rooms in the old palace.

Indus Valley (££/£££)
Lalitha Mahal tel: 2473437 fax: 2473590
www.ayurindus.com
Unusual Ayurvedic resort hotel with 25 rooms. Good vegetarian restaurant and authentic treatments.

Parklane Restaurant (££)
2720 Sri Harsha Road tel: 2430400
www.parklanemysore.com
Travellers congregate night and day at this courtyard restaurant on a hotel-lined road close to the Maharajah's Palace. For good reason too: the food is reliable, with Western staples such as pancakes or Indian and Chinese menus. There's live music in the evenings. Service is eager rather than excellent.

Nilgiri Hills
*Taj Garden Retreat (£££)
Hampton Manor, Church Road, Upper Coonoor
tel: 0423 230021/220021/42
fax: 0432 232775/222775
Lovely old colonial mansion with cottages and garden. Excellent multi-cuisine restaurant, sports (no pool), trekking, helpful staff.

Tamil Nadu (£)
Charing Cross Road, Udagamandalam
tel: 0423 2444370 fax: 0423 2444369
Spacious Tamil Nadu Tourism hotel. Cottages in garden. Restaurant, coffee shop and bar. Exchange.

Periyar National Park
(STD code 04869)
Periyar House (£)
Sanctuary, Thekkadi tel: 222026
KTDC's budget hotel, halfway between park entrance and boat jetty.The best of the 44 rooms face the lake, most are simple but clean and comfortable and there's a dormitory. Restaurant (buffet), bar, boats, exchange, massage, car and bicycle rental.

*Spice Village (£££)
Thekkadi Road tel: 222314 fax: 222317
www.cghearth.com
Cottage complex with lovely gardens, including a spice garden. Pool, travel desk, international cuisine and service to match. A peaceful place. 52 rooms.

Puduchcheri (Pondicherrry)
Ram Guest House (£)
546 MG Road
tel: 2220072 email: ramguest@hotmail.com
www.ramguest.fr.st
Ram Guest House is on the main road through Pondicherry but at the quieter, train station end. The rooms are on several floors, based around an interior courtyard. Rates are reasonable and rooms are clean and tidy. Service is friendly and helpful.

Rendezvous (££)
30 Suffren Street
tel: 2330238
Pondicherry's best meal out is at this French/Keralan restaurant in a historic building on the corner of the town's Heritage Walk. The rooftop dining area has bamboo struts, pot plants and background jazz, while the à la carte menu of well-rehearsed French classics andIndian specialties won't disappoint. Fresh fish is a sensible option. French wine and Indian beer is also served.

283

Thiruvananthapuram (Trivandrum)
(STD code 0471)
*Jas (£/££)
Thycaud/Aristo Junction
tel: 2324881/163–72 fax: 2321477/2324443
email: jas@md2.vsnl.net.in
Pleasant 43-room hotel towards station. Multi-cuisine roof-garden restaurant, bar, travel desk, exchange.

*Mascot Hotel (£/££)
Mascot Junction, MG Road
tel: 2318990/2438990 fax:
2317745/2437745 email:
hotelmascot@vsnl.net
Convenient for museums and tourist office, run by KTDC. 54 decent rooms. Excellent open-air restaurant, 24-hour coffee-shop for good snacks, bar, ice-cream parlour, pool, health club, travel desk, exchange.

Tiruchchirappalli
(STD code 0431)
Sangam (££/£££)
Collector's Office Road tel: 2414700/480
fax: 2415779 email: hotelsangam@vsnl.com
www.hotelsangam.com
Near central bus-stand. Garden, multi-cuisine restaurant, 24-hour coffee-shop, bar, exchange, health club, travel desk, 24-hour room service. 54 rooms

Tamil Nadu (£)
McDonald's Road, opposite bus-stand,
Cantonment tel: 2414346
fax: 241 5725
Simple accommodation in 44 rooms in good central location. Small garden, good restaurant, bar.

Index

Principal references are shown in **bold**

285

Index

Acknowledgements

Picture credits

The Automobile Association wishes to thank the following photographers and libraries for their assistance in the preparation of this book:
ALAMY 64b (© Jayne Fincher Photo Int), 196 (Dinodia Images); FREDRIK ARVIDSSON 3, 5a, 6b, 9b, 10/11, 12a, 13c, 14b, 15a, 16b, 16c, 18a, 18c, 19b, 20a, 22b, 25a, 25b, 26/7, 27, 29b, 35a, 35b, 36b, 38b, 40b, 41a, 41b, 44b, 46a, 46b, 76, 77, 78, 79, 80, 81, 82/3, 84/5, 86/7, 87, 88, 94, 99a, 99b, 101, 102, 103, 106, 107, 109a, 117, 119, 120, 124, 124/5, 125, 131, 144/5, 147, 148/9, 155, 158a, 158b, 159, 165, 166, 166/7, 175, 176, 177, 178a, 178b, 181, 182a, 184a, 184b, 185, 186/7, 187, 197, 200/1, 204, 205a, 205b, 207, 209, 210, 213a, 213b, 214a, 214b, 214c, 215, 216/7, 219, 220, 222, 223, 224a, 224b, 225, 226, 227, 228, 230, 231, 232b, 233b, 234, 234/5, 236, 237, 238, 239, 240b, 243, 244, 246, 247, 248a, 248/9, 250a, 250b, 253a, 261, 268; LAWRENCE ARVIDDSON-PUJOL 21b, 43; J BALDWIN 8b; THE BRIDGEMAN ART LIBRARY 31b Lord Hastings, Govenor of India by Thomas Gainsborough (1727-88) (Museo de Arte, Sao Paulo/Giraudon), 32a & 33b Conche & faience bangles and ear studs, Harappa, 2300-1750 BC (National Museum of India, New Delhi), 32b Copper vase, Harappa, 2300-1750 BC (National Museum of India, New Delhi), 36a Vairochana Buddha (wall painting), Balawaste, 7th-8th century (National Museum of India, New Delhi), 38a Nataraja (King of Dancing, one of the representations of Siva), bronze, late Chola, 12th century, Tamil Nadu (National Museum of India, New Delhi), 39 Somaskanda, Bronze, Chola, 10th century, Tamil Nadu (National Museum of India, New Delhi), 45a Red Fort at Agra during construction, from the 'Akbarnama', Mughal, 1565 (illustrated text), (Victoria and Albert Museum, London), 45b Shah Jahan (1628-57) and Qudsia Begum; the Begum pours away the wine, Kalam Delhi School, late 19th century, (gouache on paper) Delhi (Cheltenham Art Gallery & Museums, Gloucester), 46a Coat of Arms of Old East India Company, © Guildhall Library, City of London; 48/9 A Hunting Party in India by Willian Daniell (1769-1837), (Maidstone Museum & Art Gallery, Kent), 48 Storming of Delhi in 1857, from 'The Campaign in India, 1857-8', engraved by George McCulloch (fl. 1859-1901) 1859 (litho) by George Franklin Atkinson (1822-59) (after) (British Library, London), 113a Raja Sarupsingh (1842-61) of Udaipur, on a boar hunt, by Tara Chand, Rajasthan, 1855 (Victoria and Albert Museum, London); FIONA DUNLOP 17, 123, 148, 150b, 194, 198b, 206, 218, 240a, 241, 245, 248b, 253b; E.T. ARCHIVE 31a, 33a; MARY EVANS PICTURE LIBRARY 42a, 42c, 44a, 46/7 47; GETTY IMAGES 12b (Time Life Pictures), 13t (Time Life Pictures), 64a; ROBERT HARDING PICTURE LIBRARY 50a; HULTON GETTY PICTURE COLLECTION 50b, 151b; ILLUSTRATED LONDON NEWS 183; IMPACT PHOTOS 196 (Ben Edwards); MAGNUM PHOTOS 51a (Henri-Cartier Bresson); OTTO PFISTER 180; PHOTODISC 84, 100a, 100b; PICTURES COLOUR LIBRARY 141, 192, 229; REX FEATURES 137a, 137b; SPECTRUM COLOUR LIBRARY 61, 142a, 221, 242/3, 242; TRIP/DINODIA 168a, 168b, 169a, 169b, 182b; ROBERT VAN DER BERGE 143.

All remaining pictures are held in the Association's own library (AA PHOTO LIBRARY) and were taken by Douglas Corrance, with the exception of:
FREDRIK ARVIDSSON 2, 5b, 8a, 10, 14a, 15b, 16a, 18b, 24b, 28a, 30a, 49, 67, 86b, 114/5, 116, 118, 126a, 126b, 127a, 127b, 127c, 128, 129, 132, 133, 134, 135, 136, 138/9, 139, 140, 142b, 149, 150a, 151a, 152/3, 153, 156, 157, 160/1, 161, 162, 163, 174, 188, 189, 190, 191, 195, 233a, 259, 262, 267; JILL GOCHER 11b, 118/9; JIM HOLMES 232a; KEN PATERSON F/Cover cr, 37, 252b; NEIL SETCHFIELD 252t; STEVE WATKINS F/Cover cl, B/Cover l

Author's Acknowledgements

The author would like to thank the following for all their help: Nicola and Ramesh Durvasula; Sheikh Altaf and Nazir Butt at Magic India in Delhi; Yasin Zargar at Indus Travel in London; GS Sachdev, Government of India Tourist Office in London; Shankar Dandapani of SD Enterprises in Wembley; Maggi Nixon of Oberoi Hotels in London and teh Oberoi Hotels in India; Government of India Tourist Offices in Delhi, Varanasi, Aurangabad and Bhubaneshwar; Rajasthan Tourist Development Corporation; Mr Jethi at the Maharao of Kutch tourist office; Yuvraj Digvijay Singh.

Contributors

Revision verifiers: Robin Barton
Additional research and text: Carol Sykes